VICARIOUS LIABILITY IN THE COMMON LAW WORLD

This book is the one place to find unprecedented access to case-law, doctrinal debates and comparative reflections on vicarious liability from across the common law world. The doctrine of vicarious liability, that is strict liability for the torts of others, represents one of the most controversial areas of tort law. Unsurprisingly it is a doctrine that has been discussed in the highest courts of common law jurisdictions. This collection responds to uncertainties as to the operation of vicarious liability in twenty-first century tort law by looking at key common law jurisdictions and asking expert scholars to set out and critically analyse the law, identifying factors influencing change and the extent to which case-law from other common law jurisdictions has been influential. The jurisdictions covered include Canada, England and Wales, Australia, Singapore, Ireland, Hong Kong and New Zealand.

In providing critical analysis of this important topic, it will be essential and compelling reading for all scholars of tort law and practitioners working in this field.

Volume 42 in the series Hart Studies in Private Law

Vicarious Liability in the Common Law World

Edited by
Paula Giliker

•HART•
OXFORD • LONDON • NEW YORK • NEW DELHI • SYDNEY

HART PUBLISHING

Bloomsbury Publishing Plc

Kemp House, Chawley Park, Cumnor Hill, Oxford, OX2 9PH, UK

1385 Broadway, New York, NY 10018, USA

29 Earlsfort Terrace, Dublin 2, Ireland

HART PUBLISHING, the Hart/Stag logo, BLOOMSBURY and the Diana logo are trademarks of Bloomsbury Publishing Plc

First published in Great Britain 2022

A catalogue record for this book is available from the British Library.

A catalogue record for this book is available from the Library of Congress.

ISBN: HB: 978-1-50993-907-7
ePDF: 978-1-50993-909-1
ePub: 978-1-50993-908-4

Typeset by Compuscript Ltd, Shannon

FOREWORD

'Vicarious' liability, from the Latin *vicarius*, suggests a liability of one that deputises for a liability of another. But as soon as the surface is scratched the doctrine becomes very difficult to understand. This outstanding book spans a range of jurisdictions which have developed vicarious liability by reference to each other but with a result that no two jurisdictions have taken precisely the same approach: Canada, England and Wales, Australia, Ireland, Singapore, Hong Kong, New Zealand, and Scotland.

This book is bristling with insights concerning the history of vicarious liability, the relationships which should count for the purposes of vicarious liability, the torts to which vicarious liability should apply, and the degree of connection required between the tortious action and the defendant for the purposes of vicarious liability. But, perhaps most importantly, every chapter assesses these questions in the context of justifications for vicarious liability.

Part of the enormous value of this book is that it provides great insight for the future of an area of law that, despite the best efforts from the judiciary and the academic and practising branches of the profession, remains a mess. As Giliker observes in a masterful opening chapter (p 18), none of the legal systems has found a 'magic solution that renders vicarious liability straightforward and easy to apply'. This book shows the problems that have arisen, how they have arisen, and provides powerful insights into how to solve them. One deep insight may be that one reason for the confusion surrounding 'vicarious liability' is that it is attempting to do the work of up to three discrete doctrines.

First, some vicarious liability cases seem comfortably to be based upon agency reasoning: acts of an agent are attributed to a principal who is responsible for them. As Glofcheski observes in relation to the law in Hong Kong, it has been taken as implicit that a person should be liable if they employ another to perform tasks for the person's benefit (pp 147–48). But the use of vicarious liability to describe the imposition of responsibility based upon a relationship of agency is, as Giliker says, controversial (p 4).

Secondly, other vicarious liability cases seem to be based on reasoning more comfortably associated with non-delegable duties, which, as Todd observes, arise where one person has assumed responsibility for the safety of another (p 191). Non-delegable duties are duties to protect against a risk by ensuring that care is taken, rather than duties merely to take reasonable care not to act as to foreseeably cause injury. Fleming described non-delegable duties as a disguised form of vicarious liability (Giliker, p 58). And vicarious liability may sometimes be a disguise for non-delegable duties. Indeed, the breadth of vicarious liability in Canadian law may be partly due to the narrowness of the Canadian approach to non-delegable duties (Neyers and Kiss, p 34). And in her review of the position in Australia, Beuermann astutely observes that in instances of institutional liability for child sexual abuse the concept of a non-delegable duty of care might be more appropriate than that of vicarious liability (p 98; see also Ryan, pp 117–18; Glofcheski, pp 167–69).

Thirdly, cases which perhaps most accurately fit the description of vicarious liability are those in which the liability of a defendant is based upon an attribution to the defendant of the liability of another. In this sense, as Campbell and Lindsay observe, 'one cannot be vicariously liable if no delict [wrong] has been committed' (p 197). Whether or not 'enterprise liability', which is carefully explained in many of the chapters should be accepted as the basis for vicarious liability, one of the many significant insights that might be drawn from this book is that the 'labyrinthine' (Tan, p 144) doctrine of vicarious liability will be far easier to understand if it is disentangled from other doctrines. The outworking of vicarious liability by reference to its rationale will be guided by the clear and cogent comparative learning contained in this superb book.

J J Edelman,
Justice of the High Court of Australia
Canberra,
30 May 2022

PREFACE

The doctrine of vicarious liability, that is, strict liability for the torts of others, represents one of the most controversial areas of common law tort law – it is strict, not fault-based liability; covers both intentional and negligent wrongs; and, in the systems covered in this book, is expanding, imposing greater burdens on employer and public authority defendants. Unsurprisingly it is a doctrine that has been discussed in the highest courts of most common law jurisdictions. In the jurisdictions covered in this edited collection, we will see discussion of cases from the Supreme Court of Canada, UK Supreme Court, High Court of Australia, Supreme Court of Ireland, Court of Appeal of Singapore, Hong Kong Court of Final Appeal, New Zealand Supreme Court and Scottish Court of Session. What is distinctive about this area of law (and triggered by its evolving and controversial nature) is that these courts actively discuss and are influenced by case law from other common law jurisdictions. The UK Supreme Court, therefore, in *Lister v Hesley Hall Ltd*[1] in 2001 found the Canadian decisions of *Bazley v Curry*[2] and *Jacobi v Griffiths*[3] to be 'luminous and illuminating'.[4] The Singapore Court of Appeal in *Ng Huat Seng v Munib Mohammad Madni*[5] noted with approval the fine-tuning of the framework of the doctrine undertaken by the UK Supreme Court and *Ng Huat Seng* was in turn cited with approval by Baroness Hale in *Barclays Bank plc v Various Claimants*.[6] In contrast the High Court of Australia in *Prince Alfred College v ADC*[7] expressly rejected the approach advocated in the UK decision of *Mohamud v Wm Morrison Supermarkets plc*,[8] judging it to be wrongly decided, but only after a thorough discussion of UK and Canadian authorities. Despite the introduction of no-fault liability, the New Zealand courts are still willing to consider relevant decisions from around the common law world and are likely to cite and to rely on those they see as best suited for their local needs. If this seems somewhat incestuous, what it illustrates is the ongoing relationship of common law jurisdictions beyond the now terminated jurisdiction of the Privy Council and the independence of the States in question. What was once a hierarchical relationship is now

[1] [2001] UKHL 22, [2002] 1 AC 215.
[2] [1999] 2 SCR 534, (1999) 174 DLR (4th) 45.
[3] [1999] 2 SCR 570, (1999) 174 DLR (4th) 71.
[4] *Lister* (n 1) [27].
[5] [2017] SGCA 58, [2017] 2 SLR 1074.
[6] [2020] UKSC 13, [2020] AC 973 [24] and [26].
[7] [2016] HCA 37, (2016) 258 CLR 134 [83], although it argued that its approach was consistent with the reasoning in more recent Canadian cases and the result in *Lister*, although it differed in its process of reasoning: [82].
[8] [2016] UKSC 11, [2016] AC 677.

more egalitarian with judgments considered on their merits. One further important perspective can be gained from Scotland – a distinct legal system but one whose private law final court of appeal is the UK Supreme Court. Again, decisions from England and Wales are cited in the Scots courts and have actively influenced its law of delict, not however without critical 'feedback' from the Scots courts.

In view of the interface between the supreme courts of different common law jurisdictions and ongoing uncertainty as to the tests for vicarious liability and its future direction, it is timely to bring together leading scholars from these jurisdictions to ask: where are we now with vicarious liability? This book therefore responds to uncertainties as to the operation of vicarious liability in twenty-first century tort law by looking to these different common law jurisdictions[9] and asking expert authors to outline the current law in their jurisdiction and the extent to which case law from other common law jurisdictions has influenced contemporary law. Authors were also asked to address the law *contextually* and consider the extent to which extra-legal factors such as sexual abuse scandals, state compensation schemes, insurance provision etc may have influenced how courts decide cases. Given the ongoing debate of the role of theory in this area of law, notably the influence of ideas of enterprise risk as a justification for a more expansive interpretation of the test for vicarious liability, authors were also asked to consider to what extent express or implicit reference to policy has influenced the application of the law.

As might be anticipated such an ambitious schema has required exceptional national reporters and I have been indeed extremely fortunate in the contributors involved in this project who represent either leading or up-and-coming leading tort law scholars in the jurisdictions they represent. Their scholarship and erudition have truly enriched this volume and it has been a great pleasure to work with such talented scholars. In addition to their excellent contributions to this book, the contributors participated in an online workshop organised by the University of Bristol School of Law and sponsored by the Society of Legal Scholars Small Projects and Events Fund in April 2020 in which their papers were presented live to an online audience across the world from New Zealand to Canada. My great thanks go to our sponsors, our contributors, our excellent audience whose questions tested the contributors and to the practical assistance offered by Paige Spicer at the University of Bristol and University of Bristol PhD student, Katie Mccay and to Professor Ken Oliphant, Head of the University of Bristol School of Law and noted tort law scholar, for his generous opening speech.

It is hoped that the chapters in this collection will prove a source of interest, inspiration and assistance to those seeking to increase their understanding of the doctrine of vicarious liability in tort. As a comparative lawyer my mantra

[9] In terms of Scots law, a mixed common/civil law jurisdiction, although with strong common law overtones in this area of law. The Scots law contributors in chapter nine comment on the strong gravitational pull that English authority has exerted on vicarious liability north of the border although, they note, it is not a one-way street.

has always been: why only look at one system when you can gain inspiration and ideas from others? True, caution might be needed, particularly if you are dealing with non-common law systems with which you are unfamiliar or perhaps a language in which you are not fluent,[10] but a study of common law jurisdictions sharing a common language, historical ties and common legal heritage is a different case entirely. This study should therefore be of interest to academics, students, researchers, but also judges and practitioners who increasingly look to other common law jurisdictions for guidance. In the words of Lord Wilberforce:

> When the judicial approach to an identical problem … has been spelt out with such articulation in a country, one not only so closely akin to ours in legal approach, the fabric of whose legal doctrine in this area is so closely interwoven with ours, … we should be unwise not to take the benefit of it.[11]

Happy reading!
Paula Giliker
Bristol, February 2022

[10] Notably common lawyers often treat civil law systems with caution, see J Stapleton, 'Benefits of Comparative Tort Reasoning: Lost in Translation' in M Andenas and D Fairgrieve (eds), *Tom Bingham and the Transformation of the Law* (Oxford, Oxford University Press, 2009). Personally, I do not share this pessimism, although recognise the challenges of engaging in such work.

[11] *Buttes Gas & Oil Co v Hammer (No 3)* [1982] AC 888, 936–37.

CONTENTS

LIST OF CONTRIBUTORS

Dr Christine Beuermann is Senior Lecturer at the University of Newcastle, UK.

Dr Mat Campbell is Lecturer in Law at the University of Glasgow, Scotland.

Professor Paula Giliker is Professor of Comparative Law at the University of Bristol, UK.

Professor Rick Glofcheski is Professor of Law at the University of Hong Kong.

Jerred Kiss is Student-at-Law, at the University of Western Ontario, Canada.

Dr Bobby Lindsay is Lecturer in Private Law at the University of Glasgow, Scotland.

Professor Jason W Neyers is Professor of Law at the University of Western Ontario, Canada.

Dr Desmond Ryan is Associate Professor in Law at Trinity College Dublin, Ireland.

Professor David Tan is Professor of Law at the National University of Singapore.

Professor Stephen Todd is Professor of Law at the University of Canterbury, New Zealand.

1

Vicarious Liability in the Common Law World

An Introduction

PAULA GILIKER

> … any system of law would be short-sighted if it did not seek to learn lessons from the way in which courts in other countries have handled problems, particularly if the solution adopted elsewhere has worked well.
>
> K Stanton, 'Comparative Law in the House of Lords and Supreme Court' (2013) 42 *Common Law World Review* 269, 270

I. Introduction

Vicarious liability,[1] that is strict liability for the torts of others, represents a core principle of our common law of torts. It is a doctrine found throughout the common law world[2] and, as this book will demonstrate, an area of law where common law courts have drawn assistance from other apex courts, notably from the Supreme Court of Canada and the UK Supreme Court, but also other jurisdictions such as the Singapore Court of Appeal and High Court of Australia. This book will demonstrate the importance of a multi-jurisdictional common law approach, focussing on common law jurisdictions where there has been cross-citation from across the common law world and where senior courts have developed the law with reference to that of other common law jurisdictions. As will be shown, this is not simply a case of former colonies referring to the 'parent' jurisdiction of

[1] Pollock claims to have been the first to coin the phrase (see M DeWolfe (ed), *Holmes-Pollock Letters* (Cambridge, Harvard University Press, 1941) vol 1, 233).

[2] The common law world signifies the expansion of the common law tradition throughout the world as a result of the British empire: see H Patrick Glenn, *Legal Traditions of the World: Sustainable Diversity in Law* 5th edn (Oxford, Oxford University Press, 2014) ch 7 who notes the impact of this process of military, economic and legal domination.

England and Wales but of a more egalitarian exchange of ideas from jurisdictions faced with a common problem.

In this introductory chapter, I will address two issues. First, what do we mean by vicarious liability and what are the key debates that continue to challenge jurists? The roots of vicarious liability can be traced back to the early medieval idea of holding a master responsible for his servant's wrongs,[3] but it is a doctrine that came into its own following the industrial revolution (and the parallel growth of the insurance industry),[4] by permitting injuiry victims to bring claims against employers when the tort was committed by employees in the course of their employment. While early cases focused on employee negligence,[5] twenty-first-century cases, while still including matters such as traffic accidents,[6] as we will see in this book, have increasingly focused on vicarious liability for intentional torts, notably sexual abuse (the tort of battery). While early case law was reluctant to impose liability for intentional torts which could not be attributed to a misguided attempt to benefit the employer,[7] generally contemporary vicarious liability has responded to revelations across the world of historic institutional child sexual abuse by developing its principles to provide victims with the possibility of pursuing not only the culprit (who is often difficult to trace due to lapse of time or even is deceased) but the institution that employed the abuser in question. Employment relationships have also changed dramatically over time, from that of master and servant, to employer and employee, to workers now hired on temporary or zero hours contracts or working for different employers via agencies. The challenges for vicarious liability in the twenty-first century are thus very different from those of previous centuries, requiring the courts not only to address the tests determining the relationships giving rise to vicarious liability and the scope of liability, but also how to justify contemporary extensions to the doctrine. The aim of this work is to provide comparative insights into how the key debates driving vicarious liability today have been addressed by common law courts to assist jurists and practitioners alike.

Secondly, in the final part of this chapter, I will address what benefits may be gained by examining vicarious liability in the common law world, setting out the

[3] C Sappideen and P Vines, *Fleming's The Law of Torts* 10th edn (Pyrmont NWS, Lawbook Co, 2011) 19.10.

[4] See J Bell, 'Convergence and Divergence in the Development of Fault Liability' in J Bell and D Ibbetson (eds), *European Legal Development: The Case of Tort* (Cambridge, Cambridge University Press, 2014) 174–75; GE White, 'The Emergence and Doctrinal Development of Tort Law, 1870–1930' (2014) 11 *University of St Thomas Law Journal* 463.

[5] See eg the nineteenth/early twentieth century cases of *Limpus v London General Omnibus Co* (1862) 1 Hurl & C 526, 158 ER 993 and *Beard v London General Omnibus Co* [1900] 2 QB 530 concerning traffic accidents involving horse drawn buses and over-enthusiastic staff injuring members of the public.

[6] See eg the Hong Kong case of *Ming An Insurance Co (HK) Ltd v Ritz-Carlton Ltd* (2002) 5 HKCFAR 569 where the negligent driving of a hotel doorman, who had 'borrowed' one of the hotel's courtesy limousines to fetch food for himself and fellow staff members, injured two pedestrians.

[7] *Cheshire v Bailey* [1905] 1 K.B. 237, overruled in *Morris v CW Martin & Sons Ltd* [1966] 1 QB 716. See now *Lloyd v Grace, Smith & Co* [1912] AC 716.

structure and methodology of the book and what the chapters that follow seek to achieve. As will be seen, the underlying philosophy of this book is that by seeking insights from native lawyers, experts in their field, we can get insights far deeper than the 'law in books' approach.[8] This work seeks therefore not only to inform – setting out the modern application of vicarious liability in tort and its contemporary justifications across the common law world – but to provoke discussion, analysis and debate. It does so by providing ideas, new sources of authority and access to debates in jurisdictions from Canada to England and Wales and Ireland to Hong Kong and Singapore to New Zealand and Australia with the additional perspective of the Scots courts.[9]

Let us start, however, with the basics: what is vicarious liability and why is it continuing to trouble the apex courts of common law jurisdictions across the world?

II. What Is Vicarious Liability? The Key Debates

Lord Phillips remarked in the leading UK case of *Various Claimants v Catholic Child Welfare Society (CCWS)*,[10] that '[v]icarious liability is a longstanding and vitally important part of the common law of tort'. It is a rule of responsibility that holds one party legally responsible for the torts of another. It involves three stages: the commission of a tort, by a person for whom the defendant is held responsible (the relationship test) when that person is acting in the course of employment (the scope of employment or connection test). In this section, I will outline the three questions that form the key debates that will be explored in the chapters that follow. First, what relationships give rise to vicarious liability? Are similar tests utilised across the common law world? Secondly, when will the commission of the tort be regarded as sufficiently connected to this relationship so as to trigger vicarious liability? Finally, and perhaps one of the most difficult questions, *how* do we justify imposing vicarious liability on defendants who are not personally at fault? In so doing, I will give a brief historical overview to place contemporary debates in historical context. As this book will show, there are not necessarily easy answers to any of these questions, but it is how the courts address these questions, and the factors that influence their approach, which will be the focus of the discussion in the chapters that follow.

[8] W Ewald, 'Comparative Jurisprudence (I): What Was it Like to Try a Rat' (1995)143 *University of Pennsylvania Law Review* 1889, 2109 by which he means a black letter, primarily textualist, conception of law.

[9] Scotland represents a mixed legal jurisdiction (common law/civil law), but its law of delict (tort) is subject to decisions of the UK Supreme Court. It therefore provides an alternative perspective on contemporary common law developments.

[10] *Various Claimants v Catholic Child Welfare Society* [2012] UKSC 56, [2013] 2 AC 1 [34].

A. What Kinds of Relationships Give Rise to Vicarious Liability?

In the vast majority of cases, the relationship that gives rise to vicarious liability will be that of employer and employee,[11] although the doctrine does extend to other relationships, notably those specified by statute[12] and, more controversially, agency.[13] Traditionally, then, the relationship test has been formulated in the context of master/servant, now employer/employee, relationships. In feudal times, this operated narrowly and, as Wigmore identified, represented the idea of responsibility for deeds which the master had commanded or to which he had consented.[14] Baker has quite rightly questioned whether this is what we would now regard as vicarious liability since, under the command theory, the servant's acts, if the master commanded them, would be considered his own acts. He notes, however, that this could no longer be argued by the end of the seventeenth century where the master could be made vicariously liable for acts which he did not command, provided that they were for his benefit and in the course of employment.[15] The end of the seventeenth century, therefore, acts as a transition point where, as commerce and industry expanded, the notion of the 'servant' at the beck and call of the master became increasingly outdated.[16] This later led to broader conceptions of the employment relationship to reflect changing employment practices and the increasing sophistication of industry. As time progressed, one classic debate concerned the liability of surgeons, traditionally seen as independent and therefore not subject to vicarious liability, but in the twentieth century accepted as part of the staff for which the hospital could be held vicariously liable.[17] Kahn-Freund in the 1950s recognised that the law should respond to the social conditions of the present, not the past; technical and economic developments having nullified the assumption that the labourer worked only under the directions and instructions on his employer.[18] A broader understanding was therefore

[11] ibid [35].

[12] See eg Partnership Act 1890 s 10 (UK); Partnership Act 1890, s 10 (Ireland); Partnerships Act, RSO 1990, s 11 (Ontario); Partnership Law Act 2019, s 23 (New Zealand); Partnership Act 1892, s 10 (NSW).

[13] While unsuccessful in *Morgans v Launchbury* [1973] AC 127, cases relying on agency arguments can be found across the common law world, see, for example, *Soblusky v Egan* [1960] HCA 9, (1960) 103 CLR 215; *Ormrod v Crosville Motor Services Ltd* [1953] 1 WLR 409; *S v Attorney-General* [2003] 3 NZLR 450; *Moynihan v Moynihan* [1975] 1 IR 192 (head of household delegating duties to a family member).

[14] JH Wigmore, 'Responsibility for Tortious Acts: Its History. II. Harm Done by Servants and Other Agents: 1300–1850' (1894) 7 *Harvard Law Review* 383, 391. See also WS Holdsworth, *A History of English Law* Volume 3 (London, Methuen, 1908) 383–87.

[15] J Baker, *Introduction to English Legal History*, 5th edn (Oxford, Oxford University Press, 2019) 437.

[16] Holmes commented that the series of cases decided by Lord Holt (which includes *Middleton v Fowler* (n 32) and *Hern v Nichols* (1708) 1 Salk 289, 91 ER 256 form the starting point for modern decisions: OW Holmes, 'Agency' (1891) 4 *Harvard Law Review* 345, 362.

[17] Compare *Hillyer v The Governors of St. Bartholomew's Hospital* [1909] 2 KB 820 with the later case of *Cassidy v Ministry of Health* [1951] 2 KB 343.

[18] O Kahn-Freund, 'Servants and Independent Contractors' (1951) 14 *MLR* 504, 505–06.

needed of the 'employment' relationship which led to changes in the latter half of the twentieth century, notably with tests examining the degree of integration of the worker into the workplace[19] and the economic realities of the parties' situation examining the totality of the parties' relationship.[20]

One key debate addressed in this book is the extent to which changes in work practices now threaten the dominance of the traditional employment relationship. In the past, the courts regarded the contract of employment (as opposed to a contract for services) as the primary indicator of the relationship needed to trigger vicarious liability. Yet, employers now will often 'contract out' essential services such as cleaning, refuse collection and even administrative jobs such as IT provision or human resources. Those providing these services will often step into posts previously held by full-time employees. While use of agency or temporary staff may be financially beneficial to both employers and the staff they hire,[21] when these staff injure victims tortiously, the question arises whether vicarious liability continues to apply. Mulcahy in her book, *The Gig Economy*,[22] comments on how our work patterns have changed dramatically in one generation. In the past, she notes, most workers could expect to be full-time employees in secure full-time jobs, working for just one or two companies over the course of their careers. In contrast, today's employees can look forward to holding multiple jobs over the course of their careers and must accept that their lives will be made up of what she optimistically terms 'a variety of diverse work and work experiences'.[23] She adds:

> If we think of the current world of work as a spectrum, anchored by the traditional corporate job and career ladder on one end, and unemployment on the other end, then the broad range and variety of alternative work in between is the Gig Economy. The Gig Economy includes consulting and contractor arrangements, part-time jobs, temp assignments, freelancing, self-employment, side gigs, and on-demand work through platforms.[24]

How do we deal with victims injured by such workers? McKendrick in 1990 pointed out that if this new flexible workforce of casual workers and 'temps' were excluded from vicarious liability, there was a danger that the social purposes of the doctrine, such as loss distribution, would be undermined.[25] He identified a new

[19] *Stevenson Jordan & Harrison Ltd v MacDonald & Evans* [1952] 1 TLR 101, 111 per Denning LJ.

[20] *Market Investigations v Minister of Social Security* [1969] 2 QB 173, 185 per Cooke J; *Stevens v Brodribb Sawmilling Co Pty Ltd* [1986] HCA 1, (1986) 160 CLR 16, 29 per Mason J; *671122 Ontario Ltd v Sagaz Industries Canada Inc* [2001] 2 SCR 983, (2001) 204 DLR (4th) 542, [46]–[48] per Major J.

[21] eg for taxation purposes. Morgan also argues that there is an industry of volunteers that work alongside paid employees, carrying out the same tasks, receiving the same training, and wearing the same uniform and that the law must hence evolve to accept non-contractual employees for the purposes of vicarious liability: P Morgan, 'Recasting Vicarious Liability' (2012) 71 *CLJ* 615, 649.

[22] D Mulcahy, *The Gig Economy* (New York, AMACOM, 2017).

[23] ibid 2.

[24] ibid 1.

[25] E McKendrick, 'Vicarious Liability and Independent Contractors – A Re-examination' (1990) 53 *MLR* 770.

class of workers who were closely associated with the enterprise and in the same position as employees where the imposition of vicarious liability could be justified, although he also noted concerns as to the vagueness of this categorisation.[26]

Kidner also argued that the drift to casualised forms of working required a relationship test that could take account of new kinds of employment.[27] So how, therefore, should a legal system treat the claim of a person injured by the negligence of a bicycle courier making a delivery, identifiable only by the company name on his tabard?[28] Or that of the school-leaver sexually abused in the course of a mandatory health check prior to taking up employment when the check is delegated to an independent doctor?[29] Tan, in chapter six, argues that the law of vicarious liability must evolve to meet the exigencies of the contemporary work arrangements in the gig economy that include outsourcing and part-time contracts.

Changing patterns of employment give rise to further related questions. How should legal systems deal with workers sent by one employer to assist another with its operation where both employers seem to exercise some degree of control over the worker? Should joint vicarious liability be permissible despite the violence such a construction inflicts on traditional ideas of the employer/employee relationship?[30] The rise of claims of historic child sexual abuse against religious organisations such as the Roman Catholic Church has also raised questions whether priests – who are not technically employees – should be subject to vicarious liability. If, as we will see below, a wide interpretation of the course of employment test permits abuse potentially to be regarded as in the course of employment, can the relationship test extend to tortfeasors who are not strictly employees?[31]

As will be explored in this book, these are questions to which there is no straightforward answer and where courts have sought assistance from other common law courts facing the same dilemmas.

[26] ibid 781.

[27] R Kidner, 'Vicarious Liability: For Whom Should the Employer Be Liable?' (1995) 15 *Legal Studies* 47.

[28] See *Hollis v Vabu Pty Ltd* [2001] HCA 44, (2001) 207 CLR 21, discussed in chapter four.

[29] *Barclays Bank plc v Various Claimants* [2020] UKSC 13, [2020] AC 973, discussed in chapter three.

[30] Again, different approaches can be identified to this problem across the common law world, contrast, for example, *Viasystems (Tyneside) Ltd v Thermal Transfer (Northern) Ltd* [2005] EWCA Civ 1151, [2006] QB 510 with its rejection in *Day v The Ocean Beach Hotel Shellharbour Pty Ltd* [2013] NSWCA 250, (2013) 85 NWSLR 335, and, more recently, *Hallmark Construction Pty Ltd v Harford* [2020] NSWCA 41.

[31] See *Doe v Bennett* [2004] 1 SCR 436, (2004) 236 DLR (4th) 577 (Canada), *CCWS* (UK) and *Trustees of Roman Catholic Church v Ellis* [2007] NSWCA 117, (2007) 70 NSWLR 565, discussed in later chapters.

B. To Which Torts Should Vicarious Liability Apply? The Course of Employment/Connection Test

The scope of liability is also fundamental to our understanding of the doctrine of vicarious liability. It determines the breadth of this strict liability doctrine. If we can assume that, in most cases, employees are not hired to commit torts, then *when* should the employer be held answerable for its employees' torts? The answer to this question has changed over time. Initially, courts focused on whether the employer/master had commanded his servant to do the very act which harmed the victim, but this came to be regarded as far too narrow by the late seventeenth century when wider formulations came to be utilised.[32] By the nineteenth century, the courts were starting to develop the course of employment test with the terms 'scope' or 'course' of employment' coming into play in response to a changing industrialised society.[33] The doctrine did not apply, however, where the employee was 'on a frolic of his own'. As stated in the leading case of *Joel v Morison:* 'the master is only liable where the servant is acting in the course of his employment … but if he was going on a frolic of his own, without being at all on his master's business, the master will not be liable'.[34] Such case law raised a number of issues, notably to what extent liability would be dependent on the employee's acts being for the employer's benefit?[35] Would it include, for example, wilful acts that were for the employee's own benefit? Such questions were resolved to a certain extent by *Lloyd v Grace, Smith & Co* in 1912,[36] but as we will see in this book, have yet to be fully resolved by common law legal systems.

The key debate that will be addressed in this book is the extent to which the Salmond test for course of employment, stated initially in Salmond's successful 1907 textbook but adopted across the common law world, continues to influence modern law. Under the Salmond test, vicarious liability will only arise if the

[32] Wigmore (n 14) 392–94. See *Middleton v Fowler* (1698) 1 Salk 282, 91 ER 247, for example, which argued that 'no master is chargeable with the acts of his servant, but when he acts in execution of the authority given by his master'; 'authority' here replacing the language of 'command' and, in the view of Swain, moving the doctrine closer towards the modern doctrine of vicarious liability: W Swain, 'A Historical Examination of Vicarious Liability: A "Veritable Upas Tree"?' (2019) 78 *CLJ* 640, 645.

[33] See eg *Sleath v Wilson* (1839) 9 C & P 607, 612, 173 ER 976, 979: 'acting in the course of his employment'. See also *Ellis v Turner* (1800) 8 TR 531, 101 ER 1529 and, generally, A Bell, 'Scope of Employment: Connecting Closely with the Past' (2021) 137 *LQR* 254.

[34] (1834) 6 C & P 501, 503, 172 ER 1338, 1339 per Parke B.

[35] See eg *Turberville v Stampe* (1698) 1 Ld Raym 264, 265, 91 ER 1072, 1073 per Holt CJ: 'his master shall be liable … for it shall be intended that the servant had authority from his master, it being for his master's benefit' and *Duncan v Findlater* (1839) 6 Cl & F 894, 910, 7 ER 934, 940 per Lord Brougham: 'by employing him I set the whole thing in motion; and what he does, being done for my benefit and under my direction, I am responsible for the consequences of doing it'.

[36] [1912] AC 716 which accepted that an employer could be liable for the dishonesty or fraud of his employee if done within the course of employment, no matter if done entirely for the employee's own benefit.

employee's tort represented 'either (a) a wrongful act authorised by the master or (b) a wrongful and unauthorised mode of doing some act authorised by the master'.[37] Lunney argues that it was Salmond's ability to encapsulate a sophisticated idea in a neat verbal formula that endeared him to generations of students, practitioners and judges alike.[38] It also made the test easily transmissible. In the New Zealand case of *Pettersson v Royal Oak Hotel Ltd*,[39] for example, the Salmond test was cited in argument where a barman had responded to a drunken customer by throwing broken pieces of a glass at him, injuring another customer in the process. Such an act was regarded as an improper mode of doing his job of keeping order in the bar and avoiding altercations. The Privy Council (on appeal from the Supreme Court of Canada) in *Canadian Pacific Railway Co v Lockhart*[40] equally used Salmond as its starting point for its analysis. Lunney attributes the longevity of the Salmond formulation to its elegance and seductive systemising of the law, despite its difficulties in explaining cases such as *Lloyd v Grace, Smith & Co*.[41]

Difficulties with the application of the Salmond test come to the fore in relation to deliberate acts of misconduct by employees.[42] As Lord Toulson commented in the UK case of *Mohamud*, even on the most generous interpretation of the test, it would be impossible to describe intentional torts such as sexual abuse as improper modes of caring for children.[43] Common law systems therefore face a choice: either to reject claims involving torts so heinous that they would fail the Salmond test or reformulate the test to include such claims. One of the issues discussed in this book is how the common law courts have responded to this challenge. And respond they have had to do. Revelations of historic institutional child sexual abuse across the common law world have given rise to claims

[37] JW Salmond, *The Law of Torts* 1st edn (London, Stevens and Haynes, 1907) 83. This test was repeated in each edition until its final edition in 1996: RFV Heuston and RA Buckley, *Salmond and Heuston on the Law of Tort* 21st edn (London, Sweet and Maxwell, 1996) 443.

[38] M Lunney, 'Professor Sir John Salmond (1862–1924): An Englishman Abroad' in D Nolan and J Goudkamp (eds), *Scholars of Tort Law* (Oxford, Hart Publishing, 2020) 125.

[39] *Pettersson v Royal Oak Hotel Ltd* [1948] NZLR 136. Contrast, however, its application in the Australian case of *Deatons Pty Ltd v Flew* [1949] HCA 60, (1949) 79 CLR 370 (unprovoked attack by a barmaid on customer not wrongful mode of doing authorised act nor incidental to her employment).

[40] *Canadian Pacific Railway Co v Lockhart* [1942] AC 591, 599 per Lord Thankerton, approved by the SCC in *WW Sales Ltd v City of Edmonton* [1942] SCR 467. The Salmond test was expressly endorsed in the Irish context in cases such as *Reilly v Ryan* [1991] 2 LR 247, 249 per Blayney J. See also PC (Singapore) in *Keppel Bus Co v Sa-ad bin Ahmad* [1974] 1 WLR 1082, 1084: 'There is no dispute about the law … the well-known passage from *Salmond on the Law of Torts* … which was approved in *Canadian Pacific Railway* … it is not necessary to repeat it'.

[41] Lunney (n 38) 125.

[42] Rose argued in 1977 that universal and rigid adherence to the Salmond test had obscured the central question of *whether* vicarious liability should extend to intentional harm: FD Rose, 'Liability for an employee's assault' (1977) 40 *MLR* 420.

[43] *Mohamud v Wm Morrison Supermarkets plc* [2016] UKSC 11, [2016] AC 677 [39]. See also *Trotman v North Yorkshire County Council* [1999] LGR 584, 591 per Butler-Sloss LJ: 'in the field of serious sexual misconduct, I find it difficult to visualise circumstances in which an act of the teacher can be an unauthorised mode of carrying out an authorised act'.

against these institutions that they should be held vicariously liable for the torts of their employees.[44] All systems have also faced questions of the extent to which the employer should be held responsible for acts of violence between workers in the workplace. As we will see, the reaction to these challenges has not been uniform. Salmond has proven hard to shift as an underlying test. In *Bazley v Curry*[45] and *Lister v Hesley Hall Ltd*,[46] the Supreme Court of Canada and UK House of Lords preferred a test of 'close connection' (that is, whether the tort was closely connected to the tasks the employee was asked to do) to the traditional Salmond test, on the basis the latter could not be stretched to cover cases of child sexual abuse. Nevertheless, the courts justified this move by referring to text in Salmond itself which argued that a master would be liable for acts which he had not authorised 'provided they are so connected with acts which he has authorised, that they may be rightly regarded as modes – although improper modes – of doing them'.[47] While systems such as Hong Kong[48] and Singapore[49] have embraced the *Bazley/Lister* connection test, other systems, notably Australia,[50] have proven more resistant.

A further question for jurisdictions to ponder is the fact that the Salmond test does work in relation to non-intentional torts even if it has been subject to criticism for lack of precision.[51] Should the courts, then, adopt different tests for 'course of employment' for negligence and intentional torts? Or even restrict the test to cases of institutional child sexual abuse? Glofcheski suggested in 2004 that if confined to intentional misconduct (the context of *Lister* and *Bazley*), the close connection test could indeed be viewed as a merely incremental adjustment necessary to address the injustice of vulnerable groups of tort victims being left without a remedy.[52]

[44] This is a global problem, see eg Canada ('The Catholic Church in Canada is worth billions, a Globe investigation shows. Why are its reparations for residential schools so small?' *The Globe and Mail*, 7 August 2021), Australia ('Why was their trust betrayed?: Australia apologises to child sexual abuse victims' *Guardian Australia*, 22 October 2018), UK ('Survivors demand action on "epidemic" of child sexual abuse affecting millions in UK' *The Independent*, 4 July 2021) and Ireland ('A church haunted by the abused' *Irish Independent*, 22 November 2020).

[45] *Bazley v Curry* [1999] 2 SCR 534, (1999) 174 DLR (4th) 45, discussed in more detail in chapter two.

[46] *Lister v Hesley Hall Ltd* [2001] UKHL 22, [2001] 1 AC 215, discussed in more detail in chapter three.

[47] Salmond (n 37) 83–84. See Lord Steyn in *Lister* ibid [15], who argued that Salmond's explanation is the germ of the Canadian close connection test used in *Bazley*.

[48] See *Ming An Insurance Co (HK) Ltd v Ritz-Carlton Ltd* (2002) 5 HKCFAR 569, discussed by Glofcheski in chapter seven.

[49] *Skandinaviska Enskilda Banken AB (Publ) Singapore Branch v Asia Pacific Breweries (Singapore) Pte Ltd* [2011] SGCA 22, [2011] 3 SLR 540, discussed by Tan in chapter six.

[50] Note the debate in *New South Wales v Lepore* [2003] HCA 4, (2003) 212 CLR 511, for example. In the now leading case of *Prince Alfred College v ADC* [2016] HCA 37, (2016) 258 CLR 134, the HCA was dismissive of attempts in *Bazley* to link the close connection test to that of Salmond: 'The requirement of connection might be based on what had been said by Salmond … However, the risk-allocation aspect of the theory is based largely on considerations of policy … Such policy considerations have found no real support in Australia': [59]. See, further, Beuermann in chapter four in this book.

[51] See, eg, PS Atiyah, *Vicarious Liability in the Law of Torts* (London, Butterworths, 1967) 181.

[52] R Glofcheski, 'A Frolic in the Law of Tort: Expanding the Scope of Employers' Vicarious Liability' (2004) 12 *Tort Law Review* 18, 29.

To what extent, then, do we have an uniform test for 'course of employment' or, as it is increasingly termed in certain common law jurisdictions, a common test of 'close connection'? This question will be answered in the chapters that follow.

C. How Do We Justify the Imposition of Vicarious Liability?

While the doctrine of vicarious liability is well-established,[53] its place in the law of torts, dominated by ideas of corrective justice,[54] remains controversial. As Lord Nicholls commented in the UK case of *Majrowski*,

> [t]his principle of vicarious liability is at odds with the general approach of the common law. Normally common law wrongs, or torts, comprise particular types of conduct regarded by the common law as blameworthy … The general approach is that a person is liable only for his own acts.[55]

Stevens argues that difficulties in justifying vicarious liability derive from the fact that orthodoxy is wrong – what is attributed is the action, not the liability.[56] However, such arguments (also known as the master's tort thesis) were rejected by the House of Lords in *Staveley Iron & Chemical Co Ltd v Jones*[57] and are not followed across the common law world.[58] Atiyah, in his leading monograph, re-iterated the problems we face in seeking to justify vicarious liability: it runs counter to two fundamental principles of the common law of torts – that we should only be liable for our own acts or omissions and that liability should be based on fault. 'These principles', he stated, 'are so deeply rooted in legal thinking that any departure from them seems at first sight impossibly unjust'.[59]

One final key debate, then, in which the contributors must engage, is how does a legal system justify such a principle? Early cases make reference to the phrases '*respondeat superior*'[60] and '*qui facit per alium facit per se*',[61] but without

[53] 'Any idea of repealing vicarious liability would seem to us preposterous, inconceivable': GT Schwartz, 'The Hidden and Fundamental Issue of Employer Vicarious Liability' (1996) 69 *Southern California Law Review* 1739, 1745.

[54] See, for example, EJ Weinrib, 'Corrective Justice in a Nutshell' (2002) 52 *University of Toronto Law Journal* 349. It is equally difficult to reconcile with rights-based reasoning: see R Stevens, *Torts and Rights* (Oxford, Oxford University Press, 2007) 244: 'The challenge vicarious liability poses for a rights-based account of the law is twofold. First, liability appears to be imposed upon a party who has not infringed a right of the claimant. Secondly, the policy justifications commonly given for imposing the losses caused by the employee's wrong upon the employer are based upon the assumption that the law of torts is concerned with ensuring compensation for loss, not vindicating rights'.

[55] *Majrowski v Guy's and St Thomas's NHS Trust* [2006] UKHL 34, [2007] 1 AC 224 [7]–[8].

[56] Stevens (n 54) ch 11.

[57] *Staveley Iron & Chemical Co Ltd v Jones* [1956] AC 627, 643 (Lord Reid).

[58] See eg *Majrowski* (n 55) [15] (Lord Nicholls) and *Hollis v Vabu Pty Ltd* (2001) 207 CLR 21 [34]–[35].

[59] Atiyah (n 51) 12.

[60] Let the master answer.

[61] He who acts through another does the act himself.

any real sense of providing a theoretical basis for the doctrine.[62] Lord Reid summed up these phrases neatly in *Staveley Iron and Chemical Co Ltd v Jones*[63] when he commented that 'the former merely states the rule badly in two words, the latter merely gives a fictional explanation of it'. Lord Nicholls in *Majrowski*[64] took the view that whatever its historical origin, it was important to identify the factors influencing the doctrine today and that a combination of different policy factors seem to be shaping the law. Noted jurist, Fleming, described vicarious liability as a doctrine that 'cannot parade as a deduction from legalistic premises but should be frankly recognised as having its basis in a combination of policy considerations'.[65] Lord Toulson more recently in *Mohamud*[66] acknowledged that one could not explain vicarious liability without referring to competing legal theories, changes in the structure and size of enterprises and changes in social attitudes and the courts' sense of justice and fairness, not least in relation to new problems arising from revelations of child sexual abuse by people in a position of authority.

Justifying vicarious liability requires, therefore, the court to provide a contemporary explanation for a doctrine which has grown and developed over the centuries. One of the most dynamic justifications in recent years has been that of enterprise risk, promoted in US law and economics literature.[67] The Supreme Court of Canada in the important case of *Bazley* in 1999 explained that:

> The employer puts in the community an enterprise which carries with it certain risks. When those risks materialise and cause injury to a member of the public despite the employer's reasonable efforts, it is fair that the person or organisation that creates the enterprise and hence the risk should bear the loss.[68]

On this basis, it is argued, where the risk of injury is closely associated with the wrong that occurred, it is just that the entity that operates the enterprise (and in many cases profits from it) should internalise the full cost of operation, including the commission of torts. Lord Phillips commenting on UK law in 2012 found that:

> Starting with the Canadian authorities a common theme can be traced through most of the cases … Vicarious liability is imposed where a defendant, whose relationship with the abuser put it in a position to use the abuser to carry on its business or to further its

[62] Bell (n 33) 276 identifies a number of different justifications in the seventeenth and eighteenth centuries.

[63] [1956] AC 627, 643. Note also criticism by Fullager J in *Darling Island Stevedoring and Lighterage Co Ltd v Long* (1957) 97 CLR 36, 56–57.

[64] *Majrowski* (n 55) [9].

[65] JG Fleming, *The Law of Torts* 9th edn (Sydney, LBC Information Services, 1998) 410.

[66] *Mohamud* (n 43) [10].

[67] See eg AO Sykes, 'The Economics of Vicarious Liability' (1983–84) 93 *Yale Law Journal* 1231; AO Sykes, 'The Boundaries of Vicarious Liability: An Economic Analysis of the Scope of Employment Rule and Related Legal Doctrines' (1988) 101 *Harvard Law Review* 563; GC Keating, 'The Idea of Fairness in the Law of Enterprise Liability' (1997) 95 *Michigan Law Review* 1266. See, generally, GL Priest, 'The Invention of Enterprise Liability: A Critical History of the Intellectual Foundations of Modern Tort Law' (1985) 14 *Journal of Legal Studies* 461.

[68] *Bazley* (n 45) [31].

> own interests, has done so in a manner which has created or significantly enhanced the risk that the victim or victims would suffer the relevant abuse … Creation of risk is not enough, of itself, to give rise to vicarious liability for abuse but it is always likely to be an important element in the facts that give rise to such liability.[69]

However, not all jurisdictions have proven so supportive. The High Court of Australia in *Prince Alfred College v ADC*, for example, noted that *Bazley* reasoning, seen as largely based on considerations of policy, has not attracted significant support in Australia.[70]

Enterprise liability reasoning has the dual benefits of providing a justification for extending the liability of enterprises (taken to include charitable and non-profit-making institutions) for a broad range of torts, the risk of which they create by using employees in the operation of their enterprise, while, it is argued, distributing losses fairly and efficiently throughout society and encouraging employers to exercise a greater degree of care with respect to the appointment and supervision of employees.[71]

However, as will be seen in the chapters that follow, the merits of enterprise risk reasoning have been a matter of contention across common law legal systems. While it may provide an easy means by which to expand the doctrine, there are associated dangers, not least that any person (independent contractor or employee) working for an employer has the potential risk of causing harm which indicates the need for a very generous interpretation of the relationship test.[72] There is also the issue, as indicated by Fleming above, that common law courts have been reluctant to opt for one policy justification. Lord Phillips listed in *CCWS*,[73] in addition to enterprise risk, arguments based on control, delegation of duty and deeper pockets[74] that have influenced the courts.[75] Equally the benefit/burden argument,[76] that is, that those who set in motion and profit from the activities of their employees should compensate those who are injured by such activities even when performed negligently, continues to have a general appeal.[77]

[69] *CCWS* (n 10) [86]–[87].

[70] *Prince Alfred College* (n 50) [59].

[71] C Witting, 'Modelling Organisational Vicarious Liability' (2019) 39 *Legal Studies* 694 argues that deterrence works best in medium and large sized organisation permitting 'mediated' deterrence: 700–01.

[72] D Brodie, 'Enterprise Liability: Justifying Vicarious Liability' (2007) 27 *OJLS* 493.

[73] *CCWS* (n 10) [35].

[74] The argument has been criticised in that it is not a 'policy' justification as such, but a practical way of ensuring victims obtain compensation. G Williams, 'Vicarious Liability and the Master's Indemnity' (1957) 20 *MLR* 220, 232 describes it as a purely cynical theory that the master should be liable because he has a purse worth opening.

[75] For a discussion of policy grounds for vicarious liability, see Atiyah (n 51) ch 2; A Gray, *Vicarious Liability: Critique and Reform* (Oxford, Hart Publishing, 2018) chs 5–8; P Giliker, *Vicarious Liability in Tort: A Comparative Perspective* (Cambridge, Cambridge University Press, 2010) ch 8.

[76] *Qui sentit commodum debet sentire et onus* (he who enjoys the benefit ought also to bear the burden).

[77] See *Viasystems* (n 30) [55] per Rix LJ. This may be seen as a principle of natural justice (see Williams (n 74) 230) or, alternatively, as a loose formulation of enterprise risk.

We may, therefore, want to distinguish between enterprise risk in its strict law and economics sense and more general reference to ideas of 'risk' by the courts. Atiyah, for example, argues that employers should be vicariously liable for torts 'which can fairly be regarded as reasonably incidental risks to the type of business he carries on',[78] but should we take this as early advocacy of the *Bazley* approach or rather a more instinctive sense that it would be just to hold employers liable for risks that experience tells us are inherent in the nature of the business? Are the common law courts by relying on enterprise risk as a justification engaging with law and economics reasoning or rather relying on a simple formula that supports their instinctive reaction to the case at hand?

These questions will be addressed in the chapters that follow and are important to the future of the doctrine. In expanding vicarious liability, the apex courts in each common law jurisdiction are increasingly being called upon to justify their approach. It is difficult to create a test that is predictable and clear if its underlying rationale is in a state of flux. Equally we might want to question whether the same justification should be used for all torts. Should we seek different justifications for intentional and non-intentional torts? Or argue that torts involving sexual abuse and flagrant abuse of power require their own particular rationale and justification?[79] There is no simple answer to any of these questions but, by reviewing the debates across the common law world, the reader will gain a clearer idea of what is at stake and different approaches, some more successful than others.

III. Examining Vicarious Liability in the Common Law World

The aim of this book is to address the key debates discussed above from the perspective of leading common law jurisdictions: Canada, England and Wales, Australia, Ireland, Singapore, Hong Kong and New Zealand. These represent common law jurisdictions from the global North and South, drawn together by their common law legal heritage. As Patrick Glenn has argued, it is important to conceive the 'common law' not simply as a set of rules passed around the world, but as a legal tradition that not only accepts matters such as the centrality of judicial decision-making and the doctrine of *stare decisis*, but also represents a type of legal thinking, regardless of the diversity of the societies in question.[80]

These particular jurisdictions have been chosen for a number of reasons. First, they share, as has been stated, a common legal tradition, in that they are legal systems whose law is based on English law and connected by reason of colonisation

[78] Atiyah (n 51) 171.

[79] See, for example, Lord Phillips' discussion of risk and sexual abuse in *CCWS* (n 10) [87].

[80] Glenn (n 2) ch 7. See also G Samuel, 'Common Law' in JM Smits (ed), *Elgar Encyclopedia of Comparative Law* 2nd edn (Cheltenham, Edward Elgar, 2012) who describes the distinctive way of thinking of the common lawyer.

under the British Empire.[81] They also have a long history of citing each other's case law,[82] and of academic interaction. As this book will show, there is a community of common law private lawyers (of which the authors in this book are leading members) whose academic scholarship is shared across the common law world. Anyone writing on vicarious liability, therefore, would be wise to consider not only scholars in their own jurisdiction, but those across the common law world to gain insights into the operation of this doctrine and its future development.

Secondly, given that similar versions of the doctrine of vicarious liability may be found in all the jurisdictions considered in this book, vicarious liability represents an area of law ripe for comparative reflection. Indeed, in recent years, there has been a remarkable level of cross-citation between these jurisdictions. As we will see in the chapters that follow, the UK Supreme Court in recent years has relied on case law from Canada (notably *Bazley*), New Zealand[83] and Singapore,[84] while the courts of Ireland, Singapore, Hong Kong and New Zealand frequently refer to UK case law, the Canadian case of *Bazley* also proving influential. While disagreeing with the UK and Canadian response, the High Court of Australia nevertheless discusses their leading cases at length, regarding them as having the status of persuasive authority. What is important (and comes out throughout the chapters that follow) is that in citing decisions from other common law jurisdictions, these cases are not seen as 'foreign' law, but rather as living law that may be useful in the practical process of dispute resolution.[85] This is not to deny differences. The systems addressed in this book *are* different, but the key point is that they continue to demonstrate sufficient commonalities to render a comparative study useful in providing inspiration for change (or indeed quite the opposite!)

This book also includes the perspective from Scots law. While it represents an English-speaking 'mixed' legal system (civil/common law),[86] its law of delict is subject to decisions of the *UK* Supreme Court, although English appeals to the UK Supreme Court are technically non-binding in Scotland. While Scots lawyers

[81] M Siems, *Comparative Law* 3rd edn, (Cambridge, Cambridge University Press, 2022) 50–52.

[82] In contrast, citation of other common law jurisdictions such as India and African states such as Nigeria is infrequent. The common law status of India is also a matter of some dispute eg Menski argues that India is often mistakenly portrayed as a common-law country thereby ignoring the complex mixture of various legal systems that constitutes Indian law: WF Menski, *Comparative Law in a Global Context* (Cambridge, Cambridge University Press, 2006) 203. See also Menski's ch 6 on African laws.

[83] *S v Attorney-General* [2003] NZCA 149, [2003] 3 NZLR 450, cited in *Armes v Nottinghamshire CC* [2017] UKSC 60 [66] and [70].

[84] *Ng Huat Seng v Munib Mohammad Madni* [2017] SGCA 58, [2017] 2 SLR 1074, cited in *Barclays* (n 29) [26].

[85] HP Glenn, 'Persuasive Authority' (1987) 32 *McGill Law Journal* 261, 289.

[86] VV Palmer (ed), *Mixed Jurisdictions Worldwide: The Third Legal Family* 2nd edn (Cambridge, Cambridge University Press, 2012), R Zimmermann, D Visser and K Reid (eds), *Mixed Legal Systems in Comparative Perspective: Property and Obligations in Scotland and South Africa* (Oxford, Oxford University Press, 2005).

keep pace where possible with their larger neighbouring jurisdiction, it should be noted that this is a relationship that works both ways and that, in hearing appeals from Scotland, there is clearly the potential for Scottish legal principle to influence English tort law. The 2013 vicarious liability decision of the Inner House of the Scottish Court of Session in *Vaickuviene v Sainsbury*,[87] for example, has been cited by the English courts.[88] The UK Constitutional Reform Act 2005, section 27(8) requires that the Supreme Court justices must have knowledge or experience of the practice of law in each part of the United Kingdom including, of course, Scotland.[89] Indeed, the current President of the UK Supreme Court, Lord Reed, who decided a number of influential vicarious liability cases, previously practised at the Scottish Bar and served as a senior judge in Scotland for 13 years. Given this fertile relationship, a Scots perspective on developments on vicarious liability in the common law world serves to enhance the content and quality of the discussions raised in this book.

The book does not, however, include a chapter on United States law. This is deliberate and reflects the fact that its case law on vicarious liability is rarely cited by other common law courts. This limited level of cross-citation can be attributed to a number of reasons. First, the United States was never part of the Commonwealth and its law not subject to appeals to the Privy Council which served to maintain the influence of the English common law across the common law world.[90] While the right of appeal to the Privy Council was abolished in Ireland (1933) and Canada (1949) in the first half of the twentieth century, other systems covered in this book retained the right of appeal until much later: Australia and Singapore (1980s), Hong Kong (1997) and New Zealand (2003). These jurisdictions therefore have a far closer affinity with each other. Secondly, and perhaps more fundamentally, unlike the law of England and Wales or even Australia,[91] there is no 'United States' law of vicarious liability as such. Stapleton comments

[87] *Vaickuviene v J Sainsbury plc* [2013] CSIH 67, [2013] IRLR 792 (the question of vicarious liability arising when one supermarket shelf-stacker stabbed another to death).

[88] See, for example, *Mohamud v WM Morrison Supermarkets plc* [2014] EWCA Civ 116, [2014] IRLR 386 and *Graham v Commercial Bodyworks Ltd* [2015] EWCA Civ 47, [2015] ICR 665 (which also cited *Wilson v Exel UK Ltd* [2010] CSIH 35).

[89] This means that, in practice, appointments to the Supreme Court will seek to ensure that there is continued representation from both Scotland and Northern Ireland: www.supremecourt.uk/about/appointments-of-justices.html.

[90] Indeed, the Privy Council continues to provide persuasive dicta on the application of vicarious liability in hearing appeals from states such as Jamaica (*Bernard v Attorney General of Jamaica* [2004] UKPC 47, *Brown v Robinson* [2004] UKPC 56) and the British Virgin Islands (*Attorney General of the British Virgin Islands v Hartwell* [2004] UKPC 12). Lord Reed in *Wm Morrison Supermarkets plc v Various Claimants* [2020] UKSC 12 cited all three UKPC decisions in setting out the law: [23] and [39]–[40].

[91] The High Court of Australia has distinguished the 'common law of Australia' which is declared by the HCA as the final court of appeal from the position in the United States which is fragmented into different systems of jurisprudence, possessing different content and subject to different authoritative interpretations: *Lange v Australian Broadcasting Corporation* [1997] HCA 25, (1997) 189 CLR 520 [39].

that, in the US, there is a multiplicity of tort law jurisdictions and hence potentially dozens of final pronouncements on a point of common law tort law.[92] While there are state-based laws of vicarious liability, these will lack the authoritative status of a national supreme court. On this basis, although there is significant commonality across jurisdictions, the application of the law will not be identical. Comparative lawyer Jan Smits also notes a lack of interest in foreign law which he attributes to the fact that inter-state comparison (ie among the 53 American jurisdictions) is much more important than comparison with legal systems outside the United States.[93] Researchers therefore tend to refer to restatements of law produced by the American Law Institute[94] which provide both an overview of US law and an influential source widely cited and used by the courts. This leads to my third point which is that the key reference point for those researching US law in this field is the ALI Restatement on the Law of *Agency*: Restatement (3d) of Agency (2006). Treating liability as 'agency'[95] rather than 'vicarious liability' raises conceptual disparities – not least in relation to whether we are dealing with primary or secondary liability – which, despite overlapping ideas of employer/employee relationships and scope of employment,[96] render it less useful as a comparator for other common law courts. The Restatement further does not define who is an employee nor address the employee/independent contractor distinction.[97] Gray nevertheless argues that regardless of the limited utility of its case law, US academic literature is often helpful, particularly in relation to the theory of enterprise risk.[98] The leading common law case on enterprise risk – *Bazley v Curry*[99] – relied on US authority when setting out the principle. US literature will therefore be cited in this book when proven to be influential across the common law world.

[92] J Stapleton, 'Benefits of Comparative Tort Law Reasoning: Lost in Translation' (2006) 1(3) *Journal of Tort Law* 1, 24. She also commented that US tort law is further fragmented by local state legislative reforms. See also Siems (n 81) 74–77, who outlines the difficulties of using US law as a common law comparator.

[93] JM Smits, 'Comparative Law and its Influence on National Legal Systems' in M Reimann and R Zimmermann (eds), *The Oxford Handbook of Comparative Law* 2nd edn (Oxford, Oxford University Press, 2019) 505, describing the current position as 'parochial'.

[94] The ALI is an independent US organisation that produces Restatements of Law, Model Codes and Principles of Law to clarify, modernise and otherwise improve the law (www.ali.org/).

[95] See Holmes' famous article, 'Agency', discussed above. *Restatement of the Law (3d) Agency* defines agency as: '§ 1.01 Agency is the fiduciary relationship that arises when one person (a "principal") manifests assent to another person (an "agent") that the agent shall act on the principal's behalf and subject to the principal's control, and the agent manifests assent or otherwise consents so to act'. For a recent discussion, see R Van Loo, 'The Revival of Respondeat Superior and Evolution of Gatekeeper Liability' (2020) 109 *Georgetown Law Journal* 141.

[96] See *Restatement of the Law, Agency 3d* § 2.04 *Respondeat Superior*: 'An employer is subject to liability for torts committed by employees while acting within the scope of their employment.' An 'employee' is defined as 'an agent whose principal controls or has the right to control the manner and means of the agent's performance of work,' (§7.07(3)(a)). An employee 'acts within the scope of employment when performing work assigned by the employer or engaging in a course of conduct subject to the employer's control': (§7.07(2)).

[97] Gray (n 75) 90. Note also his helpful discussion of US law: 88–95.

[98] ibid 93.

[99] *Bazley* (n 45).

IV. Structure and Methodology of the Book

The chapters in this collection will set out the modern doctrine of vicarious liability in each common law jurisdiction. As indicated above, the book will address each system in turn, starting with the legal systems generating the most influential case law (Canada, England and Wales, Australia) and then moving to smaller legal systems across the common law world. In each chapter, the author(s) will seek to:

- Set out the current test for vicarious liability and key case-law sources and academic authority;
- Examine the justifications for vicarious liability, notably the influence of arguments of enterprise risk;
- Highlight the extent to which global concerns (eg revelations of institutional child sexual abuse and changing patterns of employment) and local/political concerns have influenced the application of the test;
- Consider, as relevant, specific local factors such as statutory intervention, state-based compensation schemes and the availability of liability insurance;
- Consider the influence of case-law from other common law jurisdictions;
- Make, when possible, predictions for the future.

Given the ambition of this text and the need for localised knowledge, no single author would be able to achieve these objectives. Leading scholar(s) from each jurisdiction will therefore focus on their own domestic law, providing insights and critical commentary from their position as a local expert but also as a distinguished academic working in the field of vicarious liability with a track record of exploring its application across the common law world. The aim also was to involve scholars at different stages of their careers and, where possible, encourage diversity. By including multiple contributors, the aim is to provide both a snapshot of vicarious liability across the common law world, but also a deeper understanding of its operation and future application.

The book will conclude with a comparative chapter. This will reflect on the debates and developments discussed in this book and draw out comparative insights to assist scholars and practitioners working in this area of law. Given that this is an area of law where the law is unsettled, the final chapter will provide a clear overview of the insights to be gained from reviewing vicarious liability across the common law world.

V. Final Remarks

Vicarious liability in tort continues to test our skills as jurists in determining its scope, its theoretical basis and how best to express its test(s). No legal system in this book has found a magic solution that renders vicarious liability straightforward and easy to apply. However, it is submitted, it is these challenges that make this book exceptionally timely. At a time of uncertainty, we need to think beyond national boundaries and look for wisdom and inspiration elsewhere. Where better than looking at other common law jurisdictions with similar key case law authorities and historic ties? For academics, students, researchers, judges and practitioners seeking to navigate this area of law, this book offers a way forward – providing an overview of the law in key common law jurisdictions, addressing contemporary debates and providing potential solutions. My hope is that the reader enjoys this journey through the common law of vicarious liability as much as I have in editing the book and working with an engaging, talented and erudite team of contributors.

2

Vicarious Liability

The Revolution in Canada

JASON W NEYERS AND JERRED KISS*

I. Introduction

Over the course of the past two decades, a series of decisions from the House of Lords and the UK Supreme Court has resulted in vicarious liability undergoing a far-reaching and rapid 'transformation' in England.[1] Although this transformation has been provocative and controversial – one need only examine Professor Giliker's contribution to this collection in chapter three[2] or turn to the law journals to find an abundance of recent literature considering the topic[3] – from the point of view of Canadian scholars, much of it is unsurprising. The reason for this subdued reaction lies in the fact that vicarious liability had already undergone

* This research was funded in part by an Insight Grant from the Social Sciences and Humanities Research Council. The authors thank Paula Giliker, Bret Gillespie, John Murphy, Stephen Pitel and Robert Stevens for specific comments on the draft and thank the participants at the *Vicarious Liability in the Common Law World* workshop hosted by the University of Bristol for their discussion of the ideas presented herein. The usual disclaimer applies.

[1] P Giliker, 'Can the Supreme Court Halt the Ongoing Expansion of Vicarious Liability? *Barclays* and *Morrison* in the UK Supreme Court' (2021) 37 *Journal of Professional Negligence (PN)* 55, 55.

[2] See, also, P Giliker, 'Vicarious Liability "On the Move": The English Supreme Court and Enterprise Liability' (2013) 4 *Journal of European Tort Law* 306; P Giliker, 'Vicarious Liability, Non-Delegable Duties and Teachers: Can You Outsource Liability for Lessons?' (2015) 31 *PN* 259; P Giliker, 'A Revolution in Vicarious Liability: *Lister*, the Catholic Child Welfare Society Case and Beyond' in S Worthington, A Robertson and G Virgo (eds), *Revolution and Evolution in Private Law* (Oxford, Hart Publishing, 2018).

[3] Beyond the work of Professor Giliker and the material we cite in this article, see B Lindsay, 'Fostering in a New Age of Vicarious Liability' (2018) 22 *Edinburgh Law Review* 294; J Lee, 'The Supreme Court, Vicarious Liability and the Grand Old Duke of York' (2020) 136 *LQR* 553; C Purshouse, 'Halting the Vicarious Liability Juggernaut: *Barclays Bank Plc v Various Claimants*' (2020) 28 *Medical Law Review* 294; R Buxton, 'Vicarious Liability in the Twenty-first Century' (2020) 97 *CLJ* 217; E Gordon, '*Mohamud* Explained and Re-Understanding "Close Connection" in Vicarious Liability' (2020) 79 *CLJ* 401.

its own revolution in the Canadian common law.[4] Moreover, given that many of the UK's recent vicarious liability decisions have tended to follow the path blazed by the Supreme Court of Canada,[5] Canadian jurists have arguably become acclimated to what, from the point of view of English scholars, might appear to constitute radical developments. Indeed, if asked to compare the UK Supreme Court's recent vicarious liability decisions with the Canadian jurisprudence, perhaps the most straightforward answer either one of us could provide is: 'been there, done that'.

In this chapter, we aim to more fully explore the contours and result of the Canadian vicarious liability revolution.[6] In doing so, we hope to be able to provide judges and scholars in other jurisdictions, who are considering whether to accelerate the development of the doctrine[7] or whether to 'apply the brakes'[8] on recent developments, with guidance as to how Canadian courts have addressed the perennial issues that surround the scope of vicarious liability.[9] In Section II, we describe how, beginning in the late 1990s, the Supreme Court of Canada's approach to vicarious liability began to evolve. Section III explores the social context surrounding the court's decisions and examines the key drivers of the court's overhaul of vicarious liability. Section IV describes the current two-pronged test for establishing vicarious liability in Canada. After outlining this test, Section V then examines the influence Canadian jurisprudence has had across the Commonwealth. In Section VI, we review the Supreme Court of Canada's current theoretical justifications for vicarious liability. Finding these theories wanting, in Section VII we offer a principled justification for the modern doctrine of vicarious liability developed by the court. Section VIII concludes.

[4] For an examination of vicarious liability in Quebec civil law see N De Stefano, 'A Comparative Look at Vicarious for Intentional Wrongs and Abuses of Power in Canadian Law' (2020) 98 *Canadian Bar Review* 1.

[5] See the discussion at Section V below.

[6] For greater detail, see JW Neyers, 'Vicarious Liability' in E Chamberlain and SGA Pitel (eds), *Fridman's The Law of Torts in Canada* 4th edn (Toronto, Thomson Reuters, 2020).

[7] As perhaps is occurring in Australia. For a discussion see the contribution by Beuermann to this collection. See also J Goudkamp and J Plunkett, 'Vicarious Liability in Australia: On the Move?' (2017) 17 *Oxford University Commonwealth Law Journal* 162; H Crawford, 'A Step in the Right Direction? Vicarious Liability for Intentional Wrongdoing of Employees in *Prince Alfred College Incorporated v ADC*' (2017) 24 *Torts Law Journal* 179; P Giliker, 'Analysing Institutional Liability for Child Sexual Abuse in England and Wales and Australia: Vicarious Liability, Non-Delegable Duties and Statutory Intervention' (2018) 77 *CLJ* 506; C Beuermann, *Reconceptualising Strict Liability for the Tort of Another* (Oxford, Hart Publishing, 2019); P Bomball, 'Vicarious Liability, Entrepreneurship and the Concept of Employment at Common Law' (2021) 43 *Sydney Law Review* 83.

[8] AJ Bell, 'Plus ça change, plus c'est la vicarious liability' (2020) 36 *PN* 150, 150.

[9] As arguably has occurred in the United Kingdom as a result of *WM Morrisons Supermarkets Plc v Various Claimants* [2020] UKSC 12 and *Barclays Bank Plc v Various Claimants* [2020] UKSC 13. For discussion see Giliker (n 1).

II. The Vicarious Liability Revolution in Canada[10]

Prior to the revolution ushered into existence by the Supreme Court of Canada's companion decisions in *Bazley v Curry*[11] and *Jacobi v Griffiths*,[12] the law concerning when one person could be held vicariously liable for the wrongs committed by another was fairly well-settled in Canadian law. In order for such liability to be imposed it was necessary to prove three things.[13] First, that a tort or other actionable wrong had been committed against the claimant-victim.[14] Second, that the person who committed the tort was the employee (or agent)[15] of the person sought to be made vicariously liable, as opposed to an independent contractor.[16] Third, that the tort was committed while the employee or agent was acting in the course of their employment or agency.[17] A complicated but fairly stable body of law had evolved which explained each of these requirements. For example, in relation to the second requirement courts examined the extent to which the employer controlled the actions of the putative employee,[18] whether the putative employee was an integral part of the employer's business rather than being merely accessory to it,[19] and the extent to which the putative employee was an entrepreneur.[20] In relation to the third requirement, Canadian courts used the Salmond test to determine when a tort was considered to have occurred in the course of employment.[21] The test was as follows:

> A master is not responsible for a wrongful act done by his servant unless it is done in the course of his employment. It is deemed to be so done if it is either (1) a wrongful act

[10] This part follows the analysis in, and draws heavily on, C Brown, S Pitel and J Neyers, 'The Impact of Recent Legal Developments on Liability Insurance' (2006) 32 *Advocates Quarterly* 1.
[11] [1999] 2 SCR 534 (*Bazley*).
[12] [1999] 2 SCR 570 (*Jacobi*).
[13] See S Wildeman, 'Vicarious Liability for Sexual Assault: The Two New Tests for Scope of Employment in *B(PA) v Curry* and *T(G) v Griffiths*' (1998) 7 *Dalhousie Journal of Legal Studies* 1, 5–7 discussing the pre-*Bazley* law.
[14] *Staveley Iron & Chemical Co Ltd v Jones* [1956] AC 627 (HL); *British Columbia Ferry Corp v Invicta Security Service Corp* (1998) 58 BCLR (3d) 80 (CA).
[15] The agency could either be for profit or gratuitous: see *Morgans v Launchbury* [1973] AC 127 (HL); *Gramak Ltd v O'Connor* (1974) 1 OR (2d) 505 (CA).
[16] See *671122 Ontario Ltd v Sagaz Industries Canada Ltd* [2001] 2 SCR 983 (*Sagaz*).
[17] See LN Klar, *Tort Law* 3rd edn (Toronto, Carswell, 2010) 579–80, 586; GHL Fridman, *The Law of Torts in Canada* 2nd edn (Toronto, Carswell, 2002) 276.
[18] See *Quarman v Burnett* (1840) 6 M & W 499; *St John (City) v Donald* [1926] SCR 371; *Bright & Co Ltd v Kerr* [1939] SCR 63; *Hôpital Notre-Dame de l'Espérance v Laurent* [1978] 1 SCR 605.
[19] *Stephenson Jordan & Harrington Ltd v MacDonald & Evans* [1952] 1 TLR 101, 111 (Denning LJ); *Armstrong v Mac's Milk Ltd* (1975) 55 DLR (3d) 510 (Ont HC); *Mayer v J Conrad Lavigne Ltd* (1979) 105 DLR (3d) 734 (Ont CA); *McCrindle v Westin Ltd* (1985) 35 CCLT 183 (Ont HC).
[20] *Montreal v Montreal Locomotive Works Ltd* [1947] 1 DLR 161 (PC).
[21] Embraced in *WW Sales Ltd v City of Edmonton* [1942] SCR 467.

> authorized by the master, or (2) a wrongful and unauthorized mode of doing some act authorized by the master.[22]

For the second branch of the Salmond test, the courts developed three categories of cases in which they considered that an act met its requirements: negligence (since it is a 'method of performing an act' rather than being a distinct or different act),[23] fraud committed within the employee's actual or apparent authority, even if the employee acted in their own interest,[24] and intentional torts which could be classified as an overzealous but good faith performance of the contract of employment.[25]

Bazley and *Jacobi*, however, were cases involving sexual abuse of children by employees. In contrast to the established categories, sexual abuse cases posed difficulties for the second branch of the Salmond test since, as the English Court of Appeal had noted in similar circumstances, it is difficult to define such abuse as an unauthorised mode of performing an authorized act.[26] Therefore, in order to find the employer vicariously liable, it would be necessary for the Supreme Court of Canada to re-examine the concept of 'course of employment'.

In *Bazley* the defendant was a non-profit foundation that operated a residential care facility for the treatment of emotionally troubled children. It provided, through its employees, total intervention into all aspects of the lives of the children. After performing a background check, the foundation hired Curry to work in its facility, unaware that he was a paedophile. Curry subsequently sexually assaulted Bazley, a child in his care. When the foundation discovered the abuse, it discharged Curry from his employment. Subsequently, Bazley sued the foundation to recover for the injuries he suffered as a result of Curry's tort.

Rather than following orthodoxy, the Supreme Court of Canada unanimously held that the foundation was vicariously liable for Curry's tort, thereby expanding the concept of vicarious liability for a wrong committed by an employee. Instead of asking whether the wrong was an 'unauthorized way of performing an authorized act', *Bazley* called on courts to ask whether there was a 'significant connection' between the risk to the community created by the employer's enterprise and the harm that occurred.[27] Merely providing the opportunity for harm to occur was said not to be enough.[28] The court also stated that the rules of vicarious liability

[22] RFV Heuston and RA Buckley, *Salmond & Heuston on The Law of Torts* 19th edn (London, Sweet & Maxwell 1987) 521–22. For a discussion of the use of the test in Canada pre-*Bazley* see Wildeman (n 13) 34ff.

[23] *Kooragang Investments Pty Ltd v Richardson & Wrench Ltd* [1981] 3 All ER 65 (PC) 69.

[24] *Lloyd v Grace, Smith & Co* [1912] AC 716 (HL).

[25] Compare *Deatons Pty Ltd v Flew* [1949] HCA 60, (1949) 79 CLR 370; *Daniels v Whetstone Entertainments Ltd* [1962] 2 Lloyd's Rep 1 (CA); *Lakatosh v Ross* (1974) 48 DLR (3d) 694 (Man QB). See also Wildeman (n 13) 38–40.

[26] *Trotman v North Yorkshire County Council* [1999] LGR 584 (CA). See also *McDonald v Mombourquette* (1996) 152 NSR (2d) 109 (CA) and the discussion in Wildeman (n 13) 47–50.

[27] *Bazley* (n 11) [37]–[39].

[28] See *EDG v Hammer* (1998) 53 BCLR (3d) 89 (SC), aff'd [2003] 2 SCR 459.

were justified by the policies of fair compensation and deterrence.[29] The imposition of vicarious liability was said to further the policy of compensation since it improves the innocent victim's chances of finding a solvent defendant. As to the question of the fairness of this compensation, the court stressed that this was provided by the concept of enterprise risk:

> Vicarious liability is arguably fair in this sense. The employer puts in the community an enterprise which carries with it certain risks. When those risks materialize and cause injury to a member of the public despite the employer's reasonable efforts, it is fair that the person or organization that creates the enterprise and hence the risk should bear the loss. This accords with the notion that it is right and just that the person who creates a risk bear the loss when the risk ripens into harm. While the fairness of this proposition is capable of standing alone, it is buttressed by the fact that the employer is often in the best position to spread the losses through mechanisms like insurance and higher prices, thus minimizing the dislocative effect of the tort within society.[30]

As to the second policy consideration – deterrence of future harm – the court reasoned that by holding employers liable without proof of fault, they would be induced to take actions that would reduce the number of torts committed by their employees and agents. According to the court:

> Beyond the narrow band of employer conduct that attracts direct liability in negligence lies a vast area where imaginative and efficient administration and supervision can reduce the risk that the employer has introduced into the community. Holding the employer vicariously liable for the wrongs of its employee may encourage the employer to take such steps, and hence, reduce the risk of future harm.[31]

Applying this reasoning to the facts, the court held that the foundation materially enhanced the risk of harm to children since 'it is difficult to imagine a job with a greater risk for child sexual abuse'.[32] The close and intimate nature of the interaction between Curry and the children made the sexual assault a wrong that occurred in the course of his employment. The foundation was thus held vicariously liable.

In *Jacobi*, the court followed the reasoning in *Bazley* but arrived at a different conclusion. A non-profit club for boys and girls had hired Griffiths to supervise its volunteer staff and to organize recreational activities and outings for the children. It was later discovered that Griffiths had sexually abused several of the children

[29] *Bazley* (n 11) [34]. Because compensation is one of the goals of the doctrine, courts will not hold an employer 'vicariously' liable for punitive damages unless there is reprehensible conduct specifically referable to the employer: see *Blackwater v Plint* 2005 SCC 58 [90]; *McCabe v Roman Catholic Episcopal Corp*, 2019 ONCA 213. If that is the rule, is the liability really vicarious? For a survey of this issue across the Commonwealth, see S Todd, 'Vicarious Liability, Personal Liability and Exemplary Damages' in S Degeling, J Edelman and J Goudkamp (eds), *Torts in Commercial Law* (Sydney, Thomson Reuters Australia, 2011); A Gray, *Vicarious Liability: Critique and Reform* (Oxford, Hart Publishing, 2018) ch 11 and Professor Todd's contribution to this volume, chapter eight.

[30] *Bazley* (n 11) [31].

[31] ibid [33].

[32] ibid [58].

at his home. In a four-to-three decision, the court held that the club could not be vicariously liable for Griffiths's tort since there was not a close enough connection between Griffiths's employment and the wrongdoing: his employment did not materially increase the risk of the abuse. The risk only increased once Griffiths substantially deviated from his contract and invited the victims to his home.

III. Societal Influences on Canada's Test for Vicarious Liability

Bazley and *Jacobi* constitute two of the common law world's most 'significant'[33] vicarious liability decisions. In order to fully understand them, however, one needs to appreciate the context in which they arose. As we discuss below, Nolan's recent remark that '[t]he most significant driver' of vicarious liability's transformation in the UK has 'been the desire of courts to reshape the law so as to provide meaningful redress to victims of child sexual abuse in institutional settings' applies with equal force in Canada.[34] The goal of providing child sexual abuse victims with monetary compensation, in other words, shaped the law in Canada similar to the way that it shaped the law in the United Kingdom.

Perhaps the best place to start in order to appreciate the context of *Bazley* and *Jacobi* is 1984, the year in which a government-sponsored report (the 'Badgley Report') investigating the prevalence of child sexual abuse in Canada was released.[35] The Badgley Report's findings were shocking. It found that one in two girls and one in three boys under the age of 18 were victims of unwanted sexual advances. Importantly for the present discussion, it also found that a substantial number of the perpetrators of this abuse (about one in four) were people in positions of trust (such as institutional figures).[36] Far from child sexual abuse being the result of a few isolated wrongdoers, then, the Badgley Report revealed that it was rampant across Canadian society.[37]

The Badgley Report was just the tip of the iceberg. Soon after the report was released, a number of shocking news stories relating to institutional child sexual abuse began to substantiate many of the report's findings. For example, news of sexual abuse perpetuated at an Ontario reformatory school began to make

[33] D Brodie, *Enterprise Liability and the Common Law* (Cambridge, Cambridge University Press, 2010) 1.

[34] D Nolan, 'Reining in Vicarious Liability' (2020) 49 *Industrial Law Journal* 609, 609. See also, Giliker, above n 7, which also discusses the experience in Australia.

[35] Committee on Sexual Offences Against Children and Youth, *Sexual Offences Against Children* (Ottawa, Minister of Supply and Services, 1984).

[36] ibid 2.

[37] The Badgley Report was cited by the Supreme Court of Canada on several occasions around the time it released *Bazley* and *Jacobi*, largely in the criminal law context. See eg *R v B(G)* [1990] 2 SCR 3, 14–15; *R v L(WK)* [1991] 1 SCR 1091, 1100; *R v Downey* [1992] 2 SCR 10, 17, 32–34; *R v Marquard*, [1993] 4 SCR 223, 257–58; *R v L(DO)* [1993] 4 SCR 419, 439–41; *R v O'Connor* [1995] 4 SCR 411, [120]; *R v Audet* [1996] 2 SCR 171, [6], [14] and [49]; *R v F(WJ)*, [1999] 3 SCR 569 [13].

headlines in the early 1990s.[38] Similarly, in 1989 news of sexual abuses at Mount Cashel – a Newfoundland orphanage run by the Congregation of Christian Brothers – quickly 'exploded'[39] across Canadian media outlets.[40] Together, these news stories, in conjunction with other appalling headlines,[41] provided Canadians with concrete evidence of the child sexual abuse epidemic indicated in the Badgley Report.

Around the same time that the Badgley Report's findings were beginning to ripple across Canadian society, revelations of systemic sexual abuse at church- and government-run residential schools of Indigenous children and youth were also becoming well-known.[42] While it is impossible to do the topic justice here, residential schools were institutions established by the Canadian government under the Indian Act[43] in an attempt to assimilate Indigenous children.[44] While the federal government was responsible for establishing these schools, their day-to-day operations were largely left in the hands of religious institutions, 'who [...] had an interest in converting the "heathen Indian" to Christianity'.[45] Sadly, in addition to stripping Indigenous children of their language and culture – something undoubtedly devastating in its own right[46] – sexual abuse was rampant in residential schools. When Canada's Royal Commission on Aboriginal Peoples released its final report in 1996, for instance, it described the sexual abuse occurring in them as 'pervasive'.[47]

[38] D Pugliese, 'Archbishop Apologizes to Alfred Victims; Catholic Church Trying to Stop Such Abuses' *Ottawa Citizen* (23 September 1990). Recently some Canadian politicians have called for a public inquiry into the abuses which took place in Ontario's reformatory schools. See 'MP Calls for Inquiry into Abuse at Alfred Training School' *CBC News* (30 January 2018), online: www.cbc.ca/news/canada/ottawa/david-sweet-training-school-inquiry-1.4507764.

[39] TJ Trothen, *Shattering the Illusion: Child Sexual Abuse and Canadian Religious Institutions* (Waterloo, Wilfrid Laurier Press 2012) 6.

[40] Vicarious liability was recently imposed on the Archdiocese of St John's for the abuse perpetuated in Mount Casphel. See *John Doe (GEB #25) v The Roman Catholic Episcopal Corporation of St John's*, 2020 NLCA 27, leave to appeal to SCC refused, 39343 (14 January 2021).

[41] See eg the stories of institutional sexual abuse contained in N Underwood, 'The Abuse of Children', *Maclean's* (27 November 1989), online: The Abuse Of Children | Maclean's | NOVEMBER 27, 1989 (macleans.ca).

[42] Trothen, *Shattering the Illusion* (n 39) 6.

[43] RSC, 1985 c I-5. Despite 'inspiring universal antipathy', the Indian Act continues to apply in Canada: see M Morden, 'Theorizing the Resilience of the Indian Act' (2016) 59 *Canadian Public Administration* 113, 113.

[44] E Adjin-Tettey, 'Righting Past Wrongs Through Contextualization: Assessing Claims of Aboriginal Survivors of Historical and Institutional Abuses' (2007) 25 *Windsor Yearbook of Access to Justice* 95, 99.

[45] ibid.

[46] For a comprehensive overview of the legacy of residential schools in Canada see M Florence, *Righting Canada's Wrong: Residential Schools* (Toronto, James Lorimer & Company, 2015); E Furniss, *Victims of Benevolence: The Dark Legacy of the Williams Lake Residential School* (Vancouver, Arsenal Pulp Press, 2002). For a particularly compelling personal account see E Clearsky, 'Destruction of a Language and Culture: A Personal Story' (2011) 5 *Diaspora, Indigenous, and Minority Education* 260.

[47] G Erasmus and R Dussault, *Report of the Royal Commission on Aboriginal Peoples* (Volume 1, The Commission, 1996), 359. See also Truth and Reconciliation Commission of Canada, *What We Have Learned: Principles of Truth and Reconciliation* (Winnipeg, National Centre for Truth and Reconciliation Centre, 2015).

Suffice it to say, then, that the 1980s and 1990s were characterised by an increasing number of revelations of institutional child sexual abuse. Equally important to the present discussion, however, is what emerged in the *aftermath* of these revelations. On this point, the work of Feldthusen is apposite. Research by Feldthusen in the early 1990s revealed that as institutional child sexual abuse was becoming more openly acknowledged in Canada, many victims were turning to Canada's civil justice system in order to bring their assailants to justice.[48] Institutional child sexual abuse, in other words, was quickly transforming from something that was not even talked about in Canada, to something that was becoming openly litigated in Canadian courtrooms. For instance, one particularly illuminating study by Feldthusen found that '[p]rior to 1985 there had been only a handful of civil actions pertaining to sexual abuse. Since then [ie, between 1985–1996], more than 50 Canadian sexual battery and related judgments have been reported.'[49] Importantly, many of these claims related to institutional child sexual abuse.

Unfortunately, most of these claims were unable to provide child sexual abuse victims with meaningful compensation.[50] As soon became apparent, many of the perpetrators of child sexual abuse were judgment-proof by the time of trial.[51] Hence, while child sexual abuse litigation still had the potential to provide victims with positive therapeutic effects, its ability to result in an award of damages was often limited.[52]

Unsurprisingly, this is where vicarious liability entered the picture. Because so many perpetrators of child sexual abuse were insolvent, victims began to seek out ways to extend liability beyond the particular assailant and onto a third-party (often the assailant's employer).[53] And while 'traditional actions in negligence and more innovative actions for breach of fiduciary duty'[54] proved sufficient to establish third-party liability in some cases, the doctrine which many third-party liability cases soon came to turn on was vicarious liability. Vicarious liability, in other words, soon became the main way – indeed often the only way given how Canadian courts developed non-delegable duties[55] – victims could obtain access to meaningful compensation.

The more that victims began to invoke the doctrine of vicarious liability, however, the more it became apparent that the principle was in need of Supreme

[48] B Feldthusen, 'The Civil Action for Sexual Battery: Therapeutic Justice?' (1993) 25 *Ottawa Law Review* 203, 205–06.

[49] B Feldthusen, 'The Canadian Experiment with the Civil Action for Sexual Battery' in N Mullany (ed), *Torts in the Nineties* (Sydney, LBC Information Services, 1997) 274.

[50] ibid 277.

[51] B Feldthusen, 'Civil Liability for Sexual Assault in Aboriginal Residential Schools: The Baker Did It' (2007) 22 *Canadian Journal of Law and Society* 61, 80.

[52] Feldthusen (n 49) 275.

[53] Wildeman (n 13) 3.

[54] ibid 4.

[55] See the discussion of non-delegable duties below at IVC.

Court of Canada clarification. On the one hand, some judges were employing a strict conception of the traditional Salmond test to determine whether vicarious liability could be imposed. Because, as noted above, that test only imposed vicarious liability where a tortious act could be perceived as an unauthorised 'mode' of performing an authorised act, judges who applied a rigid conception of the traditional Salmond test rarely imposed liability.[56] Instead, perpetrators were often held, in the classic language, to have engaged in a frolic of their own.[57]

On the other hand, however, no doubt in an effort to provide innocent sexual abuse victims with access to a meaningful remedy, other courts began to reject the traditional Salmond test in the context of institutional child sexual abuse claims.[58] Indeed, the rejection of the traditional Salmond test was most notably embraced by the British Columbia Court of Appeal in *Bazley*, where the court unanimously held that the Salmond test's 'unauthorized mode of an authorized act' requirement was inappropriate in the sexual abuse context.[59] Instead, the court held that more broad-based tests focusing on either an employee's conferred authority (Huddart JA) or proximity (Newbury JA) were more appropriate.

This, then, was the context in which the Supreme Court of Canada granted leave to appeal in *Bazley* and *Jacobi*. In a span of less than two decades the problem of institutional child sexual abuse had transformed from something which was 'largely kept hidden'[60] to something litigated in Canadian courtrooms. The challenge for the Supreme Court, therefore, was to consider how to best refine the Canadian doctrine of vicarious liability so that it could provide meaningful yet fair compensation for institutional child sexual abuse victims. As noted above, the Supreme Court responded by transforming the Salmond test into one of significant connection in *Bazley* and *Jacobi*. And although it initially appeared as if *Bazley* and *Jacobi* might represent the culmination of the vicarious liability revolution in Canada, the cases in fact turned out to be merely its beginning. Thus, in a series of subsequent decisions over 15 years,[61] the Supreme Court re-evaluated all aspects of the doctrine – mostly widening liability in favour of third party victims, but occasionally 'applying the brakes' to ensure the revolution did not go too far.[62]

[56] See eg the decision of the Nova Scotia Court of Appeal in *McDonald v Mombourquette* (1996) 152 NSR (2d) 109.

[57] *Joel v Morrison* (1834) 172 ER 1338 (Ex), 1339.

[58] Wildeman (n 13) 7.

[59] (1997) 30 BCLR (3d) 1.

[60] J Steed, *Our Little Secret: Confronting Child Sexual Abuse in Canada* (Toronto, Random House Canada, 1994).

[61] See *Jacobi*, above n 11, *B(KL) v British Columbia* [2003] 2 SCR 403 (*B(KL)*); *John Doe v Bennett* [2004] 1 SCR 436 (*Bennett*); *Blackwater*, above n 29; *EB v Order of the Oblates of Mary Immaculate in the Province of British Columbia*, 2005 SCC 60 (*Oblates*); *3464920 Canada Inc v Strother* [2007] 2 SCR 177 (*Strother*).

[62] See *Oblates*, above n 61 and *Sagaz*, above n 16.

IV. The Current Test for Vicarious Liability in Canada

Post-*Bazley*, vicarious liability for the torts (or other actionable wrongs)[63] of another will be imposed if two requirements (in addition to the commission of the wrong) are met. First, there must be a sufficiently close relationship between the defendant and tortfeasor so as to make vicarious liability appropriate. Second, the tort committed must be sufficiently connected to the duties entrusted to the tortfeasor by the defendant.[64] Here, we review both of these elements starting with the second requirement given its historical role as the genesis of the Canadian vicarious liability revolution.

A. Sufficiently Close Conduct[65]

As we have seen, cases involving allegations of vicarious liability for sexual abuse prompted the re-examination of the Salmond test and raised squarely the issue of whether an employer could be vicariously liable outside the traditional categories of negligence, fraud and good faith performance. In *Bazley*, the Supreme Court was especially critical of two aspects of the Salmond test. The first criticism was that from a policy perspective, the results of the cases appeared arbitrary: why for example was there vicarious liability for theft or fraud but not generally for sexual battery?[66] The second was that it was often difficult to distinguish between an unauthorised mode of performing an authorised act and a truly independent act.[67]

Rather than engaging in 'semantic discussions',[68] the court in *Bazley* suggested that the correct way to deal with this issue was first to determine whether there were any precedents that 'unambiguously determine' whether vicarious liability should be imposed.[69] Should an answer not be forthcoming from the precedents,

[63] Such as equitable wrongs (see *Strother*, above n 61) or a civilly actionable breach of a statute, so long as the statute does not expressly or impliedly indicate otherwise (see *Ari v Insurance Corp of British Columbia*, 2015 BCCA 468). For discussion, see B von Tigerstrom, 'Direct and Vicarious Liability for Tort Claims Involving Violation of Privacy' (2018) 96 *Canadian Bar Review* 539, 560–62.

[64] See for example *B(KL)*, above n 61, [19]; *Bennett*, above n 61, [20]; *LR v Bromley Estate* 2013 NLCA 24 [11]; *Kassian Estate v Canada (Attorney General)* 2015 ONCA 544, [11].

[65] This part follows the analysis in, and draws heavily on, Neyers (n 6) 331–52 and E Chamberlain and SGA Pitel (general eds), *Introduction to the Canadian Law of Torts* 4th edn (Toronto, LexisNexis, 2020) 24–27.

[66] *Bazley*, above n 11, [23].

[67] ibid [16].

[68] ibid [41].

[69] ibid [15]. What constitutes an 'unambiguous precedent' is often in the eye of the beholder: see *Solis v del Rosario*, 2015 ABCA 227 [15].

the court held that judges should be guided by the following principles, which it succinctly summarised in *Blackwater v Plint*:

> Vicarious liability may be imposed where there is a significant connection between the conduct authorized by the employer or controlling agent and the wrong. Having created or enhanced the risk of the wrongful conduct, it is appropriate that the employer or operator of the enterprise be held responsible, even though the wrongful act may be contrary to its desires … The fact that wrongful acts may occur is a cost of business. The imposition of vicarious liability in such circumstances serves the policy ends of providing an adequate remedy to people harmed by an employee and of promoting deterrence. When determining whether vicarious liability should be imposed, the court bases its decision on several factors, which include: (a) the opportunity afforded by the employer's enterprise for the employee to abuse his power; (b) the extent to which the wrongful act furthered the employer's interests; (c) the extent to which the employment situation created intimacy or other conditions conducive to the wrongful act; (d) the extent of power conferred on the employee in relation to the victim; and (e) the vulnerability of potential victims.[70]

As the subsequent jurisprudence makes clear,[71] the significant connection or close connection test is now the sole test used by Canadian courts to determine whether a particular tort was committed in the course of a particular actor's employment. Thus, the ultimate question is whether what the actor did was significantly or closely connected with what they were employed to do so as to lead to the conclusion that the employer should be vicariously responsible.

The exclusive nature of Canada's significant or close connection test means that, unlike in English law, there is no different test to be applied to determine whether an employer should be vicariously liable for fraudulent misrepresentations.[72] This also means that Canadian courts can be predicted to be unreceptive to recent suggestions made by the UK Supreme Court[73] that sexual abuse cases have their own more expansive variation of the sufficient connection test that does not necessarily apply outside of that type of case.[74] In applying its new test, Canadian courts have found that in certain circumstances retaliatory batteries,[75]

[70] *Blackwater*, above n 29, [20].

[71] See *Jacobi*, above n 11; *B(KL)*, above n 61, *Bennett*, above n 61; *Blackwater*, above n 29; *Oblates*, above n 61; *Strother*, above n 61.

[72] *Armagas Ltd v Mundogas SA* [1986] AC 717 (HL); *Hockley Mint Ltd v Ramsden* [2018] EWCA Civ 2480. Interestingly, some Singaporean commentators have recently suggested that courts in that jurisdiction have incorporated the English approach to vicarious liability for deceit *into* the close connection test. In other words, despite using different language, the test for vicarious liability for deceit is said to be substantively the same in both countries (see Ng SH, 'Blurred Lines: No Distinction Between Agency and Vicarious Liability in Fraud' (2020) 15 *Singapore Comparative Law Review* 109; C-H Tan, 'Authority, Vicarious Liability and Misrepresentation' (2012) 1 *Singapore Journal of Legal Studies* 92). Notably, no similar argument concerning the Canadian jurisprudence has been proposed. For an analysis of Singapore, see the contribution of Tan to this volume, chapter six.

[73] See eg D Brodie, 'Vicarious Liability and Bifurcation: Reflections on *WM Morrison Supermarkets v Various* Claimants' (2020) 24 *Edinburgh Law Review* 389.

[74] *Morrison*, above n 9, [23] and [36].

[75] *Cimpean v Payton* [2008] OJ No 2665 (QL) (SCJ).

sexual abuse[76] and breach of fiduciary duty or fraud[77] can be so closely connected to an employee's duties to justify the imposition of vicarious liability. In other instances, however, courts have found that these same wrongs (battery,[78] sexual abuse[79] and fraud[80]) are not sufficiently connected to what the employee was employed to do, thus making the imposition of vicarious liability inappropriate.

B. Sufficiently Close Relationship[81]

As noted above, in order to impose vicarious liability, there must also be a sufficiently close relationship between the tortfeasor and the person sought to be made vicariously liable. The paradigmatic relationship of sufficient closeness is that between an employer and employee. However, as the Supreme Court of Canada made clear in *John Doe v Bennett* (a case in which it imposed vicarious liability on a bishop for the sexual abuse committed by a priest), vicarious liability is not limited to such relationships.[82] Conversely, the paradigmatic relationship that is not close enough for the imposition of vicarious liability is between an employer and an independent contractor. Therefore, in modern Canadian law courts must be able to distinguish between relationships for which there can be vicarious liability (which we will call relationships 'akin to employment') from those relationships for which there can generally be no vicarious liability (which we will call independent contractor relationships).

Interestingly, although it is now clear that independent contractor relationships are not sufficiently close to impose vicarious liability in Canada, *Bazley*'s emphasis on policy briefly led some commentators to speculate whether the vital distinction between relationships 'akin to employment' and independent contractors might be in jeopardy.[83] For example, would not innocent victims be better compensated,

[76] See *Bennett*, above n 61; *Blackwater*, above n 29.

[77] *Strother*, above n 61; *Mignault v Palmer* 2013 MBQB 300.

[78] *Reddemann v McEachnie* 2005 BCSC 915.

[79] *Oblates*, above n 61; *TI v Lakovic* 2017 ONCA 446.

[80] *Bank Leu AG v Gaming Lottery Corp* (2003) 231 DLR (4th) 251 (Ont CA); *Solis v del Rosario* 2015 ABCA 227.

[81] This part follows the analysis in, and draws heavily on Neyers (n 6) 305–13 and Chamberlain and Pitel (n 65) 19–22.

[82] Above n 61.

[83] AE Spafford, 'The Enterprise Risk Theory: Redefining Vicarious Liability for Intentional Torts' (LLM thesis, University of Toronto, 2000) 71–73. As a result of *Cox v Ministry of Justice* [2016] UKSC 10 (*Cox*) and *Various Claimants v Catholic Child Welfare Society* [2012] UKSC 56 (*CCWS*), lower courts in England also began questioning whether there should be vicarious liability for independent contractors (see eg A Silink, 'Vicarious Liability of a Bank for the Acts of a Contracted Debtor' (2018) 34 *PN* 46; A Silink and D Ryan 'Vicarious Liability for Independent Contractors' (2018) 77 *CLJ* 458; Yiqiang Shao, 'Evolution of Vicarious Liability: How the Independent Contractor Defence was Lost' (2019) 6 *Public Interest Law Journal of New Zealand* 63, all of which discuss *Barclays Bank plc v Various Claimants* [2018] EWCA Civ 1670). Upon appeal, however, the UK Supreme Court restored orthodoxy by holding that vicarious liability cannot be imposed on independent contractors: see *Barclays*, above n 9.

and employers better deterred, if vicarious liability were imposed for the torts of their independent contractors?[84] However, just two years after *Bazley*, in *671122 Ontario Ltd v Sagaz Industries Canada Inc*, the Supreme Court reaffirmed that the traditional distinction was in fact consistent with the policies of fair compensation and deterrence:

> Vicarious liability is fair in principle because the hazards of the business should be borne by the business itself; thus, it does not make sense to anchor liability on an employer for acts of an independent contractor, someone who was in business on his or her own account. In addition, the employer does not have the same control over an independent contractor as over an employee to reduce accidents and intentional wrongs by efficient organization and supervision. Each of these policy justifications is relevant to the ability of the employer to control the activities of the employee, justifications which are generally deficient or missing in the case of an independent contractor.[85]

In light of the difficulties that courts had in making this distinction in the past, however, the court proposed an amalgamated test which incorporated what it saw as the best elements of the traditional control, organisation and entrepreneur tests. Thus, going forward the court concluded that:

> The central question is whether the person who has been engaged to perform the services is performing them as a person in business on his own account. In making this determination, the level of control the employer has over the worker's activities will always be a factor. However, other factors to consider include whether the worker provides his or her own equipment, whether the worker hires his or her own helpers, the degree of financial risk taken by the worker, the degree of responsibility for investment and management held by the worker, and the worker's opportunity for profit in the performance of his or her tasks.[86]

The court also indicated that the list it offered was non-exhaustive and that the relative weight of each factor would depend on the circumstances.[87] Subsequent Canadian jurisprudence has highlighted several other factors that may be relevant to the determination, such as: (1) who was responsible for paying for professional fees, liability insurance and continuing education; (2) the number of other clients worked for; (3) the existence of territorial, exclusive dealings or non-compete clauses in the agreement with the employer; (4) controls on sub-delegation; and (5) the method of renumeration (salary versus commission).[88]

[84] See D Brodie, 'Enterprise Liability: Justifying Vicarious Liability' (2007) 27 *OJLS* 493, 505–06 where *Sagaz*, above n 16 and *B(KL)*, above n 61 are criticised for failing to extend vicarious liability to independent contractors in light of the policies adopted in *Bazley*, above n 11. See also S Waddams, *Dimensions of Private Law: Categories and Concepts in Anglo-American Legal Reasoning* (Cambridge, Cambridge University Press, 2003) 105.

[85] *Sagaz*, above n 16, [35].

[86] ibid [47].

[87] ibid [48].

[88] *Canada Post Corp v Carroll* (2012) 383 NBR (2d) 326 (CA) [55]; *Rush v De Ruiter* 2018 ONSC 1210 [73]–[80]; *Braiden v La-Z-Boy Canada Ltd* 2008 ONCA 464; *Sytsma v Keleshian* 2016 ONSC 460 [37].

Although the *Sagaz* factors work well in the business environment for which they were designed, the Supreme Court of Canada has held that they are less relevant to non-commercial settings. Instead, the key question in these settings is whether the tortfeasor was acting in a representative fashion on behalf of the entity sought to be made vicariously liable.[89] Thus in *B(KL) v British Columbia* the Supreme Court found that the provincial government could not be held vicariously liable for torts committed by foster parents against foster children since (1) the government did not have day-to-day control of the organisation and management of foster parents' homes, (2) foster parents provided their own equipment and (3) foster parents are not held out as or generally perceived as government agents.[90] The court also noted that imposing vicarious liability in the foster parent context would not further vicarious liability's policy goal of deterrence.[91] To the contrary, it thought that imposing vicarious liability might promote a *harmful* form of deterrence because it could result in governments removing children from foster homes in favour of 'less efficacious institutional settings'.[92]

Another issue unaddressed in *Sagaz* was whether someone in a relationship akin to employment could have more than one employer for the purpose of vicarious liability. In *Blackwater v Plint*, the Supreme Court of Canada was faced with the issue of who was vicariously liable for the sexual abuse committed by a dormitory supervisor at a residential school run by the United Church (which nominated the principal, paid for the religious staff and donated the land) and the Government of Canada (which funded the school's operation, hired the principal, chose the students and set detailed standards for instruction).[93] The court unanimously concluded that where there is a relationship akin to a partnership or joint venture, joint vicarious liability is the natural solution.[94] As the court stated: 'if an employer with *de facto* control over an employee is not liable because of an arbitrary rule requiring only one employer for vicarious liability, this would undermine the principles of fair compensation and deterrence'.[95] Although the ratio of *Blackwater v Plint* might be read narrowly as applying only to quasi-partnerships or joint ventures,[96] the fact that the imposition of joint vicarious liability is consistent with both the enterprise liability justification of the doctrine and the modern

[89] *B(KL)*, above (n 61) [21]. See also *LR v Bromley Estate* 2013 NLCA 24 [124]–[126] (NLCA).

[90] ibid [23]–[25]. Interestingly, English courts have come to the opposite conclusion: see *Armes v Nottinghamshire County Council* [2017] UKSC 60.

[91] ibid [26].

[92] ibid.

[93] *Blackwater*, above n 29.

[94] ibid [38]. Merely providing funding for a school, however, is not enough for joint vicarious liability: see *Aksidan v Canada* (2008) 291 DLR (4th) 378 (BCCA).

[95] *Blackwater*, above n 29, [38]. The court apportioned liability 75 per cent to Canada and 25 per cent to the church on the basis that Canada was the more senior partner in the joint enterprise (see [65]–[73]). For criticism see J Neyers, 'Joint Vicarious Liability in the Supreme Court of Canada' (2006) 122 *LQR* 195, 198–99.

[96] See *John Doe (GEB #25) v Roman Catholic Episcopal Corp of St John's*, above n 40, [101]–[103].

English jurisprudence on this issue,[97] means that our courts are likely to impose joint vicarious liability on a regular basis moving forward.

C. Non-Delegable Duties

Before moving on to discuss the impact of Canadian vicarious liability developments on other Commonwealth jurisdictions, a brief discussion of non-delegable duties is called for. Only a brief discussion is warranted because, to date, claimants have had little success when it comes to imposing liability by way of a non-delegable duty in Canada.

In Canadian law, claimants seeking to impose liability on non-delegable duty grounds may advance two alternative arguments. First, a claimant may argue that there is clear statutory language which suggests that the legislature intended to impose a specific *statutory-based* non-delegable duty on a defendant. In *Blackwater*, for example, the claimant argued that the Government of Canada was under a statutory duty to ensure the safety and welfare of residential school students pursuant to sections 113 and 114 of the Indian Act. Section 113 stated that the

> Governor in Council may authorize the Minister … (a) to establish, operate and maintain schools for Indian children.' Section 114 went on to provide that '[t]he Minister may … (c) enter into agreements with religious organizations for the support and maintenance of children who are being educated in schools operated by those organizations.

In interpreting these provisions, the Supreme Court held that they did not support the inference of a statutory-based non-delegable duty for two reasons. First, it held that the use of the permissive term 'may' as opposed to the directive term 'shall' did not point towards an obligation as strong as a duty.[98] Second, it held that the power of the Government of Canada to enter into agreements with religious organisations concerning the care and education of Indigenous children suggested that the duty was in fact 'eminently delegable'.[99] The claimant's non-delegable duty argument was therefore dismissed.[100]

The second way in which a claimant may try to impose liability on a defendant is for a breach of a non-delegable duty imposed by the *common law*. However, in contrast to other jurisdictions which have embraced overarching and liberal tests when it comes to such non-delegable duties,[101] the Canadian approach is

[97] *CCWS* (n 83).

[98] *Blackwater*, above n 29, [50].

[99] ibid.

[100] See also *B(KL)* (n 61) and *Reference re Broome v Prince Edward Island*, 2010 SCC 11, where statutory-based non-delegable duty arguments were similarly rejected.

[101] See eg *Woodland v Swimming Teachers Association* [2013] UKSC 66; *Burnie Port Authority v General Jones Pty Ltd* [1994] HCA 13, (1994) 179 CLR 520; *Management Corp Strata Title Plan No 3322 v Tiong Aik Construction Pte Ltd* [2016] 4 SLR 521 (CA). For an academic overview of the law concerning non-delegable duties across the common law world see A Yoong, 'Challenges in the Evolution of the Doctrine of Non-delegable Duty' (2018) 25 *Tort Law Review* 143.

best described as categorical and conservative. That is, claimants must generally show that their case fits within a pre-existing common law non-delegable duty category. In *B(KL)* McLachlin CJ explained the Supreme Court's approach in these terms:

> It may be that there is no single common law concept of non-delegable duty. Instead, the phrase seems to have been used to describe a number of situations in which special, non-delegable duties arise. If this is correct, then rather than seeking to state the doctrine in terms of a single principle, we should look to the different situations in which such duties have been found – an approach consonant with the traditional methods of the common law.[102]

Unfortunately for claimants, this categorical approach to non-delegable duties means that the concept has limited utility and application. This is because most of Canada's recognised non-delegable duties – such as an employer's duty to ensure a safe system of work[103] or a property owner's duty to maintain lateral support to their neighbour's land[104] – are narrow in scope. In other words, they are only relevant to highly specific factual scenarios. Thus, unless and until the Supreme Court of Canada comes to adopt a more general and liberal test concerning the imposition of common law-based non-delegable duties,[105] claimants will continue to be required to seek compensation for sexual abuse through the use of vicarious liability principles.[106]

V. The Influence of Other Common Law Jurisdictions

When it comes to assessing the influence of other common law jurisdictions, timing is everything. Prior to *Bazley*, Canada, much like the rest of the Commonwealth, was an *importer* of English legal doctrine. Even after our judicial independence from the Privy Council in 1949,[107] Canadian courts more or less applied the settled vicarious liability rules that had been developed by the

[102] (n 61) [31].
[103] *Marshment v Borgstrom* [1942] SCR 374.
[104] *Dalton v Henry Angus & Co* (1881) 6 App Cas 740 (HL); *Reid v Linnell* [1923] SCR 594.
[105] See eg *Woodland v Swimming Teachers Association* (n 101).
[106] In *Das v George Western Limited* 2018 ONCA 1053 the Court of Appeal for Ontario reviewed the UK's more flexible test for the establishment of common law-based common law duties. Given the nature of the case before it, however, it did not need to determine whether that framework ought to be incorporated into Canadian law.
[107] Although the Supreme Court of Canada became the court of last resort for Canadian civil matters in 1949, cases which were heard before that date could continue to the Privy Council. The last case from the Supreme Court appealed to the Privy Council was *Earl F Wakefield Company v Oil City Petroleums (Leduc) Ltd* [1958] SCR 361. In *Ponoka-Calmar Oils Ltd v Earl F Wakefield Co* [1960] AC 18 (PC) their Lordships upheld the decision of the Supreme Court and dismissed the appeal: see WG Morrow, 'The Last Case' (1978) 16 *Alberta Law Review* 1.

English courts, even as divergences in other areas of tort law started to widen.[108] Thus, in light of this history, the traditional Salmond test remains the starting point for understanding Canadian law's evolution on this topic. In the post-*Bazley* period, however, Canada has largely been an *exporter* of legal doctrine and ideas relating to vicarious liability. Indeed, it is notable that the UK Supreme Court's decisions in *Mohamud v WM Morrison Supermarkets Plc*[109] and *Cox v Ministry of Justice*[110] – both of which have been the subject of extensive judicial and academic commentary in that jurisdiction[111] – have only been cited once in Canada.[112] By contrast, and as articulated in more detail below, Canadian jurisprudence continues to be cited across the Commonwealth. This suggests that, for better or for worse, it is the Supreme Court of Canada that has been the 'prime mover' in this area of law.

Without a doubt, *Bazley* and *Jacobi* have had the greatest influence abroad. In *Bazley* and *Jacobi*, it will be remembered, the Supreme Court attempted to refine the concept of course of employment so that it could better resolve child sexual abuse cases. With reference to the twin policy considerations of fair compensation and deterrence, the court decided that the best way forward was to require a significant or close connection between conduct authorised by the defendant and the wrong committed by the primary wrongdoer.[113] Given that courts in other jurisdictions were struggling with this same issue one can see why they would be attracted to *Bazley* and *Jacobi*. The Supreme Court's approach offered them a promising new way to deal with the 'difficulty'[114] posed by the traditional Salmond test in sexual abuse cases.

Indeed, it took less than two years for the House of Lords to latch onto much of the Supreme Court of Canada's reasoning. In *Lister v Hesley Hall Ltd*, the Law Lords were confronted with facts similar to those found in the 'luminous and illuminating judgments' in *Bazley* and *Jacobi*.[115] A warden at a boarding house was found to have committed a string of sexual assaults against pupils attending the institution. In response, the victims sought to make the boarding house vicariously liable. While the Law Lords felt that it was 'unnecessary to express views on the full range of policy considerations examined in [*Bazley* and *Jacobi*]',[116]

[108] See eg the Supreme Court of Canada's rejection of *Murphy v Brentwood District Council* (1990), [1991] 1 AC 398 (HL) in *Winnipeg Condominium Corporation No 36 v Bird Construction Co* [1995] 1 SCR 85 (a case involving pure economic loss in negligence for shoddy goods and structures).

[109] *Mohamud v WM Morrison Supermarkets Plc* [2016] UKSC 11.

[110] *Cox* (n 83).

[111] See eg P Morgan, 'Certainty in Vicarious Liability' (2016) 75 *CLJ* 202; P Giliker, 'Vicarious Liability in the UK Supreme Court' (2016) 7 *UK Supreme Court Yearbook* 152; M Tutin, 'Vicarious Liability: An Ever Expanding Concept?' (2016) 45 *Industrial Law Journal* 556.

[112] *Heikkila v Apex Land Corp* 2016 ABCA 126 [12]. The court did not engage in an analysis of either decision.

[113] *Bazley* (n 11) [41].

[114] *Lister v Hesley Hall Ltd* [2001] UKHL 22 [16] (Lord Steyn).

[115] ibid [27].

[116] ibid [27] (Lord Steyn). See also [60] (Lord Hobhouse).

they nevertheless agreed that the second branch of the Salmond test should be interpreted so as to require a 'significant connection' between conduct authorised by the defendant and the wrong committed by the primary wrongdoer.[117] Importantly for the claimants, the Law Lords also held that the significant connection test was met. Lord Steyn, for example, found that the sexual abuse was 'inextricably interwoven with the carrying out by the warden of his duties'.[118] Vicarious liability was therefore imposed on the basis of *Bazley*'s significant connection test.

As it turns out, *Lister* was only the beginning of an ongoing judicial discussion concerning *Bazley* and *Jacobi* in the UK. Indeed, *Bazley* has been cited by the House of Lords or UK Supreme Court five times since *Lister*.[119] It has also been cited in several Court of Appeal and Privy Council decisions,[120] and in numerous trial court judgments.[121] In these cases, courts have been receptive of *Bazley*'s significant or close connection test but, nevertheless, continued to disavow its references to policy considerations. That said, as the UK Supreme Court recently noted in *Barclays Bank Plc v Various Claimants*, it seems that some of *Bazley's* policy considerations have managed to seep their way into step one of the UK's test for vicarious liability which, like the Canadian test, asks whether there is a 'sufficiently close relationship' between the defendant and primary wrongdoer.[122] In *Barclays*, however, the Supreme Court appears to have attempted to severely restrict the applicability of policy factors at step one of the analysis.[123] Whether the judgment will be successful in this regard remains to be seen.[124]

The influence of *Bazley* and *Jacobi* has not been limited to the UK. For instance, the *Bazley/Jacobi* approach to vicarious liability has also been followed by apex courts in both Singapore[125] and New Zealand[126] in recent years.

[117] See eg ibid [70] (Lord Millett).

[118] ibid [29].

[119] In *Barclays* (n 9) [11]; *Armes* (n 90) [65]–[67]; *Mohamud v WM Morrison Supermarkets Plc* [2016] UKSC 11 [40] (Lord Toulson) [56] (Lord Dyson); *Various Claimants v Catholic Child Welfare Society* [2012] UKSC 56 [64]–[75]; *Dubai Aluminum Co Ltd v Salaam* [2002] UKHL 48 [23].

[120] For the Court of Appeal decisions see eg *Graham v Commercial Bodyworks Ltd* [2015] EWCA Civ 47; *JGE v Trustees of the Portsmouth Roman Catholic Diocesan* [2012] EWCA Civ 938; *Weddal v Barchester Healthcare Ltd* [2012] EWCA Civ 25; *MAGA v Roman Catholic Archdiocese of Birmingham* [2010] EWCA Civ 256; *Gravil v Carrol* [2008] EWCA Civ 689; *Mattis v Pollock* [2003] EWCA Civ 887. For the Privy Council decisions see eg *Brown v Robinson* [2004] UKPC 56; *Bernard v Attorney General of Jamaica* [2004] UKPC 47.

[121] In *DSN v Blackpool Football Club Ltd* [2020] EWHC 595 (QB); *Bellman v Northampton Recruitment Ltd* [2016] EWHC 3104 (QB); *GB v Stoke City Football Club Ltd* [2015] EWHC 2862 (QB); *Vertical Leisure Ltd v Polepus Ltd* [2015] EWHC 841 (IPEC); *JGE v English Province of Our Lady Charity* [2011] EWHC 2871 (QB); *Pena v Tameside Hospital NHS Foundation Trust* [2011] EWHC 3027 (QB); *N v Chief Constable of Merseyside* Police [2006] EWHC 3041 (QB).

[122] *Barclays* (n 9) [10].

[123] Indeed, the court stated that the use of policy factors should only be employed in 'doubtful cases' (see ibid [27]).

[124] For discussion see Giliker (n 1).

[125] In *Skandinaviska Enskilda Banken AB (Publ) Singapore Branch v Asia Pacific Breweries (Singapore) Pte Ltd* [2011] SGCA 22; *Ng Huat Send v Mohammad* [2017] SGCA 58.

[126] In *S v Attorney-General* [2003] NZCA 149 (S).

The High Court of Australia has also engaged with *Bazley* at length on several occasions.[127] And while the High Court has not adopted 'precisely the same approach to vicarious liability as that laid down in *Bazley*', in its most recent analysis of the issue in *Prince Alfred College Inc v ADC*[128] it held that many of the factual circumstances on which the Supreme Court of Canada placed weight remain 'highly relevant to whether a given defendant ought to be held vicariously liable'.[129]

Beyond *Bazley* and *Jacobi*, *B(KL)*[130] has also been the subject of judicial discussion in other common law jurisdictions. In contrast to *Bazley* and *Jacobi*, however, *B(KL)* has received a much more critical response. In *Armes v Nottinghamshire CC*, for instance, the UK Supreme Court rejected *B(KL)*'s reasoning. The majority justified their departure from *B(KL)* largely on the ground that the Supreme Court of Canada's decision reflected the Canadian jurisprudence's emphasis on 'the deterrence of tortious behaviour [as] one of the principal justifications for the imposition of vicarious liability'.[131] They also noted that the New Zealand Court of Appeal unanimously imposed vicarious liability on the state for torts committed by foster parents in *S v Attorney-General*.[132] Nevertheless, while disavowing the Supreme Court of Canada's reliance on deterrence, the majority in *Armes* still emphasised the Canadian court's second policy factor – namely, fair compensation – in order to reach its conclusion.[133] Given *Barclays*'s recent call to restrict the use of policy at stage one of the vicarious liability analysis to 'doubtful cases',[134] perhaps *Armes* would be approached differently today. Alternatively, *Armes* may indeed be one of those 'doubtful cases' in which policy remains relevant.[135]

VI. The Supreme Court's Theoretical Justifications for Vicarious Liability[136]

As we have seen, in *Bazley* the Supreme Court of Canada reasoned that vicarious liability is justified by the policies of fair compensation and deterrence.[137]

[127] See *Hollis v Vabu Pty Ltd* [2001] HCA 44; *New South Wales v Lepore* [2003] HCA 4; *Sweeney v Boylan Nominees Pty Ltd* [2006] HCA 19; *Leichhardt Municipal Council v Montgomery* [2007] HCA 6; *Prince Alfred College Inc v ADC* [2016] HCA 37.

[128] *Prince Alfred College Inc*, ibid.

[129] J Goudkamp, 'International Impact and Influence: Three Landmark Cases from the Canadian Law of Obligations' (2018) 87 *Supreme Court Law Review* 255, 273.

[130] *B(KL)* (n 61).

[131] *Armes* (n 90) [67].

[132] *S* (n 126).

[133] *Armes* (n 90) [61]–[63].

[134] *Barclays* (n 9) [27].

[135] For a similar view see Giliker (n 1).

[136] This part follows the analysis in, and draws heavily on, Neyers (n 6) 300–04.

[137] *Bazley*, above n 11, [34].

This combined enterprise risk and deterrence justification has been applied in numerous Supreme Court of Canada decisions and now forms the bedrock of the court's justification of the doctrine.[138] Of these policies, however, enterprise risk has taken on the most significance in subsequent judgments.[139]

Unfortunately, although the use of an enterprise risk justification is a valiant attempt to explain vicarious liability, like all the other proffered policy explanations,[140] it is not a successful justification of the doctrine. As Gray has pointed out:

> The acid test for any theory that is used to explain and justify existing legal principle is that it does *in fact* rationally explain at least the key aspects of that principle as it is currently applied in the courts. On this basic and fundamental test, the theory of enterprise risk fails.[141]

There are at least five reasons for this failure. First, enterprise risk cannot explain why vicarious liability is limited to torts committed by employees and agents rather than to all accidents caused by them in the pursuit of the enterprise's goals.[142] As Williams argued:

> In an action against the master for the negligence of the servant, it is necessary to prove the servant's negligence. This should not be the case if the underlying reason for the law is to impose upon an undertaking the social loss caused by its operations. A loss caused without negligence is just as much a loss as one caused by negligence. For example, neither a trading firm nor its vanmen can avoid some traffic accidents; yet these accidents are part of the social cost of the firm's activities.[143]

Second, the enterprise risk rationale has difficulty explaining why employees remain personally liable for their torts after these torts have been ascribed to the

[138] See for example *B(KL)*, above n 61; *Bennett*, above n 61; *Blackwater*, above n 29; *Oblates*, above n 61; *Strother*, above n 61.

[139] See *Bennett*, above n 61, [20]; *Blackwater*, above n 29, [20]. Moreover, as Ozer notes, enterprise risk sits on top of the Supreme Court of Canada's conceptual hierarchy: S Ozer, 'The Role of Enterprise within Vicarious Liability: Courageous or Unprincipled Judicial Reasoning?' (2012) 2 *Southampton Student Law Review* 143, 152.

[140] For discussions as to why the policies of deterrence, compensation, loss-spreading and enterprise risk are unable to explain vicarious liability see JW Neyers, 'A Theory of Vicarious of Liability' (2005) 43 *Alberta Law Review* 287, 292–301; T Baty, *Vicarious Liability* (Oxford, Clarendon Press, 1916) 146–54; P Atiyah, 'Personal Injuries in the Twenty-First Century: Thinking the Unthinkable' in P Birks (ed), *Wrongs and Remedies in the Twenty-First Century* (Oxford, Clarendon Press, 1996) 16; JW Neyers and D Stevens, 'Vicarious Liability in the Charity Sector' (2005) 42 *Canadian Business Law Journal* 371, 396–404; Goudkamp and Plunkett (n 7) 168–69; Gray (n 29) ch 7.

[141] A Gray, 'A Critique of the Enterprise Risk Theory of Vicarious Liability' (2019) 62 *Canadian Business Law Journal* 181, 194 (emphasis in original). See generally Gray (n 29) ch 6. See also A Beever, 'Particularism and Prejudice in the Law of Tort' (2003) 11 *Tort Law Review* 145, 150 (the test of a good explanation is that it justifies not only why a doctrine begins but also why it stops where it does).

[142] See WA Seavey, 'Speculations as to "Respondeat Superior' (1934) *Harvard Law Essays* 433, 451; AO Sykes, 'An Efficiency Analysis of Vicarious Liability under the Law of Agency' (1981) 91 *Yale Law Journal* 168, 173; R Stevens, *Torts and Rights* (Oxford, Oxford University Press, 2007) 259; Goudkamp and Plunkett (n 7) 169; Gray (n 29)138.

[143] See G Williams, 'Vicarious Liability and the Master's Indemnity' (1957) 20 *MLR* 437, 442.

enterprise, since the rationale supposes that it is the enterprise which created the risk and which, therefore, should bear the burden.[144]

Third, the rationale cannot explain why an employer can seek indemnity from their employee for any damages paid to a tort victim to satisfy a vicarious liability claim – in essence foisting enterprise liabilities back onto individuals.[145]

Fourth, enterprise risk cannot explain why vicarious liability is limited to certain legal relationships, since, if the rationale is taken seriously, there would be generalised strict liability for the creation of risks – which is certainly not the law.[146] This means that the enterprise risk theory cannot explain the liability imposed as being truly vicarious since under the Supreme Court's formulation the enterprise itself has committed a legal wrong.[147]

Fifth, the enterprise risk theory is fundamentally inconsistent with the current common law system of responsibility, which is based around persons (natural or legal) rather than enterprises.[148] Imagine a case where an employee of a bakery, which is run as a sole proprietorship, commits a tort against a third party. In such a situation the current law is that all of the assets of the vicariously responsible employer including personal assets (such as a boat or cottage) or assets used for the furtherance of other enterprises (such as equipment used in construction business also run as a sole proprietorship) are available to compensate the tort victim. If the enterprise risk theory were taken seriously, however, only those assets which were used in the bakery enterprise would be available for execution by the tort creditor since it was only that enterprise that created the risk of harm.[149] In other words, accepting enterprise liability requires a drastic change in how one thinks about the scope of legal responsibility and would mandate the creation of doctrines to individuate enterprises in order to avoid leaping arbitrarily to the conclusion that all the assets of the enterprise's owner are liable.[150] As Lord Hope of Craighead questioned: 'What, if enterprise liability is to be the governing principle, is an enterprise?'[151]

[144] See the judgment of La Forest J in *London Drugs Ltd v Kuehne & Nagel International Ltd* [1992] 3 SCR 299 where he argued for the abolition of the employee's personal liability. See also J Stapleton, *Product Liability* (London, Butterworths, 1994) 193; Neyers (n 140) 299.

[145] See HC Klemme, 'The Enterprise Liability Theory of Torts' (1976) 47 *University of Colorado Law Review* 153, 201; Gray (n 29) 124. On the employer's right to an indemnity, see *Lister v Romford Ice & Cold Storage Co* [1957] AC 555 (HL); *Co-operators Insurance Association v Kearney* [1965] SCR 106.

[146] See GT Schwartz, 'The Hidden and Fundamental Issue of Employer Vicarious Liability' (1995) 69 *Southern California Law Review* 1739, 1750.

[147] R Stevens, 'A Servant of Two Masters' (2006) 122 *LQR* 201, 202; A Ataner, 'How Strict is Vicarious Liability? Reassessing the Enterprise Risk Theory' (2006) 64 *University of Toronto Faculty Law Review* 63, 84.

[148] Neyers and Stevens (n 140) 400–01.

[149] As seems to have been the case in the Roman law and medieval civil law where, in many commercial circumstances, 'there was an equivalence between the value of the property and the owner's liability from it'. See D Johnston, 'Limiting Liability: Roman Law and the Civil Law Tradition' (1995) 70 *Chicago-Kent Law Review* 1515, 1536.

[150] See R Flannigan, 'Enterprise Control: The Servant-Independent Contractor Distinction' (1987) 37 *University of Toronto Law Journal* 25, 53 where he discusses the need to individuate enterprises.

[151] Lord Hope, 'Tailoring the Law on Vicarious Liability' (2013) 129 *LQR* 514, 526.

For these five reasons, enterprise risk fails the 'acid test' and is a poor explanation of vicarious liability despite its continued acceptance by the Supreme Court of Canada. This raises the question of whether the current law is justifiable.

VII. Justifying the Revolution?

Given that it was generally thought that there was no satisfactory explanation of vicarious liability prior to the *Bazley* revolution,[152] and given that, as we have just seen, the enterprise risk justification utilised by the Supreme Court of Canada does a poor job explaining the starting and stopping points of the current doctrine in a coherent fashion, one might think that the *Bazley* revolution would ipso facto be unjustifiable as a matter of legal principle. However, this view is mistaken. Just beneath the surface discussion of the policies of (fair) compensation, enterprise risk and deterrence lies a principled justification for the modern Canadian doctrine of vicarious liability. Moreover, the fact that the English law has been greatly influenced by the Canadian jurisprudence suggests that this explanation could also potentially justify the modern English position.[153]

As a result of *Bazley* and subsequent Supreme Court of Canada cases, it is clear that the older principled explanations of vicarious liability that relied on either: (1) the subrogation of the tort victim to the employees' contractual right of indemnification from their employers for harms suffered in the course of their employment,[154] or (2) the attribution of servants' acts to their masters so long as those acts could be seen to be unauthorised mode of an authorised act,[155] are no longer viable interpretive theories. The subrogation theory could not survive the general expansion of vicarious liability to relationships that are non-contractual and merely 'akin to employment'.[156] Similarly, neither the subrogation, nor the attribution, theory could accept that vicarious liability would encompass intentional wrongdoing, like sexual battery, which could not be understood as being in the course of employment under the traditional Salmond test. As the English Court of Appeal noted in *Trotman v North Yorkshire County Council*, sexual abuse is 'far removed from an unauthorised mode of carrying out a teacher's duties on behalf of his employer. Rather it is a negation of the duty of the council to look after children for whom it was responsible'.[157] Is another explanation possible in light of the last twenty years of legal development?

[152] See the authority cited in n 140, above.
[153] Though given the constraints of space we do no more than advert to that possibility here.
[154] Neyers (n 140); Neyers and Stevens (n 140).
[155] Stevens (n 142).
[156] See ibid 269.
[157] See also ibid 270: '[t]eachers are employed to care for children, not to abuse them. It is the very opposite of what they have been authorized to do'.

Our argument is that the modern Canadian law of vicarious liability is justified on the venerable agency principle that an '[employer] should not be able by using [a representative] to put themselves in a better position than that in which they would have been if they had dealt personally'.[158] That such an explanation of the modern law might be possible should not come as a surprise since, as Bell has noted, similar concerns interacted with, and informed, many of the formative cases of vicarious liability:

> The historical precedents speak to a ... careful expansion in liability where the incidents may all be explained in terms of their accounting for threats necessary and inhering to the creation and operation of master-servant relationships ... The cases ensured that there need not be "an end to all dealing but with the master" by functioning to give something of the same security to strangers that they would enjoy if the master acted personally.[159]

Understanding how such a principle operates to justify the modern Canadian law of vicarious liability requires a critical examination and explanation of two important concepts. The first is the idea of a 'representative'. The modern law expanding the reach of the doctrine beyond employee-employer relationships, but stopping short of imposing liability for independent contractors,[160] is consistent with this principle since it recognises that the concept of someone representing someone else is wider than the strict concept of employment. As Lord Phillips stated, relying on the borrowed servant case of *Donovan v Laing, Wharton and Down Construction*[161] and the concept of servants *pro hac vice*, for 'over 200 years, the courts have recognised that the existence of a contract of employment is not always the touchstone of the relationship that can give rise to vicarious liability'.[162] For example, there is nothing strange in thinking that in some situations and for some purposes a volunteer represents a charity,[163] that a religious official represents their church,[164] or that an agent represents their principal.[165] Stopping short of imposing vicarious liability for independent contractors also makes sense, since independent contractors are not acting as representatives, a point that, as we have seen, was emphasized by the Supreme Court of Canada in *B(KL)* in denying

[158] Taken from Peter G Watts and FMB Reynolds, *Bowstead & Reynolds on Agency* 22nd edn (London, Thomson Reuters, 2020) §8-210. We have changed 'principal' to 'employer' and 'agent' to 'representative' to make it clear that we believe that the principle applies beyond the contractual realm and to individuals who would not ordinarily be classified as true agents (who are persons who exercise the legal powers of another): see R Leow, 'Understanding Agency: A Proxy Power Definition' (2019) 78 *CLJ* 99. Other terms might also be used. For example, J Bell, 'The Basis of Vicarious Liability' (2013) 72 *CLJ* 17, 19 suggests the term 'auxiliary'.

[159] AJ Bell, 'Scope of Employment: Connecting Closely With the Past' (2021) 137 *LQR* 254, 277.

[160] *Sagaz* (n 16); *Barclays* (n 9).

[161] *Donovan v Laing, Wharton and Down Construction* [1893] 1 QB 629 (CA).

[162] Lord Phillips, 'Vicarious Liability on the Move' (2015) 45 *Hong Kong Law Journal* 29, 32.

[163] *S(C) (Next Friend of) v Miller* 2002 ABQB 152 (Alta QB).

[164] *Bennett* (n 61); *Various Claimants v Catholic Child Welfare Society* [2012] UKSC 56.

[165] *Lloyd v Grace Smith* (n 24).

the vicarious liability of the government for the torts of foster parents.[166] As the renowned jurist Dixon J observed:

> The work, although done at his request and for his benefit, is considered as the independent function of the person who undertakes it, and not as something which the person obtaining the benefit does by his representative standing in his place and, therefore, identified with him for the purpose of liability arising in the course of its performance. The independent contractor carries out his work, not as a representative but as a principal.[167]

The second concept which needs further examination is that of being 'in a better legal position'.[168] If the employer had performed the activity requested of their representative themselves, then they would have been held liable if they had committed a tort while so acting. Without any rule of responsibility for the actions of others, employers would therefore be able to insulate themselves from legal liability by not acting personally, that is by using representatives to perform all activities for them.[169] As Wigmore argued:

> it is worth while noting that the Command or Authority principle may prove to be, theoretically as well as historically, the true support of the rule of responsibility for agents' torts. (1) if I command A to do act x, I ought to be liable for the natural consequences peculiar to that act taken in itself; (2) the same follows if x is a class, series, or group of acts; (3) if A does the act in a careless or otherwise wrongful way, different from that in which I expected him to do it, and not as I myself might have done it, my personal culpability is no longer clear; nevertheless, complete legal exoneration in such cases would be poor policy, for it would afford ample opportunity to shirk responsibility, merely by appointing substitutes; so that some medium must be found.[170]

In order to forestall that possibility, and to ensure that employers are not in a better position than they would have been if they had acted personally, the legal system needs rules of attribution. This entails answering two further questions.

The first question is what is being attributed: is it the representative's actions,[171] their actions and state of mind,[172] their legal liability[173] or perhaps

[166] Above in Section IV.

[167] *Colonial Mutual Life Assurance Society Ltd v Producers and Citizens Co-Operative Assurance Co-Operative of Australia Ltd* [1931] HCA 53, (1931) 46 CLR 41, 48.

[168] Of course, as a *matter of fact* people might be better off acting through representatives where that representative has greater skills or more expertise than the employer – that is often the very reason why we choose to act through representatives. The principle refers, however, to a legal position rather than a factual one. We thank Shawn Bayern for raising this issue with us.

[169] See *Bartonshill Coal Co v Reid* (1858) 3 Macq 266 (Lord Cranworth).

[170] JH Wigmore, 'Responsibility for Tortious Act: Its History' (1894) 7 *Harvard Law Review* 383, 404–05, fn 1.

[171] Stevens (n 142) 259–67. For a short summary see R Stevens, 'Vicarious Liability or Vicarious Action' (2007) 123 *LQR* 30.

[172] E Weinrib, *The Idea of Private Law* (Cambridge, Harvard University Press, 1995) 185–87; G Williams, 'Vicarious Liability: Tort of the Master or of the Servant' (1956) 72 *LQR* 522, 522.

[173] *Bazley*, above n 11. See also *Staveley*, above n 14; *Majrowski v Guy's and St Thomas's NHS Trust* [2006] UKHL 34; *Woodland v Swimming Teachers Association* (n 101) [3].

some combination of these possibilities?[174] While it will not often make a difference to liability,[175] the answer in modern law is that it is the tortious liability of the representative which is attributed.[176] This position is consistent with (1) the longstanding imposition of vicarious liability for torts, such as deceit, that have a stringent mental element (and which would be unexplainable using the attribution of actions alone) and (2) the doctrine's underlying 'no better off' rationale. For example, one justification for why in modern law a representative has to commit a tort rather than merely cause some type of non-tortious injury or other material setback to the claimant in order for there to be vicarious liability is that, if this were not the case, an employer would be worse off acting through representatives (since, if they had acted directly, they would not have been legally liable) rather than merely not being better off.

The second, and perhaps more important question, is: when should this attribution (of actions, wrongfulness or liability) be done? As Stevens notes:

> [W]hilst some sort of rules for the attribution … are essential, this does not tell us what the detailed content of those rules ought to be. At one extreme, attribution could be limited to those acts which are expressly authorized. At the other, whenever one person carries out a task on my behalf, all of these actions could be attributed to me. … Whilst some answers may be demonstrably wrong … there may be no single demonstrably right answer.[177]

The history of the common law has seen a slow widening of the rules of attribution from explicit command, to include liability for actions which were authorized (explicitly or implicitly), and then to include liability for actions which were in the course of employment as merely an unauthorised mode of an authorised act (ie, the second branch of the Salmond test).[178] The cases since *Bazley* can be seen to be extending this attribution further to include liability for activities where one of the characteristic risks of engaging in them is a tortiously caused injury to third parties. Thus, under this view, enterprise risk or characteristic risk is not a separate legal wrong of strict liability or the justification for the whole scope of vicarious liability (which, as we have seen in Section VI, is an untenable view of the law) but is rather merely the reason *why* the tortious liability of a representative is

[174] Williams (n 172) 544 suggests that it might be possible to uphold both the master's tort theory and the servant's tort theory and 'to say that the master is responsible when either fits the facts. In other words, the law may recognise both vicarious responsibility in the proper sense of the term and also a doctrine of vicarious conduct.'

[175] ibid 522; W Swain, 'A Historical Examination of Vicarious Liability: A "Veritable Upas Tree"' (2019) 78 *CLJ* 640, 661.

[176] For a history of this question, see Swain, above n 175; Bell (n 159).

[177] Stevens (n 142) 267–68.

[178] For a discussion of the history see JH Wigmore, 'Responsibility for Tortious Act: Its History' (1894) 7 *Harvard Law Review* 315 and (1894) 7 *Harvard Law Review* 383; W Swain, 'Vicarious Liability: A Pailful of Slops and Other Hazards' in K Barker and R Grantham (eds), *Apportionment in Private Law* (Oxford, Hart, 2019) 89; Swain (n 175).

attributed back to the employer.[179] Or as Bell phrases it, it operates merely as the reason for '*collapsing* the distancing involved in the master acting through a servant rather than personally, as it were *telescoping* those legal positions'.[180] This view of enterprise risk is consistent with *Oblates* where vicarious liability was limited to situations where the claimant could prove that the representative's assigned tasks created a characteristic risk of sexual battery, rather than liability being imposed solely on the basis of the overall operational characteristics of the enterprise as a whole (in that case a residential school).[181] As Binnie J stated:

> However, if, as the appellant contends, the school as organized and operated created a significant risk to every student by every employee regardless of the particulars of his or her job, this would argue for direct liability rather than vicarious liability for … misconduct. …. Taking the trial judge's approach to its logical conclusion, the respondent would be liable for all tortious acts of all of its employees, no matter how remote the wrongdoing from the job-created power or status or how distanced [the employee] was from any position of authority over, or intimacy with, the students. … [T]his … does not conform with our jurisprudence.[182]

Viewed in terms of the attribution of liability, this new understanding of 'course of employment' or 'close connection' is not arbitrary, or merely dictated by some external policy or policies (though it may be consistent with them). Instead, it gives a fuller expression than did the older rules based on command or authorization to the idea of not being legally better off by acting through representatives. As Justice Friendly, 'one of the greatest federal judges to sit on the federal appellate bench in the twentieth century',[183] stated in *Ira S Bushey v United States*:

> A policy analysis thus is not sufficient to justify this proposed expansion of vicarious liability. This is not surprising since respondeat superior, even within its traditional limits, rests not so much on policy grounds … as in a deeply rooted sentiment that a business enterprise cannot justly disclaim responsibility for [tortious] accidents which may fairly be said to be characteristic of its activities.[184]

Moreover, the modern rule is fair to employers because what is being attributed is not liability of all torts committed by representatives but only those torts whose occurrence is a characteristic risk of the activity the employer requested the representative to perform, and as such are the type of torts that experience has shown might have been committed by the employer had they acted personally in performing the very same activity.[185] An additional benefit to viewing vicarious

[179] For a similar view, see Ataner (n 147) 85: rather than being a tort, the 'enterprise risk approach merely provides courts with the tools for finding … that the employee's tortious conduct occurred in the course of employment'.

[180] Bell (n 159) 274.

[181] For a scathing criticism of this result from the enterprise risk perspective see Feldthusen (n 51).

[182] *Oblates* (n 61) [4].

[183] M Boudin, 'Friendly, J, Dissenting' (2012) 61 *Duke Law Journal* 881, 881.

[184] 398 F2d 167 (2d Cir 1968) 171.

[185] For example, (1) a characteristic risk of driving is committing the tort of negligence through inadvertence: see Williams (n 143) 442; (2) a characteristic risk of maintaining order or protecting goods

liability and enterprise risk in this principled manner is that it also deals with the common complaint that rules of attribution like *qui facit per alium facit per se* are mere unjustified fictions,[186] conjured up to explain doctrines like vicarious liability that apparently have no other explanation.[187] As Wigmore noted, rather than being an unjustified fiction, the necessity for the rule of attribution is provided by the mischief (being legally better off) that would otherwise exist absent its implementation or instantiation in the doctrine of vicarious liability.

How then does this fit with, and justify, the Supreme Court of Canada's jurisprudence relating to vicarious liability for sexual abuse (which, as we have seen, commenced the Canadian vicarious liability revolution)? Unfortunately, the answer is both simple and heart-breaking. As outlined in Section III, and as recognised by Lord Millett in *Lister v Hesley Hall Ltd*:

> Experience shows that in the case of boarding schools, prisons, nursing homes, old people's homes, geriatric wards, and other residential homes for the young or vulnerable, there is an inherent risk that indecent assaults on the residents will be committed by those placed in authority over them, particularly if they are in close proximity to them and occupying a position of trust.[188]

Phrased more directly, it is now clear that sexual abuse is a characteristic risk of caring for the vulnerable. Thus, vicarious liability is justifiably imposed on an employer where a representative is engaged in that type of activity on the employer's behalf (as in *Bazley*,[189] *Blackwater*[190] and *Bennett*[191]). Conversely, vicarious liability is not imposed where the representative's assigned tasks as a baker,[192] janitor[193] or a boys and girls club programme director[194] do not involve any intimate care and therefore could not reasonably be seen to create any characteristic risk of sexual abuse. Thinking in terms of characteristic or

is using excessive force and thereby committing the tort of battery: see *Bettel v Yim* (1978) 20 OR (2d) 617 (SCJ) (direct liability); *Poland v Parr* [1927] 1 KB 236 (CA) (vicarious liability imposed for actions of employee protecting goods from theft); *Lakatosh v Ross* (1974) 48 DLR (3d) 694 (Man QB) (vicarious liability imposed for actions of bouncer); and (3) a characteristic risk of storing, guarding or cleaning valuables is to take (some of) them and to thereby commit the tort of conversion: see *Armorie v Delamirie* (1722) 1 Strange 505, 93 ER 664; *Morris v C W Martin & Sons Ltd* [1966] 1 QB 716 (CA); *Brink's Global Services Inc v Igrox Ltd* [2010] EWCA Civ 1207. Of course, much will depend on how broadly or narrowly a particular activity is conceptualized (see Bell (n 8) 155) but this type of indeterminacy cannot be avoided whenever general principles are applied to particulars: see Weinrib (n 172) 166–67.

186 See OW Holmes, 'Agency' (1890–91) 4 *Harvard Law Review* 345. See also Goudkamp and Plunkett (n 7) 170: attribution analyses of vicarious liability are problematic unless they 'explain why the tortfeasor's acts ought to be attributed to the defendant'.

187 For additional reasons why such reasoning is not fictional see Stevens (n 142) 267–68.

188 *Lister* (n 114) [83].

189 *Bazley* (n 11).

190 *Blackwater* (n 61).

191 *Bennett* (n 61).

192 *Oblates* (n 61).

193 *EDG v Hammer* (n 28).

194 *Jacobi* (n 11).

enterprise risk also explains why cases dealing with vicarious liability for sexual battery by non-residential school teachers have seen divided outcomes in the Canadian case law since teaching seems to straddle the two architypes and small differences in assigned tasks (such as after school care, supervision of weekend programs or athletic coaching) might cause one to think that sexual abuse had become a characteristic risk of the overall activity authorised by the employer in some situations and not others.[195]

VIII. Conclusion

In this chapter we examined the vicarious liability revolution in Canada by investigating its starting point in *Bazley* and *Jacobi*, the societal factors which made such a revolution possible, and the influence that it has had in other jurisdictions. We have also detailed the present state of the law in Canada and the current Canadian orthodoxy as to the policy explanations for vicarious liability (fair compensation, enterprise risk and deterrence). Finding this current orthodoxy wanting, we argued that the modern Canadian law on vicarious liability, and by extension its contemporary English equivalent, can be justified as an embodiment of traditional principles that govern acting through others. On this view, vicarious liability is more than an incoherent 'casserole of incommensurable policy reasons'[196] and, instead, has a principled basis. Whether this understanding of vicarious liability will be taken up by the next generation of Canadian or Commonwealth judges, however, remains to be seen.

[195] Compare *H (SG) v Gorsline* (2004) 354 AR 46 (CA) and *AB v CD* 2011 BCSC 775 where vicarious liability was not imposed for sexual batteries committed by non-residential teachers on students with *John Doe v Avalon East School Board* (2004) 244 Nfld & PEIR 153 (Nfld SC) and *SL v RTM* 2013 ONSC 1448 where vicarious liability was imposed.

[196] A Dickinson, 'Fostering Uncertainty in the Law of Tort' (2018) 134 *LQR* 359, 360.

3

Vicarious Liability in England and Wales

PAULA GILIKER

The law of vicarious liability is on the move … It has not yet come to a stop.

Cox v Ministry of Justice [2016] UKSC 10 [1] per Lord Reed

The question raised by the current case, and by the parallel case of *Various Claimants v Wm Morrison Supermarkets plc*, is how far that move can take it.

Barclays Bank plc v Various Claimants [2020] UKSC 13 [1] per Baroness Hale

I. Introduction

The aim of this chapter is to provide a critical understanding of the current state of vicarious liability in England and Wales. Vicarious liability, that is, strict liability imposed on one party for the torts of another, is a doctrine that in the last 20 years has undergone significant growth, extending liability to new relationships and a broader category of intentional and non-intentional wrongs. It is an area also that has received perhaps unprecedented judicial attention. There have been six decisions of the UK Supreme Court since 2010[1] and yet questions still remain as to the scope of this doctrine.

In this chapter, I will seek to reflect on the position in England and Wales and why the scope of vicarious liability has proven so difficult for the courts to resolve. The law must now be examined in the light of the two most recent decisions of the UK Supreme Court in April 2020: *Various Claimants v Barclays Bank plc*[2] and *Various Claimants v Wm Morrison Supermarkets plc*.[3] These are important

[1] *Various Claimants v Catholic Child Welfare Society* [2012] UKSC 56; *Cox v Ministry of Justice* [2016] UKSC 10; *Mohamud v Wm Morrison Supermarkets plc* [2016] UKSC 11; *Armes v Nottinghamshire County Council* [2017] UKSC 60; *Barclays Bank plc v Various Claimants* [2020] UKSC 13; *Wm Morrison Supermarkets plc* v *Various Claimants* [2020] UKSC 12.

[2] *Barclays Bank plc v Various Claimants* [2020] UKSC 13, [2020] AC 973 (*Barclays*).

[3] *Wm Morrison Supermarkets plc v Various Claimants* [2020] UKSC 12, [2020] AC 989 (*Morrison*).

decisions that seek to explain the law, the role of policy and how courts should apply the test for vicarious liability, advocating a principled incremental approach.[4] My account will not only examine the current law and the judicial reaction to *Barclays* and *Morrison*, but place the doctrine of vicarious liability in historical and societal context. I will also seek to address factors that, in my view, have influenced the law, be they policy arguments such as enterprise risk and deeper pockets or global scandals such as revelations of historic institutional child sexual abuse that have triggered enquiries across the world. What is clear is that *Barclays* and *Morrison*, despite the best efforts of the UK Supreme Court, have not stopped the development of the doctrine of vicarious liability in England and Wales. The rationale of, and justification for, vicarious liability in England and Wales remain as open to debate as ever.

II. The Test

In *Various Claimants v Catholic Child Welfare Society*,[5] the UK Supreme Court set out the modern test for vicarious liability. It will arise where D1 commits a tort, and the claimant can establish:

> **Stage one**: a *relationship* between D1 and D2 capable of giving rise to vicarious liability; and **Stage two**: a *connection* that links the relationship between D1 and D2 and the act or omission of D1.

This establishes a principle of strict liability where D2 (typically an employer) is held liable for the torts of D1 (typically an employee) provided that they are closely connected to the employment relationship. However, since 2001, the UK courts have adopted a generous interpretation of both stages of this test. It is now clear that the doctrine applies to both intentional and non-intentional torts and that ideas such as enterprise risk have been used by the court to justify both an extension of the doctrine and the revival of the doctrine of non-delegable duties, previously assumed to be an historical oddity rather than a conceptualised doctrine.[6] The scope of these two stages will be examined below.

[4] For commentary, see D Nolan, 'Reining in Vicarious Liability' (2020) 49 *Industrial Law Journal* 609; P Giliker, 'Can the Supreme Court Halt the Ongoing Expansion of Vicarious Liability?' (2021) 37 *Journal of Professional Negligence (PN)* 55; J Lee, 'The Supreme Court, Vicarious Liability and the Grand Old Duke of York' (2020) 136 *LQR* 6.

[5] *Various Claimants v Catholic Child Welfare Society* [2012] UKSC 56, [2013] 2 AC 1 [21] (*CCWS*).

[6] See G Williams, 'Liability for Independent Contractors' (1956) 14 *CLJ* 180 and, more recently, J Morgan, 'Vicarious Liability for Independent Contractors?' (2015) 31 *PN* 235. Contra J Murphy, 'Juridical Foundations of Common Law Non-Delegable Duties' in J Neyers, E Chamberlain and S Pitel (eds), *Emerging Issues in Tort Law* (Oxford, Hart Publishing, 2007).

A. Stage One: Defining the Relationship Test

i. *From Employment to 'Akin to Employment'*

As Lord Phillips acknowledged in the *CCWS* case,[7] the relationship that gives rise to vicarious liability is in the vast majority of cases that of employer and employee under a contract of employment.[8] Vicarious liability does not apply for the acts of independent contractors.[9] However, the courts have increasingly accepted that this should be treated as a matter not of form but of substance.[10] On this basis, the court will ask whether the worker can realistically be said to be on business on his own account, taking the risk of profit or loss.[11] If we consider, then, the 'classic' case of *Ready Mixed Concrete (South East) Ltd v Minister of Pensions and National Insurance*,[12] lorry drivers, who worked for a concrete firm, were classified as independent contractors even though the lorries they drove and owned were purchased by them on hire purchase terms from a finance company affiliated to the employer and they could not sell them without the employer's permission. On balance McKenna J found the fact that they owned the vehicles in question and the risk of profit or loss lay with them indicated that they failed to satisfy the relationship test.

This bifurcation between 'employees' and 'independent contractors', however, has been challenged. The early 2010s case of *JGE*[13] introduced the concept of 'akin to employment'. Such a development was inspired by the 2004 Canadian case of *Doe v Bennett* which had found the relationship between the bishop and a priest in a diocese 'akin' to that of employer/employee.[14] In *CCWS*, Lord Phillips confirmed that a broader notion of 'employment' would be adopted which would include relationships 'akin' to employment, giving five policy reasons that usually make it fair, just and reasonable to impose vicarious liability on the employer in such cases which included deeper pockets, enterprise risk and the employer's control of the tortfeasor.[15] Any relationship that was so close in character to that of employer/employee that it was just and fair to hold the employer vicariously liable

[7] *CCWS* (n 5) [35].

[8] Other relationships include partners (Partnership Act 1890) and for an attempt to use agency to extend the liability of an (insured) car owner, see *Morgans v Launchbury* [1973] AC 127.

[9] *D & F Estates Ltd v Church Comrs* [1989] AC 177, 208 per Lord Bridge; *Salsbury v Woodland* [1970] 1 QB 324, 336 per Widgery LJ.

[10] See *Viasystems (Tyneside) Ltd v Thermal Transfer (Northern) Ltd* [2005] EWCA Civ 1151, [2006] QB 510 (*Viasystems*) [55] (Rix LJ).

[11] *JGE v English Province of Our Lady of Charity* [2012] EWCA Civ 938, [2013] QB 722 [70] per Ward LJ.

[12] *Ready Mixed Concrete (South East) Ltd v Minister of Pensions and National Insurance* [1968] 2 QB 497.

[13] *JGE v English Province of Our Lady of Charity* at first instance: [2011] EWHC 2871 (QB), [2012] 2 WLR 709 [34]–[36] per MacDuff J (affirmed by the Court of Appeal: [2012] EWCA Civ 938).

[14] [2004] 1 SCR 436, (2004) 236 DLR (4th) 577 [27] per McLachlin CJ.

[15] *CCWS* (n 5) [35].

could give rise to vicarious liability.[16] Whilst initially seen as a response to the so-called 'errant priest' problem,[17] this extension has proved useful in responding to organisational changes in the workplace with the increased casualisation of labour with employers contracting work out and replacing permanent employees with agency and temporary staff. Courts will now examine whether the worker in question was working on behalf of an enterprise or on his or her own behalf and, if the former, how central his or her activities were to the enterprise and whether these activities were integrated into the enterprise's organisational structure.[18] On this basis, the brother teachers in a religious school in *CCWS* were akin to employees of the religious organisation to which they belonged.[19] The Supreme Court in later decisions confirmed that even prisoners serving in the prison kitchen as part of their rehabilitation could be regarded as 'akin to employees' (*Cox v Ministry of Justice*),[20] as were foster parents volunteering[21] to undertake the care of children placed under local authority control (*Armes v Nottinghamshire CC*).[22]

The Court of Appeal in *Barclays Bank Plc v Various Claimants*[23] had been prepared to go further and extend the relationship to an independent doctor carrying out health checks on potential bank employees in his own surgery. The examinations, during which the abuse had taken place, had been at the instigation of the bank, with the doctor paid a fee per examination. The Court argued that, as a result of changes in employment structures, operations intrinsic to a business enterprise which were routinely performed by independent contractors over long periods, accompanied by precise obligations and high levels of control, should be regarded as akin to employment.[24] If this removed the bright line between employees and independent contractors, this was, in the view of Irwin LJ, a price worth paying.[25] Commentators expressed concern, however, that this made the dividing line between 'employee' and 'independent contractor' increasingly porous.[26]

In the Supreme Court in *Barclays*, Baroness Hale adopted a different approach:

> There is nothing … in [prior decisions of the] Supreme Court … to suggest that the classic distinction between employment and relationships akin or analogous to

[16] ibid [47].

[17] That is, that the Roman Catholic Church could avoid vicarious liability by claiming that priests abusing children were not their employees but office-holders.

[18] *CCWS* (n 5) [49].

[19] The Court found there to be joint vicarious liability between the religious organisation and the school for the tortious actions of the teachers.

[20] [2016] UKSC 10, [2016] AC 660.

[21] Only expenses are covered in such arrangements.

[22] *Armes v Nottinghamshire CC* [2017] UKSC 60, [2018] AC 355.

[23] *Barclays Bank Plc v Various Claimants* [2018] EWCA Civ 1670, [2018] IRLR 947.

[24] Ibid [45].

[25] Ibid [61]: 'ease of business cannot displace or circumvent the principles now established by the Supreme Court'.

[26] A Silink, 'Vicarious Liability of a Bank for the Acts of a Contracted Doctor' (2018) 34 *PN* 46.

> employment, on the one hand, and the relationship with an independent contractor, on the other hand, has been eroded ... The question therefore is, as it has always been, whether the tortfeasor is carrying on business on his own account or whether he is in a relationship akin to employment with the defendant.[27]

The Court of Appeal decision in *Barclays* was emphatically overturned. The doctor, it was held, was not at any time an employee of the bank, nor anything close to an employee. He was in business on his own account as a medical practitioner with a portfolio of patients and clients. One of those clients was the bank.[28]

The 2017 case of *Armes*, interestingly, was described as a 'difficult' case.[29] Here, the application of the 'independent business' test had been influenced by the five policy incidents set out by Lord Phillips in *CCWS*. The Court conceded that in 'doubtful' cases, these policy concerns might be helpful in identifying a relationship sufficiently analogous to employment to make it fair, just and reasonable to impose liability. Otherwise, however, the courts should focus on the details of the relationship: 'Where it is clear that the tortfeasor is carrying out his own independent business it is not necessary to consider [policy]'.[30] The claim for vicarious liability in *Barclays Bank* failed.

*ii. Post-*Barclays *Case Law*

Cases subsequent to *Barclays Bank* have struggled with the suggestion that policy need not be considered unless it is unclear whether the tortfeasor is carrying out his own independent business. In *JXJ v The Province of Great Britain of the Institute of Brothers of the Christian Schools*,[31] a pupil had been sexually abused by a lay night watchman and gardener who worked for a religious school. With parallels to *CCWS* (where the religious organisation *was* held vicariously liable for the abuse by brother-teachers), the High Court found that only the school in this case would be vicariously liable for his torts.[32] In what was a straightforward case (the employee had no religious affiliation), the court nevertheless supported its conclusion by examining the policy justification for an 'akin to employment' relationship.[33] In contrast, in *SKX v Manchester CC*,[34] Cavanagh J rejected the opportunity to extend *Armes* and placed exemplary emphasis on Baroness Hale's judgment in *Barclays Bank*: 'If the wrongdoer is carrying out an independent business of his own or that of a third party, then there will be

[27] *Barclays* (n 2) [24] and [27].
[28] ibid [28].
[29] ibid [23].
[30] ibid [27].
[31] *JXJ v The Province of Great Britain of the Institute of Brothers of the Christian Schools* [2020] EWHC 1914 (QB).
[32] McKinstry was an integral part of the work, business and organisation of the school, but not of the Institute: ibid [141] per Chamberlain J.
[33] ibid [144].
[34] *SKX v Manchester CC* [2021] EWHC 782 (QB), [2021] 4 WLR 56.

no vicarious liability and there will be no need to consider [policy]'.[35] Vicarious liability for sexual abuse would not arise simply by virtue of a local authority placing the victim in a privately run children's home. The home was not part of the local authority's organisation and was not integrated into its structure.

More recently, in *Hughes v Rattan*,[36] the Court of Appeal also echoed the test in *Barclays* in rejecting the argument that the owner of a dental practice had a relationship akin to employment with three self-employed dentists who worked for his practice. Following *Barclays*, the critical question, said the Court, had reverted to being whether the alleged tortfeasor's relationship with the defendant could properly be described as being 'akin' (or 'analogous') to employment, with the focus being on the contractual arrangements between tortfeasor and defendant.[37] In contrast, however, the Court found that the dentist who owned the practice did owe patients of the practice a non-delegable duty of care in respect of the treatment they had received from the associate dentists.

Cases such as *Hughes* indicate that the approach advocated by Baroness Hale in *Barclays* is being taken seriously by the courts, although it is noted that *JXJ* (and indeed *Hughes* at first instance)[38] justified their factual findings with reference to policy.

B. Stage Two: Defining the Connection Test

i. A Test of Close or Sufficient Connection?

Stage two of the vicarious liability test plays a specific role in confining liability to torts *connected* to the relationship linking the tortfeasor and employer. It also provides a justification for liability: this defendant should pay because the tort was connected with the tasks he/she asked the employee to perform. Traditionally, the employer would only be liable for torts committed 'in the course' of the employee's employment. Under the Salmond test – stated by Sir John Salmond in the first edition of his textbook, *The Law of Torts*[39] – a wrongful act by, what he then termed, 'a servant' would only be in the course of his employment if is amounted to either (a) a wrongful act authorised by the master or (b) a wrongful and unauthorised mode of doing some act authorised by the master.

As Lord Toulson explained in *Mohamud v Morrison Supermarkets plc*,[40] although Salmond's formula was applied in many cases over the course of the twentieth

[35] ibid [50].

[36] *Hughes v Rattan* [2022] EWCA Civ 107 (vicarious liability point obiter on the facts), overturning the High Court on this point: [2021] EWHC 2032 (QB), [2022] 1 WLR 194.

[37] ibid [88] per Bean LJ.

[38] [2021] EWHC 2032 (QB) [130] per Heather Williams QC. See also *Blackpool FC Ltd v DSN* [2021] EWCA Civ 1352 [129].

[39] JW Salmond, *The Law of Torts* (London, Stevens and Haynes, 1907) 83–84, repeated in later editions.

[40] *Mohamud v Morrison Supermarkets plc* [2016] UKSC 11, [2016] AC 677 (*Mohamud)*.

century, it was not universally satisfactory, particularly in cases concerned with deliberate acts of misconduct.[41] Faced with a claim of sexual abuse, which could not legitimately be described as a wrongful mode of doing an act authorised by the employer, the House of Lords in *Lister v Hesley Hall Ltd* in 2001[42] opted for a broader test. In the words of Lord Steyn, vicarious liability would arise where the employee's torts could be said to be so closely connected with his employment that it would be fair and just to hold the employers vicariously liable.[43] Lord Nicholls in *Dubai Aluminium Co Ltd v Salaam* clarified the close connection test further in 2002:

> … the wrongful conduct must be so closely connected with acts the partner or employee was authorised to do that, for the purpose of the liability of the firm or the employer to third parties, the wrongful conduct *may fairly and properly be regarded* as done by the partner while acting in the ordinary course of the firm's business or the employee's employment.[44]

In *Mohamud*, however, Lord Toulson offered a simplified version of this test:

> In the simplest terms, the court has to consider two matters. The first question is what functions or 'field of activities' have been entrusted by the employer to the employee, or, in everyday language, what was the nature of his job … Secondly, the court must decide whether there was *sufficient* connection between the position in which he was employed and his wrongful conduct to make it right for the employer to be held liable under the principle of social justice.[45]

This version of the test – seeking a 'sufficient' (note the change of terminology) connection –was unsurprisingly widely regarded as rendering the test easier to satisfy. Such a view was supported by the generous application of the test in *Mohamud* itself, where a vicious racist attack on a customer who had merely inquired about printing facilities at the supermarket kiosk was deemed to satisfy the test. Plunkett, for example, commented that given the 'extremely liberal understanding of the "close connection" test [in *Mohamud*], it is now difficult to conceive of many circumstances that will fall outside it.'[46] Morgan queried whether the course of employment test could now simply be described as a test of causation and whether the argument in *Lister* that the mere opportunity to cause injury to the claimant should not give rise to vicarious liability could still be sustained.[47]

[41] ibid [25].

[42] *Lister v Hesley Hall Ltd* [2001] UKHL 22, [2002] 1 AC 215 (*Lister*), taking inspiration from the test utilised by the Supreme Court of Canada in *Bazley v Curry* [1999] 2 SCR 534 and *Jacobi v Griffiths* [1999] 2 SCR 570.

[43] *Lister* ibid [28].

[44] *Dubai Aluminium Co Ltd v Salaam* [2002] UKHL 48, [2003] 2 AC 366 [23] (emphasis in text).

[45] *Mohamud* (n 40) [44]–[45] (emphasis added).

[46] J Plunkett, 'Taking Stock of Vicarious Liability' (2016) 132 *LQR* 556, 561.

[47] P Morgan, 'Certainty in Vicarious Liability: A Quest for a Chimaera?' (2016) 75 *CLJ* 202.

This impression appeared to be shared by the courts. In *Bellman v Northampton Recruitment Ltd*,[48] a drunken brawl between the managing director of a company and a colleague during a post-Christmas party drinking session at a local hotel was regarded as 'sufficiently' connected to the MD's 'field of activities' to render it just for vicarious liability to arise. In the curious case of *Levitt*[49] a fight and a chase around a building site culminating in one labourer striking the other with a scaffolding pole was equally 'sufficiently' connected to the field of activities of the worker, despite the fact that it is hard to think of a more obvious frolic of one's own. In *Various Claimants v Morrison Supermarkets plc* in the Court of Appeal,[50] the fact that the tortfeasor had committed the tort with the express aim of harming his employer against whom he held a grudge did not prevent the court finding that his misuse of private information was sufficiently connected to his field of activities. As a senior IT auditor, the tort was deemed to be connected by time, place and nature to his job despite the fact that the criminal disclosure had been made via his personal USB stick on his home computer. 'The solution', said the Court of Appeal, 'is to insure against such catastrophes; and employers can likewise insure against losses caused by dishonest or malicious employees'.[51]

The UKSC in *Morrison* overturned the Court of Appeal and reaffirmed its adherence to a test of close connection as stated in *Dubai Aluminium* above:

> … in the light of the circumstances of the case and the relevant precedents, Skelton's wrongful conduct was not so closely connected with acts which he was authorised to do that, for the purposes of Morrisons' liability to third parties, it can fairly and properly be regarded as done by him while acting in the ordinary course of his employment.[52]

This is clearly a tighter formulation than that used in *Mohamud*, notably bringing back into the test the notion of authority. Earlier cases such as *Bellman* were reviewed and, although its reasoning was criticised, the result was found to be valid on the facts.[53] The result in *Mohamud* equally was approved, but its reasoning, while not expressly criticised, was admitted to have given rise to 'misunderstandings' which the Supreme Court sought to correct. 'Misunderstandings' might be regarded as an understatement. Both courts and commentators had regarded *Mohamud* as approving a more liberal approach to the connection test. Equally comments in *Mohamud* that the tortfeasor's motive had been irrelevant[54] had given rise to concerns that 'frolic' cases might now satisfy the connection test. *Morrison*, however, 'clarifies' that what appeared to be a looser test of 'sufficient' connection was, in fact, not intended to represent a departure from the test stated in *Lister* and *Dubai Aluminium*. The Court specifically denied that the test was one

[48] *Bellman v Northampton Recruitment Ltd* [2018] EWCA Civ 2214, [2019] ICR 459.
[49] *Levitt v Euro Building and Maintenance Contractors Ltd* [2019] EWHC 2926 (QB).
[50] *Various Claimants v Morrison Supermarkets plc* [2018] EWCA Civ 2339, [2019] QB 772.
[51] ibid [78].
[52] *Morrison* (n 3) [47] per Lord Reed.
[53] ibid [46].
[54] *Mohamud* (n 40) [48].

of temporal or causal connection between the employment and the wrongdoing or one of social justice.[55] Equally while the employee's motive had been irrelevant on the facts of *Mohamud* where the court had already determined that his conduct was furthering the employer's business,[56] it *would* be relevant when the question of close connection remained open (as was the case in *Morrison* itself).

Courts were further directed to refer to previous court decisions to identify the factors or principles which point towards or away from vicarious liability in the case before the court. This will lead, stated the Court, to cases being decided on a basis which is principled and consistent.[57] The Court also rejected any reference to policy in deciding the close connection test. Policy was relevant when discussing the akin to employment test (for 'doubtful' cases as seen in *Barclays*), but not in relation to the connection test. The only exception would be sexual abuse cases where a 'tailored' version of the close connection test would apply.[58]

*ii. Post-*Morrison *Case Law*

Subsequent cases indicate that while the broader message of *Morrison* has been heard, the sexual abuse exception remains a potential area for ongoing expansion. The Court of Appeal in *Chell v Tarmac Cement and Lime Ltd*[59] confirmed that 'frolic' cases would remain outside the connection test. This case involved a practical joke on a building site in which a workman had struck pellets with a work implement (hammer) causing another workman to suffer hearing loss. Use of a work implement and background tensions in the workplace were not enough to satisfy stage two of the test. However, in cases involving sexual abuse, the lower courts have been quick to address the need for a tailored approach. In *Trustees of the Barry Congregation of Jehovah's Witnesses v BXB*,[60] the Court of Appeal faced a difficult case where a religious leader (elder) had raped a congregation member while she was trying to advise him about his personal problems as a friend. The case was complicated by the fact that she had been asked to do so by a senior elder of the congregation who was also her attacker's father. The rape had not occurred while the elder had been performing any sort of religious duty and indeed took place in the elder's family home after the parties' respective families had met for lunch. Nevertheless, the Court of Appeal applied the 'tailored' open-textured test and examined all aspects of the parties' relationship, with specific reference to the

[55] *Morrison* (n 3) [26].

[56] Lord Toulson was therefore merely stating that why he chose so to act did not matter.

[57] *Morrison* (n 3) [24].

[58] ibid [23] and [36], citing *CCWS* (n 5) [83] and [85].

[59] *Chell v Tarmac Cement and Lime Ltd* [2022] EWCA Civ 7, especially [28], approving [2020] EWHC 2613 (QB). See J Cainer, 'Horseplay, Affray and Going Astray – Vicarious Liability for Intentional Wrongdoing in the Workplace' (2021) 37 *PN* 108 for questions left open by this litigation.

[60] *Trustees of the Barry Congregation of Jehovah's Witnesses v BXB* [2021] EWCA Civ 356, [2021] 4 WLR 42 (*BXB*).

power and authority the defendants had conferred on the tortfeasor. In the words of Nicola Davies LJ:

> … the tailored version of the test applies in cases in which adults are alleged to have been sexually abused as it does in such cases involving children because the rationale for the test is the same. …. On the facts of this claim, what is relevant for the purpose of the close connection test is the conferral of authority by the Jehovah's Witness organisation upon its elders, coupled with the opportunity for physical proximity as between an elder and publishers in the congregation.[61]

This led to a particularly generous interpretation of the test. The authority conferred on the elder, both by virtue of his office and the actions of fellow elders who had turned a blind eye to his openly sexually inappropriate behaviour towards female congregation members, indicated that the connection test had been satisfied. This more generous version of the test will therefore focus on the nature of the parties' relationship, notably on signs of power and/or dependency which create a risk of wrongdoing.[62] In *AB v Chethams School of Music*,[63] the High Court took as its starting point that the close connection test will be applied differently in cases concerned with the sexual abuse of children. Here abuse of a pupil had taken place within school premises and in the teacher's car and flat while he was acting as the pupil's teacher and guardian. Given the pastoral role of the teacher and the authority conferred on him by the school,[64] the court found a strong causative link between the employment relationship and the assaults.

Such case law strongly indicates that sexual abuse cases involving adult and child victims will in future be regarded as a separate category of vicarious liability claims in England and Wales. It might be questioned to what extent it is justifiable to treat such claims differently from, say, serious physical assaults and other intentional harm.[65] Can the 'tailored' approach be confined to sexual abuse cases? Time will tell.

C. Reflecting on *Barclays* and *Morrison*: A New Direction?

In *Barclays* and *Morrison*, the UK Supreme Court sought to provide guidance on the application of the two-stage test for vicarious liability in England and Wales. In *Barclays*, the Court re-emphasised the classic distinction between employees and independent contractors, indicating that, in most cases, the 'akin to

[61] ibid [84].

[62] ibid [95] per Males LJ who acknowledged that its application would need to take account of the differences between children and adults.

[63] *AB v Chethams School of Music* [2021] EWHC 1419 (QB).

[64] ibid [83].

[65] Cases such as *Armes* (n 22), for example, involved physical and sexual abuse but was treated as a sexual abuse case. To what extent, then, can claimants access the 'tailored' test by alleging sexual abuse in addition to other injuries?

employment' test can be resolved by reference to the details of the relationship. Only in doubtful cases should reference be made to wider policy factors stated by Lord Phillips in *CCWS*. In *Morrison*, the Court re-established that it was a case of 'close', not 'sufficient', connection and that while *Mohamud* was regarded as correctly decided, its simplified version of the test was deemed better stated by Lord Nicholls in *Dubai Aluminium*, which, in addition to stating a test of close connection, also advised courts to follow existing case law precedents for guidance. Reference to the Lord Philips policy factors was deemed irrelevant on the facts of *Morrison*, although a concession was made that they may be relevant in sexual abuse cases.

However, cases subsequent to *Barclays/Morrison* do suggest ongoing uncertainties in the law. The *Mohamud* sufficient connection test is still cited by the courts and the attempt to limit reference to policy factors has not been wholly successful. The courts in 'akin to employment' cases have demonstrated an understandable tendency to justify their conclusions by reference to policy even though on a strict reading of *Barclays* this is not needed. Old habits, it would seem, die hard. Counsell and Cainer also argue that the particular challenges often faced by sexual abuse victims in establishing the qualifying relationship means that many, like Ms Armes, are likely to fall within the category of 'doubtful cases', permitting invocation of policy grounds for liability.[66] One might also speculate to what extent the 'tailored' connection test for sexual abuse cases can be ring-fenced from the rest of vicarious liability, particularly for cases involving, for example, serious physical abuse of vulnerable parties. What is becoming increasingly clear is that while in *Barclays* and *Morrison* the UK Supreme Court sought to bring greater certainty to this area of law, a number of unanswered questions remain, not least how to deal with sexual abuse cases and the degree to which the courts can and should refer to policy in developing the law.

III. Vicarious Liability and Non-Delegable Duties

The expansion of vicarious liability, notably post-*CCWS*, has been mirrored by the revival of the non-delegable duty (NDD) in the 2010s. The NDD is a form of primary, not vicarious, liability: a defendant will be held *personally* liable to victims for the negligence of employees or independent contractors to whom he or she has delegated the performance of the NDD in question.[67] By holding the employer accountable for a failure to ensure that reasonable care is taken towards the victim, the NDD bears an obvious resemblance to vicarious liability. In both cases, the immediate cause of the injury will be the tortious act of another. Fleming

[66] J Counsell and J Cainer, 'Historical Sexual Abuse Claims: Is Vicarious Liability "on the Move" Again?' [2020] *Journal of Personal Injury Law* 225, 228.

[67] MA Jones (ed), *Clerk and Lindsell on Torts* 23rd edn (London, Sweet and Maxwell, 2020) [6-67].

famously called NDDs a 'disguised form of vicarious liability',[68] and while the English courts continue to argue that there is a conceptual distinction between the two forms of liability, litigants will often raise NDD arguments alongside those of vicarious liability to strengthen their case. Significantly, NDDs provide a fall-back should the claimant fail to establish the stage one relationship test for vicarious liability – even if the tortfeasor is an independent contractor to whom vicarious liability does not apply, an employer may be held responsible if it is found to owe a non-delegable duty directly to the claimant.

In the 2013 case of *Woodland v Essex CC*,[69] the Supreme Court outlined an NDD based on based on assumption of responsibility. Lord Sumption identified three critical characteristics of this distinctive category of NDD:

(i) There is an antecedent relationship between the defendant and the claimant.
(ii) It imposes a positive or affirmative duty to protect a particular class of persons against a particular class of risks and is not simply a duty to refrain from acting in a way that foreseeably causes injury.
(iii) The duty is by virtue of that relationship personal to the defendant.[70]

It will arise where the defendant has assumed responsibility to protect a claimant who is especially vulnerable or dependent on the protection of the defendant from harm and where the claimant has no control to whom the defendant delegates performance of functions which are an integral part of the positive duty assumed towards the claimant.[71] The *Woodland* NDD has been used to impose liability on institutions such as schools (*Woodland* itself), immigration centres[72] and dental practices[73] for the torts of independent contractors. However, the NDD was rejected in relation to the local authority foster care case of *Armes* in 2017 which argued that such duties are exceptional and have to be kept within reasonable limits.[74] In particular, the statutory framework for local authority fostering in *Armes* rendered the imposition of a non-delegable duty on the local authority 'too broad … the responsibility with which it fixes local authorities is too demanding'.[75] Questions have also been raised of the extent to which the *Woodland* NDD (which concerned a negligence claim) should be extended to intentional torts. While the Supreme Court (obiter) indicated in *Armes* that it had no objection in principle to such an NDD,[76] there is currently no binding authority supporting such a duty.

[68] JG Fleming, *The Law of Torts* 9th edn (Sydney, LBC Information Services, 1998) 434.
[69] *Woodland v Essex County Council* [2013] UKSC 66, [2014] AC 537.
[70] ibid [7]. This category is in addition to a separate general category of NDDs which include anomalous cases such as inherently hazardous activities and dangers on the public highway.
[71] ibid [23].
[72] NDD in relation to healthcare provision to detainees in an immigration centre: *GB v Home Office* [2015] EWHC 819 (QB). However, *Razumas v Ministry of Justice* [2018] EWHC 215 (QB) concluded that healthcare cannot be characterised as an essential or mainstream function of a prison.
[73] *Hughes* (n 36).
[74] *Armes* (n 22) [32].
[75] ibid [49].
[76] ibid [51].

Armes is significant, however, in that it favours vicarious liability rather than the NDD as a justification for imposing liability on a local authority for abuse occurring during foster care. As seen above, by adopting a broad interpretation of the 'akin to employment' relationship, there was no need to develop an NDD to ensure Ms Armes received compensation. This decision has received criticism from commentators such as Tofaris[77] and Deakin[78] who have argued that *Armes* should have been a non-delegable duty case, drawing on a body of literature that indicates that non-delegable duties provide a more suitable response to child abuse cases. The source of the debate can be traced back to *Lister* itself.[79] Here, it was clearly arguable that the company running the children's home could have been held liable on the basis of an NDD to ensure that reasonable care was taken of the children.[80] Instead the House of Lords chose to expand the doctrine of vicarious liability, although traces of NDD reasoning can be found in the judgments.[81] By 2017, the path taken had made its imprint in the law with extension of the stage one relationship test further emphasising that vicarious liability was the easiest means of establishing liability in such cases. Decisions such as *JGE* and *Armes* made any further attempts to establish an NDD for sexual abuse pointless.

It remains to be seen whether the reassertion of the employee/independent contractor distinction in *Barclays* will serve to revive the NDD argument in the law of England and Wales. Given the above analysis, and indeed the retention of *Armes* as good authority, one might think this unlikely. *Barclays* itself could easily have been re-interpreted as an NDD case – the bank owing an NDD to potential employees to ensure that reasonable care was taken in their pre-employment health checks – but this was not even argued in the Supreme Court.[82] The *Woodland* NDD remains under-theorised and in a common law system, despite the best efforts of academics, it would require a litigant brave (and wealthy) enough to bring a case for the law to change.[83] At best, then, the NDD will be raised alongside vicarious liability. The recent case of *Hughes v Rattan*[84] does, however, present an example where an NDD was argued alongside vicarious liability and the Court of Appeal chose to favour the former and reject the latter. Applying *Barclays*, the

[77] S Tofaris, 'Vicarious Liability and Non-Delegable Duty for Child Abuse in Foster Care: A Step too Far?' (2016) 79 *MLR* 884.

[78] S Deakin, 'Organisational Torts: Vicarious Liability versus Non-Delegable Duty' (2018) 77 *CLJ* 15.

[79] *Lister* (n 42).

[80] See T Weir, *An Introduction to Tort Law* 2nd edn (Oxford, Oxford University Press, 2006) 112–13; N McBride and R Bagshaw, *Tort Law* 6th edn (Harlow, Pearson, 2018) 842.

[81] See eg Lord Hobhouse in *Lister* (n 42) [54]–[55].

[82] R Buxton, 'Vicarious Liability in the Twenty-First Century' (2020) 79 *CLJ* 217.

[83] See P Giliker, 'Analysing Institutional Liability for Child Sexual Abuse in England and Wales and Australia: Vicarious Liability, Non-Delegable Duties and Statutory Intervention' (2018) 77 *CLJ* 506, 529–30.

[84] *Hughes* (n 36). Contrast *SKX v Manchester CC* (n 34) where arguments based on a non-delegable duty owed by a local authority for abuse suffered by children placed in a private children's home were rejected on the authority of *Armes*: [90].

Court rejected the argument that three self-employed Associate Dentists working for the defendants' practice were 'akin to employees' but nevertheless found the *Woodland* criteria to be met. While it might be argued that negligent treatment in a dental practice by independent dentists falls more readily within the *Woodland* concept of an NDD, it remains to be seen to what extent future case law takes this path and whether, crucially, the courts will accept that a duty to ensure that reasonable care is taken includes responsibility for both intentional and negligent harm, thereby extending the NDD into sexual abuse cases.

IV. Understanding Vicarious Liability in England and Wales

In this section, I will outline some of the influences that underlie the substantive law examined above. As we have seen, the test for vicarious liability may be stated easily; its application, however, has proven more difficult to anticipate. As Judge LJ stated in *Mattis v Pollock*, it is a test that 'requires a deceptively simple question to be answered'.[85] The reason why vicarious liability has proven so unpredictable in English law is the fact that its application has been influenced by a number of factors in recent years. While initially reticent to address these factors, in *CCWS*, the UK Supreme Court openly acknowledged five policy factors that would serve to justify the imposition of vicarious liability. However, as we will see, other factors beyond these five policy grounds have made an impression on the law we see today. In this section I will examine the influence of the Phillips policy factors and other broader policy concerns and track the extent to which they have shaped the law analysed above. It will be argued that *Barclays* and *Morrison* represent a reaction against the rapid extension of vicarious liability in recent years and reflect a more general retrenchment of private law in favour of incremental principled legal development, as seen recently in relation to the duty of care concept in the tort of negligence.[86] While such steps appear successful in relation to the tort of negligence, as seen, it has proven far harder to rein in policy-based reasoning in the context of vicarious liability.

A. Vicarious Liability and Public Policy

While Glanville Williams wrote cynically in 1957 that '[v]icarious liability is the creation of many judges who have had different ideas of its justification or social

[85] *Mattis v Pollock (trading as Flamingos Nightclub)* [2003] EWCA Civ 887, [2003] 1 WLR 2158 [19].

[86] See, eg, *Michael v Chief Constable of South Wales Police* [2015] UKSC 2, [2015] AC 1732 [130] and *Robinson v Chief Constable of West Yorkshire Police* [2018] UKSC 4, [2018] AC 736 which urged an approach based on common law precedent and the incremental development of the law by analogy with established authorities.

policy, or no idea at all',[87] this has not prevented scholars from attempting to find a means to rationalise the doctrine.[88] Swain argues, convincingly, that one of the reasons why rationalising vicarious liability is problematic is that it has existed historically through very different social and economic conditions and thus rests on insecure and shifting doctrinal foundations.[89] Atiyah, in his celebrated work, *Vicarious Liability in the Law of Torts*,[90] sought to place vicarious liability in the modern context, finding what he termed a social justification for vicarious liability – that it acts as an instrument of loss distribution fuelled by the wide-spread practice of insurance against tortious liability.[91] As to the scope of liability, Atiyah suggested that the employee should be liable for 'all those torts which can fairly be regarded as reasonably incidental risks to the type of business he carries on'.[92] The idea of risk justifying the imposition of strict liability can be traced back to nineteenth century case law such as *Duncan v Findlater*[93] and received a modern boost from its use by the Supreme Court of Canada in 1999 in *Bazley v Curry*.[94] The SCC, influenced by the US law and economics movement, argued that enterprise risk might be seen as the primary justification for vicarious liability:

> … [t]he employer puts in the community an enterprise which carries with it certain risks. When those risks materialize and cause injury to a member of the public despite the employer's reasonable efforts, it is fair that the person or organisation that creates the enterprise and hence the risk should bear the loss … It must be possible to say that the employer *significantly* increased the risk of the harm by putting the employee in his or her position and requiring him to perform the assigned tasks.[95]

Thus interpreted, vicarious liability will have, it is argued, associated normative effects, notably acting as a deterrent, inducing employers to exercise a greater degree of care in relation to the appointment and supervision of employees and ensuring fair and efficient compensation for wrongs.[96] While the House of Lords in *Lister* adopted the *Bazley* close connection test, it paid little attention to

[87] G Williams, 'Vicarious Liability and the Master's Indemnity' (1957) 20 *MLR* 220, 231.

[88] See W Swain, 'A Historical Examination of Vicarious Liability: A "Veritable Upas Tree"?' (2019) 78 *CLJ* 640 for an overview of why, historically, no single clear explanation for vicarious liability has been found.

[89] ibid 648–50.

[90] PS Atiyah, *Vicarious Liability in the Law of Torts* (London, Butterworths, 1967).

[91] ibid ch 2. He argued that spreading the burden of liability amongst the enterprise's customers and insurers is 'the most rational justification that can be offered for vicarious liability today': 27.

[92] ibid 171.

[93] *Duncan v Findlater* (1839) 6 Cl & F 894, 910, 7 ER 934, 940 per Lord Brougham, although described as an isolated example by Swain (n 88) 647.

[94] *Bazley v Curry* [1999] 2 SCR 534, (1999) 174 DLR (4th) 45.

[95] ibid [31] and [42] (emphasis in text).

[96] ibid [46]. See, further, AO Sykes, 'The Boundaries of Vicarious Liability: An Economic Analysis of the Scope of Employment Rule and Related Legal Doctrines' (1988) 101 *Harvard Law Review* 563, 577–78.

its underlying reasoning,[97] but, by 2012, the Supreme Court in *CCWS* was openly addressing the role of risk as a justification for the expansion of the doctrine since *Lister* in 2001.

Yet in stating his five policy grounds for vicarious liability, it is noticeable that risk forms only part of Lord Phillips' list, stated below:

(i) The employer is more likely to have the means to compensate the victim than the employee and can be expected to have insured against that liability (*deeper pockets argument*);
(ii) The tort will have been committed as a result of activity being taken by the employee on behalf of the employer (*delegated task argument*);
(iii) The employee's activity is likely to be part of the business activity of the employer (*enterprise liability argument*);
(iv) The employer, by employing the employee to carry on the activity will have created the risk of the tort committed by the employee (*enterprise risk argument*); and
(v) The employee will, to a greater or lesser degree, have been under the control of the employer (*control argument*).[98]

What is interesting is the mixture of the pragmatic (deeper pockets), the traditional (control) and the conceptual (enterprise liability and risk). Deeper pockets, while lacking what Lord Reed called in *Cox* a 'principled' justification for vicarious liability,[99] nevertheless facilitates victim compensation. This is enhanced by the existence of insurance cover enabling employers, required at law to be insured or self-insure, to pay.[100] *CCWS* reflected, however, a trend towards more conceptualised explanations, relying increasingly on risk-based reasoning to justify extensions of vicarious liability, notably in cases of historic sexual abuse. Vicarious liability, held Lord Phillips, is imposed

> where a defendant, whose relationship with the abuser put it in a position to use the abuser to carry on its business or to further its own interests, has done so in a manner which has created or significantly enhanced the risk that the victim or victims would suffer the relevant abuse.[101]

Risk-based reasoning extended, however, into non-abuse cases such as *Cox* where the UK Supreme Court examined whether the defendants had, in the exercise of their mission or enterprise, placed the tortfeasor in a position where the commission of the tort was an inherent risk of the activities assigned to him.[102]

[97] For criticism, see P Giliker, 'Rough justice in an unjust world' (2002) 65 *MLR* 269. For a discussion of enterprise risk as an explanation of UK law, see D Brodie, *Enterprise Liability and the Common Law* (Cambridge, Cambridge University Press, 2010). For a detailed critique, see A Gray, *Vicarious Liability: Critique and Reform* (Oxford, Hart Publishing, 2018) ch 6.

[98] *CCWS* (n 5) [35].

[99] *Cox* (n 20) [20]: 'The mere possession of wealth is not in itself any ground for imposing liability'.

[100] See Employers' Liability (Compulsory Insurance) Act 1969. Such concerns are reflected in early attempts to protect (pre-NHS) charitable hospitals from vicarious liability for fear of depleting limited resources: AL Goodhart, 'Hospitals and Trained Nurses' (1938) 54 *LQR* 533.

[101] *CCWS* (n 5) [86].

[102] *Cox* (n 20) [31].

Lord Toulson in *Mohamud* noted that risk-based reasoning had been prominent since *Lister* as the social underpinning of vicarious liability: 'The risk of an employee misusing his position is one of life's unavoidable facts'.[103]

Risk, however, while facilitating the expansion of vicarious liability on employers whose enterprises[104] create the risk of harm to others, has a tendency to promise more than tort law can offer. If your enterprise creates a risk of harm, then surely all those who act on your behalf should trigger liability, even if they are true independent contractors?[105] Why should it be confined to tortious behaviour? Why should it indeed be confined to the employment context and not extend to any risk-creating behaviour?[106] These are questions that have troubled systems such as the French legal system which more openly relies on risk, underpinned by widespread insurance cover, to support a generous scheme of vicarious liability in tort (*fait d'autrui*). More recently, attempts have been made to curtail unrestrained risk-based reasoning on the basis that it threatens core tort law principle.[107]

Barclays and *Morrison* represent a reaction to risk-based reasoning – it is to be restrained, except, potentially, in the sexual abuse context (where *CCWS* made it clear that it was relevant) and in doubtful 'akin to employment' cases. We can, however, go further than this. As we have seen, the English courts have never fully committed to one particular explanation of vicarious liability despite the arguments from scholars.[108] In *Armes* itself, the Supreme Court used all five of the Phillips policy grounds to justify its treatment of the 'akin to employment' test. There have also been other instigators for legal change beyond the five Phillips grounds which, I will argue, have been influential in shaping the law we see today. These will be examined below. Such factors may not be openly acknowledged, but arguably have influenced resort to notions of risk in that it provides an easy justification for the extension of vicarious liability these factors require.

B. Vicarious Liability and Broader Policy Concerns

i. The Global Child Sexual Abuse Scandal

While the spread of insurance served to encourage courts to expand vicarious liability in the twentieth century, undoubtedly it has been revelations of child

[103] *Mohamud* (n 40) [40].

[104] This term is to be taken loosely given that many so-called enterprises will have charitable status eg residential schools; religious organisations.

[105] D Brodie, 'Enterprise Liability: Justifying Vicarious Liability' (2007) 27 *OJLS* 493.

[106] C McIvor, 'The Use and Abuse of the Doctrine of Vicarious Liability' (2006) 35 *Common Law World Review* 268.

[107] Discussed in P Giliker, 'Examining Vicarious Liability Comparatively: A Risky Business?' in S Turenne (ed), *Essays in Honour of John Bell* (Cambridge University Press, forthcoming).

[108] See, for example, JW Neyers, 'A Theory of Vicarious Liability' (2005–06) 43 *Alberta Law Review* 287; R Stevens, 'Vicarious Liability or Vicarious Action?' (2007) 123 *LQR* 30; P Morgan, 'Recasting

sexual abuse that have encouraged the courts to widen the doctrine further in the twenty-first.[109] The connection test dates from *Lister* (2001). This case, which overturned previous authority that an employer could not be vicariously liable for sexual abuse by an employee,[110] arose at a time when the British public had been rocked by revelations of physical and sexual abuse which had occurred in North Wales children's homes between 1974 and 1990, as detailed in the 2000 Waterhouse Report.[111] Sadly revelations did not cease, including the notorious Jimmy Savile scandal in 2012,[112] leading the UK government to establish in 2015 an Independent Inquiry into Child Sexual Abuse (IICSA).[113] The inquiry, which is still ongoing, seeks to investigate whether public bodies and other non-state institutions have taken their duty to protect children from sexual abuse seriously. To date it has published more than 15 investigation reports with over 30,000 correspondents getting in touch. Abuse scandals involving the Catholic Church have also had an impact on English law.[114] While the point had been conceded in earlier case law, in the light of the potential volume of claims, the Church's lawyers came to adopt more aggressive litigation tactics, arguing that priests as office-holders, not employees, were not covered by vicarious liability. In *JGE*,[115] as described above, the Court of Appeal effectively removed that barrier by developing the notion of the relationship 'akin to employment'. Judicial intervention has also rendered it easier for victims of historic sexual abuse to circumvent limitation periods for intentional torts[116] and rendered it possible for an unincorporated association to be vicariously liable for the tortious acts of one or more of its members.[117]

Vicarious Liability' (2012) 71 *CLJ* 615; C Beuermann, *Reconceptualising Strict Liability for the Tort of Another* (Oxford, Hart Publishing 2019); Gray (n 97) ch 8.

109 P Giliker, 'A Revolution in Vicarious Liability: *Lister*, the *Catholic Child Welfare Society* Case and Beyond' in S Worthington, A Robertson and G Virgo (eds), *Revolution and Evolution in Private Law* (Oxford, Hart Publishing, 2017); Nolan (n 4) 609.

110 *Trotman v North Yorkshire CC* [1998] ELR 625.

111 R Waterhouse, *Lost in Care Report of the Tribunal of Inquiry into the Abuse of Children in Care in the Former County Council Areas of Gwynedd and Clwyd since 1974* (London, Stationery Office, 2000). The £13m inquiry took evidence from more than 650 people, contained 700 allegations of abuse involving 170 individuals and found that there had been 'appalling mistreatment' of children.

112 Savile had been a media personality who, after his death in 2011, was revealed to be a serial sexual abuser who had used his fame and charitable work for the NHS to gain access to victims. The NHS published 44 reports in relation to Savile's abuse on hospital and hospice premises: 28 reports in June 2014 and 16 in February 2015: www.gov.uk/government/collections/nhs-and-department-of-health-investigations-into-jimmy-savile. The BBC inquiry was published in 2016: 'The Dame Janet Smith Review' (www.bbc.co.uk/bbctrust/dame_janet_smith).

113 Independent Inquiry into Child Sexual Abuse (www.iicsa.org.uk). For an overview of the impact of child sexual abuse on victims, see truth-project-dashboard-december-2020.pdf (iicsa.org.uk).

114 See eg *Maga v Trustees of the Portsmouth Roman Catholic Diocesan Trust* [2010] EWCA Civ 256; [2010] 1 WLR 1441 (*Maga*); *CCWS* (n 5).

115 *JGE* (n 11).

116 *A v Hoare* [2008] UKHL 6, [2008] 1 AC 844; F Burton, 'Limitation, Vicarious Liability and Historic Actions for Abuse: A Changing Legal Landscape' [2013] *Journal of Personal Injury Law* 95

117 *CCWS* (n 5) [20].

Judicial willingness to act, changing limitation rules and moulding the test for vicarious liability to ensure that victims of abuse are not caught out on legal 'technicalities' such as the need for a contract of employment or the Salmond 'authorised mode' test, has been remarkable. Lord Phillips in *CCWS* in 2012 openly acknowledged concern at the possibility of widespread sexual abuse of children within the entertainment industry[118] – undoubtedly a reference to the Savile scandal – demonstrating awareness of the abuse scandal at the highest level. The sexual abuse of children, he argued, is now recognised as a widespread evil.[119] Lord Hope commented extra-judicially on the role of the courts towards such abuse: '[c]hild sexual abuse is an ugly phenomenon. There is a heavy responsibility on our legal system to deal as fairly and justly as it possibly can with the consequences'.[120]

Risk-based reasoning has undoubtedly provided courts with the means to extend vicarious liability and respond to abuse claims. Lord Phillips, for example, in *CCWS* commented that while creation of risk is not enough, of itself, to give rise to vicarious liability for abuse, it is always likely to be an important element in the facts that give rise to such liability.[121] The risk rationale is therefore being used to facilitate a particular goal with the courts providing a judicial response to the scandal of sexual abuse in the absence of any official State-based response. It is interesting that the Supreme Court's response in *Morrison* in seeking to rein in policy-based reasoning has nevertheless not sought to overturn this particular line of authority.

ii. Criminal Injuries Compensation Scheme

Another influential factor (linked to i) is the absence of any State-based compensation scheme dealing with claims of sexual abuse. The Criminal Injuries Compensation Scheme does provide compensation for people who have been physically or mentally injured because they were the victim of a violent crime in England and Wales,[122] but, since its introduction in 1964, its scope and coverage, and the benefits available under it, have been progressively reduced, rendering such awards far lower than comparable tort awards.[123] Compensation is subject to a tariff scheme, which details a compensation amount for each injury, with a maximum award of £500,000.[124] There are also other restrictions. In most cases,

[118] ibid [85].
[119] ibid [83].
[120] Lord Hope, 'Tailoring the Law on Vicarious Liability' (2013) 129 *LQR* 514, 525.
[121] *CCWS* (n 5) [87]. See, recently, *AB v Chethams School of Music* [2021] EWHC 1419 (QB) [88].
[122] See P Cane and J Goudkamp, *Atiyah's Accidents, Compensation and the Law* 9th edn (Cambridge, Cambridge University Press, 2018) 12.4.
[123] ibid 304.
[124] Criminal Injuries Compensation Scheme 2012 (amended). If the total amount of the claim is less than £1,000, no award will be made.

victims are expected to apply as soon as it is reasonably practicable for them to do so, normally within two years of the crime,[125] and report the incident giving rise to the criminal injury to the police as soon as reasonably practicable. The victim's own conduct is also taken into consideration including his/her willingness to co-operate with the Criminal Injuries Compensation Authority (CICA) which can refuse or reduce a payment if the victim has an unspent criminal record.[126]

The limitations of this State-based scheme have forced abuse victims to look to tort law as an alternative to recovery under the Scheme and thereby have acted as an indirect incentive to the courts to intervene. Although there have been some reforms to assist abuse victims, for example, abolition in 2019 of the 'same roof' rule which prevented awards to pre-1979 victims where the parties concerned lived together as members of the same family (thus penalising many victims of historic child sexual abuse),[127] as Miers notes, the UK government continues to focus on the affordability and financial sustainability of the Scheme.[128]

iii. The Gig Economy and the Changing Notion of 'Employee'

Another influence inciting legal change has been recognition by the courts of changes in employment practices. This is evident in recent employment law cases such as *Uber BV v Aslam*[129] where the UK Supreme Court sought to respond to changes in the labour market arising from the gig economy. As Lord Leggatt commented in that case, 'New ways of working organised through digital platforms pose pressing questions about the employment status of the people who do the work involved'.[130] While, then, the trigger for recognition of relationships 'akin to employment' was the need to ensure that office holders such as priests fell within the doctrine of vicarious liability, its underlying rationale is now accepted to be the need for vicarious liability to recognise changes in the hiring practices of enterprises and the increasing complexity and sophistication of the organisation of enterprises in the modern world.[131] The very nature of contracted-out labour, for

[125] Criminal Injuries Compensation Scheme 2012: [87]. However, allowances are made for those claiming for childhood sexual or physical abuse or who cannot claim earlier due to issues with mental or physical health.

[126] For the difficulties this may cause abuse victims, see N Sugarman, 'The Criminal Injuries Compensation Scheme 2012 and its Impact on Victims of Crime' [2016] *Journal of Personal Injury Law* 231. Grounds for withholding or reducing the award are listed in the 2012 Scheme: [22]–[29]. IICSA, *Accountability and Reparations Investigation Report* (2019) notes that the current CICA rules fail to recognise the impact of child sexual abuse and, specifically, that abuse may have directly contributed to instances of offending: Conclusions [18].

[127] D Miers, 'Historic Child Sexual Offences and the Criminal Injuries Compensation Scheme' [2019] *Journal of Personal Injury Law* 277.

[128] ibid 282.

[129] [2021] UKSC 5, [2021] ICR 657. See J Fulbrook, 'Reverberations from *Uber v Aslam* in Personal Injury Claims?' [2021] *Journal of Personal Injury Law* 59.

[130] *Uber* ibid [1].

[131] Lord Dyson in *Mohamud* (n 40) [55].

example, may signify, as in *Viasystems*,[132] that the employee in question is so much a part of the work, business or organisation of both the agency and its client that it would be just to hold both vicariously liable (joint vicarious liability). The move, therefore, from a relationship test based on a finding of a contract of employment to a more functionalist approach which examines the role played by the tortfeasor in the defendant's workplace highlights judicial awareness of changing employment practices. This is to be welcomed and, while not a policy ground per se, is nevertheless an important influence on the modern interpretation of the relationship test.

C. Understanding Vicarious Liability Comparatively

In examining the reasoning above, one further influence has yet to be appraised: that of other common law jurisdictions. The influence of the Supreme Court of Canada (SCC) has been particularly noteworthy. The 1999 cases of *Bazley v Curry*[133] and *Jacobi v Griffiths*[134] are regularly cited by the English courts, but cases such as *Doe v Bennett*[135] and *Blackwater v Plint*[136] have also proven influential in developing the 'akin to employment' test[137] and dual vicarious liability respectively.[138] Lord Steyn in *Lister* remarked that he had been greatly assisted by the 'luminous and illuminating' judgments of the SCC in *Bazley* and *Jacobi* and that wherever such problems are considered in future in the common law, these judgments should be the starting point.[139] While initially reticent to examine the enterprise risk reasoning underlying the *Bazley* test of close connection,[140] as we have seen, by the time of *CCWS* in 2012, such reasoning was accepted as part of the justifications for the doctrine.

In contrast, other common law jurisdictions have received less attention. *Barclays* did, however, refer to the Singaporean case of *Ng Huat Seng v Munib Mohammad Madni*[141] for its insights on the effects of *Cox* and *CCWS* on the employee/independent contractor distinction; its dicta being used to provide a critical commentary on English case law. What is perhaps more surprising is that Australian law, which is commonly regarded by English judges as a useful

[132] *Viasystems* (n 10) [80] per Rix LJ.
[133] *Bazley* (n 94).
[134] *Jacobi v Griffiths* [1999] 2 SCR 570, (1999)174 DLR (4th) 71.
[135] *Doe v Bennett* [2004] 1 SCR 436, (2004) 236 DLR (4th) 577.
[136] *Blackwater v Plint* [2005] 3 SCR 3, (2005) 258 DLR (4th) 275.
[137] MacDuff J in *JGE* [2011] EWHC 2871 (QB), [40].
[138] *CCWS* (n 5) [67].
[139] *Lister* (n 42) [27].
[140] ibid [27] and [60] per Lords Steyn and Hobhouse.
[141] *Ng Huat Seng v Munib Mohammad Madni* [2017] SGCA 58, [2017] 2 SLR 1074, cited in *Barclays* (n 2) [26].

comparator,[142] has received limited attention. Its leading cases of *New South Wales v Lepore*[143] and *Prince Alfred College v ADC*[144] seem to have made little impression on the English courts. There are reasons, however, we can identify for this. Lord Phillips in *CCWS* was critical of *Lepore* for its 'bewildering variety of analysis';[145] a criticism that Australian commentators are quick to acknowledge.[146] His Lordship dismissed the case on the basis that only two justices had been prepared to follow the Canadian and English approach. This division deepened when the High Court of Australia in *PAC* condemned *Mohamud* as wrongly decided and established its own test for 'course of employment'.[147] While the HCA's argument in favour of a principled and incremental approach might be viewed as similar in some ways to the argument used in *Barclays* and *Morrison*, no reference to *PAC* is made in either case. In retaining *Mohamud* as good authority, therefore, Australian authority is not regarded as helpful, despite a number of academic articles drawing attention to the parallels between the two jurisdictions.[148]

In examining the use of comparative material in English cases, a number of comments may be made. First, reference tends to be made to cases that have been highlighted in English journals by well-known and respected commentators. Lords Steyn and Hobhouse expressly credit Peter Cane's note on *Bazley* and *Jacobi* in *Lister*.[149] It is equally possible to link reference to *Ng Huat Seng* in *Barclays* with David Tan's note in *the Law Quarterly Review* two years' earlier[150] and indeed reference to *Blackwater v Plint* in *CCWS* with Jason Neyers' note also in the *Law Quarterly Review*.[151] Equally, counsel in *JGE* may well have noted that commentaries on the earlier case of *Maga* highlighted the utility of reference to *Doe v Bennett*.[152] While this is good news for those writing case notes in the *LQR*, this suggests a less than scientific form of comparative law!

[142] K Stanton, 'Comparative Law in the House of Lords and Supreme Court' (2013) 42 *Common Law World Review* 269 found Australia to be the most cited common law jurisdiction.

[143] *New South Wales v Lepore* [2003] HCA 4, 212 CLR 511, although *Lepore* has been cited in relation to non-delegable duties where, in contrast to vicarious liability, Australian authority has been widely cited see eg *Woodland* (n 69) [21].

[144] *Prince Alfred College v ADC* [2016] HCA 37, (2016) 258 CLR 134 (*PAC*).

[145] *CCWS* (n 5) [82]. In contrast, he noted that *Bazley* and *Jacobi* have had a significant influence on the English jurisprudence ([63]), finding further assistance from the application of *Bazley* in *Doe v Bennett* (n 135).

[146] See eg P Vines, 'Responsibility for Teachers' Sexual Assault: Non-Delegable Duty and Vicarious Liability' (2003) 27 *Melbourne University Law Review* 612.

[147] *PAC* (n 144) [83].

[148] See eg D Ryan, 'From Opportunity to Occasion: Vicarious Liability in the High Court of Australia' (2017) 76 *CLJ* 14; J Goudkamp and J Plunkett, 'Vicarious Liability in Australia: On the Move?' (2017) 17 *Oxford University Commonwealth Law Journal* 162.

[149] P Cane, 'Vicarious Liability for Sexual Abuse' (2000) 116 *LQR* 21.

[150] D Tan, 'Taking Two Bites at the Cherry: Vicarious Liability and Non-Delegable Duty' (2018) 134 *LQR* 193.

[151] JW Neyers, 'Joint Vicarious Liability in the Supreme Court of Canada' (2006) 122 *LQR* 195.

[152] K Williams, 'Vicarious Liability of the Roman Catholic Church for Sexual Abuse by a Priest' (2010) 26 *PN* 113; P Giliker, '*Lister* Revisited: Vicarious Liability, Distributive Justice and the Course of Employment?' (2010) 126 *LQR* 521.

Second, *Bazley* is unusual in that its influence has gone beyond the instrumental,[153] that is, validating the view of the Court that the law needs to be changed. While the House of Lords in *Lister* adhered to the usual practice of 'borrowing' a test of close connection without paying too much attention to its underlying reasoning and rationale, by *CCWS*, enterprise risk was being discussed by the court as a rationale for extending liability. Lord Phillips in *CCWS* argued that a common theme can be traced back to 'the Canadian authorities': that vicarious liability is imposed where a defendant, whose relationship with the abuser put it in a position to use the abuser to carry on its business or to further its own interests, has done so in a manner which has created or significantly enhanced the risk that the victim or victims would suffer the relevant abuse.[154]

Finally, the influence of *Bazley* can be explained for three reasons. First, good timing. In providing a means of justifying vicarious liability for those responsible for the acts of abusers, it gifted the English courts a means to circumvent the Salmond test without doing too much violence to existing law. Second, its explanation of enterprise risk chimed with reference to risk by English commentators such as Atiyah and long-standing reference to risk in case law. No attempt was made to address whether Atiyah's reference to the incidental risks of employees in the workplace coincided exactly with the law and economics concept of enterprise risk, although commentators have made it clear that enterprise risk acting alone does not explain the doctrine of vicarious liability being applied by the courts. Third, it gave access to factually useful examples with which courts could analogise (and it is interesting to see how often the facts of *Bazley* and *Jacobi* are set out in judgments). Comparative law theorists, however, should not get too excited by this example. It is not representative of the general approach of the English courts. No attempt is made to put *Bazley* in context with reference to its subsequent application in the Canadian courts. It is treated as stand-alone authority – its stature based on its utility in enabling *English* law to develop in a way regarded as fair and just by the courts.

V. Conclusions

Vicarious liability in England and Wales has been subject to expansion since 2001 with an unprecedented number of House of Lords/Supreme Court decisions attempting to determine the parameters of this doctrine. As we have seen, despite such judicial activity, the application of the two-stage test of relationship and connection remains subject to uncertainty. Why are the English courts struggling, then, with vicarious liability? Three main reasons can be found to explain

[153] See J Bell, 'The Relevance of Foreign Examples to Legal Development' (2011) 21 *Duke Journal of Comparative and International Law* 433.

[154] *CCWS* (n 5) [83].

the current position. First, as we have seen, there are a number of factors that have influenced the courts and this, inevitably, leads to uncertainty as the courts seek to determine to what extent policy (and which policy?) should influence the decision in a particular case. One category of case does stand out where policy-based reasoning has dominated – that of sexual abuse. The Canadian case of *Bazley* has provided both the test and the theoretical underpinning – enterprise risk – to justify expansion of vicarious liability for sexual abuse reaching a result that the courts regard as fair and just. *Barclays* and *Morrison* have sought to address uncertainty by advocating a more conservative, principled approach that develops past case law incrementally and minimises the role of policy. However, this chapter has noted problems with this approach. In treating abuse claims as a 'special case', a risk-based test of close/sufficient connection will survive *Morrison*. This raises the question how easy it will be to ring-fence this category of claims. Post-*Barclays* case law also demonstrates that courts have found it difficult to exclude policy considerations when dealing with the 'akin to employment' test even in cases which do not seem 'doubtful' on the facts. It is unclear to what extent *Barclays* and *Morrison* will slow down the ongoing momentum of vicarious liability.

Second, and perhaps more fundamentally, we can identify uncertainty inherent in the two-stage test itself. The tests for 'relationship' and 'connection' are often difficult to apply. For example, in extending the relationship test to include relationships functionally analogous to employment to reflect changes in workplace practice, the law inevitably becomes less clear. The 'connection' test indeed has always been problematic. Lord Nicholls commented in *Dubai Aluminium*[155] that:

> This 'close connection' test focuses attention in the right direction. But it affords no guidance on the type or degree of connection which will normally be regarded as sufficiently close to prompt the legal conclusion that the risk of the wrongful act occurring, and any loss flowing from the wrongful act, should fall on the firm or employer rather than the third party who was wronged.

The two-stage test has permitted expansion in the law, enabling it to adapt to changing times, but with flexibility goes unpredictability.

Finally, we might argue that the very nature of vicarious liability – the absence of a single clear policy justification; its adaptation over time to reflect the changing values of society; its uneasy relationship with fault-based liability – creates a doctrine without a clear sense of identity. Fleming described it as a doctrine that 'cannot parade as a deduction from legalistic premises but should be frankly recognised as having its basis in a combination of policy considerations'.[156] Bigwood and Dietrich argued recently that more precision will only be possible if a clearer and more confined rationale can be agreed which would leave less scope for

[155] *Dubai Aluminium* (n 44) [25].
[156] Fleming, *The Law of Torts* (n 68) 410.

variable decision-making.[157] The chameleon-type existence of vicarious liability is both its strength and weakness as a doctrine.

The imposition of vicarious liability remains, therefore, in practice a highly fact sensitive exercise. The 2020 cases of *Barclays* and *Morrison* attempt to provide a clearer legal framework, but, with hindsight, do not go far enough. In retaining controversial authority such as *Mohamud* and *Armes*, and the policy-based approach for 'akin to employment' and sexual abuse cases, problems remain. Another visit to the UK Supreme Court for further guidance therefore seems not simply likely but inevitable.

[157] R Bigwood and J Dietrich, 'Uncertainty in Private Law: Rhetorical Device or Substantive Legal Argument?' (2021) 45 *Melbourne University Law Review* 60, 83–4.

4

Vicarious Liability in Australia

CHRISTINE BEUERMANN

I. Introduction

Comparative research is difficult. For any comparison to be meaningful, the parameters of the research need to be determined with care and skill. It is a credit to Paula Giliker that she has engaged in comparative research so successfully for so long. The experience of writing this chapter has provided me with an opportunity to reflect more broadly upon the nature of my research and I thank Paula for extending the invitation to be involved in this project.

A wealth of different common law jurisdictions are explored in this book. Despite these riches, the comparison in this chapter will focus on the operation of the doctrine of vicarious liability in Australia and England and Wales for a number of reasons. First, the federal nature of the Australian Commonwealth means that there is not one, but several, jurisdictions in play, making any comparison with Australia inherently multi-faceted. Second, the High Court of Australia in *Prince Alfred College v ADC*[1] made a pointed effort to distinguish the approach it was taking to the two-stage test for vicarious liability from that adopted by the UK Supreme Court in *Mohamud v Wm Morrison Supermarkets plc*.[2] The comparison was therefore considered significant by the High Court itself. Finally, the Royal Commission into Institutional Responses to Child Sexual Abuse[3] in Australia has resulted in significant statutory changes. Two Australian jurisdictions have introduced changes that reflect aspects of the approach taken to the determination of vicarious liability by the courts in England and Wales.[4]

Recent revelations of historic child sexual abuse suffered in institutions charged with the care of children have placed considerable pressure on the doctrine of

[1] *Prince Alfred College v ADC* [2016] HCA 37, (2016) 258 CLR 134 (*Prince Alfred College*).

[2] *Mohamud v Wm Morrison Supermarkets plc* [2016] UKSC 11, [2016] AC 677 (*Mohamud*). Both cases focused on the stage 2 course of employment test rather than the stage 1 relationship test, discussed further in chapter one.

[3] The '*Royal Commission*' was announced by ex-Prime Minister Julia Gillard in 2012 and commenced its work in 2013. The *Redress and Civil Litigation Report* was published in 2015 followed by a Final Report titled *Beyond the Royal Commission* in 2017.

[4] Specifically, the 'akin to employment' test adopted at the first stage of the vicarious liability inquiry; s 6G Civil Liability Act 2002 (NSW); s 49I Civil Liability Act 2002 (Tas).

vicarious liability to adapt.[5] These differences make an interesting point of comparison. As it is not feasible to fully explore the historic development of vicarious liability in Australia and England and Wales within the scope of a single chapter,[6] this analysis will focus primarily on the development of the doctrine of vicarious liability in Australia since the decision of the High Court in *Prince Alfred College*; the most recent attempt by the High Court of Australia to clarify the law in this area.

Given the tendency of courts to utilise the doctrine of vicarious liability to respond to the pressures of child sexual abuse cases, this chapter will also focus on vicarious liability rather than liability for breach of a so-called 'non-delegable duty of care'. It will be seen throughout the chapter that the approach taken by courts in both Australia and England and Wales to determining vicarious liability in cases of child sexual abuse differs to the approach taken by the courts in other cases of vicarious liability. Whether it is appropriate to continue to use the term vicarious liability to refer to both these approaches and the form of strict liability for the tort of another that results from the application of those different approaches will be briefly considered.[7]

In terms of structure, the interplay between the common law and the more recent statutory developments makes the study of vicarious liability in Australia complex. This situation will more than likely intensify in coming years as opportunities for the new statutory framework in respect of institutional child sexual abuse to affect the development of the common law arise. As Dietrich and Field have noted, vicarious liability 'is a nuanced and interesting story of a complex interaction between statute and common law'.[8] It is, however, first necessary to understand how the common law developed before interrogating the impact of statutory developments. This chapter will therefore start with an examination of the common law position in Australia and then examine the nature and potential impacts of the statutory frameworks introduced in response to the Royal Commission into Institutional Responses to Child Sexual Abuse.

II. Common Law

Prior to the decision of the High Court of Australia in *Prince Alfred College*, there was no clear direction as to whether an institution in Australia could be held vicariously liable for the sexual abuse of a child within its care by an individual engaged

[5] As per Lord Phillips' now notorious declaration in *Various Claimants v Catholic Child Welfare Society* that 'the law of vicarious liability is on the move': [2012] UKSC 56, [2013] 2 AC 1 [19].

[6] For an overview of the historical background and the development of the common law test for vicarious liability, see chapter one of this volume.

[7] The term I have adopted elsewhere to refer to the form of strict liability for the tort of another imposed in cases of child sexual abuse is 'conferred authority strict liability'. See C Beuermann, 'Conferred Authority Strict Liability and Child Sexual Abuse' (2015) 37 *Sydney Law Review* 113.

[8] J Dietrich and I Field, 'Statute and Theories of Vicarious Liability' (2020) 43 *Melbourne University Law Review* 515, 520.

by the institution to work with the child. The earlier decision of the High Court in *New South Wales v Lepore*[9] had left the law in an entirely unsatisfactory state.[10] The High Court was conscious of this fact in *Prince Alfred College*[11] and, despite being presented with factual limitations and pleading anomalies not dissimilar to those in *Lepore*,[12] endeavoured to provide lower courts with more useful guidance.[13]

This section will examine the guidance provided by the High Court of Australia in *Prince Alfred College* as to the operation of the test for vicarious liability in Australia. It concerns only the second – 'scope of employment' – stage of the vicarious liability inquiry; there being no question as to the first – relationship – stage given that the teacher was an employee. The High Court has yet to be presented with the opportunity to consider the first stage of the vicarious liability inquiry in the context of child sexual abuse. This section will then consider a series of subsequent cases in which lower courts have attempted to apply that guidance. It will be seen that, despite the stated efforts of the High Court to methodologically distance the Australian approach from that taken by the UK Supreme Court, there is significant overlap, both in language used and decisions reached.

A. Guidance from the High Court of Australia: *Prince Alfred College v ADC*

All comments on vicarious liability made by the High Court of Australia in *Prince Alfred College* were dicta. The appeal by the College to a finding of vicarious liability by the Full Court of the Supreme Court of South Australia for the sexual abuse of the respondent by a teacher employed by the College was ultimately allowed on the basis that no extension of the limitation period should have been granted by the Full Court.[14]

All judges on the High Court in *Prince Alfred College* were of the view that, in certain circumstances, it was possible for an institution charged with the care of a child to be held vicariously liable for the abuse of that child by an employee. The circumstances where such liability might arise were described in the joint judgment given by French CJ and Kiefel, Bell, Keane and Nettle JJ[15] in the following terms:

> Consequently, in cases of this kind, the relevant approach is to consider any special role that the employer has assigned to the employee and the position in which the employee

[9] *New South Wales v Lepore* [2003] HCA 4, (2003) 212 CLR 511 (*Lepore*).

[10] For a detailed discussion of the decision of the High Court of Australia in *Lepore*, see Beuermann, above n 7.

[11] *Prince Alfred College* (n 1) [3].

[12] For further discussion of the limitations of the case see C Beuermann, 'Vicarious Liability: A Case Study in the Failure of General Principles' (2017) 33 *Journal of Professional Negligence* 179.

[13] *Prince Alfred College* (n 1) [10].

[14] ibid [120].

[15] This judgment will be referred to as the 'principal joint judgment', a second joint judgment being given by Gageler and Gordon JJ.

> is thereby placed vis-à-vis the victim. In determining whether the apparent performance of such a role may be said to give the 'occasion' for the wrongful act, particular features may be taken into account. They include authority, power, trust, control and the ability to achieve intimacy with the victim. The latter feature may be especially important. Where, in such circumstances, the employee takes advantage of his or her position with respect to the victim, that may suffice to determine that the wrongful act should be regarded as committed in the course or scope of employment and as such render the employer vicariously liable.[16]

Key phrases in this guidance include:

- 'cases of this kind'
- 'special role … in which the employee is thereby placed vis-à-vis the victim'
- '"occasion" for the wrongful act'
- 'authority, power, trust, control and the ability to achieve intimacy with the victim'
- 'takes advantage of his or her position with respect to the victim'.

Each of these phrases need to be carefully unpacked. In addition to guidance on what lower courts were supposed to do when deciding cases of vicarious liability, the High Court offered guidance on what *not* to do. As the latter provides important context for the former, it will be considered first.

First, lower courts were *not* to resort to general principles to guide their decision making. In the High Court's view, 'the search for a more acceptable general basis for [vicarious] liability has thus far eluded the common law of Australia'.[17] This meant that lower courts had to 'continue with the orthodox route of considering whether the approach taken in decided cases furnishes a solution to further cases as they arise'.[18] Enterprise liability was particularly noted by the High Court as a general principle that did *not* apply in Australia.[19]

Secondly, lower courts were *not* to base decisions on the idea of 'there being a connection between the wrongful act and the employment'.[20] In the High Court's view, 'a test of connection does not seem to add much to an understanding of the basis for an employer's liability'.[21] Nor, for that matter, did a consideration of whether imposing liability on an employer was 'fair, just and reasonable'. The High Court of Australia had previously criticised the use of such reasoning in the context of liability for breach of a duty of care and found it appropriate to remind lower courts that such reasoning was similarly not appropriate in the context of vicarious liability.[22]

[16] *Prince Alfred College* (n 1) [81].
[17] ibid [46].
[18] ibid.
[19] ibid [59]. The concept was introduced via the Canadian cases and first referred to by the High Court of Australia in *Hollis v Vabu Pty Ltd* [2001] HCA 44, (2001) 207 CLR 21.
[20] *Prince Alfred College* (n 1) [68].
[21] ibid.
[22] See references to *Sullivan v Moody* [2001] HCA 59, (2001) 207 CLR 562; *Prince Alfred College* (n 1).

Finally, lower courts were *not* to follow the reasoning of the UK Supreme Court in *Mohamud*.[23] As the High Court of Australia explained:

> This is because such a test of vicarious liability, requiring no more than sufficiency of connection – unconstrained by the outer limits of the course or scope of employment – is likely to result in the imposition of vicarious liability for wrongful acts for which employment provides no more than an opportunity.[24]

This view was based on an interpretation of Lord Toulson's judgment in *Mohamud* as requiring little more than a causal link between an employee's 'field of activities' and the 'sequence of events'.[25] It should be noted that the UK Supreme Court subsequently sought to clarify this interpretation as misguided in *Various Claimants v Wm Morrison Supermarkets plc*.[26] The clarified approach adopted by the UK Supreme Court will be discussed further below.

The first thing to note of the positive guidance given to lower courts by the High Court in *Prince Alfred College* was that it was limited to 'cases of this kind'. This is an important qualification. It suggests that the High Court was principally focussed on providing guidance in cases of child sexual abuse.[27] It does not necessarily follow that the guidance might not apply in other types of case, just that the High Court was reserving its position as to how the law might be developed in those other types of case.[28] A similar suggestion that the approach to child sexual abuse cases might be different was recently made by the UK Supreme Court in the *Morrisons* case:

> … the close connection test has been applied differently in cases concerned with the sexual abuse of children, which cannot be regarded as something done by the employee while acting in the ordinary course of his employment. Instead, the courts have emphasised the importance of criteria that are particularly relevant to that form of wrongdoing, such as the employer's conferral of authority on the employee over the victims, which he has abused.[29]

A suggestion as to why cases of child sexual abuse might require a different approach to the determination of vicarious liability can be found in the second key phrase highlighted in the extract from *Prince Alfred College* above: a 'special role … in which the employee is thereby placed vis-à-vis the victim'. The pivotal relationship for determining vicarious liability has traditionally been the relationship between the employer and the tortfeasor, this being the focus of the first

[23] *Prince Alfred College* (n 1) [83].
[24] ibid.
[25] ibid [72].
[26] *Wm Morrison Supermarkets plc v Various Claimants* [2020] UKSC 12, [2020] AC 989 [26] (*Morrisons*).
[27] That the court intended to refer to cases of child sexual abuse specifically, and not cases of intentional torts more generally, can be seen from the discussion: *Prince Alfred College* (n 1) [38].
[28] Although note that Gageler and Gordon JJ, in a separate joint judgment, were sceptical that it was even possible to come up with a general approach for child sexual abuse cases: ibid [131].
[29] *Morrisons* (n 26) [23].

stage of the vicarious liability inquiry. It is irrelevant, for instance, that a tortfeasor employed to deliver packages is a stranger to the person they negligently run down in the course of delivering those packages; vicarious liability can still be imposed.[30] In child sexual abuse cases, the High Court is suggesting that the relationship between the defendant employer and the plaintiff victim is as important, if not more important, than the relationship between the defendant employer and the tortfeasor. This is because, by virtue of the relationship between the defendant employer and the plaintiff victim, the defendant employer can place the tortfeasor in a particular position vis-à-vis the plaintiff victim.[31] Presumably, this means that a plaintiff victim who is a stranger to the defendant employer could not recover for vicarious liability for child sexual abuse.

The first active component of the guidance issued by the High Court in *Prince Alfred College* was that the defendant must provide the 'occasion' for the wrongful act by the tortfeasor. The vagueness of the phrase is unfortunate given the weight of the task with which it is charged. Its usage can be traced to Dixon J in *Deatons Pty Ltd v Flew*,[32] the well-known Australian case of a bar maid throwing a glass at an abusive customer:

> … the barmaid was there to deal with customers and with situations and this was the manner in which she dealt with the plaintiff and the situation which he caused. It is not a case of a negligent or improper act, due to error or ill judgment, but done in the supposed furtherance of the master's interests. Nor is it one of those wrongful acts done for the servant's own benefit for which the master is liable when they are acts to which the ostensible performance of his master's work gives occasion or which are committed under cover of the authority the servant is held out as possessing or of the position in which he is placed as a representative of his master.[33]

This section demonstrates the well-established difficulties in identifying the range of circumstances that might satisfy the second 'scope of employment' stage of the vicarious liability inquiry.[34] The reference to wrongful acts 'committed under cover of the authority' is a reference to the decision of the House of Lords in *Lloyd v Grace, Smith & Co*,[35] a case in which a solicitor's clerk misappropriated the deeds of one of the solicitor's clients, having been authorised by the solicitor to collect the deeds from the client. The somewhat nonsensical idea of child sexual

[30] Provided the 'running down' was not deliberate.

[31] Future use of the phrase 'relationship between the defendant and the plaintiff/claimant' (or similar) should be taken to incorporate the additional element of the relationship created by the defendant between the tortfeasor and the plaintiff/claimant. The phrase 'relationship between the defendant and the plaintiff/claimant' is used in contrast to the relationship between the defendant and the tortfeasor which is the traditional focus of vicarious liability.

[32] *Deatons Pty Ltd v Flew* [1949] HCA 60, (1949) 79 CLR 370 (*Deatons*).

[33] ibid 380.

[34] Discussed more fully in C Beuermann, 'The Abstraction of Form and the Associated Dangers for the English Courts: The Case Study of Vicarious Liability', paper presented at Obligations IX, Form and Substance in the Law of Obligations, University of Melbourne, 17–20 July 2018, 11–13 (available from author).

[35] *Lloyd v Grace, Smith & Co* [1912] AC 716 (*Lloyd*).

abuse somehow being 'committed under cover of the authority' of an employer presumably prompted the judges giving the principal joint judgment in *Prince Alfred College* to favour the broader categorisation of circumstances in which the 'ostensible performance of his master's work gives occasion'. With breadth though comes uncertainty, and little can be found to clarify the meaning of the phrase in Dixon J's original usage.

The reliance placed by the judges giving the principal joint judgment in *Prince Alfred College* on the judgment of Dixon J in *Deatons* is, however, significant. First, it suggests that the High Court did not intend to shift the general approach to determining vicarious liability in Australia away from the traditional Salmond test.[36] The Salmond test was only mentioned twice in *Prince Alfred College* and only by way of explaining the rise of the 'close connection' test in other jurisdictions.[37] The Salmond test had been applied in *Deatons* and the general direction of the High Court in *Prince Alfred College* was that Australian courts should continue with the approach taken in that case. Specifically, the requirement to show that the tort committed by the employee in a vicarious liability case occurred within the course or scope of employment.

Second, *Deatons* was a case in which vicarious liability was *not* imposed in respect of conduct which could amount to a criminal offence. The facts could therefore be distinguished from those in *Prince Alfred College* which were thought by the judges in the principal joint judgment to be such that they could potentially give rise to vicarious liability. The distinction drawn by the High Court was that the employer in *Deatons* merely provided an opportunity for the commission of the tort, whereas the employer in *Prince Alfred College* might be seen to provide more than that; not just an 'opportunity' for the commission of a tort, but the 'occasion'.[38]

The semantic fineness of the distinction between providing an 'opportunity' or the 'occasion' for wrongdoing cannot be denied. The distinction does though provide some much-needed context to assist a plaintiff determine what more is needed to be shown to establish that an employer did the latter rather than the former. As the focus is on the position that the employer places the tortfeasor in 'vis-à-vis the victim',[39] the victim needs to show that there was some other conduct by the employer (over and above engaging the tortfeasor in the first place) that could be seen to facilitate or enable the commission of the tort by the tortfeasor in terms of the specific position the victim is placed by the employer vis-à-vis the tortfeasor.

The judges in the principal joint judgment in *Prince Alfred College* elaborated on the type of features that could attract liability when examining the position

[36] For an explanation of the Salmond test, see chapter one, 7–8.
[37] *Prince Alfred College* (n 1) [42] and [59].
[38] ibid [80].
[39] ibid [81].

an employer has placed the tortfeasor vis-à-vis the victim, specifically: 'authority, power, trust, control and the ability to achieve intimacy with the victim'. This was not intended to be a definitive list, but included examples drawn from the decided cases.[40] For instance, the reference to 'authority' appears to be derived from its usage in *Lloyd*. References to 'power', 'trust' and the 'ability to achieve intimacy with the victim' seem to have been collated from cases where vicarious liability was imposed for child sexual abuse in other jurisdictions, namely Canada and England and Wales. Notably, the judges in the principal joint judgment distinguished cases where institutions had been held vicariously liable for sexual abuse committed by teachers and boarding masters from a Canadian case where vicarious liability had been denied for child sexual abuse committed by a 'baker, boat-driver and odd-job man at a school'.[41] Whereas teachers and boarding masters are put in a position of 'power' and 'trust' and had the 'ability to achieve intimacy with the victim', this was not the case with the 'baker, boat-driver and odd-job man'. A similar distinction was drawn in the Canadian case of *G(ED) v Hammer*[42] concerning a janitor (although the case does not seem to have brought to the attention of the High Court). It followed that the employment by the institution had provided only the 'opportunity' and not the 'occasion' for the abuse.

The final element of guidance offered by the judges giving the principal joint judgment in *Prince Alfred College* was that the tortfeasor had to take 'advantage of his or her position with respect to the victim' for vicarious liability to be imposed. It was therefore not sufficient that the tortfeasor had been put in a particular position 'vis-à-vis the victim'. It also had to be demonstrated that there was the potential for the tortfeasor to use that position to commit the abuse. This suggests a requirement for some type of causative association between the employer's conduct and the commission of the tort (although not one that needs to be proved as a matter of fact). This active element of the employer's conduct is perhaps what the judges in the principal joint judgment were alluding to when they stated that the role given to the tortfeasor by the employer 'may be said to *give* the "occasion" for the wrongdoing'.

I make no attempt in this chapter to assess the quality of the guidance provided by the High Court in *Prince Alfred College* to lower courts when determining vicarious liability for child sexual abuse. The more obvious limitations of the guidance have been noted. It is though apparent that the High Court intended lower courts to take a different approach to determining vicarious liability for child sexual abuse than that taken by courts in England and Wales. The principal difference in that approach can best be described as methodological. The direction by the High Court to lower courts was to avoid general principles and start with the existing body of cases, developing the law gradually and by analogy.

[40] Consistent with the earlier guidance that lower courts were not to develop the law by reference to general principles, but by analogy with existing cases.

[41] *Prince Alfred College* (n 1) [62].

[42] *G(ED) v Hammer* [2003] 2 SCR 459, (2003) 230 DLR (4th) 554.

B. Subsequent Lower Court Decisions

An examination of subsequent lower court decisions should determine whether the High Court achieved its aim in *Prince Alfred College* of encouraging lower courts to adopt a different approach to determining vicarious liability in Australia to that taken in England and Wales. In this section, three discrete categories of case decided in Australia after *Prince Alfred College* will be examined and compared to decisions reached on similar facts in England and Wales in a similar timeframe. Those categories are: sexual abuse of adults; skylarking; and volunteers.

The analysis shows that reassuringly similar decisions were reached in the different jurisdictions despite the stated differences in approach.

i. *Case Category 1: Sexual Abuse of Adults*

The first Australian case to apply the guidance given by the High Court in *Prince Alfred College* to facts concerning the sexual abuse of an adult was *Osmond v Highway Traffic Control Pty Ltd*.[43] This was a decision of a single judge in the Victorian County Court. The plaintiff, Osmond, alleged that she had been sexually assaulted at work by a male colleague. The male colleague was more senior, having worked at the defendant company for longer, but had not been placed in a supervisory position with respect to the plaintiff by the defendant company. The alleged assault occurred at a remote location at which the plaintiff and her colleague were required to provide traffic control services together.

The judge found that the main allegations of sexual assault were made out. The vicarious liability of the defendant company (in its capacity as employer) was, however, denied. The extent to which the judge drew on the guidance issued by the High Court in *Prince Alfred College* is evident in the following extracts from his judgment:

> In my view, the facts and circumstances of this proceeding are *significantly different from those cases involving sexual assault carried out by a teacher or boarding master* at a school or a like institution. That particular form of intimate contact, in circumstances where the teacher or boarding master resides in the same premises, and where there is a disparity of power and a repository of trust, is distinctly different from the facts of the present case.[44]

> The only connection between the sexual conduct and the employment was that Mr Urquhart and Mrs Osmond were allocated together, in a vehicle, travelling through relatively remote areas. It was not as if Mr Urquhart was assigned some employment task which he carried out in an inappropriate manner. His conduct involved sexual gratification entirely divorced from his assigned role as a traffic controller. *While the*

[43] *Osmond v Highway Traffic Control Pty Ltd* [2017] VCC 1449 (*Osmond*).
[44] ibid [83] (emphasis added).

> *employment gave him the opportunity for the sexual conduct, it was entirely otherwise unconnected with his tasks and obligations.*[45]

In the first paragraph, the judge can be seen to examine the existing cases and determine if an appropriate analogy can be drawn with the facts at hand. This is in line with the direction of the High Court to develop the law on a case-by-case basis, without resort to general principles. Note also the focus of the judge on the position the defendant employer might (or might not) have placed the tortfeasor vis-à-vis the plaintiff, rather than the relationship between the defendant and the tortfeasor per se.

In the second paragraph, the judge can be seen to operationalise the distinction between the employment providing an 'opportunity' or the 'occasion' for the sexual abuse. Ultimately, the judge decided it was a case of the former and denied vicarious liability on that basis. There is no discussion by the judge as to whether the approach to vicarious liability for child sexual abuse should also be used with respect to vicarious liability for the sexual abuse of an adult.

The language used by the judge should also be noted. On several occasions, the judge referred to the need for there to be a relevant 'connection' between the employment and the tort. At no point did the judge refer to the 'course' or 'scope' of employment, as required by the second stage of the traditional Salmond test.

Similar use of the High Court's guidance in *Prince Alfred College*, though with a different result, can be seen in the more recent decision of *Johnston v State of New South Wales*.[46] Again, this is a decision of a single judge, but of the New South Wales Supreme Court. The plaintiff was a trainee police officer training to be a police prosecutor. She alleged that she was sexually assaulted by a qualified police prosecutor whilst preparing a case with the police prosecutor in a room provided by the employer. The police prosecutor was in a position superior to that of the plaintiff and it appeared from the limited evidence before the court that the plaintiff was assisting the police prosecutor in the performance of his role at the time of the assault.[47] Leaving to one side specific statutory provisions relating to Crown liability for police officers,[48] the judge found that the decision of the trial judge that the claim for vicarious liability should be dismissed should be overturned and the matter sent back to trial for a full determination. Reliance on the guidance issued by the High Court in *Prince Alfred College* is evident in the following extract from the judgment:

> In my view … this factual matrix … is closer to cases concerning an abuse of trust or authority placed by an employer in an employee, such as those canvassed in Prince Alfred College v ADC. Indeed, it is not dissimilar to the example provided

[45] ibid [86] (emphasis added).
[46] *Johnston v State of New South Wales* [2020] NSWSC 174.
[47] ibid [43].
[48] Ss 6, 8 and 9B–9E Law Reform (Vicarious Liability) Act 1983 (NSW).

at [80] of Prince Alfred College, of a criminal act committed by an employee which was facilitated by the position in which the employment placed them vis-à-vis the victim.[49]

The example in *Prince Alfred College* referred to by the judge was generic in nature and reproduced almost verbatim from the principal joint judgment in the above passage.

A preliminary analysis of *Osmond* and *Johnston* suggests that the principal factual difference between the cases was the nature of the position the tortfeasor had been placed vis-à-vis the plaintiff victim by the defendant employer.[50] Specifically, the initial facts presented to the court in *Johnston* (although the issue was not formally determined and full fact-finding had yet to be conducted) was that the tortfeasor had been placed in a supervisory position in respect of the plaintiff by the defendant employer, with the result that the tortfeasor was potentially in a position of 'authority, power, trust, control'. This factual difference accords with attempts by the High Court in *Prince Alfred College* to distinguish between facts in which a defendant employer provided not only an 'opportunity', but the 'occasion' for the sexual assault to occur.

References to the requirement for a connection between the tort and the employment are again evident in the trial judgment in *Johnston*, although Ierace J of the Supreme Court used 'scope of employment'.[51] The use of this phrase may though have been affected by the relevant legislative provisions governing the vicarious liability of the Crown for police officers which predated the first of the child sexual abuse cases.

The English Court of Appeal has also recently had the opportunity to consider a case of vicarious liability for the sexual abuse of an adult. The claimant in *Trustees of the Barry Congregation of Jehovah's Witness v BXB*[52] was a member of the Barry Congregation of Jehovah's Witness in South Wales. She was raped by an elder in the congregation. The trial judge described the role of an elder in the following terms: 'Elders are the spiritual leaders of the congregation. To be appointed an elder a publisher must first have served as a ministerial servant and demonstrated that he is spiritually suitable to be an example to others'.[53] The claimant had spent a considerable time with the elder as the claimant's husband was a publisher who was himself hoping to qualify as an elder in the congregation. The court found the Barry Congregation vicariously liable for the rape. Nicola Davies LJ gave the

[49] *Johnston* (n 46) [45] (emphasis added).

[50] Another point of distinction is the place where the sexual assault occurred, the assault in *Johnston* occurring in work premises controlled by the defendant. It is submitted that this is unlikely to be a probative factual distinction. The reason is that an employer might still owe duties to take reasonable care for the safety of employee who is working away from the employer's premises, suggesting that it is the nature of the relationship that is relevant, not where the work is being done.

[51] *Johnston* (n 46) [44].

[52] *Trustees of the Barry Congregation of Jehovah's Witness v BXB* [2021] EWCA Civ 356 (*Barry Congregation*).

[53] ibid [50].

principal judgment (agreed with by both Bean and Males LJJ). The reasons for her decision are evident in the following extracts:

> Contained within the tailored test in cases of sexual abuse is the concept of the conferral of authority upon the tortfeasor by the defendant. In my judgment, *the tailored version of the test applies in cases in which adults are alleged to have been sexually abused as it does in such cases involving children* because the rationale for the test is the same. The issue is the connection between the abuse and the relationship between the tortfeasor and the defendant. It is not the particular characteristics of the victim. On the facts of this claim, what is relevant for the purpose of the close connection test is the *conferral of authority by the Jehovah's Witness organisation upon its elders*, coupled with the opportunity for physical proximity as between an elder and publishers in the congregation.[54]
>
> In my judgment, of the findings made by the judge, critical was his acceptance of Mrs B's evidence that 'had it not been for the fact that Mark was an elder and I had received an instruction from another elder, his father, our friendship with Mark and Mary would have come to an end well before [the rape]'. Quite simply, had Mrs B felt able to end the friendship at an earlier time, Mark Sewell would not have been able to continue his close proximity to Mrs B and *she would not have felt compelled to tolerate his increasingly inappropriate and unbearable behaviour because he was an elder*.[55]

The focus on 'conferral of authority' stems from Lord Reed's use of the phrase in *Morrisons* (as set out above) as a way of explaining why a different approach might need to be taken to child sexual abuse cases.[56] Unlike the Australian decisions, Nicola Davies LJ clearly stipulates that, in her view, the approach to sexual abuse cases should be the same whether the claimant is a child or an adult.[57]

The distinction between an 'opportunity' and the 'occasion' for wrongdoing is not part of the law in England and Wales. Nonetheless, a similar decision is reached for similar reasons. As in the Australian cases, the judges in *Barry Congregation* are focussing on the facts and making analogies with existing case law. This is a more traditional common law approach to determining cases than one that starts with general principles. The judges in *Barry Congregation* are also focussing on the relationship between the defendant and the claimant and the subsequent position the defendant places the tortfeasor vis-à-vis the claimant. The analysis is put quite succinctly by Males LJ in the same case:

> In these circumstances I agree that the stage two test is satisfied. The rape was sufficiently closely connected with Mark Sewell's status as an elder that it may fairly and properly be regarded as an abuse of the authority over Mrs B conferred on him by that status, such that the defendants who had conferred that authority on him should be vicariously liable.[58]

[54] ibid [84] (emphasis added).
[55] ibid [87] (emphasis added).
[56] *Morrisons* (n 26) [23].
[57] Males LJ agreed but noted that there are some differences between adults and children, such as the susceptibility of children to grooming; *Barry Congregation* (n 52) [96].
[58] *Barry Congregation* (n 52) [106].

Note that the concept of 'authority' in these extracts appears to be used in a slightly difference sense to that in which it was first used in *Lloyd*.[59] It was not so much that the tortfeasor was authorised to do any particular act, such as receive documents; the elder was not acting in any way as agent for the Barry Congregation. Instead, the elder had been clothed by the Barry Congregation with an authority to direct or set the standards of how the other members of the Barry Congregation behaved. As the claimant in *Barry Congregation* explained:

> The Elders are like shepherds, as it were.
>
> Their directions are always followed by members of the congregation and they are very rarely criticised. There can be serious repercussions for those who disobey them. Anybody who disobeyed an Elders instruction would receive what was called a 'shepherding call'. This would involve an elder coming to see the person concerned at their house or, in a more serious case, a judicial committee would be set up in the Kingdom Hall at which the person concerned would be given instructions on how to behave. If that person continued to disobey, they would be disfellowshipped.[60]

For this reason, the facts of *Barry Congregation* are closer to *Johnston* than *Osmond*. If it was found that the police prosecutor was placed by the defendant in a supervisory position in respect of the trainee police prosecutor, he would have been able to direct the standards of how the trainee police prosecutor acted and meter out disciplinary consequences if she did not. In the language of the courts of England and Wales, the defendant had conferred authority on the police prosecutor in respect of the plaintiff. In the language of the Australian courts, the State had created the 'occasion', and not just the 'opportunity' for the sexual assault.

The case of *Various Claimants v Barclays Bank plc*[61] should be referred to in passing before leaving the cases concerning the sexual abuse of adults. The claimant in that case was a prospective employee at the bank who had been required to undertake a medical examination prior to commencing employment. During the course of the examination, the claimant was sexually assaulted. Vicarious liability was dismissed in the case on the basis that the medical examiner was an independent contractor for whom vicarious liability did not arise.[62] The focus of the UK Supreme Court in that case was therefore on the relationship between the defendant employer and the tortfeasor and not the relationship between the defendant employer and the claimant and the subsequent position the defendant employer had placed the tortfeasor vis-à-vis the claimant. This focus appears somewhat anomalous given the approach taken in the other cases involving sexual abuse of adults.

[59] *Lloyd* (n 35).
[60] *Barry Congregation* (n 52) [11].
[61] *Various Claimants v Barclays Bank plc* [2020] UKSC 13, [2020] AC 973 (*Barclays*).
[62] ibid [27]–[28].

ii. Case Category 2: Skylarking

A closely related category to cases involving sexual abuse of adults are cases involving skylarking in the workplace. These are cases involving the deliberate commission of a tort by the tortfeasor against the victim, but typically without a sexual element.[63] Often the conduct is engaged in by way of a practical joke. To the extent the cases involve the deliberate commission of a tort, similar difficulties exist in imposing vicarious liability as are present in the cases involving the sexual abuse of adults.

Kremer v Sandfire Resources NL[64] was decided by a single judge in the District Court of Western Australia. The case involved a Melbourne Cup Day social event for the employees at the defendant's mine. The event was held in a designated recreational zone at the mine. Various refreshments were served at the event, including alcohol. The plaintiff and another employee, Mr Santos, were participating in a wooden hobbyhorse relay race which involved team members running a designated portion of a circuit astride a hobbyhorse. The plaintiff alleged that Mr Santos deliberately tripped the plaintiff during the race, causing him injury to his right shoulder and arm. The trial judge was not convinced that there was sufficient evidence to conclude that Mr Santos had deliberately tripped the plaintiff.[65] There was evidence that the two men were engaged in friendly, competitive jostling before the race.[66] The trial judge held that even if he had found that Mr Santos had deliberately tripped the plaintiff, he would not have been prepared to hold the defendant employer vicariously liable. Although this was not a case of child sexual abuse, it is apparent that the trial judge was following the guidance of the High Court in *Prince Alfred College* reaching this conclusion:

> Although Mr Santos was only in a position to be able to trip Mr Kremer because he was employed by Sandfire and was present at the relatively remote mine site where the event occurred, the fact that employment affords an opportunity for the commission of a wrongful act is not of itself a sufficient reason to attract vicarious liability ... This is not a case where Mr Santos used or took advantage of the position in which the employment placed him vis-à-vis Mr Kremer. They were off-duty employees who had chosen, under no obligation, to participate in an innately light-hearted recreational event ... This is not a case where on any view Mr Santos took advantage of his position with respect to Mr Kremer so as to require a conclusion that a deliberate trip, and therefore a wrongful act was committed in the course or scope of employment so as to render Sandfire vicariously liable.[67]

[63] Although a sexual element might sometimes be present. See, for example, *McCready v Securicor Ltd* [1991] 81 NI 229, which involved the hazing of an apprentice who had an air compressor inserted in his rectum.

[64] *Kremer v Sandfire Resources NL* [2020] WADC 130 (*Kremer*).

[65] ibid [75].

[66] ibid [26].

[67] ibid [113]–[115].

The trial judge seems to have justified the use of the guidance of the High Court of Australia on the basis that the deliberate act of tripping a fellow employee could, similarly to sexual abuse, be viewed as an example of the deliberate commission of a tort amounting to a criminal act. As in the cases of sexual abuse, the trial judge focussed on the particular position the defendant had (or had not on the facts of this case) placed the tortfeasor vis-à-vis the plaintiff. The trial judge concluded that, as the tortfeasor and the plaintiff were both off-duty employees of equal rank, the employer had provided only an 'opportunity' and not the 'occasion' for the wrongdoing.

A similar decision was reached by the High Court of England and Wales in *Chell v Tarmac Cement and Lime Limited*.[68] The incident leading to the case occurred on a building site controlled by the defendant. An employee of the defendant had hit a 'target pellet' with a hammer near the ear of the unsuspecting claimant, creating a loud explosion and causing the claimant permanent hearing loss. In the words of the Martin Spencer J, the incident 'appears to have been some form of (wholly misguided) practical joke'.[69] The claimant was an employee of equal rank employed by a subcontractor engaged by the defendant to work on the same building site alongside the defendant's own employees. This complicated employment structure did not affect the potential for finding vicarious liability as it was accepted that the tortfeasor was employed by the defendant.[70]

The decision of the trial judge denying vicarious liability on the facts of the case was upheld in the High Court. Importantly, at the time of the judgment on trial, the trial judge did not have available to him the guidance of the UK Supreme Court in *Morrisons*. Martin Spencer J in the High Court held that had the trial judge had available to him such guidance, it would only have fortified the trial judge in his conclusion.[71] Specifically, the trial judge was of the view that the tortfeasor in *Chell* was on a 'frolic of his own' (similar to the barmaid in *Deatons*) and the fact that the tortfeasor was using a work hammer in the workplace was merely incidental to the pursuit of that frolic.[72] At best, the work environment merely provided a 'temporal connection', the significance of which had been downplayed by the Supreme Court in the *Morrisons* case.[73]

The nature of the analysis in *Chell* appears very different to that conducted in *Kremer*, although a similar conclusion is reached. The biggest difference is the nature of the relationship which drew the focus of the court's attention; in *Chell* it was the relationship between the defendant employer and the tortfeasor (the traditional focus of vicarious liability), whereas in *Kremer* it was the relationship between the defendant employer and the plaintiff and the position the defendant

[68] *Chell v Tarmac Cement and Lime Limited* [2020] EWHC 2613 (QB).
[69] ibid [4].
[70] ibid [17].
[71] ibid [36].
[72] ibid.
[73] *Morrisons* (n 26) [26].

employer might (or might not have) placed the tortfeasor vis-à-vis the plaintiff. One reason for the focus on the relationship between the defendant employer and the tortfeasor in *Chell* is the fact that the claimant was employed by someone other than the defendant, although in circumstances in which the claimant was not a stranger to the defendant employer (the worksite at which the tortfeasor and the claimant worked being controlled by the defendant).[74] It is submitted that another is the reticence of the UK Supreme Court to subsequently acknowledge it erred in deciding *Mohamud*.

The UK Supreme Court was given the opportunity in the *Morrisons* case to review its earlier decision in *Mohamud*. *Morrisons* involved a disgruntled employee who, having been given a dataset of sensitive personnel information in his role as internal auditor at Morrison Supermarkets, copied that dataset and subsequently released it on the internet on the day Morrisons' financial results were due to be announced. The object in releasing the dataset was solely to cause Morrisons harm. The claim for vicarious liability brought by employees of Morrisons whose data had been released had been upheld at trial and in the Court of Appeal in accordance with the earlier decision of the UK Supreme Court in *Mohamud*. The appeal to the Supreme Court was successful and the claim for vicarious liability ultimately dismissed.

As in *Chell*, the relationship which drew the focus of the Supreme Court in *Morrisons* was the relationship between the defendant employer and the tortfeasor. This is perhaps not surprising given it was highly improbable that the disgruntled employee had a personal relationship with every employee of Morrisons whose data was included in the stolen dataset. This is not, however, the relationship which drew the attention of the various courts in the other cases examined in this chapter. In those cases, the relevant relationship examined by the courts was the relationship between the defendant employer and the victims and the position the tortfeasor had been placed vis-à-vis the victims by the defendant employer. It was for this reason that Lord Reed declared that a different approach should be taken to cases of child sexual abuse.[75]

The facts of *Morrisons* were, however, not dissimilar to *Mohamud*. In *Mohamud* the defendant employer was held vicariously liable for the racially motivated attack on the claimant who had sought the assistance of the tortfeasor employee at a petrol station kiosk.[76] Although in *Morrisons* there was a relationship between the defendant employer and the claimant employees, the defendant employer had not put the tortfeasor in any particular position vis-à-vis the claimant employees (so any pre-existing relationship between the defendant employer and the claimants was arguably not relevant to the determination of liability). In *Mohamud*, the claimant was a stranger to both the defendant employer and the tortfeasor so again

[74] Prompting questions as to whether the more appropriate defendant in *Chell* was the claimant's immediate employer.

[75] *Morrisons* (n 26) [36].

[76] *Mohamud* (n 2) [48].

there was no relationship between the defendant employer and the claimant that was relevant to the determination of liability. Notwithstanding this similarity, the opposite conclusion was reached.

It follows that the finding of vicarious liability in *Mohamud* is at odds with the more recent decisions in *Chell* and *Morrisons*. The Supreme Court was alive to this incongruity and took steps in *Morrisons* to rationalise the decision it had reached in *Mohamud* but stopped short of overturning it.

First, Lord Reed (giving judgment for the court) made clear that there had been no attempt to change the law of vicarious liability in *Mohamud*.[77] 'Orthodox common law reasoning' was to be used to determine whether vicarious liability should be imposed in the courts in England and Wales, not general principles. As Lord Reed explained, the test for vicarious liability is not 'intended as an invitation to judges to decide cases according to their personal sense of justice, but require[s] them to consider how the guidance derived from decided cases furnishes a solution to the case before the court'.[78] It is difficult to envisage that Lord Reed did not have the criticism of the High Court of Australia in *Prince Alfred College* in mind when framing his judgment in such terms, particularly when he went on to state that 'the mere fact that the [tortfeasor's] employment gave him the opportunity to commit the wrongful act would not be sufficient to warrant the imposition of vicarious liability'.[79] The decision of the High Court of Australia is not, however, referred to by the UK Supreme Court in *Morrisons*.

Secondly, as noted in the discussion of *Chell* above, Lord Reed made it clear that more than a causal connection between the employment and the tort was required for vicarious liability to be imposed; a temporal connection was not sufficient.[80]

Finally, Lord Reed sought to distinguish the facts of the two cases. In Lord Reed's view, the tortfeasor in *Morrisons* at no time understood what he was doing to be somehow connected with his employment. In contrast, the tortfeasor in *Mohamud* at least started out doing what he was supposed to be doing, which was serving the claimant.[81] Whether this factual distinction is sufficient to justify the different decisions reached in the cases is open to question. To the extent that it is even possible to say that such a distinction might exist, it would sit uncomfortably with the denial of vicarious liability by the High Court in *Deatons* which might be distinguished in similar terms.

iii. Case Category 3: Volunteers

The final category of case to be examined in this chapter is volunteers. Unlike the previous two categories of case examined in this chapter, the focus is necessarily on

[77] *Morrisons* (n 26) [17].
[78] ibid [24].
[79] ibid [35].
[80] ibid [26].
[81] ibid [28].

the first, rather than the second stage, of the vicarious liability inquiry. Somewhat surprisingly, an examination of the cases suggests that the nature of the inquiry seems to be very similar at both stages, at least in the context of volunteers who sexually abuse children.

Plaintiffs A, B, C and D v Bird[82] was decided by a single judge in the Supreme Court of New South Wales. The case involved a childcare centre owned by Little Pigeon Pty Ltd. Bird owned 1 per cent of the company. The remaining 99 per cent of the company was owned by Bird's daughter. Bird was described in the promotional material for the childcare centre as a volunteer. In that capacity, he was involved in managing the centre, supervising the playground, cooking, health and safety and some maintenance.[83] It was alleged that Bird sexually abused several children whilst volunteering at the childcare centre. The alleged victims were all under the age of five. Although evidence was difficult to come by due to the young age of the victims, the claims of sexual abuse was upheld in respect of at least some of the plaintiffs.

With respect to the first stage of the vicarious liability inquiry, the judge found that although Bird was not paid for the activities he undertook at the childcare centre, he could still be considered an employee. A significant factor in this conclusion was the 'considerable authority which Mr Bird was given at the centre, which permitted him to have the same close contact which other staff employed there had with children'.[84] It is hardly a coincidence that this is the very factor that was viewed in the other cases considered this chapter as satisfying the second stage of the vicarious liability inquiry.

The judge also found that the childcare centre could still be held vicariously liable for the abuse even if Bird could only be viewed as a volunteer.[85] This is a significant finding given that vicarious liability in Australia had previously been limited to circumstances in which the tortfeasor was employed by the defendant; Australia not accepting the 'akin to employment' test introduced in England and Wales.

The influence of the High Court's guidance in *Prince Alfred College* in the determination that the childcare centre was vicariously liable for the abuse committed by Bird (regardless of whether Bird was viewed as an employee or volunteer) can be seen in the following extract from the judgment:

> On the evidence I am satisfied that Little Pigeon was vicariously liable for Mr Bird's wrongful acts. That conclusion flows from:
>
> - The actual roles which Little Pigeon assigned Mr Bird, *which placed him in a position of considerable power and trust, which he abused;*
> - That those roles gave Mr Bird the opportunity to have the close contact with children which he, Ms Clancy and other witnesses described;

[82] *Plaintiffs A, B, C and D v Bird* [2020] NSWSC 1379.
[83] ibid [24].
[84] ibid [446].
[85] ibid [424].

- The authority Mr Bird was given by effectively being left unsupervised when he had such contact, which he also abused;
- This lack of supervision permitting him to *not only achieve intimacy with his young victims, but to control them while* committing the wrongful acts he admitted and his victims disclosed; and
- It was Mr Bird's performance of the roles he was given, *which created the occasion for his wrongful acts.*[86]

The principal fact underpinning the imposition of vicarious liability in the case was once again the position Bird had been placed in vis-à-vis the victims by the defendant childcare centre. This explains the apparent overlap between the nature of the inquiries at both stage one and two of the process for determining vicarious liability. The relevant relationship for imposing strict liability in cases of child sexual abuse, as noted by the High Court in *Prince Alfred College*, is not the relationship between the defendant and the tortfeasor, but the relationship between the defendant and plaintiff. It can therefore be argued that whether the tortfeasor was in an employment relationship with the defendant is not a relevant consideration in Australia for the imposition of vicarious liability for child sexual abuse.

A similar focus on the position a volunteer is placed vis-à-vis the claimant victim by a defendant can be seen at first instance in *DSN* v *Blackpool Football Club*.[87] The claimant aged 13 had been sexually abused by a volunteer scout for Blackpool FC on a football tour to New Zealand. The judge found that the circumstances of Roper's involvement with Blackpool FC were sufficient to satisfy the first stage of the vicarious liability inquiry:

> There was no more important task for the Club than spotting and capturing young players and bringing them into a position when they were willing to sign up for a lower division side with limited resources … None of the boys, and none of the parents of the boys, … knew anything at all about Roper except that he was a Blackpool scout who ran a Blackpool feeder team at Nova Juniors from which a professional career at Blackpool might, if Roper rated them, develop. *It was on that basis that the boys were placed in his power, and that is how he was able to abuse them.*[88]

As with *Bird*, the position in which Roper was placed by the defendant with respect to the victims was seen as satisfying the first stage of the vicarious liability inquiry.[89]

Unlike Australia, courts in England and Wales have not been explicitly directed to examine the relationship between the defendant and the claimant and the position the tortfeasor has been placed vis-à-vis the claimant by the defendant. Instead, the courts have been directed, in the absence of an

[86] ibid [450] (emphases added).
[87] [2020] EWHC 595 (QB). Overturned on appeal: [2021] EWCA Civ 1352.
[88] ibid [160] (emphasis added).
[89] Similar factors were also seen as sufficient to satisfy the second stage of the inquiry: ibid [175].

employment relationship, to assess whether the relationship between the defendant and the tortfeasor is 'akin to employment'. This focus on an entirely different relationship created difficulties in *Blackpool* on appeal. Taking into account the decision of the Supreme Court in *Barclays*[90] which had been delivered after the first instance decision, the Court of Appeal held that Roper was not in a position 'akin to employment' as he was carrying on his own business and could not be controlled by Blackpool FC.[91] Although consistent with the *Barclays* decision, it is difficult to reconcile with the dicta about 'conferral of authority' in *Morrisons* and *Barry Congregation* discussed above.[92] The judges on appeal seemed to overlook that Blackpool had vested Roper with apparent (if not actual) authority to identify young players that might be of interest to Blackpool so that Blackpool could contract with those young players in the future (making Roper an introducing agent). This prospect meant that the players were more likely to do as Roper directed to increase their chance of being signed by Blackpool FC.[93]

The impact of the shift in focus from the relationship between the defendant and tortfeasor to the position the defendant places the tortfeasor vis-à-vis the claimant is self-evident. In Australia, the courts are, in essence, collapsing the two separate stages of the vicarious liability inquiry in cases of child sexual abuse by volunteers to focus on whether the defendant put the tortfeasor in a position vis-à-vis the victim that was sufficient to attract vicarious liability. It follows that a defendant may be held strictly liable for child sexual abuse in Australia regardless of whether the tortfeasor has been in an employment relationship with the defendant. Whether the position can be clarified in England and Wales will depend on the success of any appeal brought in respect of *Blackpool* and whether the Supreme Court takes the opportunity to further clarify the guidance it issued in *Morrisons* about the different approach taken with respect to vicarious liability for child sexual abuse.

C. Conclusions: Common Law Approach to Determining Vicarious Liability in Australia

A number of conclusions can be drawn from the above survey of cases decided after the High Court of Australia issued its guidance on how to determine the second stage of the vicarious liability inquiry in cases of child sexual abuse in *Prince Alfred College*.

[90] See discussion above at n 61.
[91] *Blackpool* (n 87) [129].
[92] See discussion at (n 56) above.
[93] For further discussion see C Beuermann, 'Liability for Football Scouts' (2022) 138 *LQR* 170.

First, the lower courts in Australia have embraced the guidance issued by the High Court in *Prince Alfred College*. Furthermore, the guidance has been extended to cases beyond those involving child sexual abuse to other cases in which torts have been deliberately committed. The most fruitful aspect of that guidance appears to be the direction in cases of a tort that has been deliberately committed to focus not on the relationship between the defendant and the tortfeasor, but the relationship between the defendant and the plaintiff and the position the tortfeasor has been placed vis-à-vis the plaintiff by the defendant. From the cases so far decided, it now appears that it will be difficult to establish vicarious liability in Australia for a tort that has been deliberately committed unless there are specific aspects of the relationship between a defendant and a plaintiff that suggest that the defendant has done something more than simply provide an opportunity for the tort to occur. A noted example is the defendant conferring some type of authority or power in the tortfeasor over the plaintiff. This is not to suggest that the lower courts have fallen foul of the warning issued by Gageler and Gordon JJ in *Prince Alfred College* that the guidance issued in the principal joint judgment was not an 'absolute rule' and 'that those cases in which an employer is liable or where there is no liability must and will develop in accordance with ordinary common law methods'.[94] It does though suggest that the factual circumstances giving rise to such vicarious liability are being more successfully isolated by the courts.

Second, the focus in Australia on the relationship between the defendant and the plaintiff at the second stage of the vicarious liability inquiry appears to have relieved the pressure to expand the first relationship stage of the vicarious liability inquiry, as indicated by the volunteer cases. The High Court has still not had the opportunity to consider the first stage of the vicarious liability inquiry. There may be now no need because the guidance issued by the High Court suggests that the existence of an employment relationship no longer appears critical to the imposition of vicarious liability in Australia for a tort that has been committed deliberately.

Third, despite the stated purpose of the High Court of Australia to direct lower courts to adopt a different approach for the determination of vicarious liability to that taken by the courts in England and Wales, similar decisions are being reached on similar facts. There are also similarities in the language used in the different courts to describe the circumstances leading to the imposition of vicarious liability, such as 'conferral of authority'. The Australian lower courts appear to be particularly attracted to the language of 'close connection', despite the explicit steer away from the use of such language by the High Court of Australia in *Prince Alfred College*.

Finally, it appears that uncertainty will persist in cases of vicarious liability until the courts expressly recognise that cases of and analogous to the child sexual

[94] *Prince Alfred College* (n 1) [131].

abuse cases require a different approach. This is most evident in the case of *Barclays* in which the UK Supreme Court was focussed on the relationship between the defendant and the tortfeasor, rather than the relationship between the defendant and the claimant and the position the tortfeasor had been placed vis-à-vis the claimant by the defendant. A similar error can be seen to have been made in *SKX* v *Manchester CC*[95] in which it was held that a local authority could not be held vicariously liable to a child in its care who was sexually abused by the employee of a privately-run children's home in which the child had been placed by the local authority.[96]

III. Statutory Framework

The Royal Commission into Institutional Responses to Child Sexual Abuse[97] has prompted extensive, although inconsistent, legislative reform throughout the Australian Commonwealth, its states and territories. Each of the various reforms are designed to help alleviate in some way the previous barriers faced by victims of child sexual abuse to obtaining compensation. Most of those reforms are not relevant to the subject matter of this chapter. By way of overview, those reforms include:

- A national redress scheme by which victims of child sexual abuse in an institutional setting might seek compensation and access to counselling and psychological services, in exchange for releasing the relevant institution from civil liability;[98]
- retrospective removal of limitation periods in all states and territories for claims for damages arising from child sexual abuse;[99]
- procedures that operate retrospectively in New South Wales, Victoria, Queensland, Western Australia, Tasmania and the Australian Capital Territory for nominating a proper defendant where the institution in which the child sexual abuse occurred was operated by an unincorporated association;[100]

[95] *SKX v Manchester CC* [2021] EWHC 782 (QB).

[96] The decision in *SKX* sits uncomfortably with *Armes v Nottinghamshire CC* [2017] UKSC 60, [2018] AC 355 in which a local authority was held vicariously liable to a child in its care for the sexual abuse committed by a foster parent in whose care the child had been placed.

[97] See www.childabuseroyalcommission.gov.au/.

[98] S 43, National Redress Scheme for Institutional Child Sexual Abuse Act 2018 (Cth).

[99] Though note the legislation does not affect the inherent jurisdiction of the courts to stay proceedings where a fair trial is not possible. Limitation Act 1985 (ACT) s 21C; Limitation Act 1969 (NSW) s 6A; Limitation Amendment (Child Abuse) Act 2017 (NT); Limitation of Actions Act 1974 (Qld) s 11A; Limitation of Actions Act 1936 (SA) s 3A; Limitation Act 1974 (Tas) s 5b; Limitation of Actions Act 1958 (Vic) s 27P; Limitation Act 2005 (WA) s 6A.

[100] In the absence of such a nomination, the trustees of an associated trust can be held liable in New South Wales, Queensland, Victoria and the ACT or office holders of the unincorporated associated in Queensland and Western Australia; Civil Law (Wrongs) Act 2002 (ACT) ss 114D–114E; Civil Liability Act 2002 (NSW) ss 6I–6O; Civil Liability Act 2003 (Qld) ss 33H–33I; Legal Identity of Defendants (Organisational Child Abuse) Act 2018 (Vic) s 7; Wrongs Act 1958 (Vic) s 92; Civil Liability Act 2002 (WA) pt 2A; Civil Liability Act 2002 (Tas) ss 49K–49S.

- a statutory duty of care in New South Wales, Victoria, Queensland and Tasmania imposed on institutions charged with the care of children (operating prospectively only) in which the burden of proof shifts to the institution to prove that they did act reasonably in circumstances where a child in their care was sexually abused (rebuttable presumption of breach).[101]

A thorough review of the legislative reforms introduced in response to the Royal Commission in Australia in the various jurisdictions is provided in an excellent article by Stewart and Silink.[102] The differences between the states and territories might surprise a non-Australian reader. The federal nature of the Australian Commonwealth preserves the right of the different states (less so the territories) to legislate in most areas (other than those reserved to the Commonwealth) and it remains relatively uncommon for each of the states and territories to legislate in identical or largely similar terms.[103] The legislative reforms following the Royal Commission were inserted in a sway of legislation introduced in the various states and territories after the so-called 'insurance crisis' in Australia in 2002 for which there was similarly no uniformity.[104]

This chapter will focus on two specific reforms suggested in response to the Royal Commission:

A statutory, non-delegable duty of care imposed on institutions charged with the care of children (operating prospectively only), proposed by the Royal Commission but not implemented in any Australian jurisdiction;
a statutory form of vicarious liability imposed on institutions charged with the care of children (operating prospectively only), introduced in New South Wales[105] and Tasmania.[106]

A. Proposed Non-Delegable Duty of Care

When the Royal Commission handed down its *Redress and Civil Litigation Report*[107] in 2015, the High Court of Australia had yet to hear the appeal in *Prince Alfred College*. The Royal Commission therefore had to deal with the rather

[101] Civil Liability Act 2002 (NSW) s 6F; Civil Liability Act 2003 (Qld) s 33A; Wrong Act 1958 (Vic) s 91; Civil Liability Act 2002 (Tas) ss 49F–49H.

[102] P Stewart and A Silink, 'Australian Civil Litigation Reform in Response to the Recommendations of the Royal Commission into Child Sexual Abuse' (2020) 26 *Torts Law Journal* 1.

[103] For example, model defamation laws were introduced throughout the Australian states and territories in 2005, although they have recently been reviewed following the introduction of the Defamation Act 2013 in England and Wales.

[104] See generally P Vines, 'Tort Reform, Insurance and Responsibility' (2002) 25 *University of New South Wales Law Journal* 842.

[105] ss 6G and 6H Civil Liability Act 2002 (NSW).

[106] ss 49I and 49J Civil Liability Act 2002 (Tas).

[107] A copy is available at www.childabuseroyalcommission.gov.au/sites/default/files/file-list/final_report_-_redress_and_civil_litigation.pdf.

confused state of the law governing the imposition of strict liability for child sexual abuse that existed in Australia prior to that decision.

A review of the common law developments in Canada and England and Wales in cases of child sexual abuse led the Royal Commission to conclude:

> To our minds it is time that Australian parliaments moved to impose liability on some types of institutions for the deliberate criminal acts of members or employees of the institution as well as for the negligence of those members or employees.[108]

The dual policy concerns of compensation and deterrence were given by the Royal Commission as the reason for so doing.[109]

The Royal Commission recommended that the form of strict liability that should be imposed on institutions charged with the care of children was liability for breach of a non-delegable duty of care. In the Commission's view, there was greater support amongst the judges in Australia who had heard child sexual abuse cases at the time the Royal Commission issued its Report for imposing liability for breach of a non-delegable duty of care.[110] The Royal Commission was also mindful that vicarious liability had previously been limited to imposing strict liability for the tort of employees in Australia whereas strict liability imposed for breach of a non-delegable duty of care had not been so limited.[111]

There is a strong history of imposing liability for breach of a non-delegable duty of care in Australia.[112] It was well established at the time of the Royal Commission that the relationship between a school and student, the type of relationship in issue in both *Lepore* and *Prince Alfred College*, gave rise to a non-delegable duty of care.[113] The liability that might be imposed for breach of a non-delegable duty of care was also recognised to include strict liability for the tort of another person.[114] To impose such liability, a court had to find that the defendant owed the plaintiff a non-delegable duty of care (focussing attention on the relationship between the defendant and the plaintiff) and that the duty had been breached by the commission of the tort by the tortfeasor.[115] There was no separate requirement to examine the nature of the relationship between the defendant and the tortfeasor.

To the extent the guidance subsequently issued by the High Court in *Prince Alfred College* drew the attention of lower courts to the relationship between the

[108] ibid 490.

[109] ibid.

[110] ibid, citing specifically Mason P and Davies AJA in the Court of Appeal decision in *Lepore* ((2001) 52 NSWLR 420) and McHugh J in the judgment given in the same case by the High Court (n 9).

[111] And could extend to liability for independent contractors: ibid 491.

[112] Following the judgment of Mason J in *Kondis v State Transport Authority* [1984] HCA 61, (1984) 154 CLR 672.

[113] *Introvigne v Commonwealth* [1982] HCA 40, (1982) 150 CLR 258.

[114] But also includes liability for a failure by the duty holder itself to use reasonable care. See, generally, C Beuermann, *Reconceptualising Strict Liability for the Tort of Another* (Oxford, Hart Publishing, 2019) ch 4.

[115] ibid.

defendant and the plaintiff and the position the defendant placed the tortfeasor vis-à-vis the plaintiff when imposing strict liability in cases of child sexual abuse, the Royal Commission might be viewed as fortuitously anticipating the High Court's judgment. Evidence can be found in the type of examples referred to by the Royal Commission in making its recommendation:

> We have been influenced by the decisions of the courts in which strict liability has been recognised. If the law makes a solicitor liable for the criminal act of his clerk and the dry cleaner liable for the criminal act of his employee, could it be argued that it is not appropriate for institutions to be liable for the criminal abuse of a child when in their care? If the protection of an individual's property is an important priority of the common law, the protection of children should at least have the same priority. In our opinion the community would today expect that the care of children should attract the highest obligation of the law.[116]

The example of the solicitor is drawn from *Lloyd*[117] and it was arguably the pre-existing relationship between the defendant solicitor and the claimant client, and the fact that the solicitor's clerk had been conferred authority by the solicitor to take possession of the deeds to the claimant's property, that led to the imposition of vicarious liability. The example of the dry cleaner is drawn from *Morris v C W Martin & Sons*[118] and is factually similar; a pre-existing relationship between the defendant drycleaner and the claimant client with the drycleaner conferring authority on the employee to take possession of the claimant's fur coat. In both these examples it can be argued that the strict liability imposed on the defendant was imposed by reason of the position the tortfeasor had been placed vis-à-vis the plaintiff and the plaintiff's property by the defendant.[119]

A closer examination of the report by the Royal Commission confirms, however, that the Royal Commission was as confused as to the relevant relationship that gave rise to the imposition of strict liability in cases of child sexual abuse as the Australian courts were at the time. Whilst recommending a non-delegable duty of care, the Royal Commission was similarly recommending that liability for foster care or kinship care should be excluded. The underlying reason for that exclusion was: 'the institution that arranges foster care or kinship care does not have the degree of supervision or control of the foster care or kinship care home environment to justify the imposition of a non-delegable duty'.[120] The focus in this statement is on the relationship between the institution and the tortfeasor and not the institution and the child. That this focus was misplaced was subsequently recognised by the UK Supreme Court when it imposed strict liability in *Armes v*

[116] *Redress and Civil Litigation Report* (n 106).
[117] *Lloyd* (n 35).
[118] *Morris v C W Martin & Sons* [1966] 1 QB 716.
[119] Beuermann (n 113) ch 3.
[120] *Redress and Civil Litigation Report* (n 106) 493.

Nottinghamshire CC[121] on the defendant council for the sexual abuse of a child whom it had placed with a foster carer.[122]

It appears, therefore, that the choice of a non-delegable duty by the Royal Commission, and its emphasis on the relationship between the defendant and the plaintiff was entirely coincidental. Notwithstanding, it might now be argued that imposing liability for breach of a non-delegable duty of care in cases of child sexual abuse is more appropriate than vicarious liability given the focus of the High Court in *Prince Alfred College* on the relationship between the defendant and the plaintiff and the position the defendant places the tortfeasor vis-à-vis the plaintiff.[123]

B. Statutory Vicarious Liability

Somewhat ironically, it was the subsequent decision of the High Court in *Prince Alfred College* that sounded the death knell for the Royal Commission's preferred form of strict liability in the child sexual abuse cases: liability for breach of a non-delegable duty of care. Due to flaws in the pleadings, the only viable ground of liability addressed to the High Court in that case was vicarious liability.[124] Vicarious liability was consequently identified as the potential basis for imposing strict liability on an institution in respect of child sexual abuse in Australia.

With a view to implementing the Royal Commission's recommended non-delegable duty of care on institutions charged with the care of children, but mindful of the more recent use of vicarious liability by the High Court in *Prince Alfred College*, both New South Wales[125] and Tasmania[126] introduced a statutory form of vicarious liability. The legislation in New South Wales and Tasmania is not identical but shares the same basic components. This section will focus on the legislation introduced in New South Wales, upon which the Tasmanian reforms were based.[127]

The First Reading Speech of the Civil Liability Amendment (Organisational Child Abuse Liability) Bill 2018 in the New South Wales Parliament records

[121] *Armes* (n 95).

[122] For a discussion of the case see C Beuermann, 'Up in *Armes*: The Need for a Map of Strict Liability for the Wrongdoing of Another' (2018) 25 *Torts Law Journal* 1.

[123] As I argued in my book, Beuermann, *Reconceptualising Strict Liability* (n 113).

[124] The plaintiff had not addressed the criteria that had previously been stipulated by the High Court as having to be satisfied for the High Court to overturn one of its own decisions; *Prince Alfred College* (n 1) [36].

[125] ss 6G and 6H Civil Liability Act 2002 (NSW).

[126] ss 49I and 49J Civil Liability Act 2002 (Tas).

[127] Changes were made after it became apparent there was confusion as to the meaning of the section amongst stakeholders after a consultation process; Tasmanian House of Assembly, Second Reading Speech, Hon Elise Archer MP, 10 September 2019, www.parliament.tas.gov.au/ParliamentSearch/search.

that the New South Wales legislation was intended to codify the approach of the High Court in *Prince Alfred College*.[128] This is evident from the wording of section 6H Civil Liability Act 2002 (NSW) that picks up on various phrases from the principal joint judgment in that case:

> 6H Organisations vicariously liable for child abuse perpetrated by employees
>
> (1) An organisation is vicariously liable for child abuse perpetrated against a child by an employee of the organisation if –
>   (a) the apparent performance by the employee of a role in which the organisation placed the employee supplies the occasion for the perpetration of the child abuse by the employee, and
>   (b) the employee takes advantage of that occasion to perpetrate the child abuse on the child.
>
> (2) In determining if the apparent performance by the employee of a role in which the organisation placed the employee supplied the occasion for the perpetration of child abuse on a child, a court is to take into account whether the organisation placed the employee in a position in which the employee has one or more of the following –
>   (a) authority, power or control over the child,
>   (b) the trust of the child,
>   (c) the ability to achieve intimacy with the child.

Codifying the common law would not have advanced the position of child sexual abuse victims very far. The First Reading Speech records a further intention to extend the common law position in one important respect:

> The purpose of the codification, given that the common law has already developed to this point, is to extend this test to those who are akin to employees, as has already occurred in several overseas jurisdictions. The reason for this is that the Royal Commission learned that in many cases abuse may be perpetrated against children by those who, strictly speaking, are not employees within the existing law of vicarious liability. In faith-based organisations, this could include members of the clergy or similar, and in all organisations it could include volunteers or contractors, who are often involved in the child services sector. Proposed section 6G closes this loophole by applying the existing common law in *Prince Alfred College* to those who are 'akin to an employee'.[129]

This extension would not have been necessary had the Royal Commission's initial recommendation to impose a non-delegable duty of care on institutions charged with the care of children been adopted. To make a statutory form of vicarious liability work in the circumstances, the first stage of the vicarious liability test

[128] New South Wales Legislative Assembly, Hansard, 26 September 2018, www.parliament.nsw.gov.au/Hansard/Pages/HansardResult.aspx#/docid/'HANSARD-1323879322-103787.

[129] ibid.

adopted by courts in England and Wales was consequently transplanted into the relevant legislation:

> 6G Employees include persons exercising functions akin to employees
>
> (1) In this Division –
>
> *employee* of an organisation includes an individual who is akin to an employee of the organisation.
>
> (2) An individual is *akin to an employee* of an organisation if the individual carries out activities as an integral part of the activities carried on by the organisation and does so for the benefit of the organisation.
>
> (3) However, an individual is not *akin to an employee* if –
>
> (a) the activities are carried out for a recognisably independent business of the individual or of another person or organisation, or
>
> (b) the activities carried on by the individual are the activities of an authorised carer carried on in the individual's capacity as an authorised carer.

It should be noted that the New South Wales legislation is expressed to operate in addition, and not to the exclusion, of the common law.[130]

It is difficult to see the adoption of this particular legal transplant from the law in England and Wales into a statutory form of vicarious liability in New South Wales and Tasmania as anything but regrettable. It confuses the relevant relationship which attracts strict liability for child sexual abuse, contrary to the guidance of the High Court in *Prince Alfred College*. At best, its incorporation is now defunct since the cases show that strict liability can be imposed on institutions charged with the care of children for child sexual abuse in Australia irrespective of whether an employment relationship exists between the defendant and the tortfeasor. At worst, its incorporation might influence courts to consider applying the transplant more broadly; specifically, to cases of vicarious liability where the tort in question was not committed deliberately. As has been seen in England and Wales, this has led to confusion as to the relevant relationship that triggers strict liability and an undue expansion of vicarious liability which is now having to be reassessed by the Supreme Court.[131]

IV. Conclusion

As this book more than ably demonstrates, child sexual abuse cases have prompted significant revision of the law of vicarious liability throughout the common law world. The various revisions have met with varying degrees of success. Australia undoubtedly lagged behind other countries in the common law world in developing a form of vicarious liability that could be imposed in cases of child sexual

[130] s 6G(3) Civil Liability Act 2002 (NSW).

[131] See discussion of *Barclays* (n 61).

abuse. The developments by the courts in Australia have been slow, but careful. As a result, the prospect for misstep has arguably been reduced.[132] It remains to be seen whether the lessons learned in Australia will be acknowledged by other jurisdictions. The value of books such as this is that those lessons are made apparent. Specifically, that the form of vicarious liability imposed in cases of child sexual abuse (and in respect of other torts that have been committed deliberately) is distinct because the relationship which triggers the liability is not the relationship between the defendant and the tortfeasor, but the relationship between the defendant and the plaintiff and the position the defendant has placed the tortfeasor vis-à-vis the plaintiff. Perhaps it is now time to recognise that distinctiveness and amend the nomenclature accordingly.

[132] Although the same cannot be said for the legislative responses to the Royal Commission.

5

Connecting Cautiously

Vicarious Liability in Ireland in Comparative Perspective

DESMOND RYAN

The law of vicarious liability was relatively stable, narrow and well understood for most of the 20th century until recently, and much if not all of the development of the law has occurred because of the necessity of addressing the phenomenon of historic sexual abuse of children in an institutional context.

Hickey v McGowan [2017] IESC 6, [2017] 2 IR 196 [43] per O'Donnell J

I. Introduction

The above quotation, from the leading modern vicarious liability judgment of the Irish courts, captures the context for the development of vicarious liability doctrine in recent decades in Ireland. Like all common law jurisdictions, Ireland has grappled with the question of how vicarious liability can be utilised to provide recourse via tort law to victims of the grave evil of child sexual abuse. This has been the impetus for significant development of both stages of the vicarious liability case law, namely the *Stage 1* question of the type of relationship needed to trigger vicarious liability, and the *Stage 2* question of the nature of the connection needed between that relationship and the wrong done. This chapter critically analyses these doctrinal developments in vicarious liability in Ireland and places them in comparative perspective.

Before analysing the leading recent Irish decisions, it is necessary to place them in their broader context by noting four key points. First, the relatively small size of the jurisdiction has clear implications for the volume of decided cases addressing or clarifying the law in this area, with far fewer decisions when compared with, for example, the United Kingdom courts. This dearth of judgments is all the more significant in this specific context, having regard to an early outlier Stage 1 decision of considerable controversy.[1] A practical consequence of this has been evidence of judicial unease and confusion with the concept of vicarious liability and its application, which has only recently been replaced with clearer judicial articulation of the key principles governing this area. Thus, in the first key Supreme Court decision considering the applicability in Ireland of the close connection test,[2] the Court's approach lacked the unanimity of result seen in UK and Canadian cases such as *Lister*[3] or *Bazley*[4] and hence contributed to instability in this area. Later decisions have confirmed acceptance of the close connection test but indicate caution both with the test and its application. Within the last five years, there have now been two major decisions of the Supreme Court of Ireland addressing both Stage 1[5] and Stage 2,[6] such that greater clarity has now emerged as to the applicable tests.

The second contextual point to be made at the outset is that a striking feature of modern Irish case law on vicarious liability in sexual abuse cases is its illustration of a deliberate methodological choice to engage with comparative authorities, with overt recognition by the Supreme Court of the importance of this approach,[7] and with the Court considering *Lister*,[8] *Bazley*[9] and several decisions from other jurisdictions. In turn, the vicarious liability case law of the Supreme Court of Ireland has increasingly been referred to internationally in both judicial[10] and academic[11] analysis.

Third, in a pattern mirrored in other jurisdictions, the courts in Ireland, having established modern approaches to both stages of the vicarious liability analysis against the backdrop of sexual abuse cases, have demonstrated the application of those expanded principles to other emerging areas in vicarious liability, including in consideration of changing patterns of employment and the 'gig economy' in the context of Stage 1,[12] and novel cases raising questions other

[1] *Moynihan v Moynihan* [1975] IR 192 (*Moynihan*). See below, text following n 21 onwards.

[2] *O'Keeffe v Hickey* [2008] IESC 72, [2009] 2 IR 302 (*O'Keeffe*).

[3] *Lister v Hesley Hall Ltd* [2001] UKHL 22, [2002] 1 AC 215 (*Lister*).

[4] *Bazley v Curry* [1999] 2 SCR 534, (1999) 174 DLR (4th) 45 (*Bazley*).

[5] *Hickey v McGowan* [2017] IESC 6, [2017] 2 IR 196 (*Hickey*); *Morrissey v Health Service Executive* [2020] IESC 6 (*Morrissey*).

[6] *Hickey* ibid.

[7] See for example the comment of Hardiman J in *O'Keeffe* (n 2) above, where Hardiman J observed that he would 'freely acknowledge the inspiration often to be found in English and other UK, American, Canadian and New Zealand decisions' (albeit that, unlike the majority, his judgment declined to follow *Lister* and *Bazley*: see below analysis of *O'Keeffe* in this chapter, text following n 35).

[8] *Lister* (n 3).

[9] *Bazley* (n 4).

[10] See for example the treatment of *O'Keeffe* (n 2) above, by Longmore LJ in *Maga v Trustees of the Birmingham Archdiocese of the Roman Catholic Church* [2010] EWCA Civ 256, [2010] 1 WLR 1441 (*Maga*), where Longmore LJ (at [90]) described the approach of Fennelly J in *O'Keeffe* as 'entirely consistent with the approach of English Courts'.

[11] See for example C Beuermann, *Reconceptualising Strict Liability for the Tort of Another* (Oxford, Hart Publishing, 2019) 90–92, who considers the Supreme Court of Ireland's decision in *Reilly v Devereux* [2009] IESC 22, [2009] 3 IR 660, analysed below in this chapter, in the context of her account of conferred authority strict liability.

[12] See, for example, *Ryanair DAC and Ryanair Holdings plc v Van Zwol* [2020] IECA 105 [48]–[49] per Noonan J.

than sexual abuse at Stage 2, such as whether vicarious liability can be a mechanism for addressing systemic failings concerning cervical cancer screening.[13] In the current leading cases, the courts have demonstrated engagement with the principal theoretical justifications for the imposition of vicarious liability, particularly enterprise risk.[14]

Fourth, in common with broader comparative developments in cases such as *Lepore*,[15] *Woodland*[16] and *Armes*[17] – all of which have been cited and explored in the modern Irish case law – the relationship between vicarious liability and the non-delegable duty of care has been recently considered, with a key 2020 judgment[18] engaging with this in detail.

The conclusion reached in this chapter is that, some 20 years after *Lister*, it can now be said of vicarious liability in Ireland that Stage 1 and Stage 2 of the approach are broadly aligned with the position in the United Kingdom case law but that, as regards Stage 2, Irish courts are likely to be 'more *Morrisons*[19] than *Mohamud*'.[20]

II. Stage 1: The Courts' Approach to the *Type of Relationship* Giving Rise to Vicarious Liability

On the Stage 1 question of what type of relationship is necessary to trigger vicarious liability, Irish jurisprudence has been heavily influenced by the controversial decision of the Supreme Court in *Moynihan v Moynihan*.[21] This decision reveals the clear impact of the local factor of insurance on informing the majority's approach to the question of vicarious liability.[22] *Moynihan* concerned a two-year-old girl who sustained serious personal injuries when she upturned a teapot on herself in her grandmother's home. The trial judge held that the defendant, the child's grandmother, could not be vicariously liable for the negligence of her daughter (the plaintiff's aunt) in leaving the child unattended. The majority of the Supreme Court, however, allowed the appeal. Walsh J, delivering the judgment of the majority, identified the concept of control in the relationship between the defendant and the wrongdoer as the key guiding criterion in determining whether vicarious liability could be imposed.[23] Vicarious liability was found to be possible on the facts.

[13] *Morrissey* (n 5).
[14] See for example *Hickey*, above n 5, discussed below, text following n 40.
[15] *New South Wales v Lepore* [2003] HCA 4, (2003) 212 CLR 511 (*Lepore*).
[16] *Woodland v Essex County Council* [2013] UKSC 66, [2014] 1 AC 537 (*Woodland*).
[17] *Armes v Nottinghamshire County Council* [2017] UKSC 60, [2018] AC 355 (*Armes*).
[18] *Morrissey* (n 5).
[19] *WM Morrison Supermarkets plc v Various Claimants* [2020] UKSC 12, [2020] AC 989 (*Morrisons*).
[20] *Mohamud v WM Morrison Supermarkets plc* [2016] UKSC 11, [2016] AC 677 (*Mohamud*).
[21] [1975] IR 192.
[22] In its more recent case law, the Supreme Court of Ireland has emphasised that insurance considerations should not influence legal principle in this area: *Hickey* (n 5) [45] per O'Donnell J.
[23] *Moynihan* (n 21) 197.

Placing *Moynihan* in perspective almost 50 years later, two points occur. First, the level of emphasis placed on 'control' is now increasingly difficult to sustain in light of the more modern international and Irish case law. Secondly, *Moynihan* has, over the years, been the subject of significant academic, extra-judicial and judicial criticism. Before the major judicial developments addressed below in this chapter, the authors of the leading tort textbook in Ireland, McMahon and Binchy – which is consistently cited in every major vicarious liability decision delivered by the Irish courts – had observed in the then most recent edition that while the majority judgment in *Moynihan* had laid down 'defensible rules for determining vicarious liability', the application of these rules to the facts was 'hardly convincing'.[24] In addition, the former Chief Justice of Ireland, the Honourable Mr Justice Ronan Keane, had described the decision of the majority in *Moynihan* as 'somewhat perplexing'[25] and involving a 'radical extension of vicarious liability'.[26] It seems an 'inescapable'[27] conclusion that the case turned upon the existence of an insurance policy, presumably the grandmother's household insurance.[28]

By 2008, in *O'Keeffe*, Hardiman J went much further in expressing his unease with what he described as the 'elaborate', 'legalistic' and 'highly artificial' analysis by the majority in *Moynihan* of 'the entirely casual relationship whereby the defendant's daughter had made a pot of tea in her mother's house, where she herself lived'.[29] Hardiman J went on to state that he 'much prefer[red] the more realistic analysis to be found in the dissenting judgment of Henchy J' in *Moynihan*. Noting that the plaintiff in *Moynihan* had not sued her aunt, the person alleged to be directly negligent, but only the grandmother, who was hoped to be a 'deep pocket', Hardiman J continued:

> The case appears to me to be an early example of the dismantling or muddying of the long established boundaries or limits of vicarious liability. This was done for the very humane reason of helping an innocent injured party to recover compensation, but it was done at a very considerable social cost, not often considered or discussed.[30]

To Hardiman J, *Moynihan*:

> represented a significant step on the road to the situation in which it is widely believed that every misfortune must be compensatable and that if misfortune is caused by an insolvent person, or an unascertained person, or a person not amenable, it should be compensated by the nearest solvent mark, or in the last resort by the State itself.[31]

[24] BME McMahon and W Binchy, *Law of Torts* 3rd edn (Dublin, Butterworths, 2000) 1093 at n 10.
[25] R Keane, 'Judges as Lawmakers: The Irish Experience' (2004) 4(2) *Judicial Studies Institute Journal* 1, 4 at n 10.
[26] ibid.
[27] *O'Keeffe* (n 2) [45].
[28] The issue of insurance was considered in both the majority (see especially 198) and (rather more forcefully) the dissenting (see 202–03) judgments in *Moynihan* (n 1).
[29] *O'Keeffe* (n 2) [45].
[30] ibid [46].
[31] ibid [50].

Despite the criticism it has engendered, *Moynihan* has not been overruled, and indeed, referring to *Moynihan* in the leading 2020 Supreme Court decision in *Morrissey*,[32] analysed below, Clarke CJ observed: 'It is clear, therefore, that for at least the last 45 years, the Irish courts have recognised that informal relationships involving some degree of delegated function and control can give rise to vicarious liability'.[33]

It is now necessary to place in perspective more recent approaches which have been adopted to vicarious liability Ireland at Stage 1, triggered by the need of the law to respond to the horrors of institutional sexual abuse. As has been judicially observed, '[t]he calamity of the exploitation of authority over children so to abuse them sexually has shaken society to its foundations'.[34] The first major Supreme Court decision to consider vicarious liability for child sexual abuse was *O'Keeffe*,[35] which arose out of sexual assaults of a school pupil committed by a teacher. The plaintiff sought to have vicarious liability imposed upon the Minister for Education for the wrongs committed by the teacher. Although I will explore this decision more fully below in this chapter in the context of its relevance for the Stage 2 close connection inquiry, it is important to note that the particular way in which education was historically structured and organised in Ireland had a key bearing on the Stage 1 inquiry in *O'Keeffe*. This is due to the complex nature of the relationship between the Department of Education, the school's management system and the wrongdoing teacher. This feature of the case presented distinct and formidable difficulties for the plaintiff: it was on the basis of this 'triangular' relationship that the High Court and the majority of the Supreme Court held that vicarious liability could not be imposed since there was no employment relationship between the abuser and the manager.[36]

As regards the non-application of *Moynihan*, Fennelly J preferred to express no view on that decision since the court had not been asked to overrule it, other than to observe that it was 'based on highly unusual facts' and did not establish any precedent capable of being applied to *O'Keeffe*.[37]

In *O'Keeffe*, there was a sharp divergence of approach amongst the Supreme Court. Hardiman J, having surveyed the comparative authorities including *Bazley*, *Lister* and *Lepore*, would have rejected the adoption of the close connection test. The majority judgment, delivered by Fennelly J, however, confirmed the adoption in Irish law of the close connection test, adopting a cautious and incremental approach.[38] Some years following this decision, Ms O'Keeffe succeeded before the Grand Chamber of the European Court of Human Rights in establishing a violation of Article 3 of the European Convention on Human Rights.[39]

[32] *Morrissey* (n 5).
[33] ibid [12.8].
[34] *O'Keeffe* (n 2) [182] per Fennelly J.
[35] *O'Keeffe* (n 2).
[36] ibid [248] per Fennelly J.
[37] ibid.
[38] I return to these different judgments more fully later in this chapter in the context of Stage 2.
[39] *O'Keeffe v Ireland* [2014] ECHR 96, (2014) 59 EHRR 15.

The leading modern decision on Stage 1 is now that of *Hickey v McGowan*.[40] The plaintiff in *Hickey* sought damages for assault and battery perpetrated upon him by a teacher in his primary school. For present purposes, the key issue in the case was whether vicarious liability could be imposed upon the head of or Provincial of the Marist Brothers in Ireland, the order of which the wrongdoing teacher was a member. The High Court (Ó Néill J) had answered this question in the affirmative and in doing so explicitly endorsed the approach in *Catholic Child Welfare*[41] in considering the true nature of the relationship between the Brothers and the wrongdoer. Ó Néill J continued:

> In the *CCWS* case, the relationship between the abusing Brothers and their institute was treated as '*akin to employment*'. I am persuaded to take the same view of the relationship between the second named defendant and the Marist Congregation of which he was a member. Thus, that relationship is one which can give rise to vicarious liability, and because of the closeness of connection between the teaching activities of the second named defendant and the mission on which he was sent, and which he shared with the Marist Congregation, both aspects of the '*close connection*' test are, in my view, met in this case.[42]

Ó Néill J described the reasoning of Lord Phillips in *CCWS* as 'compelling' and expressly adopted it as being 'necessary to arrive at a just outcome of the litigation'.[43]

On appeal,[44] the Supreme Court upheld the imposition of vicarious liability, and the judgment in *CCWS* was considered at length by the Irish Supreme Court.[45] O'Donnell J (as he then was), giving the lead judgment, regarded the relationship between the wrongdoer and the Marist Order as being one capable of giving rise to vicarious liability. This was because, inter alia, both the wrongdoer and the Order 'considered that he was pursuing an important and central objective of the Order in teaching … children rather than merely providing a service to the manager of the school'.[46] In a key passage of the majority judgment, O'Donnell J emphasised the cautious, incremental approach which had been adopted by Fennelly J in the *O'Keeffe* decision. O'Donnell J said:

> The relationship between members and the order, and the importance to the order of the role of members as teachers of young people, are matters which have no direct comparators in the secular world. Accordingly, I do not consider that there is anything inappropriate in addressing this question from the perspective of justice and fairness.

[40] *Hickey* (n 5).
[41] *The Catholic Child Welfare Society v Various Claimants* [2012] UKSC 56, [2013] 2 AC 1 (*CCWS*).
[42] [2014] IEHC 19, [63] (emphasis original).
[43] ibid [68].
[44] A Court of Civil Appeal was only introduced in Ireland with the enactment of the Court of Appeal Act 2014. Prior to this, decisions of the High Court in civil cases could only be appealed directly to the Supreme Court.
[45] *Hickey* (n 5).
[46] ibid [42] per O'Donnell J.

> This is not to reintroduce the unbridled discretion in individual cases so sharply criticised by Hardiman J in *O'Keeffe v Hickey*. Instead, a general question is raised in this case as to whether all persons similarly situated should be liable if certain facts are found … [I]t is now clear that there can be vicarious liability without fault for acts of sexual abuse. If so the onlooker would surely struggle to understand that the only person or body who as a practical matter may be required to compensate a plaintiff abused in this way by a member of the Marist Order, in a school staffed by the Order, should be the local parish priest … [I]n principle, once it is accepted there can be vicarious liability of acts of abuse a religious order (or its members) may be vicariously liable for acts of abuse which are sufficiently closely connected to the object and mission of the order … I reach this conclusion adopting what I consider to be the cautious and incremental approach outlined by Fennelly J in *O'Keeffe*, conscious indeed of the strength of the criticism of that approach contained in the judgment of Hardiman J in the same case.[47]

Charleton J (who partially dissented for unrelated reasons) also confirmed his agreement with the imposition of vicarious liability arising from this type of non-employment relationship, since it was 'inescapable that the relationship is equivalent to employment'[48] emphasising in a passage very redolent of the approach in *CCWS* why this was so:

> In terms of ordinary sense, the relationship between persons in religious orders is closer than in employment; the direction by their superior is stronger than that of a boss at work because he or she carries moral as well as financial authority; and the coherence of a group advancing temporal aims for spiritual purposes exceeds that of any secular organisation.[49]

Hickey confirms that it is possible to impose vicarious liability outside the confines of an employment relationship and in so doing it coheres with trends in international case law such as the decision in *CCWS* (albeit that O'Donnell J (as he then was) delivering the majority judgment did express concerns about what he referred to as 'rather freewheeling analysis'[50] advanced on behalf of the plaintiff in the context of some elements of *CCWS*).[51]

A striking feature of *Hickey* is the extensive consideration given in the judgments in the Supreme Court to the theoretical basis for the imposition of vicarious liability. Thus the concept of enterprise risk which has featured so prominently in analysis in the courts of other common law jurisdictions, such as in *Bazley*, for example, is specifically identified by O'Donnell J in *Hickey* as the core theoretical basis for the imposition of vicarious liability in a passage of some significance:

> In most such cases of imposition of liability without individual culpability, to some extent at least it can be said that the defendant creates, or permits and often benefits

[47] ibid [38]–[39] per O'Donnell J.
[48] ibid [101] per Charleton J.
[49] ibid [93] per Charleton J.
[50] ibid [43] per O'Donnell J.
[51] ibid.

> from, a situation which carries with it the risk of injury or the wrongdoing by others. In the case of the employer/employee, the employee is in a position to commit the tort because he is employed and provided with equipment which he or she may misuse. The employer chooses the general activity and it is of value to him or her. To that extent it is perhaps not unfair that an employer should bear the risk of wrongdoing, even wrongdoing which he or she may forbid and indeed genuinely abhor. This is, I would add, irrespective of whether the employment is for profit or can be labelled an enterprise.[52]

O'Donnell J's judgment specifically rejects[53] the relevance of considerations of the means to compensate the victim which had been referred to in *CCWS* but later downplayed in *Cox*.[54] Similarly, insurance considerations were regarded as not being strictly relevant, at least as a matter of principle.[55]

The *Bazley* enterprise risk approach is also strongly in evidence in the judgment of Charleton J in *Hickey v McGowan*, who cites the relevant paragraph of McLachlin J's judgment in *Bazley* to the effect that '[h]olding the employer vicariously liable for the wrongs of its employee may encourage the employer to take … steps [of imaginative and efficient administration and supervision], and hence, reduce the risk of future harm'.[56] Charleton J's judgment continues with an express acceptance of enterprise risk:

> [T]he modern approach to vicarious liability may fairly be recognised as having developed through policy considerations. Those who have control over an enterprise may not be able, as in prior times, to pretend to a knowledge or level of skill equivalent to their workforce, but are enabled to organise the manner of work and relations with those with whom it is engaged so that risks are reasonably anticipated and, through safety measures and training, are minimised. Of course, the absence of such engagement in foresight and prevention may of itself establish fault. The party, however, with the ability to assess risk and to guard against or insure against it will be the organiser of the work, usually an employer. In advancing the economic interests of the enterprise, a corresponding duty has arisen whereby those working for such an enterprise, as salaried individuals, and without the backing of capital, become as one with those who employ them. Tort liability thus pursues its part of the proper ordering of society because it incentivises an enterprise towards safety and away from wrongful conduct.[57]

Overall, the approach of the Supreme Court in *Hickey v McGowan* reveals the Court's commitment to the cautious and incremental approach adopted by Fennelly J in *O'Keeffe*.[58]

[52] ibid [42] per O'Donnell J.
[53] ibid [44].
[54] *Cox v Ministry of Justice* [2016] UKSC 10, [2016] AC 660 [20] per Lord Reed.
[55] *Hickey* (n 5) [45].
[56] Per McLachlin J in *Bazley* [33], cited in *Hickey* (n 5) [99] per Charleton J.
[57] ibid [102] per Charleton J.
[58] This point is noted by the Supreme Court in its more recent decision in *Morrissey* (n 5) [12.4] per Clarke CJ.

At the time of writing, the most recent judgment of the Supreme Court of Ireland concerning Stage 1 is the decision in *Morrissey*.[59] Ms Morrissey, who at the time of the judgment was terminally ill from cancer and who sadly passed away shortly after the decision was handed down, had undergone screening in accordance with Ireland's National Cervical Screening Programme 'CervicalCheck' in August 2009 and again in August 2012. In both instances, her smear test was reported as negative for abnormalities and she was provided with a clear result. When Ms Morrissey was later diagnosed with cervical cancer, her smears were audited and it was reported that the original results provided in respect of both tests were incorrect. Ms Morrissey and her husband instituted proceedings against the Health Service Executive ('HSE'), the body charged with the provision of health services in Ireland and with the promotion of the CervicalCheck scheme. From 2008, the HSE had contracted out the testing of samples to various multinational firms ('the laboratory defendants', who were the other two defendants in the case).

For present purposes, the High Court (Cross J) had found in favour of the Morrisseys against all three defendants and had held that the HSE was vicariously liable for the negligence of the laboratory defendants. Notably absent from that judgment, however, was any detailed consideration of the point that the other defendants were not employees of the HSE, nor in a relationship equivalent to employment as identified in *Hickey*. On appeal, the Supreme Court overturned the finding of vicarious liability. In doing so, the Court has provided significant further clarification of the position in Irish law on 'Stage 1' in the context of non-employment relationships.

The unanimous judgment of the Supreme Court, delivered by Clarke CJ, includes express consideration of the correct methodological approach which the courts should follow in approaching vicarious liability, with the Court concluding that its approach should be informed by any underlying principle, if one can be identified, but should also, to the extent that it is not possible to identify any underlying principle, adopt an incremental approach, consistent with the position evinced by O'Donnell J in *Hickey v McGowan* having regard to the earlier judgment of Fennelly J in *O'Keeffe*.[60] The key passage in this regard is the conclusion of Clarke CJ to the effect that, at Stage 1:

> [T]he ultimate question which the Court must address is as to whether the level of engagement by one party with the way in which the other party is to carry out a task entrusted to it is sufficient to conclude that there is a real extent to which it can be said that the contracted party is closely integrated into the activities of the employer not just in respect of the ends to be achieved but as to the manner in which those ends are to be pursued.[61]

[59] *Morrissey* (n 5).
[60] *O'Keeffe* (n 2).
[61] ibid [12.20].

This articulation of an integration-based approach to the Stage 1 approach represents a significant elucidation of the existing case law up to and including *Hickey*. This is likely to be the most influential element of the *Morrissey* judgment for future vicarious liability litigation.

Modern work arrangements, including in the gig economy, have of course stretched the parameters of the distinction between a contract of service and a contract for services.

As has recently been memorably captured by Noonan J in the Court of Appeal in *Ryanair DAC and Ryanair Holdings plc v Van Zwol*:

> Victorian concepts of master and servant are becoming increasingly difficult to accommodate in the context of modern employment arrangements and the advent of the 'gig economy'. The distinction between a servant and an independent contractor was once more clear cut than it now is.[62]

In a comparative context, this raises the question of whether the recent expansion of the scope of vicarious liability at Stage 1 can embrace liability for a truly independent contractor, or whether the Irish courts will follow the approach of the UK Supreme Court in *Barclays Bank*.[63] Because the 'akin to employment' approach was essentially adopted (albeit in slightly different terminology and with a degree of caution) by the Irish Supreme Court in *Hickey* when the Court spoke of '*quasi*-employment'[64] and 'equivalent to employment' relationships, it is instructive to assess the influence and impact of these developments on the orthodox exclusion of independent contractors from the ambit of persons for whom a defendant could be held vicariously liable. While the point awaits specific judicial determination, it can be confidently predicted that *Barclays* will be followed in Irish law. This is for two main reasons. First, in *Morrissey* (a judgment which pre-dated *Barclays* by less than two weeks), Clarke CJ, adopting the 'evolution by analogy'[65] approach to vicarious liability, stated:

> [T]he overall test must be one which considers whether the nature of the relationship, including the question of control, is such that it is similar in substance, if not in form, to the types of relationships which have traditionally been regarded as giving rise to vicarious liability.[66]

The above passage appears to make it highly likely that *Barclays* will be followed in Ireland. This interpretation is also consistent with the approach adopted by the Court of Appeal of Ireland in *Rice v Muddiman*,[67] where Irvine J (as she then was)

[62] *Ryanair* (n 12) [48] per Noonan J.

[63] *Barclays Bank plc v Various Claimants* [2020] UKSC 13, [2020] AC 973 (*Barclays*).

[64] See for example the judgment of Charleton J in *Hickey* (n 5), dissenting on grounds not relevant to this point, at [128], [134].

[65] *Morrissey* (n 5) [12.6] per Clarke CJ.

[66] ibid [12.16].

[67] [2018] IECA 402 [51]–[52] per Irvine J.

stated that vicarious liability could not be triggered by the wrongdoing of an independent contractor. Tellingly, the judgment in *Rice* makes no reference to the 'quasi-employment' approach in *Hickey* – arguably signifying that *Hickey* was not regarded as affecting the orthodox rule against imposing vicarious liability for independent contractors.

In summarising the current position in Ireland concerning Stage 1, a number of points can be made. First, courts will (and should) give nuanced consideration to the reality of the working relationship alleged to trigger vicarious liability and will be alive to modern working practices and the need for a pragmatic application of the Stage 1 principles that avoids rigidity and artificiality so as to do justice in an individual case. Whilst caution is clearly discernible from the recent case law analysed above, its trend is one of introducing greater flexibility into the Stage 1 inquiry, albeit with an emphasis on the need for reasoned justification. In short, the courts will adopt an 'evolution by analogy' approach that is characterised by caution and incrementalism. Secondly, it appears highly likely, for the reasons set out above, that *Barclays* also represents the correct legal position in Ireland.

III. Stage 2: The Acceptance of *Lister* in Irish Law via a 'Cautious, Incremental Approach'

As we mark the passing of the 21st anniversary of *Lister*,[68] it is worth recalling just how seismic a shift that decision ushered into the law of vicarious liability. This is vividly underlined by a consideration of the first Irish Supreme Court decision to consider *Lister*, the 2008 decision of *O'Keeffe*.[69] In *O'Keeffe*, as set out above in this chapter, there was a stark divergence of approach between the majority and dissenting positions as to the nature of the test for vicarious liability in Irish law – the majority favouring the close connection test, but Hardiman J in dissent inclining towards a much narrower conception of vicarious liability based on the orthodox Salmond test.

Hardiman J's judgment sounded a strong note of caution about following *Bazley* or *Lister*. Of the innovation in Canadian law, in particular, Hardiman J described some of the key formulations of law by the Supreme Court of Canada as 'vague in the extreme and quite unhelpful'.[70] Analysing the qualification sounded by McLachlin J in *Bazley* that 'effective compensation must also be fair, in the sense that it must seem just to place liability for the wrong on the employer',[71]

[68] *Lister* (n 3).
[69] *O'Keeffe* (n 2).
[70] ibid [123] per Hardiman J.
[71] *Bazley* (n 4) [31] per McLachlin J.

Hardiman J described this passage as 'utterly lacking in rigour, and perhaps even in meaning' so that it was 'utterly useless as a predictive tool' and 'a modern version of the 'Chancellor's foot'.[72]

The stark extent of the difference between the approach of Hardiman J in *O'Keeffe* and that taken both by the Supreme Court of Canada in *Bazley* and the House of Lords in *Lister* is perhaps best illustrated by Hardiman J's use of the description 'firmly rooted in principle and in precedent'[73] when referring to the decision of the English Court of Appeal in *Trotman v North Yorkshire County Council*.[74] Hardiman J described *Lister* as comprising 'no development of a coherent legal principle'.[75]

Hardiman J's judgment also included detailed treatment of the decision of the High Court of Australia in *Lepore*.[76] Of the various approaches espoused in the different judgments in that case, it was the approach of Callinan J in *Lepore* with which Hardiman J expressed agreement. It will be recalled that, in *Lepore*, Callinan J had rejected altogether the application of vicarious liability to such situations of intentional wrongdoing by employees.[77] In *O'Keeffe*, Hardiman J expressed his strong endorsement of the Callinan position in unequivocal terms.

In contrast with the approach adopted by Hardiman J, the judgment of Fennelly J, for the majority, expresses far greater support for the international innovations in vicarious liability, in particular the close connection test as adopted in *Lister*. Fennelly J summarised his acceptance of the close connection test as a matter of Irish law in the following passage:

> Ultimately, I am satisfied that it is appropriate to adopt a test based on a close connection between the acts which the employee is engaged to perform and which fall truly within the scope of his employment and the tortious act of which complaint is made … The close-connection test is both well established by authority and practical in its content. It is essentially focussed on the facts of the situation. It does not, in principle, exclude vicarious liability for criminal acts or for acts which are intrinsically of a type which would not be authorised by the employer. The law regards it as fair and just to impose liability on the employer rather than to let the loss fall on the injured party. To do otherwise would be to impose the loss on the entirely innocent party who has engaged the employer to perform the service. The employer is, of course, also innocent, but he has, at least, engaged the dishonest servant and has disappointed the expectations of the person to whom he has undertaken to provide the service.[78]

[72] *O'Keeffe* (n 2) [90] per Hardiman J.
[73] ibid [119] per Hardiman J.
[74] *Trotman v North Yorkshire County Council* [1998] EWCA Civ 1208, [1999] LGR 584.
[75] *O'Keeffe* (n 2) [95] per Hardiman J.
[76] *Lepore* (n 15).
[77] ibid [342] per Callinan J.
[78] *O'Keeffe* (n 2) [243] per Fennelly J.

As would later be emphasised by the Supreme Court in a key 2020 judgment,[79] the approach of Fennelly J emphasises the incremental approach of the common law in the context of the close connection test.

Finally, on the question of the status in Irish law of *Lister* and *Bazley*, Geoghegan J described the Canadian innovation as perhaps 'the leading modern case'[80] and went on to conclude, in dissent, that he would have allowed Ms O'Keeffe's appeal on the basis of an application of 'the general modern principles underlying vicarious liability.'[81]

In the subsequent decision of the Irish Supreme Court in *Reilly v Devereux*,[82] the close connection test was further confirmed, albeit that vicarious liability was again not imposed. The case involved the question of whether vicarious liability could be imposed for sexual assault perpetrated by an army sergeant on a subordinate. In delivering the judgment of the Court, Kearns J emphasised how the plaintiff in the appeal in *Reilly* relied almost exclusively on the principles laid down in *Bazley*.[83] In so doing, three parallels were sought to be drawn between the factual backgrounds in *Bazley* and *Reilly*. First, the environment of the defence forces was such that the normal rules of adult interaction did not apply, since the disparity in rank between the plaintiff, who was a gunner, and the perpetrator, a sergeant major, led to a situation where the latter 'exercised great power over the plaintiff and could command unquestioning obedience from him'. Secondly, it was argued that 'an element of intimacy and camaraderie was encouraged in the [a]rmy in circumstances where employees worked in close quarters together'. Finally, it was suggested that within a culture where complaining was both discouraged and 'largely fruitless', a person in the plaintiff's position was particularly vulnerable to the wrongful exercise of power by a superior officer.[84]

Rejecting the attempt to draw these parallels between the facts of *Bazley* and *Reilly*, Kearns J did not accept that the nature of the employment relationship in *Reilly* supported the imposition of vicarious liability. The relationship between the plaintiff and defendant 'could hardly be more different'[85] from that between a schoolteacher and a child at a residential school; nor was there intimacy or a quasi-parental role implicit in the relationship as had been the case in *Bazley*. This judgment sits in contrast with the apparent emergence in recent years of a 'tailored test', apparently equally applicable to adults, in cases of sexual abuse in English law.[86]

[79] *Morrissey* (n 5).
[80] *O'Keeffe* (n 2) [174] per Geoghegan J.
[81] ibid [181].
[82] *Reilly* (n 11).
[83] ibid [27] per Kearns J.
[84] ibid.
[85] ibid [32] per Kearns J.
[86] See, for example, *Barry Congregation of Jehovah's Witnesses v BXB* [2021] EWCA Civ 356, [2021] 4 WLR 42, which is, at the time of writing, under appeal to the Supreme Court.

Whilst *Reilly* brought some further clarity to the question of the acceptance of the close connection test in Ireland, the situation has now been put beyond any doubt whatsoever in light of the leading modern vicarious liability decision in Ireland of *Hickey*,[87] decided in 2017. One of most significant aspects of that judgment is the analysis of O'Donnell J of the divergent approaches of Fennelly J and Hardiman J respectively in *O'Keeffe*. Thus, O'Donnell J observed:

> Although both judgments were careful not to reach any concluded position in that regard in the absence of any defendant in a position to argue the case, it is certainly much more likely that such a manager could have been found liable under Fennelly J's close connection test, and unlikely, perhaps highly unlikely that a manager could be found liable under Hardiman J's adherence to a strict 'unauthorised mode of performance of the task' test. *I think it is clear however that the judgment of Fennelly J. must be taken now to represent the law. This is not simply because it was agreed to by two other members of the Court, but, it must be recalled, Geoghegan J. delivered a judgment in which he would have dismissed the appeal and held the State parties to be vicariously liable.*[88]

The italicised wording above provides extremely important clarification as to the status in Ireland of the close connection test and greatly adds to clarity in this area of the law. O'Donnell J drew the following conclusions on the application of *O'Keeffe* to *Hickey*:

> First, as already observed, the judgment of Fennelly J., and the close connection test must be taken to represent the law in Ireland. Second, even though there was not a residential component to the school and the children were not particularly vulnerable, it seems clear that that test was satisfied in this case. The abuse took place during the very act of teaching in the classroom. Indeed, this seems to have been tacitly accepted in this case insomuch as the case proceeded on the assumption that the manager employer was vicariously liable for the abuse. It follows therefore that there was a close and sufficient connection between the teaching carried out and the criminal abuse. Third, and perhaps most importantly, the issue which divided the Court in *O'Keeffe* does not therefore arise here. The question is not whether the act done is one for which a person is otherwise vicariously liable for the acts of another should be responsible i.e. whether on this occasion the employer or anyone else should be liable for an act of sexual abuse. That issue must be taken to be satisfied in this case both on an application of the close connection test in general, and the attribution of liability to the manager in particular.[89]

In conclusion, then, after initial division within the Supreme Court in *O'Keeffe*, it has now come to be unequivocally accepted that the close connection test does represent the law in Ireland.

[87] *Hickey* (n 5).
[88] ibid [25] per O'Donnell J (emphasis added).
[89] ibid [27] per O'Donnell J.

IV. Judicial Consideration of the Relationship between Vicarious Liability and the Non-Delegable Duty of Care

In common with approaches in other jurisdictions,[90] the major recent decision of *Morrissey* involved consideration of both vicarious liability and the non-delegable duty of care. The Supreme Court's decision in *Morrissey* in 2020 represents the first occasion on which *Woodland*[91] has been adopted into Irish law. Clarke CJ engaged in a detailed consideration of the features identified by Lord Sumption in *Woodland*[92] which Clarke CJ set out and then proceeded to analyse in detail.[93] This is a significant new contribution to Irish jurisprudence. As with the approach to vicarious liability in *Morrissey*, Clarke CJ addressed head-on the question of how courts should confront novel questions concerning the non-delegable duty of care:

> While the United Kingdom case law sets out quite detailed criteria for assessing whether such a duty can be said to exist in particular circumstances, it does seem to me to be necessary to consider the appropriate approach to be adopted in determining whether the concept of a non-delegable duty should be extended to a category of case which has not yet been the subject of a specific ruling by the courts. In that context, it is appropriate to refer back to the overall analysis set out in the section of this judgment concerning vicarious liability which suggests that a court should be informed by any underlying principle, if there be one, but should also, to the extent that it is not possible to identify any underlying principle, adopt an incremental approach.[94]

Concluding that it was not necessary for the purposes of *Morrissey* to determine whether all of Lord Sumption's categories 'have a counterpart in Irish law', Clarke CJ did identify 'potentially at least one underlying principle behind the concept of the non-delegable duty, being that such a duty derives from a particular relationship between the parties'. Given that that underlying principle did not clarify the parameters of the *type of relationship* which will be held to give rise to a non-delegable duty, Clarke CJ concluded that 'the incremental approach by analogy provides the best assistance to the Court in attempting to map out the parameters of the circumstances which give rise to such a duty'.[95]

Morrissey considers the crucial distinction drawn in *Woodland* between cases where the defendant has assumed a responsibility to perform a function, on the one hand, and where the defendant has merely assumed a responsibility to arrange for its performance, on the other. The judgment includes analysis of

[90] As, for example, the United Kingdom in *Armes* (n 17).
[91] *Woodland* (n 16).
[92] ibid [23] per Lord Sumption, discussed by Giliker in more detail in chapter three.
[93] *Morrissey* (n 5) [13.11]–[13.26] per Clarke CJ.
[94] ibid [13.15] per Clarke CJ.
[95] ibid [13.18].

Myton v Woods[96] and *Armes*[97] and ultimately upholds the imposition of primary liability but, crucially, on a different, and more confined, basis than that on which it had been imposed by the trial judge. This is evident in the conclusion of Clarke CJ when he says:

> [I]t seems to me that the HSE is primarily liable for any negligence which might be found against the laboratories. I propose that the Court should reach such a somewhat narrower basis than that adopted by the trial judge because, for the reasons already referred to, I would not hold the HSE to be vicariously liable for the acts of those laboratories. However, I would hold that the HSE, in the manner in which it adopted and promoted CervicalCheck, acted in a way which would lead an informed and reasonable person to assume that the HSE was undertaking responsibility for ensuring that the programme would be conducted in a non-negligent way and, further, I would hold that there was nothing in the circumstances of the operation of the programme which would lead a reasonable person to conclude that the HSE had absolved itself of any obligations in respect of the screening part of the programme.[98]

Morrissey is thus a key development in Irish law. Its consideration of *Woodland* and *Armes* strongly suggests that those authorities will inform the development of the non-delegable duty analysis in this jurisdiction, although it remains to be seen whether the approach to vicarious liability in *Armes* will be followed in this jurisdiction or whether it may be regarded as too great a leap in the context of the cautious and incremental approach to vicarious liability confirmed in *Morrissey*.

V. Conclusion

The vicarious liability developments in Ireland analysed in this chapter reveal the dynamism and momentum of this area of law. The analysis undertaken allows a number of conclusions to be drawn. First, the clear influence of judicial and academic analysis in comparative perspective is openly acknowledged in, and readily discernible from, the key Irish judgments analysed above. Second, in approaching modern vicarious liability challenges, the courts in Ireland have confirmed that they will proceed with caution and having regard to the incremental tradition of the common law. That having been said, the courts have – after initial disagreement in *O'Keeffe*[99] – unambiguously confirmed the application of the close connection test in Irish law. As regards the Stage 1 inquiry, the language of 'equivalent to employment' and 'quasi-employment', and indeed the result reached in *Hickey*,[100] demonstrate that there is a flexibility at Stage 1 that is very similar to

[96] (1980) 79 LGR 28.
[97] *Armes* (n 17).
[98] *Morrissey* (n 5) [13.26] per Clarke CJ.
[99] *O'Keeffe* (n 2).
[100] *Hickey* (n 5).

the *CCWS*[101] approach. Whilst *Morrissey* was not concerned with the same issue as *Barclays*, a close reading of the former judgment, particularly having regard to previous *dicta* in *Hickey*,[102] suggests that Irish law will follow *Barclays* and that the distinction between employees and truly independent contractors for vicarious liability purposes remains good law.

At the time of writing, no reported decision in Ireland has yet considered *Mohamud*.[103] Based on the evidence of the approach in *Hickey*, *Mohamud* would appear difficult to reconcile with the cautious reservation expressed in the modern Irish cases. It can be confidently predicted that it will be the tenor and import of the later *Morrisons*[104] decision which will likely be considered far more consistent with the cautious, incremental approach evinced in the Irish case law to date.

Meanwhile, the successful invocation of a non-delegable duty of care in recent case law is likely to re-invigorate that area of tort doctrine in cases where vicarious liability is unavailable.

To conclude by returning full circle to the same passage with which this chapter opened, it must be recalled that, in his judgment in *Hickey*,[105] O'Donnell J sounded the following note of caution: 'Vicarious liability is not on the move, at least not of its own volition. If it moves, it is by the decision of judges which must be reasoned and justified'.[106] Considering these salutary dicta, the key question for future courts will be this: Can further movement in vicarious liability be sufficiently reasoned so as to justify 'connecting cautiously' with existing precedent?

[101] *CCWS* (n 41).
[102] Including the statement of Charleton J in *Hickey* (n 5) [99] that '[i]n any defendable analysis of a relationship based on control giving rise to vicarious liability, the distinction between a contract of service and a contract for services must not be blurred'.
[103] *Mohamud* (n 20).
[104] *Morrisons* (n 19).
[105] *Hickey* (n 5).
[106] ibid [43] per O'Donnell J.

6

Enterprise Risk and Vicarious Liability in Singapore

DAVID TAN

I. Introduction

It has been said that limited liability is 'the corporation's most precious characteristic'[1] and that the desire to avoid liability has determined the shape of the modern business organisation.[2] At the same time, businesses in the twenty-first century are increasingly relying on call centres, online third-party sellers, sales agents, brokers, ride-sharing contract drivers, debt collectors, delivery services and many other external providers that may harm third parties. The expanding scope of vicarious liability to meet the changes in the structure of work organisations of modern industry has seen a concerted movement away from the traditional justifications of effective compensation and deterrence towards the enterprise risk argument as the primary policy consideration in numerous decisions handed down by the UK Supreme Court in the last decade.[3] The Court of Appeal, the highest appellate court in Singapore, has cited these decisions with approval to 'fine-tune the existing framework underlying the doctrine so as to accommodate the more diverse range of relationships which might be encountered in today's context'.[4] In a scenario where an individual is acting on behalf of an enterprise, whether a profit-maximising business or a non-profit organisation, tort law generally serves to allocate the cost of accidents amongst three parties: the enterprise, the actor/agent and the victim. While the actor/agent can be found to be personally liable to the victim in negligence or for committing an intentional tort, the victim may

[1] WW Cook, '"Watered Stock"- Commissions -"Blue Sky Laws"- Stock Without Par Value' (1921) 19 *Michigan Law Review* 583, 583.

[2] LM LoPucki, 'The Death of Liability' (1996) 106 *Yale Law Journal* 1, 4.

[3] eg *Barclays Bank plc v Various Claimants* [2020] UKSC 13, [2020] AC 973 (*Barclays Bank*); *Cox v Ministry of Justice* [2016] UKSC 10, [2016] AC 660 (*Cox*); *Various Claimants v Catholic Child Welfare Society* [2012] UKSC 56, [2013] 2 AC 1 (*Catholic Child Welfare Society*).

[4] *Ng Huat Seng v Munib Mohammad Madni* [2017] SGCA 58, [2017] 2 SLR 1074 [63] (*Ng Huat Seng*).

not be able to recover compensation from an insolvent tortfeasor. As delegation of the performance of activities is so pervasive in modern organisational relationships, it is pertinent to develop a set of efficient rules for the law of vicarious liability to better increase social welfare outcomes and to manage actor/agent risk-taking.

When examining whether vicarious liability should be imposed on party A for the acts of party B, courts typically follow a two-stage inquiry. Stage 1 involves an evaluation of the relationship between A and B – whether they were in an actual or deemed employer-employee relationship. Stage 2 considers whether the tortious act of B was within the scope of employment. The expansionary phase of vicarious liability beyond the traditional strictures of an employer-employee relationship began in the early 2010s as the English courts fell under social pressure to provide redress to victims of sexual abuse that happened in educational institutions and religious organisations. In 2012, the UK Supreme Court in *Various Claimants v Catholic Child Welfare Society* declared a more flexible approach to Stages 1 and 2 of the test, and held that: (i) the relationship that could properly give rise to vicarious liability need not be one of a formal employment contract so long as it was akin to the relationship between an employer and employee (Stage 1); and (ii) a close connection between the tortious act and the tortfeasor's relationship with the defendant would satisfy the scope of employment test (Stage 2).[5] This was affirmed in subsequent decisions of *Cox v Ministry of Justice*,[6] *Mohamud v WM Morrison Supermarkets plc*,[7] *Armes v Nottinghamshire County Council*,[8] *WM Morrison Supermarkets plc v Various Claimants*[9] and *Barclays Bank plc v Various Claimants*.[10] In September 2017, in a rare five-member full bench decision of the Singapore Court of Appeal in *Ng Huat Seng v Munib Mohammad Madni*, the unanimous judgment delivered by Chief Justice Sundaresh Menon considered the recent English judicial pronouncements on the law of vicarious liability and non-delegable duties, and affirmed the application of *Catholic Child Welfare Society* in Singapore law.[11] In the last decade, for negligence cases, hitherto the highest appellate court in Singapore has sat on only two occasions as a five-member bench: one dealing with the applicable standard of care for determining medical negligence in Singapore,[12] and the other on the recognition of loss of genetic affinity as recoverable damage.[13] In May 2020, the issue of vicarious liability came before the Court of Appeal again, but the claims against the defendants were time-barred, and

[5] *Catholic Child Welfare Society* (n 3).
[6] *Cox* (n 3).
[7] *Mohamud v WM Morrison Supermarkets plc* [2016] UKSC 11, [2016] AC 677 (*Mohamud*).
[8] *Armes v Nottinghamshire County Council* [2017] UKSC 60, [2018] AC 355.
[9] *WM Morrison Supermarkets plc v Various Claimants* [2020] UKSC 12, [2020] AC 989 (*Morrisons*).
[10] n 3.
[11] *Ng Huat Seng* (n 4) [61]–[66].
[12] *Hii Chii Kok v Ooi Peng Jin London Lucien* [2017] SGCA 38, [2017] 2 SLR 492.
[13] *ACB v Thomson Medical Pte Ltd* [2017] SGCA 20.

the court did not consider it necessary to deal with the issue.[14] It should also be noted that in 2020, the UK Supreme Court in its unanimous decision in *Barclays Bank*, cited *Ng Huat Seng* as affirming contemporary English jurisprudence that 'the classic distinction between employment and relationships akin to or analogous to employment, on the one hand, and the relationship with an independent contractor, on the other hand, has [not] been eroded', and that the English decisions 'did not present a new analytical framework'.[15]

From the onset, vicarious liability is 'at odds with the general approach of the common law' by deviating from fault as the core basis for liability.[16] There still appears to be no unanimity between judges and academics about the rationale behind vicarious liability, as Glanville Williams foreshadows in an earlier comment that vicarious liability is 'the creation of many judges who have different ideas of its justification or social policy, or no idea at all'.[17] More than two decades ago, the House of Lords has commented that it was 'not useful to explore the historical origins of the vicarious liability of an employer in the hope of finding guidance in the principles of its modern application';[18] instead judges have resorted to overt policy considerations to resolve the complex issues before them. The extension of the close connection test in Stage 2 of the vicarious liability test by the House of Lords in *Lister v Hesley Hall* in 2002 had already attracted its fair share of criticism – in particular by academic commentators who insist on doctrinal purity and a strict adherence to the Salmond formulation.[19] On the other hand, the *Lister* test – at least the version propounded by Lord Steyn – has been hailed as 'an intellectually satisfying and practical criterion'[20] by the Singapore Court of Appeal and has been consistently applied across many cases throughout the Commonwealth, including Singapore, involving intentional torts.[21] While courts have not jettisoned the longstanding principle that an employer may be vicariously

[14] *IPP Financial Advisers Pte Ltd v Saimee bin Jumaat* [2020] SGCA 47, [2020] 2 SLR 272 [104].

[15] *Barclays Bank* (n 3) [24] and [26].

[16] *Majrowski v Guy's and St Thomas's NHS Trust* [2006] UKHL 34, [2007] 1 AC 224 [8] (Lord Nicholls). See also P Giliker, *Vicarious Liability in Tort: A Comparative Perspective* (Cambridge, Cambridge University Press, 2010) 2.

[17] G Williams, 'Vicarious Liability and the Master's Indemnity' (1957) 20 *MLR* 220, 231.

[18] *Lister v Hesley Hall Ltd* [2001] UKHL 22, [2002] 1 AC 215 [34] (*Lister*) (per Lord Clyde).

[19] eg C McIvor, 'The Use and Abuse of the Doctrine of Vicarious Liability' (2006) 35 *Common Law World Review* 268.

[20] *Skandinaviska Enskilda Banken AB v Asia Pacific Breweries (Singapore) Pte Ltd* [2011] SGCA 22, [2011] 3 SLR 540 [75] (Skandinaviska). See also *Ming An Insurance Co (HK) Ltd v Ritz-Carlton Ltd* [2002] 3 HKLRD 844 [19] (Ming An). The courts in Singapore do not appear to refer to *Lister* in cases involving negligence. It is worth noting that the Singapore courts are not particularly deferential toward the decisions of the UK Supreme Court or the House of Lords. The Court of Appeal has previously rejected the assumption of responsibility test for duty of care cases involving pure economic loss: *Anwar Patrick Adrian v Ng Chong & Hue LLC* [2014] SGCA 34; [2014] 3 SLR 761. But it would independently assess the merits of a particular approach and has adopted the English Woodland test (discussed by Giliker in chapter three of this volume) for the evaluation of the existence of a non-delegable duty of care: *Ng Huat Seng* (n 4).

[21] eg *Ming An* (n 20); *Bernard v Attorney-General of Jamaica* [2004] UKPC 47; *Mattis v Pollock (trading as Flamingos Nightclub)* [2003] EWCA Civ 887, [2003] 1 WLR 2158.

liable for the tortious act of an employee but not for the acts of an independent contractor – this was adamantly insisted upon by the Singapore Court of Appeal in *Ng Huat Seng* – there is a discernible trend of a liberal application of the close connection test to situations involving religious ministers and boarding school wardens sexually abusing minors. Undoubtedly, as Lord Phillips stated in *Catholic Child Welfare Society*, '[t]he law of vicarious liability is on the move',[22] and it is no surprise that this expansionary move in the English decisions post-*Catholic Child Welfare Society* have come under significant academic scrutiny.[23] Even Lady Hale in *Barclays Bank* acknowledged this as her Ladyship noted that the *Barclays Bank* decision as well as *Morrisons* was about 'how far that move can take it'.[24]

This chapter argues that the law of vicarious liability must evolve to meet the exigencies of the contemporary work arrangements in the gig economy that include outsourcing and part-time contracts. Section II considers how the Singapore Court of Appeal in 2011 has gravitated towards an overarching rationale of 'enterprise risk' in *Skandinaviska Enskilda Banken AB v Asia Pacific Breweries (Singapore) Pte Ltd*. Section III evaluates how the Court of Appeal in 2017 has more explicitly endorsed the English developments on vicarious liability and in a manner that is consistent with the *Skandinaviska* approach. Section IV suggests that a more explicit articulation of the paradigm of 'internalising externalities' can assist courts in deciding the appropriate legal responsibility to be assigned to entities – whether profit-maximising companies, volunteer organisations or religious bodies – that benefit from carrying on an enterprise that necessarily creates or significantly enhances risks to others.

II. The Genesis of the 'Enterprise Risk' Approach: *Skandinaviska Enskilda Banken AB v Asia Pacific Breweries (S) Pte Ltd*

Vicarious liability is not a tort, yet it lies within the province of all common law systems of tort law. It has been recognised for centuries as a rule of responsibility which obliges the defendant to be liable for the torts committed by another party even though the defendant is not personally at fault. Vicarious liability derived originally from mediaeval notions of headship of a household, including wives and servants; their status in law was absorbed into that of the master. It has been

[22] *Catholic Child Welfare Society* (n 3) [19].

[23] eg, D Nolan, 'Reining in Vicarious Liability' (2020) 49 *Industrial Law Journal* 609; P Morgan, 'Vicarious Liability and the Beautiful Game – Liability for Professional and Amateur Footballers?' (2018) 38 *Legal Studies* 242; P Giliker, 'Analysing Institutional Liability for Child Sexual Abuse in England and Wales and Australia: Vicarious Liability, Non-Delegable Duties and Statutory Intervention' (2018) 77 *CLJ* 506; A Silink and D Ryan, 'Vicarious Liability for Independent Contractors' (2018) 77 *CLJ* 458.

[24] *Morrisons* (n 9) [1].

spoken of in the archaic terms of master/servant and *respondeat superior* and discussed in the modern language of employer/employee/independent contractor. Liability is imposed on the defendant not because the defendant was found to be at fault, but as a result of the defendant's relationship with the *tortfeasor* rather than the victim. Vicarious liability runs counter to the notions of corrective justice and individual responsibility that underpin much of tort law, yet it is fast becoming the first port of call for judges anxious to find someone to bear the burden of paying compensation.

In 2011, Chief Justice Chan Sek Keong delivering the judgment for the Court of Appeal in *Skandinaviska Enskilda Banken AB v Asia Pacific Breweries (S) Pte Ltd*, endorsed the approach taken by the Supreme Court of Canada where McLachlin CJ restated the rationale of vicarious liability as follows:

> Vicarious liability is based on the rationale that the person who puts a risky enterprise into the community may fairly be held responsible when those risks emerge and cause loss or injury to members of the public. Effective compensation is a goal. Deterrence is also a consideration. The hope is that holding the employer or principal liable will encourage such persons to take steps to reduce the risk of harm in the future.[25]

But the confidence of two Chief Justices in their pronouncements is not so widely shared. Courts and academic commentators have often lamented about the enigmatic nature of the law of vicarious liability. No one denies the existence of the doctrine, but its multifarious policy objectives and the scope of its application are notoriously unclear. Giliker astutely notes that

> vicarious liability rests at the heart of the modern law of tort, despite its status quo as a cuckoo in the nest of corrective justice. It provides a solvent target for claims and, supported by the defendant's ability to insure or self-insure, is perceived as a means by which everyday risk may be spread within various sectors of society.[26]

While it might not be possible to identify a singular overarching policy objective, there is consensus that generally, when determining whether vicarious liability should be imposed on party A for the acts of party B, courts follow a two-stage inquiry. Stage 1 entails an analysis of the relationship between A and B – whether they were in an actual or deemed employer-employee to which vicarious liability may attach.[27] Independent contractors – that is, those performing work under a contract for service – may be nonetheless held to be in a *deemed* employment relationship *if* an enterprise exercised adequate control over the method

[25] *Skandinaviska* (n 20) [70] (citing *Roman Catholic Episcopal Corporation of St George's v John Doe (a pseudonym) and John Doe (a pseudonym)* [2004] 1 SCR 436 [20] (*John Doe v Bennett*)) (emphasis added). The Singapore Court of Appeal has frequently referred to a number of Canadian decisions in the area of tort law, especially in duty of care jurisprudence: eg *See Toh Siew Kee v Ho Ah Lam Ferrocement (Pte) Ltd* [2013] 3 SLR 284; *Ngiam Kong Seng v Lim Chiew Hock* [2008] 3 SLR(R) 674.

[26] Giliker (n 16) 19.

[27] *Mersey Docks & Harbour Board v Coggins & Griffith (Liverpool) Ltd* [1947] AC 1 (*Mersey Docks*); *Hawley v Luminar Leisure Ltd* [2006] EWCA Civ 18 (*Hawley*).

of performance of tasks and, in certain circumstances, if the tortfeasor was additionally presented to the public as an 'emanation' of the enterprise;[28] otherwise, the independent contractor defence applies.[29] Stage 2 determines the scope of the employer's or deemed employer's liability, and requires that the wrongful act be committed in the course of employment. Commonwealth common law courts have traditionally applied the Salmond test:

> A master is not responsible for a wrongful act done by his servant unless it is done in the course of [the servant's] employment. It is deemed to be so done if it is either (1) a wrongful act authorised by the master, or (2) a wrongful and unauthorised mode of doing some act authorised by the master.[30]

However, there is arguably a third limb as Salmond himself intimated: 'a master … is liable even for acts which he has not authorised, provided they are so connected with acts he was authorised, that they might be rightly regarded as modes – although improper modes – of doing them'.[31] This explanation forms the basis of the 'close connection' test presently applied by the UK Supreme Court,[32] the Supreme Court of Canada[33] and the Singapore Court of Appeal.[34]

Skandinaviska was a case concerned with Stage 2 and the ambit of the close connection test. Chief Justice Chan observed that the close connection test which imposes vicarious liability only when it would be fair and just to do so requires the court to 'openly confront the question of whether liability should lie against the employer, rather than obscuring the decision beneath semantic discussions of "scope of employment" and "mode of conduct"'.[35] In *Skandinaviska*, an elaborate fraud was perpetrated by an employee of Asia Pacific Breweries ('APB') over a period of more than four years against two claimant banks, where it was unanimously held on the facts that APB was not vicariously liable to the banks for the fraud as the financial institutions had failed to take reasonable precautions. Nevertheless, the Court of Appeal agreed that the applicable test for determining whether vicarious liability should be imposed on an employer for torts committed by an employee during an unauthorised course of conduct was the 'close connection' test,[36] and the application of this test should be guided by the

[28] *Hollis v Vabu* [2001] HCA 44, (2001) 207 CLR 21, 42.

[29] While technically this is not a 'defence', but a rule or principle, the courts in Singapore have explicitly referred to the 'independent contractor defence' where assessing Stage 1, eg *Lim Seng Chye v Pex International Pte Ltd* [2019] SGHC 28 [47]–[55].

[30] RFV Heuston and RA Buckley, *Salmond and Heuston on the Law of Torts* 21st edn (London, Sweet & Maxwell, 1996) 443. The test first enunciated in JW Salmond, *The Law of Torts* (London, Stevens & Haynes, 1907) 83. See also *Lister* (n 18) [15] (Lord Steyn).

[31] Salmond ibid 83–84.

[32] eg *Lister* (n 18); *Dubai Aluminium Co Ltd v Salaam* [2002] UKHL 48; *Catholic Child Welfare Society* (n 3); *Mohamud* (n 7).

[33] eg *Bazley v Curry* [1999] 2 SCR 534; *Jacobi v Griffiths* [1999] 2 SCR 570; *EB v Order of the Oblates of Mary Immaculate in the Province of British Columbia* [2005] 3 SCR 45.

[34] *Skandinaviska* (n 20).

[35] ibid [75] (citing *Bazley* (n 33) [41]).

[36] ibid [75].

rationale that 'a person who employs another to advance his own interests and thereby creates a *risk* of his employee committing a tort should bear responsibility for any adverse consequences resulting therefrom'.[37]

Chief Justice Chan emphasised that the policy consideration of deterrence from future harm

> which is aimed at promoting efficiency in business enterprises through deterrence, is a legitimate one. However, like victim compensation, it rests on the fundamental premise that the employer is best placed, relative to everybody else, to manage the risks of his business enterprise and prevent wrongdoing from occurring.[38]

In this respect, the Court of Appeal's judgment in *Skandinaviska* provides a solid basis for courts in Singapore to incorporate an overarching 'enterprise risk' framework into the tests applied at Stages 1 and 2 of the vicarious liability analysis. Chan CJ unequivocally approved of a two-prong approach to examining whether a close connection existed for the purposes of imposing vicarious liability on an employer for the intentional wrongdoing for an employee: first, the court should consider the factual matrix by applying the five factors proposed by McLachlin J in *Bazley*;[39] and second, policy considerations of effective victim compensation and deterrence of future harm in the light of better management of enterprise risks should guide the court's determination of whether it would ultimately be fair and just to impose vicarious liability.[40] The *Bazley* factors, relevant in determining whether the requisite degree of connection exists in a particular case, include: (a) the opportunity that the enterprise afforded the employee to abuse his or her power; (b) the extent to which the wrongful act may have furthered the employer's aims (and hence be more likely to have been committed by the employee); (c) the extent to which the wrongful act was related to friction, confrontation or intimacy inherent in the employer's enterprise; (d) the extent of power conferred on the employee in relation to the victim; (e) the vulnerability of potential victims to wrongful exercise of the employee's power.[41]

III. The Affirmation of the 'Enterprise Risk' Approach: *Ng Huat Seng v Munib Mohammad Madni*

In *Ng Huat Seng*, the parties owned neighbouring residential properties that were located along a slope. The appellants' house was the lower property: the ground level of their house was two metres lower than the ground level of the respondents' house, which lay further up the slope. The properties were separated by a boundary

[37] ibid [77] (emphasis added).
[38] ibid [70].
[39] ibid [87]–[88]; [95].
[40] ibid [77]–[83]; [92]–[93].
[41] *Bazley* (n 33) [41].

wall located on the boundary between the two plots. The respondents purchased their property in 2010 intending to demolish the existing house there and build another in its place. They appointed Esthetix Design as the main contractor on a turnkey basis to carry out the required demolition, design and reconstruction works. The main contractor was responsible for engaging other subcontractors and applying for necessary approvals to complete the works. On 5 September 2011, while demolition works were taking place on the respondents' property, some debris from the respondents' property fell onto the boundary wall and damaged it. Some of the debris also ricocheted off the boundary wall and caused damage to the appellants' property, including damage to windowpanes and air-conditioning condensing units. In 2012, the appellants commenced proceeding in negligence, and argued inter alia that the respondents were vicariously liable for the negligence of Esthetix, and alternatively, if the independent contractor defence applied, the demolition works were ultra-hazardous activities and respondents therefore owed a personal non-delegable duty to ensure that reasonable care was taken in the performance of the demolition works.

A. Vicarious Liability

On the Stage 1 issue, Chief Justice Menon held that:

> while we accept that the *Christian Brothers* case and *Cox* recognise that the doctrine of vicarious liability can be applied outside the strict confines of an employment relationship, it becomes evident … that their essential contribution was to fine-tune the existing framework underlying the doctrine so as to accommodate the more diverse range of relationships which might be encountered in today's context.[42]

The Court of Appeal noted that, at its core, these relationships must be sufficiently close relationships 'akin to employment' and possess the same fundamental qualities as those which inhere in employer-employee relationships. What this means is an affirmation of jettisoning a formalist approach to the definition of an employee, and the acknowledgment that a worker can be classified as an 'employee' solely for the purposes of vicarious liability. The court emphasised that these cases do not suggest that 'vicarious liability can be imposed on a defendant for the lapses committed by a person who was engaged as an *independent contractor*'.[43] It simply would not be fair, just and reasonable to hold a defendant liable for the acts by a *true* independent contractor, who, by definition, is not furthering the defendant's enterprise, but engaged in his or her own enterprise. Hence it was clear that the notion of 'akin to employment' clarifies or supplements the employee/independent contractor distinction and does not supersede it.

[42] *Ng Huat Seng* (n 4) [66].
[43] ibid [64] (emphasis in original).

Menon CJ emphasised that the focus of Stage 1 is on finding the existence of a 'special relationship' between the defendant and the tortfeasor, and 'whatever might be the nature of that special relationship, its very antithesis is a relationship under which the tortfeasor is engaged by the defendant as an independent contractor'.[44] In this regard, the five factors or criteria listed by Lord Phillips in *Catholic Child Welfare Society* would help to guide the Singapore courts in determining *the types of relationships* within which it would be fair, just and reasonable to impose vicarious liability.[45] If the defendant and the tortfeasor were not bound by an employment contract but their relationship had these same incidents, then that relationship properly be characterised as being akin to the relationship between an employer and employee:

(a) the employer would be more likely than the employee to have the means to compensate the victim and could be expected to have insured itself against that liability;
(b) the tort would have been committed as a result of activity undertaken by the employee on behalf of the employer;
(c) the employee's activity would likely be part of the business activity of the employer;
(d) the employer, by employing the employee to carry out the activity, would have created the risk of the tort being committed by the latter; and
(e) the employee would, to a greater or lesser degree, have been under the control of the employer at the time the tort was committed.[46]

Under the *Ng Huat Seng* approach, it appears that the element of control has been assigned a less important role than in previous case law in Singapore; it is now one of five factors to be considered. Indeed, control may not be wholly determinative in determining the existence of an employer/employee relationship for the purposes of imposing vicarious liability, but on some of the present authorities the question of control appears to be at the crux of the test to be applied. In *Awang bin Dollah v Shun Shing Construction & Engineering Co Ltd*, the Singapore Court of Appeal in 1997 recognised that in cases dealing with employer's vicarious liability for damage caused by a tortfeasor to a third party,

> an 'employer' in such a case means not only the party who actually employs the employee, but also the one who at the material time exercises or has the right to exercise control over the employee in respect of the work he was engaged to perform, notwithstanding that there is no contract of employment between him and the party who exercises or has the right to exercise control.[47]

It was clear from the unanimous decision in *Awang bin Dollah* that, in Singapore law, one may be held vicariously liable for the torts committed by one engaged

[44] ibid [42].
[45] ibid [62].
[46] ibid [54] (referring to *Catholic Child Welfare Society* (n 3) [35]).
[47] *Awang bin Dollah v Shun Shing Construction & Engineering Co Ltd* [1997] 3 SLR 677 [19].

under a contract for services (as opposed to a contract for employment), as indicated by LP Thean JA:

> where the workman is not employed by the main contractor but by a sub-contractor, the main contractor may be liable as the 'employer' of the workman, if he exercises or has the right to exercise control over the workman in respect of the work upon which he was engaged to perform.[48]

This decision was not mentioned in *Ng Huat Seng*. However, in a 2021 decision by the Singapore High Court, the intermediate appellate court, in *Munshi Mohammad Faiz v Interpro Construction Pte Ltd*, applied *Ng Huat Seng* in coming to the conclusion that Singapore law recognised dual vicarious liability in a 'borrowed employee' situation,[49] invoking four rationales in its reasoning – effective victim compensation, deterrence, enterprise liability and loss distribution.[50] The court also referred to the Canadian authority of *Blackwater v Plint* where the Canadian Supreme Court held that both the Government of Canada and the United Church of Canada were jointly vicariously liable for the wrongful acts of the supervisor.[51] Hence under Singapore law, for Stage 1, where more than one defendant can satisfy the special relationship test articulated in *Ng Huat Seng*, dual or joint vicarious liability may be imposed; in some situations, the courts still continue to apply a more traditional control test as articulated in *Mersey Docks*.[52]

Stage 2 is concerned with determining 'whether there is a sufficient connection between the relationship between the defendant and the tortfeasor on the one hand, and the commission of the tort on the other'.[53] The 'scope of employment' limitation is often viewed as a proxy for enterprise causation. In *Catholic Child Welfare Society*, Lord Phillips had focused on the finding of a strong causative link in establishing a close connection and had cautioned that the creation of risk was not enough, of itself, to give rise to vicarious liability. Menon CJ concurred, and highlighted that in addition to the special relationship between the tortfeasor and the defendant: 'the defendant must in some way have *created or significantly enhanced, by virtue of that relationship, the very risk that in fact materialised* in order to be held vicariously liable for the tortfeasor's wrongful acts'.[54]

[48] ibid [20]. This is essentially the test articulated by the House of Lords in *Mersey Docks* (n 27). The test was affirmed by the Singapore Court of Appeal in 2014, although the court also commented that the control test is neither the only test applicable nor even necessarily the decisive factor. See *BNM (administratrix of the estate of B. deceased) v National University of Singapore* [2014] 4 SLR 931 [24], [28]–[29].

[49] *Munshi Mohammad Faiz v Interpro Construction Pte Ltd* [2021] SGHC 26 [63]–[64] (*Munshi*). As a matter of authority, this issue has not been expressly decided by the Singapore Court of Appeal, but there was a High Court case accepting that it was permissible under Singapore law. *Chen Qiangshi v Hong Fei CDY Construction Pte Ltd* [2014] SGHC 177 [197]–[198], [201]–[202].

[50] *Munshi* (n 49) [64]. The court also referred to the Canadian authority of *Blackwater v Plint* [2005] 3 SCR 3 where the Canadian Supreme Court held that both the Government of Canada and the United Church of Canada were jointly vicariously liable for the wrongful acts of the supervisor.

[51] *Munshi* (n 49) [66] (citing *Blackwater* (n 50) [36]–[38]).

[52] eg *Lim Seng Chye v Pex International Pte Ltd* [2019] SGHC 28 [50]–[54].

[53] *Ng Huat Seng* (n 4) [44].

[54] ibid [66] (emphasis added).

On the facts of *Ng Huat Seng*, Esthetix Design was clearly an independent contractor and could not be deemed to be in a relationship akin to employment to be brought within the ambit of vicarious liability. The court concluded that an independent contractor relationship will generally exclude the application of the doctrine *and* that the defendant must, pursuant to its relationship with the tortfeasor, either have created or significantly increased the risk of harm that ensued. This was a similar finding by the UK Supreme Court in *Barclays Bank* that the doctor who sexually assaulted the prospective employees during their medical examinations was 'in business on his own account';[55] the Supreme Court also cited *Ng Huat Seng*'s statement of the independent contractor rule with approval.[56]

This enterprise risk approach to vicarious liability in *Ng Huat Seng* was earlier articulated by the Singapore Court of Appeal in *Skandinaviska*. This '*Skandinaviska* risk paradigm' – that the person who runs an enterprise, and who obtains a benefit from appointing other individuals to conduct activities connected to the enterprise, should bear the external risks that emanate from this enterprise – was argued to be applicable to both Stages 1 and 2. It finds support in the bulk of case law despite courts generally being reluctant to refer more explicitly to risks for fear of slipping into the domain of law and economics.[57]

B. Non-Delegable Duty

In contrast, the non-delegable duty issue was more complicated and problematic. The court in *Ng Huat Seng* observed that a cardinal rule in the tort of negligence was that a person would generally be held liable only for that person's *own* carelessness, and *not* for the carelessness of others; however there were two 'derogations' from the fault-based principle: vicarious liability and non-delegable duty. Menon CJ noted that the doctrine of non-delegable duties imposed on a defendant a duty that 'extend[ed] beyond being careful, to procuring the careful performance of work delegated to others'.[58] Unlike vicarious liability which imposes secondary liability on a party based on its relationship with the tortfeasor, a party subject to a non-delegable duty would be held *personally* liable in tort even if he had non-negligently delegated the performance of certain tasks to an independent contractor who had then been negligent in performing those tasks. The court affirmed its earlier decision in *MCST Plan No 3322 v Tiong Aik Construction Pte Ltd*,[59] which applied a two-stage test for determining whether a non-delegable

[55] *Barclays Bank* (n 10) [27].

[56] ibid [26].

[57] D Tan, 'Internalising Externalities: An Enterprise Risk Approach to Vicarious Liability in the 21st Century' (2015) 27 *Singapore Academy of Law Journal* 822, 841–42.

[58] *Ng Huat Seng* (n 4) [80] (citing *Woodland v Essex CC* [2013] UKSC 66, [2014] AC 537 [5] (*Woodland*)).

[59] *MCST Plan No 3322 v Tiong Aik Construction Pte Ltd* [2016] SGCA 40, [2016] 4 SLR 521.

duty would arise on a given set of facts, that is, the claimant would have to satisfy the threshold requirement in the first stage that: (a) *either* the claimant's case fell within one of the established or recognised categories of non-delegable duties; *or* (b) that case possessed all of the five defining features outlined by Lord Sumption in *Woodland*.[60] Then at the second stage, the court would additionally take into account the fairness and reasonableness of imposing a non-delegable duty of care on the defendant in the particular circumstances of the case, as well as the relevant policy considerations in the local context of Singapore. Menon CJ emphasised that non-delegable duties should remain 'exceptional' because: 'in many instances, it would be unrealistic or even impossible for the duty-bearer to fulfil the non-delegable duty in question, and this could lead to very artificial outcomes'.[61]

In *Ng Huat Seng*, the Court of Appeal did not venture to consider whether this strict liability approach to both vicarious liability and non-delegable duties – that the defendant would be liable for the acts of a tortfeasor without the need for the claimant to prove fault on the part of a defendant – was desirable, fair, just or reasonable. A later decision on non-delegable duty in a lower court was related to analysing whether the doctrine of ultra-hazardous acts was a part of Singapore law, and even though the five defining *Woodland* features were discussed, there are still many lingering questions in terms of its application to a panoply of scenarios.[62] Take for example, in the context of educational institutions, when one accepts that an educational authority or school owes a non-delegable duty for the pupils' physical safety as an established category, does the age of the pupil – and correspondingly the degree of control and vulnerability – make a difference? Is it fair, just and reasonable to hold a university or secondary school to the high standard of care commensurate with a non-delegable duty in the same manner we would readily accept for children in primary schools and kindergartens? To what extent should a school assign its academic educators to supervise competently appointed swimming instructors, rugby coaches and gymnastic teachers, who might be independent contractors possessing the requisite special skills for the specific functions?

Perhaps many of us believe that if an enterprise faces both the prospects of vicarious liability and non-delegable duty, it will be incentivised to locate and discipline potentially errant actors, and even be able to reduce tort costs through screening measures, training programs and closer monitoring. It would not be able to hide behind legal concepts like 'control', 'independent contractors' or 'in the course of employment' if it has indeed introduced risks into the community. According to Van Loo, the dominant corporate law narrative is that businesses

[60] See *Woodland* (n 58) [23].
[61] *Ng Huat Seng* (n 4) [85].
[62] *Lim Seng Chye v Pex International Pte Ltd* [2019] SGHC 28 [77]–[82].

can avoid liability by drawing organisational boundaries.[63] Witting is rightly concerned about the reality of deterrence involving large bureaucratic organisations.[64] As he points out, 'tort law's efficacy as a deterrent will depend upon who the defendants are' and '[o]rganisations and professional persons are more likely to act in rational ways and should be more easily deterred by tort rules'.[65] Ultimately, in the context of physical safety in educational institutions, sexual abuse in religious establishments and organisational liability in a healthcare system, we need to ensure that these twin legal principles operating in tandem ultimately strike an appropriate balance between public concern over protection of the young and the vulnerable and the just imposition of a financial burden on indispensable enterprises which confer significant benefits on society.

IV. 'Internalising Externalities': Extrapolating from *Skandinaviska* and *Ng Huat Seng*

A. Enterprise Risk or Enterprise Liability in Singapore

The unanimous decision of the Court of Appeal in *Ng Huat Seng* accepted that although both UK Supreme Court's decisions in *Catholic Child Welfare Society* and *Cox* recognise that 'the doctrine of vicarious liability can be applied outside the strict confines of an employment relationship', they nonetheless did not represent a radical departure from the orthodoxy that vicarious liability cannot be imposed on a defendant for the lapses committed by a tortfeasor who was engaged as an independent contractor.[66] What *Catholic Child Welfare Society* and *Cox* stood for was the provision of 'a renewed and more fine grained method for discerning the types of relationships which may give rise to vicarious liability'[67] and to accommodate the more diverse range of relationships which might be encountered in today's business realities.[68] The court did not explore the theoretical underpinnings of such a refinement further, save for a reference to Lord Phillips comments in *Catholic Child Welfare Society* being 'consistent with the approach in *Skandinaviska*'.[69] Specifically, Menon CJ approved Lord Phillips' comments as 'entirely correct':

> Vicarious liability is imposed where a defendant, whose relationship with the abuser put it in a position to use the abuser to carry on its business or to further its

[63] R Van Loo, 'The Revival of Respondeat Superior and Evolution of Gatekeeper Liability' (2020) 109 *Georgetown Law Journal* 141, 144.
[64] C Witting, 'Modelling Organisational Vicarious Liability' (2019) 39 *Legal Studies* 694.
[65] ibid 708.
[66] *Ng Huat Seng* (n 4) [64].
[67] ibid.
[68] ibid [63].
[69] ibid [66]–[67].

> own interests, *has done so in a manner which has created or significantly enhanced the risk that the victim or victims would suffer the relevant abuse. …* Creation of risk is not enough, of itself, to give rise to vicarious liability for abuse but it is always likely to be an important element in the facts that give rise to such liability.[70]

Previously in *Skandinaviska*, Chan CJ had distinguished the *rationale* of vicarious liability from the *goals or objectives* of victim compensation and deterrence. The raison d'être for vicarious liability is premised on 'efficiency': the person who runs an enterprise, and who obtains a benefit from appointing other individuals to conduct activities connected to the enterprise, should bear the external risks that emanate from this enterprise. In a 2021 decision by the Singapore High Court on the issue of imposing dual vicarious liability, Dedar Singh Gill J explicitly referred to the 'enterprise liability rationale' as '[t]hat an employer who stands to generate profits from an employee's activities ought to also bear the potential liability arising therefrom',[71] together with other rationales such as effective victim compensation, deterrence and loss distribution. This '*Skandinaviska* risk paradigm' not only holds for Stage 2, but as the author shall argue, is equally applicable to Stage 1. The term 'enterprise risk' should not be seen as a misnomer when the concept is invoked in the imposition of vicarious liability on non-profit institutions whose ability to spread losses is limited compared to profit-making enterprises. It stands for a wider proposition that *any* institution would be vicariously liable for the acts of its agents where the risk of injury could be said to be closely associated with the wrong that occurred, and it would be just, fair and reasonable that the entity that engaged in, and profited from or gained a non-economic benefit from, particular activities should internalise the full cost of operations, including potential torts.[72] In this regard, the Singapore courts appear to be more willing to consider a more overarching consideration of enterprise risk, which is sometimes referred to as 'enterprise liability' in the local decisions.

The benefit does not have to be financial in nature and can be anything of value to an organisation. In this regard, Witting is especially critical. He appreciates that *Catholic Child Welfare Society* represents the embrace of normatively important features of organisational vicarious liability that reflects the transition to a corporatised and bureaucratic world characterised by collective action, continuous planning and economies of scale where there is significant devolved decision-making, increased exercise of discretion in numerous functions, and sharing of tasks by workers.[73] Witting argues that while recent case law constructs a model of the 'deterrable organisation', the conclusion is that 'although organisations

[70] ibid [66] (citing *Catholic Child Welfare Society* (n 3) [86]–[87]) (emphasis in original).

[71] *Munshi* (n 49) [64].

[72] See also S Deakin, '"Enterprise-Risk": The Juridical Nature of the Firm Revisited' (2003) 32 *Industrial Law Journal* 97. However, Morgan has been especially critical, arguing that this form of enterprise liability suffers from the substantial flaws of being inapplicable to non-profit employers, and of actually tolerating employee wrongdoing. P Morgan, 'Recasting Vicarious Liability' (2012) 71 *CLJ* 615.

[73] Witting (n 64) 697.

are deterrable, there will be insufficient deterrence unless steps are taken to reinforce the operation of the model by a more targeted use of powers to award remedies'.[74]

While deterrence has been touted as an objective of the law of vicarious liability, Chan CJ argued that while this may hold true in many negligence scenarios,

> [i]n yet other cases, the type of tort that occurs is, realistically speaking, uncontrollable and, therefore, not amenable to deterrence. This is particularly relevant to torts committed in the course of excessively risky business enterprises, spur-of-the-moment torts and intentional torts. In such situations, it may well be possible to find that the employer has done all that is reasonable to deter the tort and yet has failed to prevent the commission of the tort. In such situations, deterrence as a justification for imposing vicarious liability loses much of its force.[75]

B. Enterprise Risk Elsewhere

The *Skandinaviska* risk paradigm finds support in the bulk of case law in Commonwealth common law jurisdictions despite courts generally being reluctant to refer more explicitly to risks for fear of slipping into the domain of law and economics. The impenetrable code of 'just, fair and reasonable' has often been used by English courts to allow for a covert consideration of whether an enterprise should internalise the risks that it has created. Earlier cases like *Morris v C W Martin & Sons Ltd*[76] demonstrate that where an employer undertakes the care of a client's property and entrusts the task to an employee who steals the property, the employer is vicariously liable. It can also be viewed from the perspective that the risk of theft by an employee is inherent in a business which involves (and benefits from) entrusting the custody of a customer's property to employees, and when this risk eventuates, the owner of the business should bear the consequences. Similarly, where the activities of businesses involve engaging individuals to deliver goods, decisions like *Ilkiw v Samuels*[77] and *Rose v Plenty*[78] show a finding

[74] ibid 695.

[75] *Skandinaviska* (n 20) [80].

[76] *Morris v C W Martin & Sons Ltd* [1966] 1 QB 716 (a firm of cleaners was held vicariously liable to a customer whose fur was stolen by one of its employees). See also *Port Swettenham Authority v T W Wu & Co (M) Sdn Bhd* [1979] AC 580 (Privy Council).

[77] *Ilkiw v Samuels* [1963] 1 WLR 991. A lorry driver was given strict instructions by his employers not to allow anyone else to drive the lorry. He allowed a third party, who was incompetent, to drive it without making any inquiry into his competence to do so. Under the second limb of the Salmond test (Stage 2), the court found that the driver was employed not only to drive, but to be in charge of the lorry as his employer's representative. The employers were held vicariously liable for the resulting accident.

[78] *Rose v Plenty* [1976] 1 WLR 141. A milk roundsman, despite strict instructions not to do so, asked a boy to help him deliver milk and let him accompany him on his float. This was clearly an unauthorised act, but the court held that it nevertheless was done in the course of delivering milk. The employer was held liable for injuries sustained by the boy when he fell off the float as a result of the roundsman's negligent driving.

of vicarious liability through an almost tortured interpretation of Stage 2 when courts have refused to openly discuss how these businesses have created risks to the community. On the other hand, Lord Nicholls in *Dubai Aluminium Co Ltd v Salaam*, explicitly states that:

> The underlying legal policy is based on the recognition that carrying on a business enterprise involves risk to others. It involves the risk that others will be harmed by wrongful acts committed by the agents through whom the business is carried on. When those risks ripen into loss, it is just that the business should be responsible for compensating the person who has been wronged.[79]

In *Hollis v Vabu*, the joint judgment of Gleeson CJ, Gaudron, Gummow, Kirby & Hayne JJ of the High Court of Australia acknowledged that all employees and independent contractors perform work for the benefit of their employers and principals respectively, but this, by itself, cannot be a sufficient indication that this person is an employee.[80] The Court referred with approval to McLachlin J's judgment in *Bazley v Curry*, who held that 'where the employee's conduct is closely tied to a risk that the employer's enterprise has placed in the community, the employer may justly be held vicariously liable for the employee's wrong'.[81]

In *Darling Island Stevedoring and Lighterage Co Ltd v Long*, Fullagar J expressed the view that the modern doctrine respecting the liability of an employer for the torts of an employee was adopted not by way of an exercise in analytical jurisprudence but as a matter of policy.[82] Lord Millett in *Lister* cited Fleming with approval, noting that vicarious liability has its basis in a combination of policy reasons and:

> Most important of these is the belief that a person who employs others to advance his own economic interest should in fairness be placed under a corresponding liability for losses incurred in the course of the enterprise.[83]

His Lordship also approved of Atiyah's observations that '[t]he master ought to be liable for all those torts which can fairly be regarded as reasonably incidental risks to the type of business he carries on'.[84]

As the most ardent supporter of adopting the enterprise risk framework for the law of vicarious liability, Lord Millett argues that if the employer-defendant's objectives cannot be achieved without a 'serious risk' of the employee-tortfeasor committing the kind of wrong which he has in fact committed, the employer ought to be liable. Moreover, the fact that his employment gave the tortfeasor the opportunity to commit the wrong is not enough to make the employer liable.

[79] *Dubai Aluminium Co Ltd v Salaam* [2002] UKHL 48, [2003] 2 AC 366 [21].
[80] *Hollis* (n 28) [40].
[81] ibid [42] (quoting *Bazley* (n 33) 548–49).
[82] *Darling Island Stevedoring and Lighterage Co Ltd v Long* [1957] HCA 26, (1957) 97 CLR 36, 56–57.
[83] *Lister* (n 18) [65] (quoting JG Fleming, *The Law of Torts* 9th edn (Sydney, LBC Information Services, 1998) 410).
[84] ibid [65] (quoting PS Atiyah, *Vicarious Liability in the Law of Torts* (London, Butterworths, 1967) 171).

The owner of the enterprise (or 'employer') is 'liable only if the risk is one which experience shows is inherent in the nature of the business'.[85]

In the context of the United States, Kraakman notes that the fundamental economic analysis of vicarious liability, developed with the aid of principal-agent models, looks to the insolvency of agents and to limitations on the ability of the parties to shift liability as the basic conditions favouring vicarious liability.[86] Most prominently, American scholars like Kornhauser,[87] Sykes[88] and Shavell[89] agree that vicarious liability for ordinary torts is more likely to increase social welfare, and to be efficient because employers/principals have greater ability to monitor or otherwise exert more control over actors/agents who perform activities that confer a benefit on the enterprise. In the early 1980s, Sykes argues that 'vicarious liability may lower social marginal costs by increasing the incentives for loss avoidance'[90] and it 'eliminates the incentives for inefficient expansion when agents are potentially insolvent by forcing enterprises to bear the full costs of their activities'.[91] Moreover, vicarious liability 'may lead to the employment of more … responsible agents with an attendant increase in loss-avoidance effort'.[92] Engaging in a similar analysis, Kornhauser concludes that:

> shifting from agent to enterprise liability will lead to a greater level of care if first, the principal can affect the probability of injury by her arrangement of the work environment; second, the principal may, at some cost, screen agents on the basis of carefulness; or third, the principal can identify the causally responsible agent more readily than courts can. In each of these three cases, the shift to enterprise liability will lead to a decrease in the number of injuries.[93]

This economic analysis approach to enterprise risk is not without its carefully delineated boundaries. According to a more recent analysis by Sharkey,

> Applying Sykes's notion of enterprise causation ensures that each business 'bears the incremental social costs associated with its operation.' Furthermore, it demonstrates

[85] ibid [65]. Indeed, Lord Millett emphasised this later in his judgment: 'In the present case the warden's duties provided him with the opportunity to commit indecent assaults on the boys for his own sexual gratification, *but that in itself is not enough to make the school liable*. The same would be true of the groundsman or the school porter': ibid [82] (emphasis added).

[86] RH Kraakman, '3400 Vicarious and Corporate Civil Liability' in B Bouckaert and G De Geest (eds), *Encyclopedia of Law and Economics: Volume II* (Cheltenham, Edward Elgar, 2000) 669, 670. The term 'agent' is used here to broadly represent all actors who perform functions for the enterprise under myriad work arrangements.

[87] LA Kornhauser, 'An Economic Analysis of the Choice between Enterprise and Personal Liability for Accidents' (1982) 70 *California Law Review* 1345.

[88] AO Sykes, 'The Economics of Vicarious Liability' (1982) 93 *Yale Law Journal* 1231; AO Sykes, 'The Boundaries of Vicarious Liability: An Economic Analysis of the Scope of Employment Rule and Related Legal Doctrines' (1988) 101 *Harvard Law Review* 563.

[89] S Shavell, 'The Optimal Level of Corporate Liability Given the Limited Ability of Corporations to Penalize their Employees' (1997) 17 *International Review of Law & Economics* 203.

[90] Sykes, 'The Economics of Vicarious Liability' (n 88) 1250.

[91] ibid 1251. Sykes further explains that '[t]he scale of enterprise activity then contracts to the point where the price of agency output covers its social marginal costs': ibid.

[92] ibid.

[93] Kornhauser (n 87) 1370.

> the inefficiency of holding an employer vicariously liable for all employee torts even when the employer cannot affect either the likelihood that the employee commits a tort or the likely amount of damages.[94]

Today, where employer insurance is usually compulsory in many sectors, a successful claim in vicarious liability is likely to result in an eventual distribution of losses throughout the relevant sector. In theory, the loss distribution will extend beyond the enterprise to the general public, for instance, the cost of higher insurance premiums being passed on to customers in the form of higher prices. Although as Cane points out that 'loss spreading … is not self-justifying',[95] it should be noted that loss spreading is an *effect* of risk internalisation. Risk internalisation as a *justification* for vicarious liability is grounded in notions of social justice and economics.[96] More recently, Van Loo has also argued that firms should internalise the full costs of their business activities in a manner that advances efficiency while balancing other values, such as distribution.[97]

C. Objections to the Enterprise Risk Approach

Witting, however, raises an interesting objection to this enterprise risk approach. He argues that with non-profit bodies, the '"benefits" of risk imposition arising from their activities accrue to third parties and not to those in charge',[98] and perhaps more charitably, he concedes that:

> [t]he best that we can say about enterprise liability is that it looks in the right direction by providing an explanation of vicarious liability that is not reliant upon agency, but which takes into account the organisational status of defendants and provides support for the imposition of liability upon profit-making businesses.[99]

This narrower view of 'benefit' has certainly been rejected by the courts in Singapore and the UK. Assuming we interrogate whether an organisation operates pursuant to ordinary profit motives, and whether, in Witting's words, 'the owners and managers of businesses operated for profit derive personal benefits from imposing risks on others',[100] one can also argue that in a publicly listed company, the benefits of risk imposition accrue to the *shareholders* of the company, rather than personally to the directors or employees of the company. Nonetheless, Witting's concern

[94] CM Sharkey, 'Institutional Liability for Employees' Intentional Torts: Vicarious Liability as a Quasi-Substitute for Punitive Damages' (2018) 53 *Valparaiso University Law Review* 1, 9 (referring to Sykes, 'The Boundaries of Vicarious Liability' (n 88) 564).

[95] P Cane, 'Justice and Justifications for Tort Liability' (1982) 2 *Oxford Journal of Legal Studies* 30, 52. See also Giliker (n 16) 236–37.

[96] See, eg, HJ Laski, 'The Basis of Vicarious Liability' (1916) 26 *Yale Law Journal* 105, 121.

[97] Van Loo (n 63) 172.

[98] Witting (n 64) 700.

[99] ibid.

[100] ibid.

with the efficacy of imposing organisational vicarious liability as a form of 'mediated deterrence' is a valid one,[101] and that a liability award can act as 'a disturbing event which serves to alert the company [or the organisation] to the existence of a dysfunction, which triggers its standard operating procedures and initiates a process of deterrence'.[102]

Let us consider a hypothetical scenario of DBS Bank, Singapore's largest bank, engaging both full-time employees and part-time paid workers (which, for convenience, we shall refer to as 'agents') to sell investment products to customers at its branches all over Singapore. These agents don uniforms and are stationed at designated investment counters in the branches. What risks has DBS introduced to the community in the pursuit of its commercial objectives? A potential or existing customer may be injured by the negligent act of an agent, whether as a result of relying on poor financial advice or having a cup of hot tea spilt on him or her. This customer may also be defrauded by the agent or sexually assaulted in a meeting room. In these circumstances, the court is likely to have no problems relying on a risk internalisation justification to support a finding of vicarious liability. In another hypothetical scenario, now involving a non-profit organisation in Singapore like the Society for the Physically Disabled or Boys' Town, these institutions are dedicated to providing important guidance, rehabilitation, counselling and training that benefit many members of society. However, they also introduce risks. Again their agents – which include full-time employees, part-time paid workers and casual volunteers – in the conduct of numerous activities on behalf on the organisations would no doubt be viewed by the beneficiaries and public as emanations of the enterprise. It does not make sense to distinguish between full-time employees, part-time paid workers and casual volunteers if they were performing identical organisational functions. There is a reasonable likelihood that these agents might commit negligent acts or intentional torts in the course of carrying out activities for these institutions.

In the private sector, compelling profit-maximising firms to internalise the costs of their agents' misconduct that accompany their productive activities can arguably result in an efficient scale of production by aligning the private costs of production with the social costs. In the twenty-first century, as the debate intensifies on whether public agencies and non-profit organisations should be held vicariously liable for the torts committed by their agents, the notion of internalising externalities nonetheless applies with equal force. Even if the enterprise is not insured, from an economic standpoint, it is still in a better position *vis-à-vis* the victim to bear the costs of the accident. From the perspective of social justice, the enterprise – even if it is a small unincorporated charitable institution seeking to assist the disadvantaged in society – should also pay for the sexual assault on children under its care. Kraakman notes that while pinning vicarious liability on

[101] ibid 701.
[102] ibid 705 (internal citations omitted).

such entities might not affect the scale of the non-market enterprise, it will still induce 'optimal caretaking, self-policing and efficient risk-bearing'.[103] According to Giliker, French law has also moved towards a recognition that an enterprise should bear the risks created by the activities of the employees in its service, thereby establishing a regime adapted to modern needs.[104]

D. Arguments for Internalising Costs and Optimal Enterprise Behaviour

Whether one is a profit-maximising firm or a non-profit institution, the enterprise has to make a decision on the level of precaution to take in the conduct of its activities, and it has to bear the costs (often quantifiable and financial in nature) of such a decision. The consumer–potential victim enjoys the benefits of such decisions, for instance, from the reduction in the probability of harm to the victim. But the benefits of taking precaution are *external* with respect to the enterprise's decision on how much precaution should be taken. If the enterprise bears the costs and benefits of its own decision, then it will decide optimally. However, when either costs or benefits are external, the decision-maker is unlikely to take into account all the costs and benefits involved. If there is a real possibility of a finding of vicarious liability, and the likelihood of paying compensation may be in fact mitigated by taking certain precautions, this may be viewed as a 'benefit' that the enterprise can properly evaluate in the decision-making process. By recognising that the overriding rationale of the law of vicarious liability is to internalise the externalities, it incentivises a socially optimal level of precaution, that is, where the sum of the cost of precaution and the expected accident cost is equal to the social cost of an accident.

The *Skandinaviska* risk paradigm implicitly embodies these attributes and ensures that both corporates and non-corporates face the full expected costs of accidents or wrongdoing. As Chan CJ notes:

> The applicability of victim compensation and deterrence as valid policy considerations in a particular case does not inevitably lead to the conclusion that the employer should be held vicariously liable; *vice versa*, the inapplicability of these considerations does not mean that the employer may not be made vicariously liable.[105]

The *Skandinaviska* test – with its two-step analysis applicable to *all* intentional torts including physical assault, sexual abuse or fraud – arguably provides a more methodical approach for courts to evaluate the existence of a close connection than Lord Phillips' succinct and elegant formulation in *Catholic Child Welfare Society*.

[103] Kraakman (n 86) 669, 673.
[104] Giliker (n 16) 238–39, 246.
[105] *Skandinaviska* (n 20) [81].

The first step involves an examination of how the facts at hand fulfil the *criteria* of opportunity, furtherance, relatedness of the wrongful act to the enterprise risks, power and vulnerability; while the second step requires an active engagement with the relevant *policy* considerations to determine whether it would be fair, just and reasonable to impose vicarious liability. This test not only covers the enterprise risk and other policy considerations that the UK Supreme Court was concerned with in *Catholic Child Welfare Society*,[106] but also resonates with Lord Phillips' recondite observations that 'the policy reasons are not the same as the criteria. One cannot, however, consider the one without the other and the two sometimes overlap'.[107] While *Ng Huat Seng* and later UK Supreme Court decisions such as *Barclays Bank* and *Morrisons* have attempted to rein in an expansive approach to imposing vicarious liability, there is still much uncertainty as to the exact scope of the doctrine in its application to the gig economy.

However, one must be cautious that enterprises should not always be compelled to internalise the costs of all risks that eventuate. One should not conflate a risk internalisation justification with a liability conclusion. The limiting mechanisms operate at Stages 1 and 2 as fact-intensive inquiries. Chief Justice Chan highlighted this in *Skandinaviska*: 'What the court has to do in each case is to examine all the relevant circumstances – *including policy considerations* – and determine whether it would be fair and just to impose vicarious liability on the employer'.[108] Where the victim may have the capacity to take precautions against certain risks – like in the case an international bank which is the victim of a commercial fraud (in *Skandinaviska*) as opposed to vulnerable children in a boarding school (in *Lister*) – it would not be fair and just to impose vicarious liability. The introduction of a 'precondition for the imposition of vicarious liability … that the victim seeking compensation should either be without fault himself, or be less at fault than the blameworthy party and/or the ultimate defendant'[109] in *Skandinaviska* arguably provides a counterbalance to the expansive proclivity of the risk internalisation paradigm. Although there had not been another case in Singapore that directly addressed this consideration, it was mentioned by lower courts in passing in subsequent decisions.[110] A risk-based approach to vicarious liability, by augmenting the ease by which victims obtain compensation, also diminishes the incentive for victims to take care of their own safety. It is perhaps fair and just that victims who have the means to protect themselves from harm but instead *increase* the risk of harm to themselves should not

[106] *Catholic Child Welfare Society* (n 3) [43] and [86].

[107] ibid [34].

[108] *Skandinaviska* (n 20) [75].

[109] ibid [78]. This notion of a moral value/conscience has been pursued by the Court of Appeal in a number of recent decisions, in particular in reshaping the law of breach of confidence. See *I-Admin (Singapore) Pte Ltd v Hong Ying Ting and others* [2020] SGCA 32; B Wong and D Tan, 'A Modern Approach to Breach of Confidence based on an Obligation of Confidence' (2020) 136 *LQR* 548.

[110] eg *Poh Chiak Ow v United Overseas Bank Ltd* [2020] SGHC 275; *Ong Han Ling v American International Assurance Co Ltd* [2018] 5 SLR 549.

be allowed to claim compensation from the enterprise. In vicarious liability cases involving fraud in Singapore, courts are more circumspect about making a finding of vicarious liability. In 2020, the Singapore High Court held that it would not be fair, just and reasonable to hold United Overseas Bank (UOB) vicariously liable for the alleged false representations made by a bank manager that resulted in the claimant's investments in a UOB-approved investment product. It appears that courts will be guided by policy considerations even as they apply the tests for Stage 1 and Stage 2. The judge noted that:

> Ultimately, vicarious liability should only be imposed where it is fair, just and reasonable to do so, having regards to the aims of effective victim compensation, deterrence of future harm, and in the light of the concept of enterprise risk. These aims should also be balanced against the competing public policy consideration militating against holding a person liable for another person's torts.[111]

Kraakman's observation provides support for the direction that the Supreme Courts of the United Kingdom and Canada are heading in *Catholic Child Welfare Society* and *Bazley*, as well as the *Skandinaviska* risk paradigm:

> In most cases strict vicarious liability is congruent with a policy of forcing firms to internalize tort costs. In fact, when principals cannot monitor their agents' behavior, the only justification for vicarious liability is the internalization of tort costs and the concomitant regulation of activity levels.[112]

If an enterprise faces the prospect of vicarious liability, it would be incentivised to locate and discipline potentially errant agents, and even be able to reduce tort costs through screening measures, training programmes and closer monitoring. It would not be able to hide behind legal concepts like 'control', 'independent contractors' or 'in the course of employment' if it has indeed introduced risky activities into the community. In *Hollis v Vabu*, McHugh J of the High Court of Australia warned that '[i]f the law of vicarious liability is to remain relevant in the contemporary world, it needs to be developed and applied in a way that will accommodate the changing nature of employment relationships'.[113] The affirmation by the Singapore Court of Appeal of the 'akin to employment' test at Stage 1 and the 'close connection' test at Stage 2 arguably represents a principled and coherent development of the law of vicarious liability for intentional torts that focuses on the enterprise risk principle as the primary explanatory factor for imposing vicarious liability.[114]

In the context of sexual abuse in educational institutions or religious enterprises, these more nuanced approaches can better strike a balance between public

[111] *Poh Chiak Ow* ibid [96] (citing *Ong Han Ling* ibid [160]).
[112] Kraakman (n 86) 669, 675.
[113] *Hollis* (n 28) 54.
[114] McIvor has earlier noted this shift but has expressed her disagreement with this approach. She contends that the 'courts are currently applying the enterprise argument to vicarious liability in a manner that is both inappropriate and disproportionate'. McIvor (n 19) 286.

concern over protection of young and vulnerable children, the just imposition of a financial burden on enterprises which introduce such risks to society and the legal desire for rules to exhibit certainty and consistency. In other commercial contexts, including organisational liability in a healthcare system,[115] the myriad contractual arrangements between the enterprise and individual professionals militate against a strict adherence to the traditional doctrinal rules in Stages 1 and 2.

By engaging bouncers as part of the business of running a nightclub, as in *Hawley*, the management has exposed its patrons to the risk of physical assaults. The use of bicycle couriers, as in *Hollis*, would subject members of the public to the risk of potential physical injuries through accidents. A financial institution that hires managers, consultants and client advisers in pursuit of commercial objectives creates the risks of fraudulent misconduct. The Catholic Church introduces the risk of sexual assaults on young children when its priests and ecclesiastical volunteers propagate the faith amongst the community. As Morgan notes:

> Volunteers may work alongside paid employees, carrying out the same tasks, receiving the same training, and wearing the same uniform. They may be equally associated with the enterprise as employees. They may be indistinguishable to members of the public, or consumers of their services, from the paid employees they work alongside.[116]

It is time to view enterprises not only as a positive wellspring of benefits to the economy and general society, but also a provenience of risks. As courts across the common law world begin to nudge towards a policy-oriented approach that has, at its heart, a risk management–cost internalisation impetus, it is important to consider more carefully the impact on the doctrinal development of Stages 1 and 2 of the test for vicarious liability. The risk approach to vicarious liability should not be carte blanche for courts to find a convenient deep-pocket enterprise to bear the costs of an accident or wrongdoing, but should guide a clearer articulation of rules that may be properly applied in every situation. Although 'risk creation' should not automatically lead to the imposition of liability, a 'risk internalisation' framework can better orientate courts to consider the factual circumstances in Stages 1 and 2 in a principled and consistent fashion.

V. Conclusion

The vicarious liability cases in Singapore in the last two decades have dealt with commercial fraud, physical injury and property damage; there were no cases on sexual abuse. While the law of vicarious liability is certainly on the move in an expansionary direction to reflect contemporary social attitudes and business

[115] See, eg, TE Chan, 'Organisational Liability in a Health Care System' (2010) 18 *Torts Law Journal* 228, 235–37.

[116] Morgan (n 72) 649.

realities, the cautionary road blocks introduced in *Barclays Bank* and *Morrisons* by the UK Supreme Court have brought some order to the litigation chaos resulting from the open-ended tests that appeal to vague notions of fairness and justice.[117] These developments are certainly in line with the Singaporean decisions; the broader *Skandinaviska* risk paradigm has been refined by the Court of Appeal in *Ng Huat Seng* and subsequent High Court decisions. Courts should also be attuned to the reality of deterrence. Some scholars have suggested that a vicarious liability regime may be more efficient than direct negligence liability where there is a significant risk of under-detection of employers' failures to take measures to prevent their employees' intentional torts, especially within large employers and institutions with a complex internal organisation.[118] Witting sagely observes that the deterrence potential of vicarious liability could be augmented by 'courts doing such things as making greater use of exemplary damages and of non-monetary orders aimed at bringing about organisational reforms'.[119] What this also means is that for internalisation and the resultant gatekeeping processes to be implemented by large organisations across an intricate network of work arrangements, the remedies would need to more accurately reflect the economic and social costs of the activity rather than simply imposing legal liability on the enterprise.

In a 2021 Singapore High Court decision, the current law for Stage 1 and Stage 2 was elegantly summarised by Justice Dedar Singh Gill as an inquiry to determine 'sufficient closeness' and 'sufficient connection' respectively.[120] What remains to be resolved in the future for Singapore courts is the overlap between a normal duty of care,[121] a non-delegable duty and vicarious liability. The courts in Singapore are no doubt taking a cue from the English developments, but confidently and quietly charting their own path through this labyrinthine area of tort law.

[117] eg Nolan (n 23) 623–24.

[118] eg Sharkey (n 94) 23–25.

[119] Witting (n 64) 713. The insurability of vicarious liability punitive damages will not necessarily thwart the deterrence cost-internalisation mechanism. Sharkey observes that to the extent that insurance can play a risk-management role by providing oversight of institutional and employer policies regarding hiring, training, and supervising employees, then the deterrence function persists. At the same time, insurance companies can engage in experience rating of their premia to further bolster the deterrence effect. Sharkey (n 94) 39. Singapore has not witnessed cases involving egregious conduct that merited a discussion of exemplary or punitive damages.

[120] *Munshi* (n 49) [39] (citing *Ng Huat Seng* (n 4) [42] and [44]).

[121] Unlike the English courts, the Singapore courts have adopted a 'single test … to determine the imposition of a duty of care in all claims arising out of negligence, irrespective of the type of the damages claimed, and this should include claims for pure economic loss'. *Spandeck Engineering (S) Pte Ltd v Defence Science & Technology Agency* [2007] 4 SLR(R) 100, [2007] 1 SLR 720 [71]. See also D Tan, 'The End of the Search for a Universal Touchstone for Duty of Care?' (2019) 135 *LQR* 200; D Tan and YH Goh, 'The Promise of Universality: The *Spandeck* Formulation Half A Decade On' (2013) 25 *Singapore Academy of Law Journal* 510.

7

Employers' Vicarious Liability in Hong Kong

RICK GLOFCHESKI

I. Introduction

Until the turn of the twenty-first century, the law of employers' vicarious liability in Hong Kong was stable. Very few cases reached the courts. There were no perceived gaps in the law. A defendant, although himself not at fault, would be liable for a tort committed against a plaintiff if it could be shown that the wrong-doer was employed by the defendant (the first limb) and committed the tort in the course of his or her employment duties (the second limb). According to the accepted formulation, employment duties would include unauthorised modes of performing authorised employment duties.[1] There were of course difficult cases at the margins, but in Hong Kong the law was sufficiently robust to catch a miscreant police officer abusing his powers to bribe a falsely accused person,[2] and more mundane cases like that of the lorry driver who, for his own convenience, ignored his employer's instructions and parked his vehicle with valuable cargo in a convenient but unsecure place.[3]

This relatively calm and predictable state of affairs changed abruptly in 2002, when, in an employee negligence case decided by the Court of Final Appeal,[4] the second limb, that the tort was committed in the course of employment, was replaced by a more flexible test introduced a year earlier in the UK House of Lords.[5] It would henceforth be sufficient if the employee's wrong was shown to be closely connected to the employment such that it was just and fair to impose vicarious liability. It was no longer necessary that the employee was carrying out authorised tasks. More change was to come, in the form of a trio of UK Supreme Court

[1] See JW Salmond, *The Law of Torts* 1st edn (London, Stevens and Haynes, 1907) 83 for the original formulation.

[2] *Kimmy Suen King On v Attorney-General* [1987] HKLR 331.

[3] *Dense Billion Ltd v Hui Ting Sung* [1996] 2 HKLR 107.

[4] *Ming An Insurance Co (HK) Ltd v Ritz-Carlton Ltd* (2002) 5 HKCFAR 569.

[5] *Lister v Hesley Hall* [2001] UKHL 22, [2002] 1 AC 215.

decisions beginning in 2012.[6] These decisions relaxed the employment contract requirement. Under this approach, a contract of employment, strictly speaking, would no longer be required, an approach now accepted by the courts of Hong Kong. It is important to note that these changes were introduced in the United Kingdom in the context of a social problem prevalent there but apparently not in Hong Kong: the sexual assault of children committed by the defendants' care workers and teachers that would have otherwise gone without a remedy under the traditional vicarious liability test. Such cases had never come before the courts in Hong Kong.[7]

An analysis of the recent case law shows that these changes to vicarious liability law have had an impact in Hong Kong in three important ways. First, there has been a substantial increase in the volume of vicarious liability litigation reaching the courts, possibly as much as a four- or five-fold increase. This can perhaps be explained on the basis of an increase in the scope of liability intended by the new developments, although it will be argued here that it is better explained on the basis of the open-endedness of the new principles, encouraging litigation that would not have taken place under the previous law. Second, there is a higher degree of unpredictability of outcome in the cases, not so much regarding the contract of employment requirement, but more so regarding the second limb, as the courts grapple with the meaning of the new law. Finally, most of the new cases concern claims brought by injured workers against their own employers. This is an important feature because, in this context, there will normally be other actions and remedies available to an injured employee, which may affect the way that the vicarious liability issue is decided.

II. Employers' Vicarious Liability: Theory and Policy

It is not easy to find a clear, let alone definitive, statement in Hong Kong case law explaining the theory and policy justification for the imposition of employers' vicarious liability. It seems to have been taken as implicit that if a person

[6] These are *Various Claimants v Catholic Child Welfare Society* [2012] UKSC 56, [2013] 2 AC 1 (*CCWS*), *Cox v Ministry of Justice* [2016] UKSC 10, [2016] AC 660 (*Cox*) and *Armes v Nottinghamshire Council* [2017] UKSC 60, [2018] AC 355 (*Armes*).

[7] This is not to say that such abuses do not take place, only that legal remedies are not sought. For an understanding of the scale of the problem and some of the reasons why legal or other help is not pursued, see *Belated Listening, Delayed Healing – an Exploratory Study of Disclosure and Help-Seeking Practices Among Adult Survivors of Child Sexual Abuse*, RainLily, 2020, and the sources contained therein, available at www.scribd.com/document/480992104/Belated-Listening-Delayed-Healing-An-Exploratory-Study-of-Disclosure-and-Help-Seeking-Practices-Among-Adult-Survivors-of-Child-Sexual-Abuse#from_embed. For the only reported case in which a legal remedy was sought, although apparently not pursued to trial, see *H v Lau Ka Yee* [2006] 4 HKLRD 579 (application to strike out the claim of vicarious liability against the diocese for a deacon's sex assaults on an altar boy dismissed on the basis that the minimum standard of an arguable case was met by the plaintiff).

employs others to perform tasks for his benefit, that person should bear responsibility for any harm caused as a result of those tasks being carried out. Beyond that presumed assumption, some of the members of the Court of Final Appeal in *Ming An Insurance Co (HK) Ltd v Ritz-Carlton Ltd*,[8] the only vicarious liability case to reach the highest court in Hong Kong, provided some comments on the justification for vicarious liability, although falling well short of a complete theory. Writing the main judgment in support of a more flexible test for the course of employment requirement, Bokhary PJ stated that the purpose of vicarious liability was to 'provide the victims of tort with recourse against persons who have the means to satisfy awards and on whom it would be just to fix liability'.[9] However broadly true, such a statement is too general and does not explain why vicarious liability is as restricted in application as it is. It does not indicate when it will be just to fix liability. It does not provide much help in cases that have to be decided at the margins. Anyway, compensation and justice are characteristics of all private law decision-making. Risk creation was identified as an important factor by Litton and Mortimer NPJs as well as Bokhary PJ. One who through his business activities creates risks should bear the consequences and will thereby be encouraged to minimise or eliminate those risks. However, risk creation is too broad and uncertain, and would logically lead to a more expansive liability extending far beyond employment to the activities of, among others, contractors and, as will be seen, this has been rejected by the courts in the UK and Hong Kong. Also, risk does not equate with wrong. Torts are only one type of risk. As pointed out by Gray, risk theory 'does not explain why vicarious liability is dependent upon proof that the employee committed a tort'.[10] The related question of who is best able to insure against the relevant risk has also been flagged in the case law.[11] For Litton NPJ in *Ming An* it was an important consideration: 'if the risk which gave rise to the damage … was created by those [business] activities … that was a risk which the employer could have insured against'.[12] However incomplete as an explanation, it is likely that risk theory favoured by the court in *Ming An* has contributed to the expansion of vicarious liability litigation in Hong Kong in the ensuing decades.

A. First Limb: A Relationship of Employment

The paradigm case of employers' vicarious liability in Hong Kong involves an employment relationship as conventionally defined in the common law. It is important to remember that the legal definition of a contract of employment is

[8] *Ming An* (n 4).
[9] ibid [13].
[10] A Gray, *Vicarious Liability Critique and Reform* (Oxford, Hart Publishing, 2018) 138.
[11] See eg *Ho Kwok Kei v AS Watson & Co Ltd* [2019] 3 HKLRD 592, discussed in the text accompanying n 35 below.
[12] *Ming An* (n 4) [42].

relevant to many purposes, including entitlement to statutory employment benefits and protections. In Hong Kong, the leading case law on contract of employment concerns workers injured at the job site seeking compensation for injury, or workers alleging wrongful termination seeking statutory employment benefits. In the context of a typical Hong Kong work arrangement, it is often difficult to distinguish between an employee and a legitimate, self-employed independent contractor. Specialist, self-employed contractors are prevalent, in particular, on construction sites, and in the transport industry, where there is a long and well-documented history of employers engaging in various avoidance strategies to side-step their labour law obligations.[13] Typically, the worker is designated in a contract as being self-employed, or otherwise presents an ambiguous profile because he is casually employed. The distinction between employment and legitimate self-employment can be razor-thin.

Adopting the approach in the leading English case, the relevant question for the Hong Kong courts is: was the worker in business on his own account?[14] Employer control over the worker continues to be an important factor in answering that question but is far from conclusive, having given way to a more nuanced approach that openly acknowledges modern labour conditions and social expectations. Integration into the organisation may be more relevant than control over how the work is done. A number of factors have been identified in the case law as relevant to the determination. However, as explained by the Court of Final Appeal in *Poon Chau Nam v Yim Siu Cheung*,[15] the determination should be approached not as a 'check-list' of indicators but on the basis of an 'overall impression'.[16] The overall impression approach entails a pragmatic, textured evaluation of the features of the relationship which, in the context of worker injury claims brought against employers, leaves plenty of room for a worker to argue that despite labelling and other avoidance strategies he was nonetheless working under a contract of employment. The overall impression approach tilts to a worker bias, certainly in the context of employee injury and benefits claims.[17] There is not yet much evidence in the case law to indicate how this pro-worker tendency in labour rights cases might affect the employment determination in a vicarious liability case, but given that the test has always been the same for both,[18] it can be assumed that a similarly generous approach will apply.

[13] See R Glofcheski and F Aslam (eds), *Employment Law and Practice in Hong Kong* 2nd edn (Hong Kong, Sweet & Maxwell Asia, 2016) 22.

[14] *Lee Ting Sang v Chung Chi Keung* [1990] 1 HKLR 764, adopting the dicta of Cooke J in *Market Investigations v Minister of Social Security* [1969] 2 QB 173.

[15] *Poon Chau Nam v Yim Siu Cheung* (2007) 10 HKCFAR 156.

[16] Adopting the approach of Mummery J in *Hall v Lorimer* [1994] 1 WLR 209.

[17] See R Glofcheski, 'Tort Law' in SNM Young and Y Ghai (eds), *Hong Kong's Court of Final Appeal: The Development of the Law in China's Hong Kong* (Hong Kong, Cambridge University Press, 2013) 532–33.

[18] There is no definitive statement in the Hong Kong case law, but this has been the practice. In *Poon Chau Nam* (n 15) a worker injury case, the Court of Final Appeal made reference to PS Atiyah, *Vicarious Liability in the Law of Tort* (London, Butterworths, 1967) ch 5, in determining the meaning of employee.

In Hong Kong there have not been any cases imposing vicarious liability on a defendant in circumstances other than where an employment relationship was established. A plaintiff who cannot establish that the wrongdoer was the defendant's employee quite simply cannot succeed in imposing vicarious liability on the defendant, although this is not for lack of trying. This remains the position despite a trio of United Kingdom Supreme Court decisions in the last decade imposing vicarious liability in circumstances of a relationship that fell short of employment but were characterised as being 'akin to employment'. *Various Claimants v Catholic Child Welfare Society*,[19] *Cox v Ministry of Justice*[20] and *Armes v Nottinghamshire CC*[21] concerned factual contexts quite different from one another but possessing some common features. The Brothers of the Christian Schools in *Various Claimants*, the prisoners in *Cox* and the foster parents in *Armes* lacked some of the recognisable characteristics that define an employment relationship, but did possess some of them. In particular, each could be said to be performing their work activities

> as an integral part of the business … carried on by the defendant and for [the defendant's] benefit … and … the commission of the wrongful act [was] a risk created by the defendant by assigning those activities to the individual in question.[22]

These decisions have created huge potential for the extension of vicarious liability to new, yet-to-be-identified relationships, beyond the conventional employment relationship that was historically the hallmark of vicarious liability.

But there are limits. According to Lord Reed in *Cox v Ministry of Justice* there would be no vicarious liability where the wrongdoer's activities could more properly be characterised as 'attributable to the conduct of a recognisably independent business of his own or of a third party'.[23] In *Barclays Bank v Various Claimants*, Lady Hale embraced Lord Reed's distinction in deciding against Barclays' vicarious liability for the sexual abuses committed by a doctor appointed by Barclays to conduct medical examinations of its prospective employees.[24] Neither Lord Reed nor Lady Hale provided a policy justification for the drawing of such a firm line. Yet there will be cases where the apparently independent business is nothing more than an organisational strategy designed to insulate the employer from liability when the reality is one of considerable subordination and integration into the defendant's business. *Singh Gurpinder v Craigside Investments Ltd*[25] is arguably such a case. The case concerned a statutory claim for a work-related injury but the same test for employment relationship would apply had it been a

[19] *CCWS* (n 6).
[20] *Cox* (n 6).
[21] *Armes* (n 6).
[22] *Cox* (n 6) [24] per Lord Reed.
[23] ibid [24].
[24] *Barclays Bank v Various Claimants* [2020] UKSC 13, [2020] AC 973 [27].
[25] *Singh Gurpinder v Craigside Investments Ltd* [2013] DCEC 1978/2011.

case of employers' vicarious liability. The plaintiff pizza delivery motorcyclist, whose sole function was to take the deliveries on a roster basis as the orders came in, was injured in a traffic accident in the course of a delivery. He possessed the basic characteristics of an employee, save for the fact that he was required to provide and maintain his own motorcycle. He was paid a $50 hourly retainer and $20 for each delivery. The court's justification for finding him to be an independent contractor, and thus not eligible for statutory injury compensation, centred on the facts that the employer did not provide the legally required employment benefits and protections (the worker was largely left to his own on that count), and that he could save time and petrol by taking shorter delivery routes. That is injustice enough from a labour rights perspective, but even if considered in the context of a vicarious liability claim, whatever be the characterisation, contractor or employee, the policy that drives vicarious liability should not be undermined on the basis of such flimsy distinctions.[26] The case predates, but anticipates, claims that will no doubt soon appear before the courts in Hong Kong arising from accidents involving ride share and food delivery platforms in which the businesses have insisted on contractor designation in the agreements with their drivers.[27]

Somewhat ironically, most of the attempts in the Hong Kong case law to argue for the imposition of vicarious liability in circumstances other than an employment relationship have concerned cases in which the wrongdoer was plainly the defendant's independent contractor or the independent contractor's employee. This, despite a very clear pronouncement from the Court of Final Appeal, albeit in a case that pre-dated *Cox v Ministry of Justice*, that there can be no vicarious liability for an independent contractor's torts.[28] That such cases are nonetheless brought demonstrates the unintended consequences of the Supreme Court case law – the indeterminacy of the akin to employment principle throwing desperate plaintiffs a life-line to cling to. In these cases, in most of which the plaintiff cited *Cox v Ministry of Justice*, the vicarious liability argument failed, largely with reference to Lord Reed's qualification in *Cox* excluding vicarious liability for the torts of an independent contractor, a position in the meantime cemented with the Supreme Court decision in *Barclays Bank v Various Claimants*.[29] Hong Kong courts have taken this qualification to draw a clear line against vicarious liability for independent contractors and their employees.

In *Li Ming Tak v Hong Kong Airport Services Ltd*,[30] the plaintiff, employed by the defendant as an airport cargo handler, was medically assessed and told by the

[26] See *Hollis v Vabu* [2001] HCA 44, (2001) 207 CLR 21 for a more robust approach, in the context of bicycle couriers.

[27] At least one such case has been initiated: 'Hong Kong woman sues Uber over 2018 accident that left one dead and four injured', *South China Morning Post*, March 1, 2021.

[28] *Luen Hing Fat Coating & Finishing Factory Ltd v Waan Chuen Ming* (2011) 14 HKCFAR 14 at [20].

[29] *Barclays* (n 24).

[30] *Li Ming Tak v Hong Kong Airport Services Ltd* [2015] 4 HKLRD 749.

defendant's panel doctor that he could return to mixed work duties. The plaintiff alleged that the advice was negligent and resulted in an exacerbation of pre-existing injuries. The plea of vicarious liability was dismissed because the panel doctor was not employed by the defendant.[31] *Cox* had not yet been decided, which may explain why there was no attempt to argue that the panel doctor was in a relationship akin to employment (he had been serving on the defendant's panel of doctors for more than 10 years). *Various Claimants v Catholic Child Welfare Society*[32] was apparently not cited by counsel.

In *Talat Zahid v Cheung Fat Metal Trading Co Ltd*,[33] the plaintiff, employed by the first defendant scrap metals company, was injured when the second defendant, an employee of the first defendant's unloading contractor (the third defendant) pressed the wrong button on a hoist causing it to strike the plaintiff. The plaintiff succeeded in his negligence claim against the first defendant, and also against the second defendant in negligence and the third defendant in vicarious liability for the second defendant's negligence. The plaintiff also sought to impose vicarious liability against the first defendant, an obviously difficult argument on these facts. He argued that since the work performed by the third defendant and its employee (unloading scrap metals with a hoist) was undertaken on behalf of the first defendant, and that this activity was integral to the first defendant's business, the first defendant, by engaging the third defendant and his employee to do the work, had created the risk of a tort being committed by them. The vicarious liability argument was rejected because it would mean that principal contractors would be liable for all injuries caused to its employees by subcontractors, and in the court's response, 'that simply cannot be right'.[34]

A factually stronger case was presented in *Ho Kwok Kei v AS Watson & Co Ltd*.[35] In March 2010, the first defendant, a supermarket chain, arranged through one of its related companies to engage transport contractors (the third defendant) to provide transport services between the first defendant's warehouses and its stores. It was a term of the agreement that the first defendant would provide some of its own vehicles for use by the third defendant. It was also a term of the agreement that the parties were independent contractors. In December 2010, the plaintiff, one of the first defendant's store managers, was assisting with the unloading of a delivery vehicle when he was injured through the negligence of one of the third defendant's drivers. It is noteworthy that until 2010, the first defendant employed its own team of drivers. The driver in the instant case had been

[31] The plaintiff failed to prove any negligence on the part of the panel doctor and his claims failed for that reason as well.

[32] *CCWS* (n 6) above.

[33] *Talat Zahid v Cheung Fat Metal Trading Co Ltd* HCPI 399/2012, [2017] HKEC 1297.

[34] *Cox* was briefly considered and vicarious liability rejected for similar reasons in *Tsoi Wing Yuk v Perfect Marble Co Ltd* (HCPI 779/2012, [2016] HKEC 818) (tortfeasor employed by the defendant's subcontractor did not take any instructions from or carry on activities for the defendant but for his employer only).

[35] *Ho Kwok Kei* (n 11).

employed by the first defendant for 15 years, until 2010, before being employed by the third defendant under the new arrangement. At the time of the accident, he was in fact driving a vehicle provided by the first defendant. The plaintiff was able to establish liability against the first defendant on the basis of a breach of the employer's duty in negligence, and against the third defendant vicariously for the negligence of its driver.[36] Although it is unclear what was to be gained given that the third defendant was obliged to carry insurance under its agreement with the first defendant, the plaintiff also claimed against the first defendant in vicarious liability for the negligence of the third defendant's driver. The plaintiff, citing *Various Claimants*, *Cox* and *Armes*, argued that the delivery of goods from the first defendant's warehouses to its stores was integral to the first defendant's business activities, and that by engaging the third defendant to make deliveries by means of its own vehicles, the first defendant had created a risk of the tort being committed by the third defendant. This was certainly a more plausible case than *Talat Zahid*, and the court appears to have been more sympathetic. However, the result was the same:

> It is clear that the application of the approach in *Cox* in a case such as the present … would be a major change in the law. It would render the distinction between an employee and an independent contractor far less significant, if not altogether obsolete.[37]

The court questioned whether it was open to the Court of First Instance to expand the scope of vicarious liability in such a fundamental way, especially as the point was not addressed by counsel. Insurance considerations were also relevant: the Court was not

> equipped with information about how the insurance system would work under the new approach and what the implications might be. It is undeniable that the law in this area may be influenced by considerations of risk allocation and in particular who would be best placed to insure against the relevant risks.[38]

Although the result was the same, this is a more thoughtful approach than that in *Talat Zahid*, leaving the issue for another day and a higher court.

Although the independent contractor/employee divide is a convenient place to draw the line, it is to be regretted that no clear policy justification was put forward in either *Cox* or for that matter in the later case of *Barclays Bank v Various Claimants*.[39] As matters stand, the rule reads more like dogma than principle. As has been seen, a contractor can meet many of the characteristics of an

[36] It should be noted that despite the finding of liability, no damages award was made. The statutory employees' compensation award obtained by the plaintiff in earlier, separate proceedings exceeded the award of common law damages after taking into account the plaintiff's contributory negligence. By virtue of s 26 of the Employees' Compensation Ordinance (Cap 282), any award of common law damages will be reduced by the amount of compensation paid under the Ordinance. Nonetheless, all of the plaintiff's common law claims were fully considered by the court.

[37] *Ho Kwok Kei* (n 11) [68].

[38] ibid [70].

[39] *Barclays Bank* (n 24) above.

akin-to-employment relationship. One may well question why a plaintiff's entitlement to damages should be affected by internal arrangements in the defendant's business structure. If the defendant sets up a delivery business and then proceeds to hire drivers to carry out the deliveries, the risks created are the same whether the drivers are employees or independent contractors. Why should the position of accident victims be adversely affected? Control cannot provide the answer, as surely the degree of control can be substantially the same whatever the employment arrangement, and anyway, control need not be total or exclusive to justify liability. The pizza delivery motorcyclist in *Singh*[40] comes to mind. Arguably there should be an examination of the substance of the relationship before determining the issue of defendant's vicarious liability.[41] The fact that a contractor is likely to have insurance coverage and that the defendant exerts less or limited influence on a contractor than on an employee, should not justify a blanket exclusion. The position is also inconsistent with cases of dual vicarious liability.[42] There, as contended by the plaintiff here, a defendant is held vicariously liable for the tort of an independent contractor's employee.

i. *Spousal Relationship as Akin to Employment?*

The suggestion that by virtue of marriage a person could be said to be in a relationship akin to employment with his or her spouse has a medieval ring to it. Yet that is the very argument that was made in two recent Hong Kong cases. As far-fetched as the argument may seem, in both cases the spousal vicarious liability argument received a sympathetic hearing, demonstrating again the open-endedness, and thus the potential for expanded liability, under the akin-to-employment principle. It is important to consider the context in which the actions were brought, the desperate plight of this category of victim, and the large-scale social evil that might otherwise go without a remedy. In these cases the plaintiffs were migrant domestic workers living in their employers' households. There are almost 400,000 such migrant domestic workers in Hong Kong,[43] almost all of them female, a huge and important part of the workforce whose legal protections are meagre and for whom employer abuses are rampant. There can be no doubt that the live-in requirement, mandatory for migrant domestic workers, poses safety hazards found only in this kind of work.[44] Female domestic workers are vulnerable to various forms

[40] *Singh* (n 25) above.
[41] This was the position taken at trial and in the Court of Appeal in *Barclays Bank v Various Claimants.*
[42] See 'Dual Vicarious Liability' section II.A.ii below.
[43] Data.Gov.HK at https://data.gov.hk/en-data/dataset/hk-immd-set4-statistics-fdh/resource/063e1929-107b-47ae-a6ac-b4b1ed460ac3.
[44] Exacerbated by long, unregulated work hours, often no private sleeping space, and a legal environment in which reporting abuse is discouraged because migrant domestic workers are required by law to return to their country of citizenship within two weeks of termination of employment.

of abuse, including sexual, on a large, but often hidden scale.[45] *Waliyah v Yip Hoi Sun Terence*[46] was a pregnancy discrimination claim for damages under the Sex Discrimination Ordinance.[47] The claimant had been forced to urinate into a pot and undergo a home pregnancy test by her employer's wife. The pregnancy test was positive and the claimant was dismissed from her employment. The plaintiff succeeded in her pregnancy discrimination claim against her employer on the basis of remedies within the framework of the Sex Discrimination Ordinance. She also sought to establish vicarious liability against her employer for his wife's conduct, relying in part on the decision in *Cox v Ministry of Justice*. The argument was not dismissed outright but nonetheless failed, in part because it was not fully addressed by counsel. In the words of the court, it:

> would entail an extension of the principle stated in *Cox* to a domestic setting so as to make a person vicariously liable for the act of his or her spouse. In the absence of any thorough arguments from both sides, I am reluctant to decide whether the common law principle can be so extended.[48]

In *X v Pang Ka Wai*[49] the plaintiff, also a migrant domestic worker, alleged that she was repeatedly raped by her employer's husband. She brought an action against the husband in trespass to the person, and sought to impose vicarious liability for the trespass on her employer, on the basis of the decisions in *Cox* and the close connection principle as applied in *Mohamud v Wm Morrison Supermarkets plc*.[50] The employer applied to strike out the claim on the argument that there can be no vicarious liability for the torts of a spouse. The court ruled that it would be premature to strike out:

> given that *Cox* and *Mohamud* are recent advances in the law on vicarious liability … This is clearly an unusual and tragic case with special circumstances regarding the family situations of both parties, and there is potential financial prejudice to the plaintiff if the 2nd defendant is not joined.[51]

By reason of the nature of the proceedings, the decisions in both *Waliyah* and *X* suffer from the absence of full argument on the akin-to-employment issue. It would have been interesting to hear the policy arguments in support of vicarious liability in this context. Certainly, these would not be easy arguments to make. If nothing else, the decisions suggest that we have yet to see the logical limits of the akin-to-employment principle.

[45] See eg 'Hong Kong's Hidden Shame', ILO Asia Pacific Migration Network, at https://apmigration.ilo.org/news/hong-kongs-hidden-shame.

[46] *Waliyah v Yip Hoi Sun Terence* [2017] 1 HKLRD 1082.

[47] Cap 480.

[48] *Waliyah* (n 46) [14].

[49] *X v Pang Ka Wai* PI Action No 44 of 2017, HCPI 44/2017.

[50] *Mohamud v Wm Morrison Supermarkets plc* [2016] UKSC 11, [2016] AC 677.

[51] *Pang Ka Wai* (n 49) [42].

ii. Dual Vicarious Liability

Can vicarious liability for the same wrong be imposed on two defendants concurrently? Can a worker serve two masters at once? It may be recalled that in both *Talat Zahid*[52] and *Ho Kwok Hei*[53] the plaintiffs made such an argument, albeit unsuccessfully. In addition to seeking to impose vicarious liability against the wrongdoer's employer, the plaintiff sought to impose vicarious liability against his own employer on the basis that the relationship between the wrongdoer and the plaintiff's employer was akin to employment. In *Various Claimants v Catholic Child Welfare Society*,[54] vicarious liability was established against both the religious order to which the tortfeasors (lay brothers) belonged, and the Diocese that managed the schools where the lay brothers committed their acts of sexual abuse against pupils. The court considered that the relevant question was not, as in *Mersey Docks and Harbour Board v Coggins & Griffith (Liverpool) Ltd*,[55] how and to what extent the defendant controls or instructs the employee in performing the work, but rather was the employee 'a part of the work, business or organisation of both employers such that it is just to make both employers answer for his negligence'.[56] On the other hand, a year later Lord Hoffmann NPJ in the Hong Kong Court of Final Appeal made a very clear ruling to the effect that

> employment is a bilateral relationship … No doubt a person may be simultaneously employed by more than one employer in respect of different services, but I know of no case in which anyone has been held to have two independent employers in respect of the same services.[57]

The comment was made not in relation to vicarious liability but in relation to a negligence claim brought by the deceased worker's estate in which it was alleged that four separate defendants, related companies, owed the employer's duty of care to the deceased to provide a safe system of work. As such, Lord Hoffmann need not be read to rule out dual vicarious liability, especially given that vicarious liability no longer requires an employment relationship strictly speaking.

Dual vicarious liability has been applied in Hong Kong. In *Chan Si Mui v Kong Hung Keung*,[58] it was applied in the case of a negligent public light bus driver in the context of complicated employment arrangements with two related companies. More typically, the dual vicarious liability argument will arise where the wrongdoer was on loan from his employer to another contractor, receiving instructions from that contractor. This context is rather different from that in *CCWS*.

[52] *Talat Zahid* (n 33) above.
[53] *Ho Kwok Hei* (n 11) above.
[54] *CCWS* (n 6) above.
[55] *Mersey Docks and Harbour Board v Coggins & Griffith (Liverpool) Ltd* [1947] AC 1.
[56] Citing Rix LJ in *Viasystems (Tyneside) Ltd v Thermal Transfer (Northern) Ltd* [2005] EWCA Civ 1151, [2006] QB 510 [79].
[57] *Chung Yuen Yee v Sam Woo Bore Pile Foundation Ltd* (2013) 16 HKCFAR 315.
[58] *Chan Si Mui v Kong Hung Keung* HCA 1800/1991, [1994] HKLY 494.

Lau Yuet Ming v Wong Ping Hang[59] was such a case. Since the borrowing employer gave instructions to the forklift operator and the general employer was entitled to give instructions, both defendants were found vicariously liable for the plaintiff's injuries caused by the negligence of the forklift operator.[60] This seems a sensible solution and consistent with the objectives of vicarious liability. Where two (or more) contractors (one of them being the general employer) give instructions, exercise some control and/or benefit from work being done, shared vicarious liability is a practical and reasonable result.

B. Second Limb: Tort Committed in the Course of Employment

i. *Employee Negligence*

As in other common law jurisdictions, vicarious liability will be imposed only if the tort was committed by the employee in the course of his or her employment. Until 2002, course of employment required that the tortious act was authorised by the employer, or was an unauthorised mode of carrying out an authorised employment activity – the so-called 'Salmond' formulation.[61] Employer authorisation was the touchstone. In *Ming An v Ritz-Carlton*,[62] the Court of Final Appeal considered a case with facts that previously would have been analysed and decided according to the line of cases commonly known as 'frolics'.[63] In *Ming An*, the second defendant was employed by the first defendant hotel as a hotel doorman. He occasionally performed duties as a 'car jockey', parking cars for the hotel's customers, and moving the hotel's courtesy limousines (owned not by the hotel, but hired with drivers from a third party) to make room for others. The second defendant took a courtesy limousine to drive a hotel bellboy to a restaurant to purchase some food for himself and other staff members. While doing so he lost control of the vehicle, mounted the pavement and struck two pedestrians. The Court of Final Appeal reversed the courts below and found vicarious liability on the application of the close connection test introduced a year earlier in the House of Lords decision of *Lister v Hesley Hall*,[64] a case of employee sexual trespass.

Writing the lead judgment, Bokhary PJ went directly to the question whether the *Lister* close connection principle should be applied in Hong Kong in the context

[59] *Lau Yuet Ming v Wong Ping Hang* DCPI 115/2010, [2012] CHKEC 134.

[60] The court cited the judgments of May LJ and Rix LJ in *Viasystems (Tyneside) Ltd v Thermal Transfer (Northern) Ltd* (n 56) in support.

[61] n 1 above.

[62] *Ming An* (n 4) above.

[63] The term frolic is attributed to Parke B in *Joel v Morison* (1834) 6 C & P 501, 503 to describe an employee who has stepped outside of the course of his employment to pursue his own purposes, an employee who has 'gone on a frolic of his own'.

[64] *Lister* (n 5) above.

of employee negligence. He described the *Lister* close connection test to be 'an intellectually satisfying and practical criterion for vicarious liability'.[65] Moreover, the new test was not to be restricted to sexual assault cases because 'the basic test for vicarious liability has never varied according to whether the employee's tort involved mere inadvertence or something worse'.[66] It should be noted that this latter statement is strictly speaking not correct in that the test for vicarious liability for employee financial fraud of a client has long been treated differently than, for instance, employee negligence.[67]

As for how to determine whether the connection is sufficiently close, risk creation was an important factor to all of the judges. Litton NPJ explained that the factors to be considered include:

> the employee's duties at the time when the tort occurred, whether he was acting in the interests of the employer or solely for himself … the business activities of the employer … and whether the risk which gave rise to the damage was created by those activities.[68]

Moreover, according to Bokhary PJ, it is necessary to 'stand back and see how the employer's activities were actually carried out and how that exposed the public to the risk of tortious harm caused by the employee'.[69] For Litton NPJ, 'the underlying idea is that the injury done by the servant must involve a risk sufficiently inherent in or characteristic of the employer's business that it is just to make the employer bear the loss'.[70] It seems to have been important to Bokhary PJ and Litton and Mortimer NPJs that the employer benefits from the employee's unauthorised act, because each of them mentioned the rather obvious point that the collection of food for employees would be of benefit to the employer. Employees nourishing themselves could of course be said to be of benefit to all employers, whatever the nature of the business. Importantly, a narrow conception of employment should be avoided: 'the matter must be looked at broadly; the court should not "dissect the servant's task into its component activities"'.[71]

Ming An was not a 'hard' case. As acknowledged by Bokhary PJ, the insurance arrangement was such that the plaintiff would have received compensation whatever the outcome in the litigation.[72] It was only a question of which insurer would cover the bill. Moreover, it was significant that none of the judgments made reference to any of the precedents in the frolic line of cases. For these reasons, it is clear that the court was intent on making a clean break, changing the law of vicarious liability across the board. It is not surprising then that in all of the employee negligence and trespassory tort vicarious liability cases decided since *Ming An*, the close connection test has been used to decide the issue of vicarious liability.

[65] *Ming An* (n 4) 579.
[66] ibid 580.
[67] See eg *Armagas Ltd v Mundogas SA* [1986] AC 717.
[68] *Ming An* (n 4) 586.
[69] ibid 582.
[70] ibid 584.
[71] Bokhary PJ ibid 585, citing Diplock LJ (as he then was) in *Ilkiw v Samuels* [1963] 1 WLR 991, 1004.
[72] *Ming An* (n 4) 576.

Although *Ming An* did not explicitly overrule the Salmond authority-based principle, that principle has been referred to in the case law only in passing in the decades since *Ming An*, and then only to trace the history of the close connection principle.[73] Employer authorisation, once the touchstone for vicarious liability, would henceforth not be a pre-condition for vicarious liability. The basic proposition from *Ming An*, that the close connection test applies to all cases of employee negligence, is now fully accepted by Hong Kong courts.[74]

According to Bokhary PJ in *Ming An*, most past cases would not be decided differently under the new rule. If this statement is correct, it is only so as regards routine employee negligence cases. It is certainly not true regarding previous cases concerning assault, in particular sexual assault, the very reason why the close connection principle was introduced. And it is not true regarding many of the negligence cases where the employee was described as having gone on a frolic of his own. One need look no further than *Ming An* itself, a case in its essentials not much different than the leading frolic case of *Storey v Ashton*,[75] where the court reached a different result.

Academic commentary at the time questioned the need to apply *Lister* to negligence.[76] According to this criticism, the analytical approach in the Canadian decision in *Bazley v Curry*,[77] from which the judgments in *Lister* drew so heavily, was tailored to address the peculiar problem of sexual assault by care-home workers against vulnerable persons in their care, and should have been so restricted. Sexual assault could not possibly satisfy the second limb of the Salmond formula, as being a wrongful mode of carrying out an authorised employment activity. Moreover, the court in *Bazley* qualified the new approach, which would be necessary only where precedent did not otherwise point the way.[78] In the meantime, the UK Supreme Court has emphasised that cases should be decided according to relevant precedents, confirming the more conventional approach.[79] Whether the ruling in *Ming An* to the effect that the close connection test applies without qualification to all cases of employer vicarious liability in Hong Kong will survive the suggested approach in *Morrison* remains to be seen.

ii. Employee Trespass

In the years following the decision in *Ming An*, it soon became apparent that the close connection test was no more certain, nor predictable of outcome, than the

[73] As in *Cheng Muk Ping v Chan's Machine Engineering Co Ltd* [2008] HKEC 1733.

[74] See eg *Lo Ping Kin v Yuen Tsz Shing* DCPI 2474/2013, where it was applied to impose vicarious liability in the context of an injury caused by the negligence of a co-worker. See also the comments of Marlene Ng J in *Chan Shek Ho v Shiu Ho Chi* HCPI 613/2014 (2018) [21].

[75] *Storey v Ashton* (1868–69) LR 4 QB 476.

[76] R Glofcheski, 'A Frolic in the Law of Tort: Expanding the Scope of Employers' Vicarious Liability' (2004) 12 *Tort Law Review* 18.

[77] *Bazley v Curry* [1999] 2 SCR 534.

[78] ibid [15].

[79] *WM Morrison Supermarkets plc v Various Claimants* [2020] UKSC 12, [2020] AC 989 [24] and [36].

previous law. This is particularly evident in the employee trespass cases, where the close connection test is now routinely applied. It is important to remember that previously most if not all trespass cases would be treated as employee frolics, save for that line of cases in which the employment requires the employee to use force where necessary in the performance of regular employment duties (night club bouncers, security guards, police officers and the like).

It is useful to frame this discussion with an appreciation of the full extent of the change wrought by *Lister v Hesley Hall*, summarised in plain language in that case by Lord Millett in a passage that is cited in the Hong Kong case law:

> It is no answer to say that the employee was guilty of intentional wrongdoing, or that his act was not merely tortious but criminal, or that he was acting exclusively for his own benefit, or that he was acting contrary to express instructions, or that his conduct was the very negation of his employer's duty.[80]

It is also useful to recall the approach of McLachlin J in *Bazley v Curry*, her comments directed specifically at intentional torts:

> The relevant factors may include, but are not limited to: (a) the opportunity that the enterprise afforded the employee to abuse his or her power; (b) the extent to which the wrongful act may have furthered the employer's aims (and hence be more likely to have been committed by the employee); (c) the extent to which the wrongful act was related to friction, confrontation or intimacy inherent in the employer's enterprise; (d) the extent of power conferred on the employee in relation to the victim; and (e) the vulnerability of potential victims to the wrongful exercise of the employee's power.[81]

Almost all of the employee trespass vicarious liability cases decided by Hong Kong courts since 2002 have concerned assaults committed at the workplace by one employee against another, either against a co-worker, a supervisor or a subordinate. It is important to note that in such cases it is possible for the plaintiff to sue the employer for negligence for failing to provide a safe place and system of work, for instance in relation to bullying. Liability for a breach of the employer's duty of care in negligence will often be a more acceptable basis of imposing liability, allowing the court to bypass the more controversial vicarious liability argument. On the other hand, in cases where employer breach of duty in negligence cannot be proved, vicarious liability under the law as it is evolving has the potential to provide a remedy where one would otherwise not be available. This could happen, for instance, where workplace tension is tacit and erupts suddenly in violence in circumstances where the employer could not have reasonably anticipated it. That was the case in two decisions heard together in the English Court of Appeal, *Weddall v Barchester Healthcare Ltd; Wallbank v Wallbank Fox Designs Ltd*.[82]

[80] *Lister* (n 5) [79].
[81] *Bazley* (n 77) [41].
[82] *Weddall v Barchester Healthcare Ltd; Wallbank v Wallbank Fox Designs Ltd* [2012] EWCA Civ 25, [2012] IRLR 307.

In both cases, a subordinate attacked a superior after receiving work-related instructions or requests not to his liking. The plaintiff succeeded in establishing vicarious liability in *Wallbank* but not in *Weddall*, on the not entirely convincing distinction that in *Weddall* the employee's violent reaction was not immediate, the employee having bicycled from home to work before assaulting the plaintiff. However, in both cases the violent responses seem equally closely connected to the employment. The rulings demonstrate the unpredictability of outcome with the new rule, which is also evident in the Hong Kong case law.

In *Li Hoi Shuen v Man Ming Engineering Trading Co Ltd*,[83] the murder and robbery of a warehouse supervisor during his sleep by two labourers with whom he was on poor terms was found to be not sufficiently connected to the employment to be fair and just to impose vicarious liability. The court acknowledged that the fact that an employee acts against his employer's interests, pursuing his own purposes, does not rule out vicarious liability. Nonetheless, the workers were employed to provide unskilled labour for the air conditioning maintenance and installation services, not to maintain discipline or to apply physical violence in the course of their employment. The Court found that the workers, in murdering the deceased, were taking revenge against their boss. The fact that the workers were unhappy with the deceased's criticism of their work, and that the murder took place in the employer-provided warehouse where all three worked, lived and slept, did not establish a sufficiently close connection with the employment. Liability was nonetheless established on the alternative basis of the employer's breach of duty in negligence in failing to provide reasonably safe accommodation.

In *Ling Man Kuen v Chow Chan Ming*,[84] the plaintiff's supervisor lost his cool and suddenly assaulted the plaintiff in the course of a meeting in which the plaintiff's recent work performance was being reviewed. The defendant's plea that what the supervisor did was an unauthorised and independent act that did not advance the defendant's business interests might well have succeeded under the previous law but was rejected on the application of the close connection principle as introduced in *Lister* and *Ming An*. The assault 'was not pre-meditated' and 'took place while the supervisor and plaintiff were engaged in duties at the very time and place demanded by the employment'[85] and thus was sufficiently connected to the employment that it was fair and just to impose vicarious liability. This was an important ruling, the court having found no breach of the employer's duty in view of the suddenness of the attack and the absence of prior warning putting the defendant on notice of the likelihood of violence.

In *Cheung Chak Fui v Sun Hing Organization Plastic*[86] the plaintiff, employed in the defendant's Shenzhen factory, was working in his office when his assistant

[83] *Li Hoi Shuen v Man Ming Engineering Trading Co Ltd* [2006] 1 HKLRD 84.
[84] *Ling Man Kuen v Chow Chan Ming* DCPI 1445/2005, [2006] HKEC 1566.
[85] ibid [70].
[86] *Cheung Chak Fui v Sun Hing Organization Plastic* (2011) HCPI 91/2008.

entered and assaulted him. The attack took place against a general background of work-related tension and inter-personal jealousies that included occasional threats of violence against the plaintiff. The court ruled against vicarious liability because the attack could not be said to be 'sufficiently inherent in or characteristic of Sun Hing's business that it is just to make Sun Hing bear the loss',[87] this despite the court's alternative finding that the employer was in breach of duty for having failed to take adequate measures to provide a safe system of work and to protect the plaintiff, having been previously notified of the threats made against the plaintiff. At first glance it might appear that a finding of breach of duty to provide a safe place of work is a contradiction of the finding that the tortious act was not sufficiently connected to the employment, but this depends on how the concept of employment is construed under the close connection test. On one view, given the deterioration of the employment environment, a close connection is made out. On another view, an act of violence by an assistant could not be said to be inherent in his employment duties as set out in his contract, even broadly interpreted. In taking the latter approach the court cited Litton NPJ in *Ming An* to the effect that the risk created must be inherent in or characteristic of the employer's business,[88] and in this case it was not. The decision on vicarious liability does not sit well with *Ling Man Kuen*, where the attack was also not inherent in the nature of the defendant's business.

The case of *Yeung Mei Hoi v Tam Cheuk Shing*[89] underlines the extent of the change, and the unpredictability of outcome wrought by *Lister* and *Ming An*. The plaintiff estate management supervisor criticised a security guard for failing to stop an unauthorised taxi from entering the estate, and for his improper wearing of his uniform. When the plaintiff tried to take a photograph of the security guard to show to the defendant employer, the security guard assaulted the plaintiff. The Court of Appeal, citing all of the leading authorities beginning with *Lister* and including *CCWS*, found a sufficiently close connection to impose vicarious liability. In the court's view the employer's system of supervision and discipline of security guards carried a risk that a subordinate might react in an unauthorised way. The connection was sufficiently close because 'at that moment of time his scope of employment required him to be subject to the supervision and discipline of the plaintiff'.[90] Moreover, 'it was fair and just to hold the employer vicariously liable because this risk can be insured against by the employer'.[91] Again the imposition of vicarious liability was important because the court at first instance found no breach of the employer's duty in negligence, and this ruling was not the subject of appeal. It is not clear why retaliation was thought to be a risk of supervision

[87] ibid [65].

[88] *Ming An* (n 4) [35], quoting from WVH Rogers, *Winfield & Jolowicz on Tort* 16th edn (London, Sweet and Maxwell, 2002).

[89] *Yeung Mei Hoi v Tam Cheuk Shing* [2015] 2 HKLRD 483.

[90] ibid 493.

[91] ibid.

here, but not in *Cheung Chak Fui*. The only distinction made was that in *Cheung* 'the assault occurred at a time when the parties were not engaged in work related discussions',[92] but as in *Weddall* and *Wallbank*, that is a very technical distinction. The retaliation was merely delayed. The decision does not seem warranted if measured against McLachlin J's criteria for intentional torts vicarious liability in *Bazley v Curry*. On the basis of this case, a Court of Appeal ruling, it is difficult to see how supervisors attacked by subordinates reacting violently to criticism cannot succeed in vicarious liability.

In *Chan Shek Ho v Shiu Ho Chi*,[93] the defendant's warehouse worker (D1), whose work included instructing truck drivers on where to park and unload their cargo, attacked the plaintiff, a self-employed truck driver delivering goods to the warehouse. The warehouse worker took issue with where and how the plaintiff, with whom he had no prior contact, unloaded his goods, and subjected him to a violent attack. The court found the attack to be sufficiently closely connected to the worker's employment because the work 'carried with it a risk that D1 might react in an unauthorised way when truck drivers refused to follow such instructions or when they parked their trucks and/or unloaded cargo in their own way rather than as instructed by D1'.[94] As in *Mohamud v Wm Morrison Supermarkets plc*, cited favourably by the court, the violence, however uncalled for, occurred in the context of performing assigned work duties. The ruling was vital because as a self-employed driver there was no employer's negligence action available to the plaintiff. However, as in *Yeung*, the risk identified by the court is one that is run in all variety of work environments. It is difficult to see any limit to the availability of the vicarious liability remedy in the context of workplace assault by an employee.

The case of *Tsang Sau Yan v v Man Shing Cleaning Service Co Ltd*[95] stands out from this thread. It concerned co-workers who were employed by the defendant as cleaners in a high-rise building. The plaintiff and her colleague came to dislike each other, in large part because of tensions arising out of a personal loan made by the plaintiff to the co-worker that was a long time in repayment. Their personal dislike led to conflicts about workplace duties. The dispute that led to the assault arose out of the sharing of plastic bags used in their cleaning work. The court found the assault to arise from a personal grudge rather than work tensions, and thus not sufficiently connected to the employment. The reasoning is rather puzzling:

> Chan was taking revenge for the personal vengeance against the plaintiff when she got the plastic bags from the Toilet. Though Chan committed the assault in the working place during the office hours, she was not acting in the interests of the defendant but solely for herself. I am not satisfied that the risk of the assault can be said to be sufficiently inherent in or characteristic of the defendant's business in cleaning.[96]

[92] ibid 494.
[93] *Chan Shek Ho v v Shiu Ho Chi* HCPI 613/2014, [2018] HKCFI 737.
[94] ibid [35].
[95] *Tsang Sau Yan v Man Shing Cleaning Service Co Ltd* (2014) DCPI 2757/2012.
[96] ibid [64].

It is not a requirement for vicarious liability in cases of assault that the wrongdoing employee be acting in the employer's interests. Nor is it a requirement that the assault be an inherent risk in the defendant's business, as demonstrated by cases like *Ling*, *Yeung* and *Chan*. The decision in *Tsang* is not in itself surprising in the context of the disputed facts, but again demonstrates the large degree of inconsistency and unpredictability in the determination of the employee assault cases.

It is easier to understand how a supervisor's use of force is connected to employment. Even under the Salmond test such conduct might qualify as a wrongful mode of performing the authorised activities of supervision and discipline. The act of supervision is a means of advancing the employer's interests. This was an important consideration in the *Bazley* criteria. The connection is less apparent when a worker attacks his boss. Nonetheless, the cases suggest the connection can be sufficiently close whether the dispute is between co-workers, or is committed by a subordinate against a supervisor. On close examination a feature that may distinguish the successful Hong Kong cases from those that failed is that identified in *Weddall v Barchester Healthcare Ltd*[97] – the immediacy of the attack. In *Ling Man Kuen* and *Yeung Mei Hoi*, the assailant's violence was an immediate reaction to something said or done by the co-worker. That feature was absent in *Li Hoi Shan* and *Cheung Chak Fui*. However, it does not explain the outcome in *Chan Shek Ho*, nor for that matter in *Tsang Sau Yan*. Nor is it a very convincing distinction. More pertinent is how closely the attack is connected to the employment duties, broadly speaking, including the employment environment.

Vicarious liability in its post-*Lister* form has emerged as an additional important tool to secure workplace safety by providing an alternative remedy in the event of injury by assault. So long as vicarious liability is being used in this way, the theoretical and policy justifications for vicarious liability may require re-evaluation, in particular, to take into account the role of vicarious liability as a tool for ensuring workplace safety and compensation in the event of injury.

iii. Employee Financial Fraud

Financial fraud committed by an employee against a client is the other line of cases that has been affected by the decisions in *Lister* and *Ming An*. As with the employee trespass line of cases, the law has been thrown into an uncertain state. Here, the controversy is not with employee status, but with the second limb, whether the tort was committed in the course of employment. It cannot be assumed that the *Ming An* close connection test applies to such cases, despite the statement by Bokhary PJ in *Ming An* that close connection is 'the basic criterion for vicarious liability in regard to all torts committed by an employee during an unauthorised course of conduct, whether intentional wrongdoing or mere inadvertence is involved'.[98]

[97] *Weddall* (n 82). *Weddall* was not cited in the Hong Kong cases.
[98] *Ming An* (n 4) 581.

There is a tension with an earlier line of authority imposing stricter conditions for vicarious liability for financial fraud as compared to negligently caused personal injury or, for that matter, employee assaults. According to that line of authority, applying principles of agency law, vicarious liability attaches only if the employee acted within his actual or ostensible authority. This position was recently confirmed in the post-*Lister* era by the English Court of Appeal, reversing the trial judge who had applied a form of the *Lister* close connection test.[99]

Importantly, liability will not attach where the fraudulent employee asserted the authority. There must be some statement or conduct by the employer that induces the plaintiff to believe the employee has the authority to undertake that kind of transaction.[100] This more onerous position is explained on the basis that fraud is a reliance-based tort,[101] but that in itself does not explain the insistence on actual or apparent authority. Reliance speaks more to causation than liability. It should also be noted that strictly speaking, if liability is to be determined on the basis of principles of agency law, these cases are not about vicarious liability but the personal liability of the principal.

The confusion as to the correct test is evident from the first such case to be considered in Hong Kong in the post–*Ming An* era. In *Ronia Ltd v Clarke*,[102] the defendant solicitor's clerk defrauded the plaintiff, the defendant's client, of a large sum of money for his own benefit. He received legal fees and forged legal documents deceiving the plaintiff into believing that legal action was being taken to pursue the plaintiff's breach of contract claims against a former business partner when it was not. The evidence showed that it was the defendant's practice to permit the clerk to interview clients and open files, and that in this case the clerk had exercised considerable management of the file. Moreover, the court found that there was a holding out by the defendant of the clerk's authority, such that the plaintiff was entitled to consider the clerk's deeds as acts representative of the defendant. The court rejected the defendant's argument to the effect that because the clerk defrauded the client to his own advantage, he was on a frolic of his own, acting outside of the scope of his authority. Suggesting uncertainty with how to reconcile earlier approaches to vicarious liability for financial fraud with the law after *Ming An*, the court touched all the bases:

> Even if there had not been actual authority, by virtue of the same factual circumstances, there has been a 'holding out' by the defendant so that the plaintiff was entitled to consider Tsang's deeds were acts representative of the defendant … for the same reason, applying the 'close connection' test, this is a case where Tsang's wrongful acts were so closely connected to his employment that it is fair and just to hold the defendant vicariously liable.[103]

[99] *Hockley Mint Ltd v Ramsden* [2018] EWCA Civ 2480, [2019] 1 WLR 1617.
[100] *Armagas Ltd v Mundogas SA* (n 67) per Lord Keith at 782H–783B.
[101] *Hockley Mint Ltd* (n 99) [63] of the joint judgment.
[102] *Ronia Ltd v Clarke* HCA 3972/2000, [2005] HKEC 326.
[103] ibid [55]–[56].

A year later, in *Wan Kwok Ling v Hou Tak Securities Ltd*,[104] a case in which a stock-broking firm's settlement clerk devised a fraudulent scheme through which she misappropriated the funds of a client for her own benefit, *Ming An* was cited but not relied upon. Vicarious liability was found on the basis of the House of Lords decision in *Armagas Ltd v Mundogas SA*:[105]

> Vicarious liability for fraud is governed by 'a set of principles and a line of authority of peculiar application' so that 'it is unnecessary to consider the development of the basis of vicarious liability in relation to torts such as negligence or trespass, which have followed a somewhat different line'.[106]

The defendant was liable, having conferred either actual or ostensible authority on the settlement clerk for the transactions concerned.

Yet in *Brassart Jacqueline Marcelle v R & P International Accounting Affairs Ltd*,[107] a case in which the employee of a financial institution enticed the plaintiff into consolidating her mortgages and taking a loan at an exorbitant interest rate, having falsely represented the terms of the loan, vicarious liability was established solely on the application of the *Ming An* close connection principle:

> The 2nd defendant, when perpetrating fraud or cheating the plaintiff, was clearly acting in his capacity of the 1st defendant's employee in the course of his employment with the 1st defendant. Applying the close connection test … namely whether an employee's tort was so closely connected with his employment that it would be fair and just to hold his employer liable, I have no hesitation to find.[108]

Neither *Ronia* nor *Wan Kwok Ling* was cited. There was no discussion of agency law principles, and no explanation as to why close connection was the relevant principle. In fact, it seems to have been a case where vicarious liability could have been established on either approach.

The opportunity was presented but the confusion was not cleared up in *Standard Chartered Bank v Wendy Lau and Annie Nie*.[109] A branch services manager employed by the defendant bank (SCB) defrauded a customer of account monies for her own benefit. The bank was found vicariously liable on the basis of the *Ming An* close connection test, but also with reference to agency law:[110]

> I accept Mr Ho's submission that Wendy's wrongdoings in question were closely connected to her employment as SCB's staff who liaised with Annie, one of its customers.

[104] *Wan Kwok Ling v Hou Tak Securities Ltd* [2006] 4 HKLRD 525.
[105] *Armagas* (n 67).
[106] ibid 536. In the same year in another stockbroking fraud case liability was imposed with refence to agency law only – see *Liu Man Lok v Ricofull Securities Ltd* [2006] 4 HKLRD 503.
[107] *Brassart Jacqueline Marcelle v R & P International Accounting Affairs Ltd* (2017) HCA 305/2015.
[108] ibid [40].
[109] *Standard Chartered Bank v Wendy Lau and Annie Nie* (2021) HCA 1478/2017.
[110] Adopting an *obiter* remark of Cheung JA in *Zhang Hong Li v DBS Bank (HK) Ltd* [2018] HKCA 435, in which both close connection and agency law principles were cited as bases of liability. On the facts of that case no fraud was proven. The approach resonates with that in *Nathan v Dollars & Sense Ltd* [2008] NZSC 20, [2008] 2 NZLR 557, cited by the CA in *Zhang*.

> Further or alternatively, SCB created an agency in which there was a risk of misconduct by Wendy, in that she was in a position to misappropriate from customers' accounts (as she did).[111]

Neither *Ronia* nor *Wan Kwok Ling* nor *Brassart* was cited. There was no explanation or discussion as to why both approaches were cited.

Most recently, in *Luk Wing Yan v CMB Wing Lung Bank Ltd*,[112] another case of fraud committed against a customer by the defendant bank's branch securities manager for his own benefit, the court applied the approach in *Armagas v Mundogas*[113] rather than that in the general employee tort line of cases. The court found that the bank employee did not have the actual or apparent authority to offer the kinds of investments in question, and any reliance on such authority by the customer was not reasonable. In passing, the court thought that:

> insofar as it is necessary to reconcile the 'close connection' test and the test of apparent authority, it seems to me that it is the apparent authority of the employee who makes the fraudulent representations that will identify the necessary close connection as might render it just to hold the employer vicariously liable.[114]

Neither *Ronia* nor *Wan Kwok Ling* nor *Brassart* nor *Standard Chartered* was cited. This decision differed from the previous in that the court reviewed the close connection line of cases at considerable length before determining that the agency law line of authority, in particular the decision in *Armagas v Mundogas*, was applicable to the instant case.

The current state of the law of employee fraud in Hong Kong is in an unacceptable state. First, the law is unclear. Cases are decided according to different legal principles, with no explanation for the different approaches, on the one hand deviating from an established line of authority from agency law, and on the other openly defying Bokhary PJ's declaration that the same test for vicarious liability applies to all employee torts. It is regrettable that none of the courts in the post-*Ming An* fraud decisions addressed the issue of the proper test for employee fraud vicarious liability clearly and head on. This would require an examination of the *Ming An* close connection principle, the reach of that decision and its appropriateness to a line of cases that had previously been treated as *sui generis*.[115] The court in *Luk Wing Yan* acknowledged the two lines of authority but did not explain why close connection was not the appropriate principle.

[111] *Standard Chartered Bank* (n 109) [116].

[112] *Luk Wing Yan v CMB Wing Lung Bank Ltd* (2021) HCA 1249/2016, [2021] HKCFI 279.

[113] *Armagas* (n 67).

[114] *Luk Wing Yan* (n 112) [142].

[115] As for instance was conducted by the Singapore Court of Appeal in *Skandinaviska Enskilda Banken AB v Asia Pacific Breweries (Singapore) Pte Ltd* [2011] SGCA 22, a case concerning a massive fraud scheme. After a lengthy analysis of the close connection line of cases beginning with *Bazley v Curry*, the court came to the view that the same test, the close connection test, applies to all cases of employer vicarious liability. In the event the court found no vicarious liability because of the limited connection with the employment, and that it would not be fair and just on the facts to impose vicarious liability.

Leaving aside the inconsistency of approach, the line of authority that says that victims of fraud can succeed only if they can prove the existence of employee actual or apparent authority does not sit well with another line of cases in which the victim is also deprived of his property by the defendant's employee. Where the plaintiff is a victim of theft committed by an employee entrusted with the plaintiff's property, the course of employment test suffices for the imposition of vicarious liability,[116] a position that has been made more plaintiff-friendly with the introduction of the close connection test.[117] One might well ask why an employer can avoid liability for his employee's tort merely because the tort was deceit, or because the employee can be said to be an agent. Justice might be better served if, in cases of fraud where no apparent authority is found, any failing on the part of the victim is treated as contributory fault resulting in apportionment rather than the complete denial of a remedy.

C. Employers' Non-Delegable Duty

We have seen from the recent UKSC decisions and a line of first instance decisions in Hong Kong that vicarious liability will not be imposed where the wrongdoer is found to be working for or conducting an independent business. The rationale for this has not been well-explained in the case law, but for now it is the law. On the other hand, there is an established principle in relation to independent contractor negligence that in its effect operates rather like employers' vicarious liability. That is the line of cases in which it is said that the employer owes a non-delegable duty of care to the plaintiff, a duty that cannot be discharged by delegation to an independent contractor. In *Woodland v Swimming Teachers Association*,[118] Lord Sumption described two broad categories of non-delegable duty: 'a large, varied and anomalous class of cases in which the defendant employs an independent contractor to perform some function which is either inherently hazardous or liable to become so in the course of his work'; and cases in which there is an antecedent relationship with the claimant from which it is possible to impute to the defendant the assumption of a positive duty to protect the claimant in circumstances where the claimant is in some way dependent on the defendant for protection from injury.[119]

It has also been said, in Hong Kong at least, that the categories of non-delegable duty are not closed.[120] This creates a strategic synergy between employers'

[116] *Morris v CW Martin & Sons Ltd* [1966] 1 QB 716; *Port Swettenham Authority v TW Wu & Co Sdn Bhd* [1979] AC 580 applying the Salmond course of employment test.

[117] As in *Brink's Global Services Inc v Igrox Ltd* [2010] EWCA Civ 1207.

[118] [2013] UKSC 66, [2014] AC 537.

[119] ibid [6]–[7].

[120] *Chong Ngan Seng v China Harbour Engineering Co Ltd* [2013] 2 HKLRD 223 [55].

vicarious liability and non-delegable duty. In a vicarious liability case that fails because the wrongdoer is found to be an independent contractor, the plaintiff can try to characterise the defendant's activity as giving rise to a non-delegable duty. That is what happened in the Court of Appeal decision in *Li Ming Tak*.[121] In that case, the court found that the panel doctor who advised the plaintiff that he was fit to return to work was not negligent, and on that basis the case failed. Nonetheless the substantive liability arguments were considered. Having found the panel doctor to be an independent contractor, the court considered the non-delegable duty argument. However, in doing so the court seems to have misunderstood the law. The court expressed doubt that Lord Sumption's criteria could be satisfied on these facts, and without a detailed examination of the criteria, rejected the non-delegable duty argument. It was unfortunate that an important argument was overlooked. It is well established that an employer's duty to employees to provide a safe system and conditions of work is non-delegable. That category predates *Woodland*. That duty could, at least arguably, extend to appointment of a panel doctor to whom an injured employee is sent for an assessment of fitness for work. The independent contractor was being asked to assess the fitness to return to work and hence the safety of the employee, the very essence of the non-delegable duty owed by the defendant to its workers. Moreover, liability in such a case does not require proof that the defendant acted unreasonably in relying on the doctor's advice, as the court seems to have assumed. The duty is to see that reasonable care was taken by the doctor, and no more.

An important development related to non-delegable duty took place in the Court of Final Appeal decision in *Luen Hing Fat Coating & Finishing Factory Ltd v Waan Chuen Ming*.[122] The defendant's independent contractor came to the defendant's factory to repair a machine, and in doing so used an unsafe method, resulting in injury to the independent contractor's employee. The defendant was found liable for that injury, not on the basis of non-delegable duty (the work was not intrinsically dangerous), but on the basis of the usual criteria used to construct a duty of care. The court ruled that it was just and reasonable to impose a duty largely because the defendant loaned its equipment for the repair work to the contractor with knowledge (from previous experience) that it would be used in an unsafe way. Justice and reasonableness were used to ground a duty of care. When the duty arises, it is in effect a duty to warn the contractor's employees of the dangerous system being used, or to take some measures to prevent the unsafe system from being used. This development is important because an employer is not (other than in cases of non-delegable duty) liable for the torts of its independent contractors, including those in which the victim is the employee of the independent contractor. Nonetheless, this looks suspiciously like a new category of

[121] *Li Ming Tak* (n 30).
[122] *Luen Hing Fat Coating & Finishing Factory Ltd v Waan Chuen Ming* (2011) 14 HKCFAR 14.

non-delegable duty slipped in through the back door. The principle has taken hold and is now routinely applied in Hong Kong.[123]

III. The Future

Although there have not been any successful vicarious liability cases in Hong Kong in which the wrongdoer was not at the time of committing the tort in a contract of employment with the defendant, that should change. Local courts have responded positively to the UKSC akin to employment initiative. It is odd that most of the attempts to enlist the new principle in Hong Kong concerned tortfeasors who were independent contractors or their employees, but it is only a matter of time before cases concerning ambiguous work relationships such as those in *Cox* and *Armes* will reach the courts. Indeed, we have already seen such arguments, in the form of the spousal relationship as akin to employment, but these took place in specialised proceedings without full argument.

Bokhary PJ's declaration that all employer vicarious liability cases should henceforth be decided according to the close connection principle is now deeply entrenched in the Hong Kong case law and is not likely to change. However, the more precedent-oriented approach signalled in *WM Morrison Supermarkets plc v Various Claimants*[124] should be welcomed and will likely have an impact in Hong Kong. It can be expected, indeed hoped, that close connection will not be treated as replacing the precedents but providing an addendum to them, to be applied where justice cannot otherwise be achieved under the old principle, in particular in cases of employee assaults, whether sexual or otherwise.

A bigger problem for the courts is how to approach cases of employee fraud committed against the defendant employer's client. The argument has been made here that a bifurcated approach which applies a different line of authority to employee fraud is unnecessary and confusing. It contradicts Bokhary PJ's declaration that the same test should apply to all employee torts. Moreover, it is inconsistent with the objectives of vicarious liability, including the enterprise risk theory that has risen to the fore as the policy justification for the expansion of vicarious liability in recent decades, here in Hong Kong and in the highest courts elsewhere. The present inconsistent approach in which judges apply close connection or agency law without explanation as to why, will probably not be resolved until the position is clarified by the Court of Final Appeal or perhaps by the UK Supreme Court.

[123] See eg *Gauchan Som Prasad v Hin Wah Construction Co Ltd* (DCPI 2398/2009, [2011] HKEC 1011); *Lam Pak Keung v Ip Tsz Ping* [2016] 3 HKLRD 139 and *Ng Tat Kuen v Tam Che Fu* (HCPI 896/2013, [2015] HKEC 2226).

[124] *Morrisons* (n 79).

It is likely that the courts in Hong Kong will hold fast to the position reinforced in recent UKSC case law, that there can be no employer vicarious liability for the tort of an independent contractor, despite the absence of a convincing policy justification. After all, this position is deeply entrenched in the Hong Kong case law and there is no reason why the courts would deviate from that when the UKSC will not. This, of course, puts pressure on the courts in making the employee/independent contractor distinction, which, in effect, determines the outcome of the vicarious liability argument, but that pressure has always been there. It also means that plaintiffs who fail to show that the wrongdoer was an employee may try to make creative arguments for non-delegable duty. In recent years only one such attempt was made but we can expect to see more.

8

Vicarious Liability in New Zealand

STEPHEN TODD

I. Introduction

The principles of vicarious liability are commonly applied in the context of accidents causing personal injury giving rise to a liability in tort. Claims of this kind in New Zealand have to be considered in the special context provided by the bar on common law actions which is part of New Zealand's accident compensation scheme. Accordingly, the impact of the scheme on those principles needs to be explained. It is certainly true that there have been fewer cases examining and applying the relevant rules since the scheme came into force back in 1974.

As regards the common law, and speaking broadly, the core elements to the doctrine of vicarious liability were laid down by the UK courts in the Victorian era,[1] and its ambit remained fairly settled until around the start of the present century. Since then, however, the doctrine has been 'on the move',[2] first by its significant expansion in key respects and, most recently, by a rowing back or at least a clarification of its expanded principles. This leads us to consider the significance in New Zealand of developments in the common law elsewhere. New Zealand has a relatively small population – reaching five million people in 2020[3] – and overseas case law can be very influential in determining open or insufficiently litigated matters. Formerly such influence came almost entirely from the UK, but since the later part of the last century the decisions from other common law jurisdictions increasingly have come to be cited. It may be that UK cases are still favoured a little, primarily for historical reasons and because the decisions tend to be well reported and readily available. But, in principle, the courts will look at any decision that they think is helpful. Nowadays it is fair to say that the New Zealand courts will consider relevant decisions from around the common law world and are likely to cite and to rely on those they see as best suited for their local adoption.

[1] For an examination of the history of the doctrine, see *Mohamud v WM Morrison Supermarkets plc* [2016] UKSC 11, [2016] AC 677 [10]–[25] per Lord Toulson.

[2] *Various Claimants v Catholic Child Welfare Society* [2012] UKSC 56, [2013] 2 AC 1 [19].

[3] www.stats.govt.nz/news/new-zealands-population-passes-5-million.

Overseas influences certainly have heavily shaped the law of vicarious liability in New Zealand. More specifically, the courts have accepted some aspects of the recent developments, and in some respects they have either gone their own way or the relevant issues remain undetermined. In this light, the broad aim of this chapter is to examine the principles of vicarious liability as laid down by the courts in this country, and to evaluate the position as it stands in the light of important decisions of the common law courts overseas.

II. Impact of the Accident Compensation Scheme

A. Ambit of the Scheme

In New Zealand, all claims for compensatory damages in tort or contract or on any other basis are subject to the provisions of the accident compensation scheme. So, all claims of vicarious liability in respect of any such causes of action equally are subject to the scheme. Accordingly, a few general words about the ambit of the scheme are needed as a precursor to the main discussion.

Any person in New Zealand who suffers personal injury in a way that is covered by the Accident Compensation Act 2001 can make a claim to the Accident Compensation Corporation for payment of accident compensation.[4] There are now 12 specific heads of cover, and these fall broadly into four categories – personal injury caused by an accident, personal injury caused by treatment, personal injury caused by employment-related disease or infection and personal injury by way of mental or nervous shock suffered as a consequence of physical injury, or by the victims of certain specified sexual offences, or which is work-related.[5] Importantly, the scheme only covers illness or disease to the extent that this is covered in the particular case as employment-related or as falling within one of the other categories.[6]

Where cover for personal injury exists, all proceedings for damages arising directly or indirectly out of a person's injury or death are barred.[7] The bar cannot be avoided by failure to make a claim, or a purported denial or surrender of rights under the 2001 Act or its predecessors, or a lack of entitlement to any particular benefit.[8] The source of any particular claim seeking compensation for personal

[4] Accident Compensation Act 2011, s 20(1) (hereafter ACA 2001). The scheme is primarily for New Zealand residents, but it also covers temporary visitors. However, non-residents are not eligible for certain benefits, and, in particular, for earnings-related compensation. Cover extends to New Zealand residents who suffer injury while abroad for which there would be cover had the injury occurred within New Zealand: ACA 2001, s 22.

[5] ACA 2001, ss 20, 21, 21B.

[6] For full discussion, see S Todd, C Hawes, U Cheer and B Atkin, *Todd on Torts* 8th edn (Thomson Reuters, Wellington, 2019) chapter 2.

[7] ACA 2001, s 317(1).

[8] ACA 2001, s 317(7).

injury is immaterial. All actions for damages for compensation for personal injury covered by the Act or a former Act are barred, whatever the nature of the conduct and whether founded on tort, contract, equity or statute. This includes all cases involving a vicarious, as opposed to a direct, liability. Personal injury actions in New Zealand against overseas defendants equally are barred.[9]

Where there is no cover, the right to sue remains. In *Queenstown Lakes District Council v Palmer*[10] Thomas J noted that the exchange of common law rights for the statutory cover was frequently spoken of as a social contract or social compact. Persons covered under the Act were denied access to the courts at common law in return for the perceived advantages of the statutory scheme. Accordingly, if a claim does not involve personal injury in any form, or if it involves personal injury but falls outside the particular categories that are covered for compensation, an action for damages, if available, can proceed in the ordinary way.

B. Exemplary Damages

A further possible basis for a common law action is where the plaintiff seeks to recover exemplary, rather than compensatory, damages. Quite early on, in *Donselaar v Donselaar*,[11] the Court of Appeal decided that actions for exemplary damages could still be maintained. Richardson J explained that proceedings for exemplary damages did not arise directly or indirectly out of a person's injury or death, where the statutory bar applied, because exemplary damages did not arise out of the plaintiff's injury and were not directed to the plaintiff's loss. In its contemporaneous decision in *Taylor v Beere*[12] the Court of Appeal confirmed that exemplary or punitive damages were intended to punish and deter a defendant guilty of outrageous or contumelious conduct. Compensatory damages might themselves have a punitive effect, but a court could make an award beyond what was properly allowed for by way of compensation in order to register its condemnation of the defendant's 'outrageous' conduct and to mark 'the contumelious disregard by the defendant of the plaintiff's rights'.

Donselaar was affirmed by the NZ Supreme Court in *Couch v Attorney-General (No 2)*.[13] The defendant contended here that without actionable compensatory damages the tort of negligence was incomplete, and so there was no tort for which exemplary damages might be awarded. On this argument *Donselaar* was wrongly decided, but Tipping J pointed out that Parliament had had several opportunities to include exemplary damages expressly within the bar and had not done so.

[9] *McGougan v DePuy International Ltd* [2018] NZCA 91, [2018] 2 NZLR 916.
[10] *Queenstown Lakes District Council v Palmer* [1998] NZCA 190, [1999] 1 NZLR 549 at 555; and see *McGougan* (n 9) [25]–[40].
[11] *Donselaar v Donselaar* [1982] 1 NZLR 97 (CA).
[12] *Taylor v Beere* [1982] 1 NZLR 81, 90 (CA).
[13] *Couch v Attorney-General (No 2)* [2010] NZSC 27, [2010] 3 NZLR 149 [84]–[90].

Furthermore, since *Donselaar*, there had been introduced into the Act an express provision that exemplary damages could be awarded despite the court's inability to award compensatory damages.[14] So the ordinary need for there to be damage to complete the tort of negligence should for this purpose be seen as satisfied by there being a case for the award of exemplary damages.[15]

III. Relationship between the Wrongdoer and the Defendant

A. Employment

Turning now to the common law, the core relationship where vicarious liability can apply is, of course, that which exists between an employer and an employee. However, recent developments overseas show that the presence or absence of an employment contract is no longer decisive and there are other relationships, akin to employment, where it is just that vicarious liability should attach. The element of control, formerly critical in determining whether a contract of employment was in existence, has become simply one part of the factual matrix which will determine whether it is just that A should be vicariously liable for the tortious act of B.

The most important and, in most cases, decisive criterion is that of control. The question is not whether the employer exercises actual control over how work is done but whether the employer exercises ultimate managerial authority or control. It is the employer's right of control over the employee so far as there is scope for control, not the exercise of a power of command.[16] Particular factors that may be relevant include whether the person performing the services provides his own equipment, whether he hires his own helpers, what degree of financial risks he takes, what degree of responsibility for investment in management he has and whether and how far he has an opportunity to profit from sound management in the performance of the work.[17] Another, related, way of looking at the question is to examine whether the person concerned is an integral part of the employer's business or is only accessory to it. The court asks whether the worker

[14] ACA 2001, s 319(1). S 319 was introduced following the decision of the Court of Appeal in *Daniels v Thompson* [1998] 3 NZLR 22, which held, broadly, that the conviction or acquittal of a defendant in a prior criminal proceeding prevented any subsequent recovery of exemplary damages, because of the risk of double punishment or double jeopardy. S 319(2) and (3) reverse the effect of this decision in personal injury cases, by providing that exemplary damages may be awarded in cases covered by the ACA despite the fact that the defendant's conduct has resulted in a criminal charge leading to either a conviction or an acquittal, but providing also that these subsections do not cut down the general reach of subsection (1).

[15] On the question whether there can be a vicarious liability to pay exemplary damages, see Section VI below.

[16] *Challenge Realty Ltd v Commissioner of Inland Revenue* [1990] 3 NZLR 42 at 62.

[17] *TNT Worldwide Express (NZ) Ltd v Cunningham* [1993] 3 NZLR 681 at 700.

is genuinely in business on his or her own account or whether he or she is 'part and parcel of' – or 'integrated into' – the enterprise of the person or organisation for whom the work is performed.[18] Where the terms of a contract are fully set out in writing which is not a sham, the true nature of the contract depends on an analysis of the rights and obligations so defined at the time of its execution.[19] The contractual description given to the relationship by the parties themselves is relevant but is not decisive.[20]

The preceding principles are entirely orthodox in drawing the long-accepted distinction between employees on the one hand and independent contractors on the other. There have been no recent developments challenging that orthodoxy.[21]

B. Relationships Analogous to Employment

A significant expansion in the kinds of relationships that can found a claim alleging vicarious liability for another's wrongdoing has been driven by cases in Canada and in the UK involving abuse committed by priests, or by other persons holding spiritual authority, in circumstances where the defendant being sued is not their employer. The first of these was *John Doe v Bennett*,[22] where the Supreme Court of Canada held that the relationship between a Roman Catholic bishop and a priest in a diocese was 'akin to an employment relationship', and that vicarious liability could be imposed on the diocesan episcopal corporation sole, which was equated with the bishop, in respect of sexual assaults committed by the priest on boys in his parish.

In the UK, similar reasoning was adopted in the Court of Appeal,[23] and thereafter in the Supreme Court in *Various Claimants v Catholic Child Welfare Society* (hereafter the *Christian Brothers* case).[24] Lord Phillips recognised that the policy reasons that usually made it fair, just and reasonable to impose vicarious liability on an employer in respect of the tort an employee committed in the course of his employment should apply equally where the relationship was akin to employment – where the defendant and the tortfeasor were not bound by a contract of employment, but their relationship had the same incidents. In the instant case the De La Salle Institute of the Brothers of the Christian Schools (the Institute) was held to be vicariously liable for sexual and physical abuse committed by its brothers while teaching at and employed by a residential institute (called St Williams) for boys who needed care and protection. The relationship between the Institute and the brothers had all the essential elements of

[18] *Challenge Realty* (n 16) 65.
[19] *TNT Worldwide Express* (n 17) 686.
[20] *Challenge Realty* (n 16) 59–60; *Bryson v Three Foot Six Ltd* [2005] NZSC 34, [2005] 3 NZLR 721.
[21] The distinction has been affirmed in the UK: see n 28 below.
[22] *John Doe v Bennett* 2004 SCC 17, [2004] 1 SCR 436.
[23] *E v English Province of Our Lady of Charity* [2012] EWCA Civ 938, [2013] QB 722.
[24] *Christian Brothers* (n 2).

the relationship between employer and employee: the Institute was subdivided into a hierarchical structure and conducted its activities as if it were a corporate body; the teaching activity of the brothers at St Williams was undertaken because the provincial head directed the brothers to undertake it; the teaching activity undertaken by the brothers also was in furtherance of the objective, or mission, of the Institute; and the manner in which the brother teachers were obliged to conduct themselves as teachers was dictated by the Institute's rules. The relationship between the teacher brothers and the Institute differed from that of the relationship between employer and employee in that the brothers were bound to the Institute not by contract, but by their vows, and the brothers entered into deeds under which they were obliged to transfer all their earnings to the Institute, but neither difference was material. Indeed, they rendered the relationship closer than that of an employer and its employees.[25]

Subsequent cases in the UK Supreme Court, applying the new test, held that a prison authority was vicariously liable for the negligence of a prisoner working in the prison kitchen[26] and also, in a decision which will be examined below, that a local authority was vicariously liable for abuse of a foster child committed by foster parents.[27] By contrast, and after some uncertainty, the distinction between employees and independent contractors has been maintained.[28] A core policy basis for the imposition of vicarious liability is found in the notion that a business should bear the risks posed by the enterprise it has introduced into the community.[29] An employer operating a business through its employees has introduced such risks for its own benefit. But a contractor operating an independent business is the appropriate risk-bearer.

C. Vicarious Liability of Fostering Authority for Foster Parents?

The key decision in New Zealand where an allegedly vicariously liable defendant was not the wrongdoer's employer is *S v Attorney-General*.[30] The plaintiff alleged

[25] St Williams had earlier been held vicariously liable in respect of the abuse committed by its employed teachers, and its claim for a contribution from the Institute accordingly succeeded.

[26] *Cox v Ministry of Justice* [2016] UKSC 10, [2016] AC 660.

[27] *Armes v Nottinghamshire County Council* [2017] UKSC 60, [2018] AC 355; see n 39 below and accompanying text.

[28] *Barclays Bank plc v Various Claimants* [2020] UKSC 13, [2020] AC 973, overturning the contrary decision of the Court of Appeal at [2018] EWCA Civ 1670. Their Lordships' decision restores the import of non-delegable duties, which may be imposed on defendant employers in respect of wrongdoing by independent contractors: see below Section VII.

[29] See especially *Skandinaviska Enskilda Banken AB v Asia Pacific Breweries (S) Pte Ltd* [2011] SGCA 22, [2011] 3 SLR 540; discussed in chapter six by Tan.

[30] *S v Attorney-General* [2003] 3 NZLR 450 (CA); and see *W v Attorney-General* (unreported, CA 227/02, 15 July 2003).

that at various times starting in the early 1960s, when he was aged about five, he had been physically abused by his foster father and sexually abused by his foster parents' son. He alleged also that after 1964, when the foster parents separated, he was regularly beaten and later sexually abused by his foster mother. In 1996, after both parents had died, S began counselling for psychological problems. In the same year he made an application for leave to issue proceedings against the Department of Social Welfare (the Department) alleging, inter alia, direct liability for negligence and breach of fiduciary duty in failing to protect him from the assaults and the abuse, and vicarious liability for assault and battery committed by the foster parents and their son. A separate claim against the son was settled before the trial.

The trial judge held, inter alia, that the bar on personal injury actions contained in the accident compensation legislation applied to the plaintiff's claims, that S had cover under the scheme and that the Crown was not liable for exemplary damages.[31] S appealed, and the Crown cross-appealed against the High Court finding that, but for the accident compensation bar, the Crown would have been vicariously liable for the conduct of S's foster parents.

The court held first that the accident compensation bar did not apply. The applicable Act – the Accident Rehabilitation and Compensation Insurance Act 1992 (a predecessor to the Accident Compensation Act 2001) – had extended cover to personal injury which was mental or nervous shock suffered as a result of particular acts, including certain sexual offences, but it was not intended to apply where, as here, the shock occurred before the Act came into force. Exemplary damages were not covered either, so in this respect a common law claim could still proceed.[32]

Second, the defendant argued that the claims were statute barred under the Limitation Act 1950. It was held that the six-year limitation period in a case alleging vicarious liability for assault and battery involving child abuse[33] commenced running when the victim first realised that he or she had not given a free and considered consent to the abuse.[34] S's realisation must have occurred by the early 1980s. However, the evidence supported the conclusion that S was under a disability which inhibited him from bringing proceedings, and on this basis the proceedings were brought in time.[35]

This brings us to the question whether the Crown could be vicariously liable in respect of the foster parents' sexual misconduct. At the time when S was decided the concept of a 'relationship analogous to employment' as founding a claim of vicarious liability had yet to be developed by common law courts overseas, and

[31] *S v Attorney-General* [2002] NZFLR 295.
[32] See further Section VI below.
[33] Limitation Act 1950, s 4(1). Leave was required if a claim was filed more than two years and less than six years after the cause of action accrued: s 4(7).
[34] Applying *T v H* [1995] 3 NZLR 37 (CA).
[35] Applying the Limitation Act 1950, s 24.

in these circumstances the members of the Court of Appeal argued the matter differently. Blanchard J, delivering the joint majority judgment, observed that the foster parents were not employees of the Department, and thought that in the circumstances the relationship was appropriately characterised as one of agency, albeit that the agency was of an unusual, indeed unique, nature. Further, his Honour was quite satisfied that the abuse occurred in the course of the agency duties of the foster parents, it being sufficiently connected with the purpose of parenting for which the placement was made.[36] These factors, together with recognition of the special obligation of protection of children imposed on the Superintendent of Child Welfare as a surrogate of the New Zealand community, rendered it fair that compensation for the innocent victim's serious injury should be borne by and distributed amongst the community. However, additional abuse by the foster parents' son could not be regarded as being conduct of an agent of the Crown. The son was not appointed as a foster parent and his assaults had no apparent connection with any parenting role, and so in this case the Crown was not vicariously liable.

Tipping J, in a separate judgment, preferred not to characterise the relationship between the parties in terms of existing categories where vicarious liability arose. In his Honour's view, the best course was to determine, as a matter of policy and analogy, whether vicarious liability should be found to exist. In the instant case the foster parents in one sense were agents of the state, in another they were employed (albeit not contractually so) by the state, and in another they were independent contractors given the large amount of freedom and discretion afforded to them in bringing up the children. However, as regards the last of these, it could well be said that while performance of the Superintendent's duties to the child could be delegated, responsibility for improper performance could not. Hence the independent contractor dimension was neutralised. It was appropriate also to bring into account the statutory environment favouring foster care over long-term institutional care, together with any associated policy concerns. And vicarious liability for children in institutions, but not for those in foster care, would produce an undesirable and potentially unjust anomaly. Accordingly, in the light of these various factors, it was appropriate that the Department should be held vicariously liable for the conduct of the foster parents.[37]

[36] See further Section IV.B below.

[37] Compare *A v Roman Catholic Archdiocese of Wellington* [2008] NZCA 49, [2008] 3 NZLR 289, where a foster child placed in a Catholic orphanage run by the Sisters of Mercy and managed by a director of Catholic Social Services alleged that the orphanage and Catholic Social Services were vicariously liable for abuse suffered by the child during holiday placements with caregivers. The Court of Appeal held that the defendants were not liable, because they had no statutory control over the child and were simply fulfilling the obligations of parents to maintain her. The orphanage was not set up to provide care during school holidays and did not inspect or supervise holiday placements. It was unreal to regard the holiday caregivers as the agents of the defendants or as performing their duties. See also *White v Attorney-General* [2010] NZCA 139 [198]–[211].

We must ask now how we should view the reasoning in *S* in the light of contrasting decisions with materially similar facts in Canada and in the UK. As regards the position in Canada, in *KLB v British Columbia*,[38] a majority in the Supreme Court of Canada held that the Government of British Columbia was not vicariously liable for physical and sexual abuse committed by the plaintiff's foster parents. In the majority's view the foster parents were in important respects independent of the government, they did not hold themselves out as government agents and nor were they reasonably perceived as such, and the government could not exercise close control over their activities.

A contrary view was taken by the UK Supreme Court in *Armes v Nottinghamshire County Council*, where, as already noted, vicarious liability was imposed on a local authority for child abuse committed by foster parents.[39] Lord Reed, giving the majority judgment, said that the picture, as a whole, pointed towards the conclusion that the foster parents provided care to the child as an integral part of the local authority's organisation of its childcare services. It could properly be said that the torts committed against the claimant were committed by the foster parents in the course of an activity carried on for the benefit of the local authority. Further, the local authority's placement of children in their care with foster parents created a relationship of authority and trust between the foster parents and the children, in circumstances where close control could not be exercised by the local authority, and so rendered the children particularly vulnerable to the risk of abuse. It could be considered fair that they should compensate the unfortunate children for whom that risk materialised. So far as the issue of control was concerned, while the foster parents controlled the organisation and management of their household and dealt with most aspects of the daily care of the children without immediate supervision, it would be mistaken to regard them as being in much the same position as ordinary parents. The local authority exercised powers of approval, inspection, supervision and removal without any parallel in ordinary family life, and in this way exercised a significant degree of control over both what the foster parents did and how they did it. And finally, most foster parents had insufficient means and no insurance cover to be able to meet a substantial award of damages, whereas the local authorities which engaged them could more easily compensate the victims of injuries which were often serious and long-lasting.

Let us evaluate the decision in *S* in light of the conflicting decisions overseas. We should recognise at the outset that the notion of the relationship between a public authority and foster parents as being founded on a special form of agency is

[38] *KLB v British Columbia* 2003 SCC 51, [2003] 2 SCR 403.

[39] Above n 27; C Beuermann, 'Up in Armes: The Need for a Map of Strict Liability for the Wrongdoing of Another in Tort' (2018) 25 *Torts Law Journal* 1; A Dickinson, 'Fostering Uncertainty in the Law of Tort' (2018) 134 *LQR* 359: S Deakin, 'Organisational Torts: Vicarious Liability Versus Non-delegable Duty' (2018) 77 *CLJ* 15; A Bell, 'The Liability of Local Authorities for Abuses by Foster Parents' (2018) 34 *Professional Negligence* 38.

unsatisfactory and should be rejected.[40] Rather, finding a relationship 'analogous to contract' is preferable and would be in line with developments elsewhere. Indeed, Tipping J's analysis in *S* is quite similar in substance, although not expressed in those terms. While the contract analogy perhaps may be criticised on the basis that it can be somewhat vague and uncertain, it nonetheless works quite well when applied to working relationships *that are not contractual* in circumstances where the 'employer' is in a controlling position. Yet should a public body's relationship with foster parents qualify? Very arguably, the better view is that taken in *KLB* and by Lord Hughes in his dissent in *Armes*. Lord Hughes maintained that the foster carers did not do what the authority would otherwise do for itself; they did something different, by providing an upbringing as part of a family. A family life was not consistent with the kind of organisation which the enterprise test of vicarious liability contemplated. Vicarious liability was necessary, and fair and just, when it applied to fix liability on someone who undertook an activity, especially a commercial activity, by getting someone else integrated into his organisation to do it for him. Employment was the classic example, and other situations might be analogous. But the extension of strict liability needed careful justification. Once one examined the nature of fostering, its extension to that activity did not seem to be either called for or justified but, rather, fraught with difficulty and contra-indicated.

The majority decision in *Armes* has been criticised as long on policy and short on principle: rather than seeking out a clear, principled basis for imposing liability on those who had committed no wrong, the judges relied on a casserole of incommensurable policy reasons and general resort to what was 'fair' and 'just' to support the doctrine.[41] Its operation thus becomes highly unpredictable, and litigants are encouraged to push at the ill-defined and expanding boundaries of liability. More particularly, Lord Reed's conclusion that foster parents were an integral part of the local authority's child care services appears to be inconsistent with one of his reasons for rejecting the claim based on a non-delegable duty owed to the claimant – that the duty of the local authority was not to provide daily care but to arrange for and monitor its performance.[42] Again, his Lordship's references to the local authority's statutory duties and powers as supporting the imposition of vicarious liability[43] contrasts with the clear position in the law of negligence, recently affirmed by Lord Reed himself, that public authorities are generally subject to the same liabilities in tort as private individuals and bodies.[44] And finally, the importance he attaches to the local authority's deeper pockets[45] undermines his own, principled, rejection of that factor in an earlier decision.[46]

[40] The basis for vicarious liability in the case of agency is considered below at Section V.
[41] Dickinson, above n 39, making the points that follow.
[42] *Armes* (n 27) [47]; see further Section VII.B.
[43] (n 27) [59]–[62].
[44] *Robinson v Chief Constable of West Yorkshire Police* [2018] UKSC 4, [2018] AC 736 [31]–[42].
[45] *Armes* (n 27) [63].
[46] See *Cox* (n 26) [20].

A factor which, conversely, can point in favour of liability, and which also was identified by Lord Reed,[47] is that of risk creation, the local authority having placed the claimant in a position where she was particularly vulnerable to abuse. But this factor cannot point to the imposition of vicarious liability where the relationship is not one that is analogous to employment. Rather, finding a relationship between a defendant and a claimant in circumstances where the defendant has assumed a degree of control over the claimant, who can be seen to be vulnerable and in need of protection, may point towards the defendant owing the claimant a non-delegable duty of care. We will come back to this possibility later on.[48]

IV. Connection between the Relationship and the Wrongdoing

A. Conduct in the Course or Scope of Employment

In orthodox terms, an employer is vicariously liable for the tort of an employee only where the tort is committed in the course of employment. The test that has been commonly applied, derived from *Salmond on Torts*,[49] has two limbs. It must be asked whether the employee's act is a wrongful act authorised by the employer or is a wrongful and unauthorised mode of doing some act authorised by the master. The first limb of this test is not really about vicarious liability, as, where a wrongful act is authorised, the employer is personally liable. The second limb raises the problem of deciding whether conduct is an unauthorised mode of doing something or is simply not authorised at all. It is a question of fact and degree whether a tortious act is so much within the scope of employment that it was generally authorised, albeit tortiously carried out.[50]

Asking whether tortious conduct was in the course or scope of employment gives expression to the need to place limits on the employer's liability, by restricting that liability to those acts which can be recognised as sufficiently connected to the employment relationship and by differentiating those cases where the employment merely gives the employee the opportunity to commit the unauthorised act. The test has been applied in a great variety of circumstances and has fostered a multitude of decisions, and, at least in cases involving negligence, it probably works as well as can reasonably be expected. Yet determining how it should apply in cases where the wrongdoer has engaged in deliberately wrongful, often criminal, conduct entirely for his or her own ends has proven especially difficult. Taking the child abuse cases as examples, it is impossible to characterise sexual abuse by

[47] *Armes* (n 27) [61].
[48] See Section VII.
[49] JW Salmond, *The Law of Torts* 1st edn (London, Stevens and Haynes, 1907) 83–84.
[50] *Commercial Union Assurance Co of NZ Ltd v Lamont* [1989] 3 NZLR 187, 212 (CA).

a teacher or priest as a wrongful mode of doing authorised work: such conduct is the very antithesis of what the teacher or priest should do. Certainly, earlier decisions tend to show that the courts were more reluctant to hold employers liable for the deliberate torts of their employees than for their negligence, although it is not clear whether this reluctance arose because the underlying policy considerations were seen to be less applicable where employees were behaving in a deliberately unlawful manner, or whether it was simply seen to be more difficult to characterise such behaviour as being one way of performing employment obligations. At all events, recent cases involving intentional conduct have preferred to ask whether the connection between the tortious conduct and the employment is sufficiently close as to justify vicarious liability.

B. Conduct Closely Connected with the Employment

In *Bazley v Curry*,[51] a decision of the Supreme Court of Canada, McLachlin J maintained that vicarious liability was generally appropriate where there was a significant connection between the creation or enhancement of a risk and the wrongful act, even if unrelated to the employer's desires. Relevant factors might include the opportunity that the enterprise afforded the employee to abuse his or her power; the extent to which the wrongful act may have furthered the employer's aims (and hence be more likely to have been committed by the employee); the extent to which the wrongful act was related to friction, confrontation or intimacy inherent in the employer's enterprise; the extent of power conferred on the employee in relation to the victim; and the vulnerability of potential victims to wrongful exercise of the employee's power. Applying these principles, a foundation operating residential care facilities for troubled children was vicariously liable for paedophilic assaults by a care-giving employee. His duties included general supervision and also intimate activities like bathing and putting the children to bed, and in these circumstances the employer was seen as having created or enhanced the risk of his sexual wrongdoing. By contrast, in *Jacobi v Griffiths*,[52] the same court held, in a majority decision, that a children's club was not vicariously liable for sexual abuse by an employee away from the club premises and outside working hours. The employment gave the opportunity to commit the assaults, but the employee was not placed in a special position of trust and the actual work created no special risk of wrongdoing.

In the UK, in *Lister v Hesley Hall Ltd*,[53] the House of Lords imposed vicarious liability on the employer of a warden of a boarding house for boys with emotional and behavioural difficulties who systematically sexually abused the

[51] *Bazley v Curry* [1999] 2 SCR 534; and see *Blackwater v Plint* 2005 SCC 58, [2005] 3 SCR 3.

[52] *Jacobi v Griffiths* [1999] 2 SCR 570; and *see B v Order of the Oblates of Mary Immaculate* 2005 SCC 60, [2005] 3 SCR 45; *Reference re: Broome v Price Edward Island* 2010 SCC 11, [2010] 1 SCR 360.

[53] *Lister v Hesley Hall Ltd* [2001] UKHL 22, [2002] 1 AC 215.

boys. The majority of their Lordships took a similar approach as in *Bazley*, seeing the discussion in that case as a clarification of the second limb of the *Salmond* test. Accordingly, they focused attention on the closeness of the connection between the employee's acts and the duties of the employment. Merely providing the opportunity for the abuse was not enough.

In *Christian Brothers*,[54] the UK Supreme Court confirmed that there needed to be proof that the defendant caused a material increase in the risk that abuse would occur and held that on the facts this was established. The relationship between the Institute and the brothers enabled the Institute to place the brothers in teaching positions. Living cloistered on the school premises were boys who were vulnerable because they were children in the school, because they were virtually prisoners, and because their personal histories made it very unlikely that if they attempted to disclose what was happening to them, they would be believed. The brother teachers were placed in the school to care for the educational and religious needs of these pupils. Abusing the boys in their care was diametrically opposed to those objectives but, paradoxically, that very fact was one of the factors that provided the necessary close connection between the abuse and the relationship between the brothers and the Institute.

In *S v Attorney-General*,[55] the close connection test was accepted by the Court of Appeal as part of New Zealand law. Applying it, the Crown was held to be vicariously liable for the sexual abuse committed by the foster parents of the plaintiff child in that case. Blanchard J was satisfied that the abuse was sufficiently connected with the purpose of parenting for which the placement was made. The Department, by placing children in private homes where they were vulnerable to a wrongful exercise of power, and where their condition necessarily was not able to be monitored as regularly and fully as in an institution, had created or increased a risk of child abuse.

Bazley, *Lister*, *Christian Brothers* and *S* all concern allegations of sexual abuse, and a key question is whether the principles they lay down should apply generally in other cases involving claims of vicarious liability. In *Mohamud v WM Morrison Supermarkets plc*,[56] the UK Supreme Court recognised that the close connection test could apply broadly in cases where the question of the link between the relationship and the wrongdoing was in issue. In this case the claimant, a man of Somali origin, inquired at the defendant's petrol station about printing documents from a USB stick, but the defendant's employee (K), who worked in the kiosk, promptly abused him using foul, racist and threatening language. The claimant then returned to his car, but K followed him to the petrol station forecourt,

[54] *Christian Brothers* (n 2).

[55] *S* (n 30).

[56] *Mohamud v WM Morrison Supermarkets plc* [2016] UKSC 11, [2016] AC 677; J Plunkett, 'Taking Stock of Vicarious Liability' (2016) 132 *LQR* 556; P Morgan, 'Certainty in Vicarious Liability: A Quest for a Chimaera' (2016) 75 *CLJ* 202; SSH Chan, 'Hidden Departure from the *Lister* Close Connection Test' [2016] *Lloyd's Maritime and Commercial Law Quarterly* 352.

told him never to come back and, ignoring instructions to stop by a supervisor, subjected him to a violent assault. The claimant sued the defendant employer, seeking damages in respect of this unprovoked assault. The claim failed both at first instance and in the English Court of Appeal, and the claimant appealed to the Supreme Court.[57]

Lord Toulson recognised that the House of Lords in *Lister* was mindful of the risk of over-concentration on a particular form of terminology and thought there was a similar risk in attempting to over-refine, or lay down a list of criteria for determining, what precisely amounted to a sufficiently close connection to make it just for the employer to be held vicariously liable. Simplification of the essence was more desirable. Taking this approach, the Supreme Court had to consider two matters. The first question, to be addressed broadly, was what functions or 'field of activities' had been entrusted by the employer to the employee, or, in everyday language, what was the nature of his job. Second, the Court had to decide whether there was sufficient connection between the position in which he was employed and his wrongful conduct to make it right for the employer to be held liable as a matter of social justice. The cases in which the necessary connection had been found were cases in which the employee used or misused the position entrusted to him in a way which injured the third party.

In the instant case it was K's job to attend to customers and to respond to their inquiries. His conduct in answering the claimant's request in a foul-mouthed way and ordering him to leave was inexcusable, but within the 'field of activities' assigned to him. What happened thereafter was an unbroken sequence of events. Following the claimant to the forecourt was all part of a seamless episode. When K again told the claimant in threatening words that he was never to come back to the petrol station, this was not something personal between them; it was an order to keep away from his employer's premises, which he reinforced by violence. In giving such an order he was purporting to act about his employer's business. It was a gross abuse of his position, but it was in connection with the business in which he was employed to serve customers. His employers entrusted him with that position, and it was just that, as between them and the claimant, they should be held responsible for their employee's abuse of it. K's motive was irrelevant. It looked obvious that he was motivated by personal racism rather than a desire to benefit his employer's business, but that was neither here nor there.

Lord Toulson's words appear to suggest that in applying the close connection test an employee's motive for acting should be disregarded. In some cases that is certainly true, but in many it is not. A key focus needs to be on the question whether the defendant has placed the wrongdoer in a position of power or authority over the victim. The existence of such a relationship can be seen as significant because of the potential it creates for abuse, providing the wrongdoer

[57] The claimant died from an unrelated illness before his appeal was heard.

with the means to inflict it.[58] A power relationship certainly exists in the abuse cases, and finding a relationship of this kind can help the courts in distinguishing between cases where the defendant has created a risk of the wrongdoing in question and those where the defendant has merely provided the opportunity for that wrongdoing. However, in cases where there is no such relationship, some other basis for imposing vicarious liability may still be found. An example is seen in deliberate assault cases where the conduct of the employee was an unauthorised interpretation or extension of the work the employee was authorised to carry out.[59]

In *Various Claimants v WM Morrison Supermarkets plc*,[60] Lord Reed explained the decision in *Mohamud* in this way. Here a rogue employee of the defendant, who was a senior IT auditor, disclosed personal information about his co-employees on the Internet when motivated by a work-related grudge. The co-employees sued in respect of an invasion of their privacy, and the question for determination was whether this disclosure was 'closely connected' with S's employment. In deciding the question, a key focus of Lord Reed's judgment was on the decision of the Supreme Court in *Mohamud* and how it should be understood. His Lordship was satisfied that that decision was not intended to effect a change in the law of vicarious liability, as was apparent when Lord Toulson's judgment was read as a whole. His Lordship had relied in particular on *Dubai Aluminium Co Ltd v Salaam*,[61] where Lord Nicholls had identified the general principle applicable to vicarious liability arising out of a relationship of employment: the wrongful conduct should be so closely connected with acts the employee was authorised to do that, for the purposes of the liability of the employer to third parties, it might fairly and properly be regarded as done by the employee while acting in the ordinary course of his employment. However, Lord Phillips had noted in *Christian Brothers* that the close connection test had been applied differently in cases concerned with the sexual abuse of children, which could not be regarded as something done by the employee while acting in the ordinary course of his employment.[62] Instead, the courts had emphasised the importance of criteria that were particularly relevant to that form of wrongdoing, such as the employer's conferral of authority on the employee over the victims, which authority he had abused.

Lord Reed emphasised that Lord Toulson in *Mohamud* was not suggesting any departure from the approach adopted in *Dubai*. Read in context, Lord Toulson's

[58] C Beuermann, 'Vicarious Liability and Conferred Authority Strict Liability' (2013) 20 *Torts Law Journal* 265 argues that the courts should recognise a distinct category of 'conferred authority strict liability', in addition to vicarious liability, to cover such relationships.

[59] *Pettersson v Royal Oak Hotel Ltd* [1948] NZLR 136 (CA); *Mattis v Pollock (t/a Flamingos Nightclub)* [2003] EWCA Civ 887, [2003] 1 WLR 2158; *Weddall v Barchester Health Care Ltd*; *Wallbank v Wallbank Fox Designs Ltd* [2012] EWCA Civ 25, [2012] IRLR 307.

[60] *Various Claimants v WM Morrison Supermarkets plc* [2020] UKSC 12, [2020] AC 989.

[61] *Dubai Aluminium Co Ltd v Salaam* [2002] UKHL 48, [2003] 2 AC 366.

[62] *Christian Brothers* (n 2) [83], [85].

comments that there was 'an unbroken sequence of events', and that it was 'a seamless episode', were not directed towards the temporal or causal connection between the various events, but towards the capacity in which the employee was acting when those events took place.[63] When he followed the claimant out of the kiosk and on to the forecourt, he was following up on what he had said in the kiosk. He ordered the claimant to keep away from his employer's premises and reinforced that order by committing the tort. In doing so, he was 'purporting to act about his employer's business' and it was 'not something personal'. Read in isolation, Lord Toulson's concluding remark that motive was irrelevant would be misleading, yet his Lordship was addressing the point that the reasons why K had become violent were unclear. His Lordship had already concluded that K was going, albeit wrongly, about his employer's business, rather than pursuing his private ends, and the reason why he had become so enraged as to assault the motorist could not make a material difference. That was all that the remark was intended to convey.

Applying this approach, Lord Reed said that it was abundantly clear that the rogue employee was not engaged in furthering his employer's business when he committed the wrongdoing in question. On the contrary, he was pursuing a personal vendetta, seeking vengeance for disciplinary proceedings against him some months earlier: he was engaged in 'a frolic of his own'.[64] In those circumstances, his wrongful conduct was not so closely connected with acts which he was authorised to do that, for the purposes of Morrisons' liability to third parties, it could fairly and properly be regarded as done by him while acting in the ordinary course of his employment. So, all the claims failed.

A key clarification in *Morrison* is that the principles applied in the sexual abuse cases should be regarded as exceptional. Without doubt, a sexual abuser is engaged not just in a 'frolic' but a very serious criminal offence entirely on his own account. In such cases, the question whether the employer has put the wrongdoer in a position which enabled him or her to exercise power or authority or control over the victim is very relevant. Whether any particular case falls within the sexual abuse category is likely to be clear in most cases, although, exceptionally, the question may need exploring. Other special categories which are similarly treated also are possible, as the discussion below concerning the vicarious liability of principals for the torts of their agents will show.

A further question concerns the field of application for the close connection test in cases of negligence. Here the *Salmond* test, asking whether negligent misconduct is a wrongful mode of doing authorised work, can operate reasonably coherently, although difficulties in its application are bound to arise out of the limitless variety of facts where the question may be put in issue. By contrast, the question whether *intentional* misconduct can be seen as a wrongful mode of doing

[63] *Morrison* (n 60) [26]–[30].
[64] *Joel v Morison* (1834) 6 C & P 501, 503.

what was authorised is certainly difficult and sometimes impossible to apply in any sensible fashion, especially in sexual abuse cases. For this reason, McLachlin J introduced the test of 'close connection' and the accompanying explanatory principles as applying in circumstances involving unauthorised and intentional wrongdoing. But should the new test be applied as well in the case of negligent wrongdoing? The answer seemingly is yes, provided there is the requisite close connection with *authorised work* – with what the wrongdoer was employed to do. We need no longer ask whether the wrongdoing is a mode of doing authorised work but whether it is closely connected with that work. The connection with what is authorised is critical. Without that link there can normally be no basis for holding the employer (or person in an analogous position) liable for the wrongdoer's harm. But exceptionally, as in sexual abuse and other special claims, misconduct entirely for the wrongdoer's own purposes may have a sufficient connection with that work.

V. Principals and Agents

A. Claims in Deceit

There is a good deal of uncertainty in the cases about the circumstances in which a principal may be held vicariously liable for the tort of an agent. In particular, some authority appears to hold that a claim of deceit should be treated differently from other types of wrongdoing in the context of the vicarious liability of a principal. In *Armagas Ltd v Mundogas SA*,[65] the House of Lords determined that where a claimant had suffered loss in reliance on the deceit of an agent, the principal was vicariously liable only if the deceitful conduct of the agent was within his or her actual or ostensible authority. And recently, in *Hockley Mint Ltd v Ramsden*,[66] the English Court of Appeal determined that that principle had not been replaced or supplemented by the law as laid down in *Lister* and *Dubai*.[67] The trial judge had taken the view that the relevant tests for determining whether a principal was vicariously liable for his agent's deceit was whether it was just and fair for liability to be imposed on the principal and whether there was a sufficiently close connection between the agent's wrongdoing and the class of acts which the agent was employed to perform. But the Court of Appeal observed that *Armagas* was the authority binding on the court and that the judge accordingly had applied the wrong legal test. He had not identified or addressed the essential ingredients of vicarious liability as required by *Armagas*: a holding out or representation by the principal to the claimant, intended to be and in fact acted upon by the claimant,

[65] *Armagas Ltd v Mundogas SA* [1986] AC 717 (HL).
[66] *Hockley Mint Ltd v Ramsden* [2018] EWCA Civ 2480, [2019] 1 WLR 1617.
[67] See Section IV.B.

that the agent had authority to do what he or she did, including acts falling within the usual scope of the agent's ostensible authority. Further, the decisions in *Lister* and *Dubai* did not concern a reliance-based tort and were not about the ostensible authority of an agent or employee. Rather, they concerned questions about the ordinary course of employment and the ordinary course of a firm's business, which was why *Armagas* was not mentioned in any of the speeches in either case.

Let us compare *Armagas* and *Hockley Mint* with *Nathan v Dollars & Sense Ltd*,[68] a decision of the New Zealand Supreme Court which does not ultimately concern the imposition of vicarious liability, but which discusses the principles of agency as they apply in this context. A borrower (R) sought to arrange a loan from a financier (D & S) to fund his business, with his parents' property being used as security. D & S's lawyer asked R to obtain his parents' signatures and to carry out other tasks in relation to the security on D & S's behalf. R forged the signature of his mother (N), following which the mortgage was registered and the loan moneys advanced. R's business later was placed in liquidation, and D & S sought to enforce its security. Blanchard J, giving the judgment of the court, recognised that it could not be said that borrowers could never act as agents for lenders. Here R had been entrusted with the task of obtaining the signatures and was D & S's agent for that purpose, having been impliedly authorised to act in a representative capacity. Whether a principal was liable for an agent's conduct depended upon whether the conduct fell within the scope of the task the agent had been engaged to perform. There needed to be a sufficiently close connection between that task and the agent's unlawful act, so that the wrong could be seen as the materialisation of the risk inherent in the task. On the facts the conduct was within the scope of the agency, even though the forgery was done exclusively for the benefit of the agent, and the fraud of D & S's agent had to be regarded as its own fraud. Accordingly, the fraud exception to the indefeasibility provisions governing title to registered land applied,[69] D & S's title as mortgagee was not indefeasible and the mortgage in its favour should be removed from the Land Register.

The decision in *Nathan* is consistent with that in *Armagas* (which the court did not mention), because *Nathan* did not concern a liability for misrepresentation concerning the agent's authority. Blanchard J noted in the course of his judgment that the son's fraud was not primarily against the principal and that it was just as much against his mother, who gained no benefit whatsoever from the transaction. This possibly suggests that the forgery was seen as a tort vis-à-vis the mother; but any potential liability to the mother would not have been for deceit. Certainly, there was no statement made by the son to the mother upon which she relied to her detriment. But *Nathan* held at least that vicarious liability could apply to an agency relationship not involving employment and applied a close connection test in determining the scope of that liability.

[68] *Nathan v Dollars & Sense Ltd* [2008] NZSC 20, [2008] 2 NZLR 557.

[69] Land Transfer Act 1952 (NZ), ss 62, 63. See now Land Transfer Act 2017 (NZ), ss 51, 52 and s 6 (definition of 'fraud').

B. Agency in Contract and in Tort

This brings us to consider whether or how the rules governing a principal's *contractual* liability should also govern the principal's *tortious* liability. There are obvious differences between these actions. A principal's contractual liability is founded upon the *principal's* conduct either in conferring actual authority or in holding someone out as acting with his or her authority. The liability of the principal does not depend upon the agent having committed a tort. By contrast, the principal's tortious liability depends upon the *agent's* conduct in committing a tort for which the principal can be strictly liable.[70]

Let us take first the position where the wrongdoer – the alleged agent – is not an employee. If the wrongdoer has no actual authority, and the alleged principal has not held that person out as an agent and thus conferred upon him or her an ostensible authority to bind the principal,[71] then he or she is not or is not deemed to be the principal's agent, there is no basis for a finding that the principal is bound as a matter of contract and, notably, there is no relationship upon which a claim for vicarious liability may be founded. But if the requisite authority or holding out exists, then the question whether the principal is vicariously liable for the agent's tort should depend on whether the wrongdoing is closely connected with the agency relationship. Suppose now that the agent is also an employee. The solution here seems to be to distinguish between his or her conduct *qua* agent and conduct *qua* employee or contractor.[72] Insofar as the agent/employee is acting as a contractual agent seeking to bind the principal, the normal requirement of actual or ostensible authority will apply. Insofar as the agent/employee is acting simply as an employee or for other purposes, the close connection test will apply in determining whether the employer/principal is vicariously liable for the employee's tort. On this reasoning the decisions in *Armagas* and also, seemingly, both *Hockley Mint* and *Nathan* can be recognised as having been correctly decided. It is clear that the alleged agent in *Hockley Mint* was not an employee of the principal, so there could be no vicarious liability without an agency relationship having been shown to exist. In *Nathan*, by contrast, the son had actual authority to act as agent from the financier, so there was an agency relationship in respect of which the close connection test could apply.

This analysis can also help explain the long-standing decision of the House of Lords in *Lloyd v Grace, Smith & Co.*[73] An employee who was employed by a

[70] Some early agency scholars took the view that the rules of contractual and tortious agency should be the same: see WA Seavey, 'Rationale of Agency' (1920) 29 *Yale Law Journal* 859; CA Wright, 'The American Law Institute's Restatement of Contracts and Agency' (1935–36) 1 *University of Toronto Law Journal* 17.

[71] While the test for rebutting ostensible authority in relation to contracts is objective, in this type of case it may be that subjective knowledge of a person's lack of authority needs to be shown: see *Thanakharn Kasikorn Thai Chamkat v Akai Holdings Ltd (No 2)* [2010] HKCFA 64, (2010) 13 HKCFAR 479 [47]–[62].

[72] P Watts, 'Agency, Forgery and the Land Register' (2008) 124 *LQR* 529, 532.

[73] *Lloyd v Grace, Smith & Co* [1912] AC 716.

solicitor as a conveyancing manager, and who was vested with authority to arrange and negotiate sales of real property, deceitfully induced the plaintiff to convey her property to himself, and in these circumstances their Lordships held unanimously that the defendants were vicariously liable for the fraud. Lord Macnaghten was satisfied that a principal was liable for the fraud of his agent committed in the course of the agent's employment and not beyond the scope of his agency, whether the fraud was committed for the benefit of the principal or not. And if we invoke modern reasoning, we can say that the underlying basis for the decision is well expressed in the notion that the agent's fraud was closely connected with his position as conveyancing manager, and that by putting him in that position the principal created the risk of the fraud being committed. But we must recognise that this is another exceptional case, and that the approach being taken here arguably is analogous to that in the sexual abuse cases. So, the principal can be vicariously liable for the fraud notwithstanding that the agent acts entirely out of self-interest and does not purport to be acting in any way for the benefit of the principal. This is because the principal has put the agent in a position of authority over the client, who is vulnerable to fraudulent conduct and who is necessarily dependent on the agent to act honestly.

VI. Claims for Exemplary Damages

A question which stands alone, of particular importance in New Zealand,[74] is whether there can be a vicarious liability to pay exemplary damages. In the UK, in *Kuddus v Chief Constable of Leicestershire Constabulary*,[75] the House of Lords was divided on the issue. Lord Hutton thought that the power to make an exemplary award in respect of conduct amounting to misfeasance in public office served to uphold and vindicate the rule of law and to deter wrongdoing by public officers.[76] But Lord Scott saw an award of exemplary damages where the defendant was not a wrongdoer and the award would be met out of public funds as not adding anything at all to the deterrent effect of a finding in favour of an injured person. A defendant should not be liable to pay exemplary damages unless he had committed punishable behaviour, a principle that left no room for an award where liability was vicarious only.[77] The English Court of Appeal later took the former view,[78] and this also seems to be the approach taken in Australia.[79] On the other hand, the

[74] See Section II above.
[75] *Kuddus v Chief Constable of Leicestershire Constabulary* [2001] UKHL 29, [2002] 2 AC 122.
[76] ibid [78]–[79].
[77] ibid [108], [131].
[78] *Rowlands v Chief Constable of the Merseyside Police* [2006] EWCA Civ 1773, [2007] 1 WLR 1065.
[79] *New South Wales v Ibbett* [2006] HCA 57, (2006) 229 CLR 638, although the decision in this case turned on the provisions of a New South Wales statute.

Supreme Court of Canada has held that punitive damages could not be awarded in the absence of reprehensible conduct specifically referable to the employer.[80]

In New Zealand, in *S v Attorney-General*,[81] Blanchard J said that it would be quite unfair to inflict a punishment upon someone who had been found not to have been complicit in the wrongdoing. The damages would not then be a reflection of the culpability of the defendant, and exemplary damages were not intended and should not be used to provide an additional monetary remedy. Furthermore, in the case of workplace injury it was debatable whether an award against an employer whose agent or employee had behaved disgracefully would provide an additional incentive to take further and effective precautions going beyond those required by an ordinary duty of care. However, the balance might possibly be different in a case in which an official of the State had deliberately, recklessly or in a grossly negligent manner, directly inflicted personal injury on the plaintiff, and whether the Crown might be held vicariously liable in such a case should be left open. On the facts it was determined that the Department of Social Welfare was vicariously liable to S to pay compensatory damages for the foster parents' sexual assaults and batteries but was not liable to pay exemplary damages.

The view rejecting vicarious liability is the better one.[82] The core objection is simple – the injustice involved in punishing innocent parties. In Lord Scott's words, '[S]ilently and without any proper or principled justification for it, a system of vicarious punishment of public employers for the misfeasances of their employees has crept into our civil law'.[83] This suggests that it is very doubtful whether, as mooted in *S*, there is room for an exception for officials of the state either.

VII. Non-Delegable Duties

A person who, in some way, has assumed responsibility for the safety of another may be held *personally* liable to the other person for failing to take care in the exercise of his or her supervisory responsibilities. In particular, a parent or a person in loco parentis may be held liable for negligence in failing to protect a child from danger.[84] Furthermore, in certain limited circumstances, the duty of a person in a supervisory or controlling position may be non-delegable, in

[80] *Blackwater* (n 51) [91]; and see *McCabe v Roman Catholic Episcopal Corp* [2015] ONCA 213.

[81] n 30 [88]–[94].

[82] See S Todd, 'Vicarious Liability, Personal Liability and Exemplary Damages' in S Degeling, J Edelman and J Goudkamp (eds), *Torts in Commercial Law* (Sydney, Thomson Reuters, 2011) 409–48.

[83] *Kuddus* (n 75) [136].

[84] See, for example, *McCallion v Dodd* [1966] NZLR 710; *Barnes v Hants County Council* [1969] 1 WLR 1563 (HL); *Tweed Shire Council v Howarth* [2009] NSWCA 103. In *A v Roman Catholic Archdiocese of Wellington* (n 37), William Young P suggested that the duty could extend to protecting children's physical and psychiatric health, including emotional abuse: provided it did not extend to anything approaching a duty to maximise or enhance children's emotional well-being, it should be reasonably manageable.

the sense that that person cannot delegate legal responsibility in circumstances where the task in question is actually performed by someone else. In *Woodland v Swimming Teachers Association*,[85] Lord Sumption observed that English law had long recognised that non-delegable duties existed but did not have a single theory to explain when or why. We will consider here the 'protective' duty that was in issue in *Woodland*, which probably is the category of real significance, and put the others to one side.[86]

A. Protective Relationships

The category of non-delegable duty in issue in *Woodland* concerned persons who have taken on a protective role in favour of another or others. Lord Sumption recognised that the relevant cases had three critical characteristics. First, the duty arose not from the negligent character of the act itself but because of an antecedent relationship between the defendant and the claimant. Second, the duty was a positive or affirmative duty to protect a particular class of persons against a particular class of risks, and not simply a duty to refrain from acting in a way that foreseeably caused injury. Third, the duty was by virtue of that relationship personal to the defendant. The work required to perform such a duty might well be delegable, and usually was. But the duty itself remained the defendant's. Five particular factors in establishing this personal duty were (i) the vulnerability of the claimant, (ii) the existence of a relationship between the claimant and the defendant by virtue of which the defendant had a degree of protective custody and control over the claimant, (iii) the claimant having no control over how the defendant chose to perform its obligations, (iv) the delegation of that custody and control to another person and (v) negligence by that person in the performance of the very function assumed by the defendant and delegated to him or her.[87] A clear instance was the non-delegable duty of employers to maintain a safe system of work for their employees,[88] and the relationships between hospitals and their patients,[89]

[85] *Woodland v Swimming Teachers Association* [2013] UKSC 66, [2014] 1 AC 537 [6]; R George, 'Non-delegable Duties of Care in Tort' (2014) 130 *LQR* 534; J Morgan, 'Liability for Independent Contractors in Contract and Tort: Duties to Ensure Care Is Taken' (2015) 74 *CLJ* 109.

[86] Lord Sumption identified liability for 'extra-hazardous acts' as another category, but described it ([6]) as 'varied and anomalous' and ripe for re-examination. Others were the non-delegable duty of a landowner to prevent the escape of water from his land (as recognised in *Rylands v Fletcher* (1866) LR 1 Ex 265 (Exch Ch) or to maintain support for neighbouring land (citing *Dalton v Henry Angus & Co* (1881) 6 App Cas 740 (HL)), and the non-delegable duty of employers of independent contractors conducting operations obstructing the highway (citing *Tarry v Ashton* (1876) 1 QBD 314 (QB)). Another important category, which Lord Sumption did not mention, is the non-delegable duty owed by a bailee to a bailor of goods.

[87] *Woodland* (n 85) [7], [23].

[88] *McDermid v Nash Dredging and Reclamation Co Ltd* [1987] AC 906 (HL).

[89] Approving the approach of Lord Greene MR in *Gold v Essex County Council* [1942] 2 KB 293, 301 (CA) and of Denning LJ in *Cassidy v Ministry of Health* [1951] 2 KB 343, 359–65 (CA).

and local education authorities and their pupils[90] fell into the same category.[91] So, in *Woodland* itself, the duty of a local education authority was held to be non-delegable in circumstances where a pupil suffered serious injury in the course of a school swimming lesson conducted by swimming instructors provided by an independent contractor.[92]

It is always important to identify the particular function or task that the body concerned has assumed a duty to perform. Lord Sumption emphasised that an education authority would not be liable for the negligence of independent contractors where its own duty was not to perform the relevant function but to arrange for its performance, as where a school provided extra-curricular activities outside school hours. Nor would the authority be liable for the negligence of those to whom no control over the child had been delegated, such as theatres, zoos or museums to which children might be taken by school staff. For example, an education authority was not liable for the negligence of a taxi firm employed by the authority to drive children to and from school, for the school had no duty to transport the children.[93] Again, a hospital was not liable for the negligence of an independent laboratory carrying out tests on tissue samples for a patient who was not being treated by the hospital.[94]

B. Personal Liability of Fostering Authority to Foster Child?

Let us return now to the case of a local authority arranging for the fostering of children in its care. In *Armes* the UK Supreme Court determined, by a majority, that the authority was vicariously liable,[95] but held, unanimously, that no non-delegable duty should be imposed. Lord Reed recognised that a local authority, in relation to a child in its care, had the powers and duties which a parent or guardian would have by virtue of their relationship to a child of which they were the parent or guardian.[96] These included the general duty to safeguard and promote the child's health, development and welfare, and the right to direct, control or guide the child's upbringing. There was ample authority that the duty of a parent or person in loco parentis was a duty to take reasonable care.[97]

[90] *State of New South Wales v Lepore* [2016] HCA 37, (2016) 258 CLR 134.

[91] His Lordship said other examples were likely to be prisoners and residents in care homes. See eg *GB v Home Office* [2015] EWHC 819 (QB) (medical treatment of detainee in an immigration removal centre); *Hughes v Rattan* [2022] EWCA Civ 107, [2022] 1 WLR 1680.

[92] The case was remitted for trial, and, in *Woodland v Maxwell* [2015] EWHC 273 (QB), the claimant established that her injuries were caused both by a lifeguard employed at the pool and by a teacher in failing to notice that she was in difficulties in the water.

[93] *Myton v Woods* (1980) 79 LGR 28.

[94] *Farraj v King's Healthcare NHS Trust* [2009] EWCA Civ 1203, [2010] 1 WLR 2139.

[95] See Section III.C.

[96] Child Care Act 1980 (UK), s 10 (repealed in 1991, in force during the relevant period).

[97] Citing *Carmarthenshire County Council v Lewis* [1955] AC 549, 566 (HL); *Harris v Perry* [2008] EWCA Civ 907, [2009] 1 WLR 19, [37]; *Surtees v Royal Borough of Kingston upon Thames* [1991] 2 FLR 559 (CA).

But there were no authorities suggesting that parents were required not merely to take personal care for their children's safety, but to ensure that reasonable care was taken by anyone else to whom the safety of the children might be entrusted. There were good reasons for adopting that approach in a domestic setting, for holding the parents liable because of a lack of care on the part of the nanny or the babysitter, or if the child were abused by a friend or a grandparent, would be liable to interfere with ordinary aspects of family life which were often in the best interests of children themselves. Further, since a non-delegable duty would render the local authority strictly liable for the tortious acts of the child's own parents or relatives, the effect of a care order, followed by the placement of the child with his or her family, would be a form of state insurance for the actions of the child's family members. His Lordship accordingly concluded that the proposition that a local authority was under a duty to ensure that reasonable care was taken for the safety of children in care, while they were in the care and control of foster parents, was too broad, and that the responsibility with which it fixed local authorities was too demanding.

It would seem perfectly appropriate for the relationship between fostering authority and child to be characterised as one where the authority had assumed a responsibility to protect the child by virtue of an antecedent protective relationship between them. Indeed, on its face the relationship looks to be a particularly apt example, whereas, for reasons suggested earlier, the relationship between local authority and foster parent does not look at all like a relationship analogous to employment that gives rise to vicarious liability. However, the Supreme Court's denial of a non-delegable duty demonstrates that persuasive reasons of policy can nonetheless negate the imposition of such a duty notwithstanding that a protective relationship can be seen to exist. Certainly, the contrast with, and any implications for, the ordinary duty of care owed by a parent or person in loco parentis points away from a duty that was non-delegable in the circumstances of the case.

This reasoning also leads to a rejection of the duty in *S*. The possible application of the concept of a non-delegable duty appeared to be recognised by Tipping J, who maintained that while performance of the Superintendent of Child Welfare's duties to the child could be delegated, responsibility for improper performance could not.[98] But the difficulty posed by the contrasting position of parents was not considered.

VIII. Vicarious Liability Compared with Non-Delegable Duties

In conclusion, let us compare the ambit of a claim alleging vicarious liability and a claim alleging breach of a non-delegable duty. In the case of vicarious liability,

[98] See also *A v Roman Catholic Archdiocese of Wellington* (n 37) [74], where William Young P said that the holiday caregivers did not perform non-delegable statutory duties imposed upon the Sisters of Mercy and Catholic Social Services.

the focus is on the relationship between the defendant and the wrongdoer, whereas the focus in the case of a non-delegable duty is on a protective relationship assumed by a defendant over a vulnerable plaintiff. However, it appears that the two forms of liability can overlap and that sometimes either principle can apply. An example might be *Lister*, where the employer was held to be vicariously liable for the employee warden's sexual abuse and, seemingly, the school could equally have been held to have been under a non-delegable duty in respect of a child it had taken into its care. On the other hand, *Christian Brothers* could not have been argued as a case of a non-delegable duty, unless the De La Salle Institute could be treated as having assumed a degree of protective custody over the claimant (and having delegated performance to its brothers). But it is hard to see any such relationship existing, the claimant being in fact in the custody of the Middlesbrough Defendants. Conversely, *Woodland* could not be argued as a case of vicarious liability, involving as it did the negligence of independent contractors. In *Woodland* itself Lord Sumption said that the case had 'nothing to do with vicarious liability, except in the sense that it [the issue on appeal] only arises because there is none'.[99]

[99] *Woodland* (n 85) [4].

9

Vicarious Liability in Scotland

MAT CAMPBELL AND BOBBY LINDSAY

I. Introduction

This chapter first surveys the doctrinal core of vicarious liability in Scotland. Generally, the present law is either settled or on a predictable trajectory: of principal interest is the manner of its evolution to date and to come. If it develops as we envisage, problems which courts will encounter, and the character of future foreign influence, are in turn foreseeable. We address these matters in the third section of the chapter, before the fourth considers under-examined issues bearing on Scots law's response to historic child abuse.

II. General Principles of Vicarious Liability

Vicarious liability involves the imposition, regardless of fault, of liability upon one defender for another defender's delict (tort). Two elementary points may be addressed briefly. First, one cannot be vicariously liable if no delict has been committed.[1] Second, vicarious liability is distinct from direct liability for breach of a personal duty.[2] This section concentrates on the basic inquiry: the requirement of a relationship capable of giving rise to vicarious liability; and the requirement that any delict be relevantly linked to that relationship.[3] Though we summarise and evaluate certain features of the current position on each of these issues, the fundamental stakes are like those in play in jurisdictions with far more law and literature of interest.[4] To say something of any real moment, it is necessary primarily to examine how vicarious liability has developed, and is likely to develop, in Scotland.

[1] *Baxter v Colvilles Ltd* 1959 SLT 325 (IH); *Sutherland v Bank of Scotland Plc* [2014] CSOH 113 [42].

[2] *Marshall v William Sharp & Sons Ltd* 1991 SLT 114 (IH) esp 119 (Lord Ross), 124–25 (Lord Dunpark), addressing a common law safe system of work case before vicarious liability.

[3] *Grubb v Shannon* [2018] SC GLA 13, 2018 SLT (Sh Ct) 193 [17], [61]–[64]; *Kennedy v Bonnici* [2021] CSOH 106, 2022 SLT 63 [55].

[4] Scholarship which could not have been produced for want of material if focused principally on Scottish sources includes C Beuermann, *Reconceptualising Strict Liability for the Tort of Another* (Oxford, Hart Publishing, 2019); A Gray, 'A Critique of the Enterprise Risk Theory of Vicarious

A. Relationships Giving Rise to Vicarious Liability

The first stage of the basic inquiry concerns the relationships from which vicarious liability arises. Chief among them is employment. Cases of borrowed employees also pose no difficulty. Beyond that, eventual recognition of dual vicarious liability seems probable, and the notion of a relationship 'akin to employment' is less novel in Scotland than perhaps hitherto thought.

i. Employment and Employment Pro Hac Vice

It is well-established that, whilst there is no general liability for the delict of one's independent contractor,[5] relationships of employment and employment *pro hac vice* give rise to vicarious liability.[6] In the mid-1940s it was recognised that the indicia of employment cannot remain frozen in time,[7] and shortly thereafter, Lord Cooper confirmed that changing social, political and employment conditions render appropriate 'a broad overhead view' of the arrangements between persons which the courts encounter.[8] Importantly, the judges are realistic about how influential should be a purported employer's level of control over a purported employee. This will be important. But it has long been acknowledged that control need not be exercised in fact. It may suffice that the employer can secure the proper discharge of the purported employee's functions should the need arise.[9] Moreover, an employment relationship may exist even where control is practically unnecessary, or beyond a purported employer's own skill.[10]

Control aside, any factor appearing relevant in a particular case must be considered, including powers of selection and dismissal, methods of and reasons for payment, financial risk, provision of tools or equipment, the general nature of a purported employee's work, party intention,[11] the collection of income tax or national insurance or, of course, the presence of a contract that might qualify as one of employment.[12] Helpful more general questions include whether service

Liability' (2019) 62 *Canadian Business Law Journal* 181; J Dietrich and I Field, 'Statute and Theories of Vicarious Liability' (2019) 43 *Melbourne University Law Review* 515. We wrote too early to consider fully Professor Elspeth Reid's account of vicarious liability in *The Law of Delict in Scotland* (Edinburgh, Edinburgh University Press, 2022), [3.01]–[3.77].

[5] *Grubb* (n 3) [48]–[49], [56]; for an exception, see, eg, *Esso Petroleum Co Ltd v Scottish Ministers* [2016] CSOH 15, 2016 SCLR 539 [14]–[24]: primary liability for independent contractors' negligent damage to neighbouring property.

[6] *King v Fife Council* 2004 Rep LR 33 (OH) [9].

[7] *Short v J&W Henderson Ltd* 1946 SC (HL) 24, 33–35, where Lord Thankerton opined that the indicia of employment may require to be restated. *Short* was a workers' compensation statute case, but is cited in vicarious liability cases such as *Kilboy v South Eastern Fire Area Joint Committee* 1952 SC 280 (IH) 285, 287.

[8] *Kilboy* (n 7) 285–87.

[9] *Short* (n 7) 33–35.

[10] *United Wholesale Grocers Ltd v Sher* 1993 SLT 284 (OH) 287.

[11] Ibid 286–87.

[12] *Grubb* (n 3) [87].

in return for remuneration is offered as opposed, for example, to an end result simpliciter; or whether a purported employee is part and parcel of another's business, rather than conducting a separate business on her own account as a true independent contractor.[13] Recent authority permits the latter question to be understood as the kernel of an 'entrepreneur test'.[14] Both questions assist in the identification of factors bearing on a given case.

There is no single test for employment *pro hac vice*. Criteria which assist in some cases will not in others.[15] But again, there exist general questions to focus the analysis. Appellate authority suggests that, broadly, the matter depends primarily on the transfer, not of actual detailed control over the manner of an employee's work,[16] but of capacity to direct, or to *delegate* to her a discretion as to, how work is done.[17] It has also been proposed that the search is for facts establishing a transfer of responsibility for conduct in the discharge of functions, and that this *may* be less likely in cases involving employees considered skilled.[18] Furthermore, an employee must expressly or impliedly accept working for a temporary employer. In this regard, it appears to have been thought that something in the nature of a contract was required.[19] But for decades it has been clear that a tripartite agreement to transfer the employee from one employer to another is not essential.[20]

Just as in much earlier times,[21] English sources on the above issues have continued freely to be cited in the courts: when the indicia of employment are recalled;[22] and in matters concerning borrowed employees.[23] Also observable in secondary sources,[24] this openness supplements learning that already exists.

[13] *Sher* (n 10) 287.

[14] See *Grubb* (n 3) [72], [99], citing *E v English Province of Our Lady of Charity* [2012] EWCA Civ 938, [2013] QB 722 [72].

[15] *Malley v London Midland & Scottish Railway* 1944 SC 129 (IH) 136, 140–41, 144–45.

[16] Though transfer is likelier where, eg, the usual employer cedes control over the employee's place, apparatus and manner of work, as observed in *Lyell v Sun Microsystems Scotland BV* [2005] CSOH 36, 2005 SCLR 786 [6](3), [14], an employers' (direct) liability case.

[17] *McGregor v JS Duthie & Sons & Co Ltd* 1966 SLT 133 (IH) 141–142 (Lord Grant), 143 (Lord Strachan), 145 (Lord Walker).

[18] *King* (n 6) [11]–[12]; *Moir v Wide Arc Services Ltd* 1987 SLT 495 (OH).

[19] *Malley* (n 15) 137 (Lord Cooper, original emphasis: 'strictly speaking, there must always be … a *tripartite* agreement'), 147–49 (Lord McKay), 149–50 (Lord Jamieson).

[20] *McGregor* (n 17) 142 (Lord Grant), 144–45 (Lord Walker).

[21] See P Simpson, 'Vicarious Liability' in K Reid and R Zimmermann (eds), *A History of Private Law in Scotland*, vol II (Oxford, Oxford University Press, 2000) 604–05, explaining English influence on the Scottish recognition of employment *pro hac vice*, tentatively dated to 1893. See also *Ogilvie v The Magistrates of Edinburgh* (1821) 1 S 24 (IH), in which the court sent away to English ports for information about 'the manner of appointing and paying pilots, and the understood freedom from responsibility on the part of those who appointed them'.

[22] For example, in *Kilboy* (n 7) 285–86, Lord Cooper relied upon both Scottish and English authority. See, similarly, *Marshall* (n 2) 121.

[23] Where the decision in *Mersey Docks and Harbour Board v Coggins & Griffith (Liverpool) Ltd* [1947] AC 1 (HL) has been highly influential. Various speeches are cited in the borrowed employee cases mentioned above.

[24] See, eg, G Cameron, *Thomson's Delictual Liability* 6th edn (London, Bloomsbury, 2021) [12.6]–[12.8], [12.18]; Reid (n 4) [3.18]–[3.22].

As the cases drawn upon here from the twentieth century onwards show, Scots law is self-sufficient as regards the principles which guide the identification of employment relationships. Those principles are easily stated, and their concreteness must at least aid their application. But it is their general open texture that makes it easy to act upon the clear licence which judges past have given to keep the law moving, and this is perhaps the most important feature of the body of authority addressed here. From a doctrinal perspective, we might look forward to refinement of what could often be rather unrestrained, multi-factorial examinations of fact situations, to see if they disclose employment.[25] Of most obvious interest in this regard will be the general questions highlighted above. They may help sharpen academic writings, pleadings and the judicial guidance which will benefit from at least some systematisation as it proliferates in further decided cases. From a practical perspective, as in other jurisdictions, newer working and employment practices will cause novel fact patterns to come before the courts;[26] and they will further occupy those advising clients. In particular, what has been called 'the orthodox employee/independent contractor distinction' will likely continue to be challenged by employers, who have 'an obvious incentive … to seek to pre-empt vicarious liability by dressing their workers in the clothing of contractors rather than employees'.[27] On top of the legal flexibility identified above, Scots law's theoretical ability to respond to this difficulty, and others, is or will be improved by developments considered under the next two headings. But in turning to them, we concentrate on the insights they yield about how the law is shaped in this jurisdiction.

ii. Dual Vicarious Liability

It is likely that, when directly considered again, dual vicarious liability will be recognised in Scots law.[28] In *Park v Tractor Shovels Ltd*,[29] part of Hatten's role was to maintain his employer's plant at a steel works. He volunteered to assist the pursuer with work on plant belonging to the latter's own employer at the same site. Hatten negligently injured the pursuer, who argued, inter alia, that both his own employer *and* Hatten's usual employer were vicariously liable. Lord Cowie accepted that it was 'at least in theory possible that although Hatten was

[25] For an academic attempt to do this elsewhere, see P Bomball, 'Vicarious Liability, Entrepreneurship and the Concept of Employment at Common Law' (2021) 43 *Sydney Law Review* 83.

[26] For earlier developments in England, Australia and Hong Kong, see P Giliker, 'Comparative Law and Legal Culture: Placing Vicarious Liability in Comparative Perspective' (2018) 6 *Chinese Journal of Comparative Law* 265, 267–71.

[27] D Nolan, 'Reining in Vicarious Liability' (2020) 49 *Industrial Law Journal* 609, 616–17. See also *Cox v Ministry of Justice* [2016] UKSC 10, [2016] AC 660 [29].

[28] Lord Jauncey's statements in *Esso Petroleum Co Ltd v Hall Russell & Co Ltd (The Esso Bernicia)* [1989] AC 643 (HL, Scot) 685–86 need not be discussed here for the reasons given in *Viasystems (Tyneside) Ltd v Thermal Transfer (Northern) Ltd* [2005] EWCA Civ 1151, [2006] QB 510 [33]–[34], [73]–[74].

[29] *Park v Tractor Shovels Ltd* 1980 SLT 94 (OH).

acting within the scope of his employment with the second defender [and usual employer, which *was* held vicariously liable], he was at the time of th[e] accident in the temporary employment of the first defenders'; but he had 'no hesitation in rejecting' that possible argument, because the heavy burden of showing that responsibility had shifted was not discharged.[30] His Lordship concluded:

> Having reached that decision it seems to me that that disposes of any question of joint liability on the part of the defenders based on vicarious responsibility. In my opinion it is not merely a tenet of the Christian faith that a man cannot serve two masters, but that it applies also to the legal doctrine of vicarious liability.[31]

Three points temper the surprise which such concision might elicit. First, how full or persuasive an argument Lord Cowie heard on the point is unclear from the *Scots Law Times* report. Second, in 1980 the conclusion pronounced perhaps appeared obvious, at least to a likely busy first instance judge, already in a pursuer's favour on established principles.[32] Third, and relatedly, the strongest support for dual vicarious liability to put before Lord Cowie was, realistically, Patrick Atiyah's famous monograph.[33] Atiyah favours dual liability as a general rule in cases of employment *pro hac vice* where the pursuer is a third party rather than one of the wrongdoer's two employers.[34] They would be left 'to dispute among themselves who should bear the burden'.[35] Authority from the United States is cited in support. But Atiyah doubts whether an English court could emulate its approach.[36] So, even if Lord Cowie had read Atiyah's book, it might have been too tentative to carry the day. It is not referred to in the report of *Park*, and any general claim about awareness of it at the bar or on the bench would be speculative.[37] In any event, its open citation, or even consultation without reference, are perhaps unlikely.[38] Then-current tendencies against the use in court of writing by living authors were not unwavering. But they were strong, and did not soften so as to be more like today's until the 1990s.[39]

[30] ibid, 100.

[31] ibid, 101.

[32] It goes too far to claim *generally* that dual vicarious liability was probably then considered impossible 'outside the academic world': WJ Stewart 'A Note on Matthew' 6, 24: The Theology of Dual Vicarious Liability' 2007 *Scots Law Times (News)* 99, 101; compare *Kastner v Toombs* (1980) 611 P 2d 62 (Alaska SC) 65; though compare, in turn, *DePratt v Sergio* (1981) 102 Wis 2d 141 (Wis SC).

[33] PS Atiyah, *Vicarious Liability in the Law of Torts* (London, Butterworths, 1967) ch 18 esp 156–57, 163–64.

[34] In the latter event, the employers' position inter se should, in Atiyah's view, depend on any contract by which the employee is lent, not delict: ibid 153–54.

[35] ibid 163.

[36] But see his views about the possibility that more than one employer might be liable, just not *vicariously*: ibid 157–58.

[37] A favourable book notice of course came long before *Park*, if it raised the book's profile at all: DM Walker 1967 *Scots Law Times (News)* 171.

[38] Undue optimism is implicit in the statement, which cannot be wrong taken literally, that '[i]t is *not impossible* that the argument taken may in some way have been infused by [Atiyah's] work': Stewart (n 32) 101, fn 25 (emphasis added).

[39] K Reid, 'Smoothing the Rugged Parts of the Passage: Scots Law and its Edinburgh Chair' (2014) 18 *Edinburgh Law Review* 315, 332–34.

We should not think ill of Lord Cowie, then. All the more so, because however well-reasoned, a case will not affect developments if it slips from memory. It appears that some have forgotten *Park*'s significance. For example, the important *Stair Memorial Encyclopaedia* records English law's acceptance of dual vicarious liability, citing *Park* only in discussion of employment *pro hac vice*.[40] The case is not mentioned at all in other widely read work, such as *Gloag & Henderson*. Perhaps with studied imprecision, this text observes that 'dual vicarious liability is yet to be recognised in Scots law', and notes that it 'may prove a useful device in cases, for example, involving agency workers'.[41] Reference is made to English authorities that have already made the move,[42] Scottish commentary on which also omits *Park*.[43]

The same pattern is visible in more recent Scottish cases. In *Bell v Alliance Medical Ltd*,[44] Lord Boyd appeared to accept as good law certain 'incremental developments' by reference to passages from *Various Claimants v Catholic Child Welfare Society*,[45] in which Lord Phillips stated that '[i]t is possible for two different defendants, D2 and D3, each to be vicariously liable for the single tortious act of D1'. And in *Grubb v Shannon*,[46] Sheriff Reid opined that the deemed transfer reasoning, usually employed to resolve cases of employment *pro hac vice*, was 'an unwieldy fiction': '[a] more principled solution may finally have been found in the concept of dual vicarious liability'. This is not an endorsement of something like Atiyah's proposal of routine dual liability in employment *pro hac vice* cases. The Sheriff's reference to *Viasystems*[47] confirms that English law provided the food for thought. These *obiter* hints plainly favour a conception of dual vicarious liability along the lines drawn south of the border. That is, now that Rix LJ's approach in *Viasystems* has been preferred to May LJ's control-centred analysis,[48] dual vicarious liability arises when practical and structural considerations suggest that a wrongdoer is recognisable as part of the work, business or organisation of more than one defender sought to be made vicariously

[40] With three other cases, for the proposition that the burden of showing 'that transfer of liability has taken place … can be discharged only in exceptional circumstances': K Miller, 'Strict Liability' in R Black (gen ed), *The Laws of Scotland: Stair Memorial Encyclopaedia*, vol XV (London, LexisNexis, 1995) [249], citing *Viasystems* (n 28) in an update appended to that paragraph. See also Cameron (n 24) [12.18], citing *Park* on employment *pro hac vice* but observing that dual vicarious liability has 'not been considered in the Scottish courts'.

[41] HL MacQueen and Lord Eassie (eds), *Gloag & Henderson: The Law of Scotland* 15th edn (Edinburgh, W Green, 2022) [25.15], fnn 97–8. See also Reid (n 4) [3.33]–[3.34].

[42] *Viasystems* (n 28); and *Various Claimants v Child Catholic Welfare Society* [2012] UKSC 56, [2013] 2 AC 1 (*CCWS*).

[43] A Barron, 'Vicarious Liability for Employees and Agents' 2006 *Scots Law Times (News)* 79; G Junor, 'Child Abuse Claims – a Reversal of View' 2013 *Scots Law Times (News)* 59.

[44] *Bell v Alliance Medical Ltd* [2015] CSOH 34, 2015 SCLR 676 [113].

[45] *CCWS* (n 42) [20]–[21] esp [20(iv)]; citing *Viasystems* (n 28).

[46] *Grubb* (n 3) [55].

[47] *Viasystems* (n 28).

[48] See *CCWS* (n 42) [45].

liable, so that each may justly be treated as assuming the burden of the beneficial relationships which they have undertaken.[49]

As seen under previous headings, and as will be seen under the next, a flexible conception exists in Scotland of employment, employment *pro hac vice*, and relationships 'akin to employment', for the purposes of vicarious liability. Once this conception is accepted, dual vicarious liability seems doctrinally unchallenging, and is rather simply conceived of as practically necessary to give effect to commonly listed policy objectives of vicarious liability on easily imaginable fact patterns. A glance beyond the British Isles shows that if the idea is accepted in principle,[50] the current English model is not the only conceivable one. One could favour routine dual vicarious liability based on a stronger normative commitment to responsibility for risks characteristic of an organisation's activities than to responsibility for the wrongdoing of persons over whom an entitlement to control exists.[51] But neither awareness of this nor appetite for further investigation are likely to be great in this jurisdiction. As has been seen, even Scottish authority contrary to courts' and commentators' current inclinations is being ignored, consciously or not, in favour of English law. On the current state of the sources – and barring valuable litigation rendering worthwhile the sort of argument and judgment-writing that please academics – it would surprise if much, if any, debate, preceded Scots law's eventual commitment to the *Viasystems* approach.[52]

iii. Relationships 'Akin to Employment'

Only relatively recently was it confirmed that vicarious liability may arise from something *called* a relationship 'akin to employment'. However, there is precursive appellate authority. In the 1990 case of *Marshall v William Sharp & Sons Ltd*,[53] a quarry manager died on site due to the negligence of an electrician, Dean. Though Dean was not an employee of the quarry's operators,[54] the Inner House held them vicariously liable for his delict. A statutory instrument required that a competent

[49] *Natwest Markets Plc v Bilta (UK) Ltd* [2021] EWCA Civ 680 [152]–[155], [185]–[187]; though the penultimate sentence in the second-cited paragraph range may neglect *Hawley v Luminar Leisure Ltd* [2006] EWCA Civ 18, [2006] IRLR 817.

[50] Which is not inevitable: *Day v The Ocean Beach Hotel Shellharbour Pty Ltd* [2013] NSWCA 250, (2013) 85 NSWLR 335 [23]–[33]; special leave refused [2014] HCASL 77; applied in *Hallmark Construction Pty Ltd v Harford* [2020] NSWCA 41 [79]–[81], [90].

[51] See the reasoning of the Supreme Court of Louisiana (a jurisdiction favoured by some Scottish academic lawyers) in *Morgan v ABC Manufacturer* (1998) 710 So 2d 1077 (La SC) 1084: where a negligent employee is lent, the lending employer remains liable under the Louisiana Civil Code, art 2320; referred to in argument and mentioned in *Viasystems* (n 28) 513 (argument), [41], [43] (May LJ).

[52] For better or worse: JW Neyers, 'Joint Vicarious Liability in the Supreme Court of Canada' (2006) 122 *LQR* 195, 197; and in comparison with the acceptance of dual vicarious liability after quite-lengthy discussion of policy and authority in *Munshi Mohammad Faiz v Interpro Construction Pte Ltd* [2021] SGHC 26 [52]–[69]; leave to appeal refused with reasons [2021] SGHC(A) 1 esp [12]–[24].

[53] *Marshall* (n 2).

[54] ibid 119, 121 (Lord Ross, with whom Lord Maxwell agreed), 125–26 (Lord Dunpark).

person be available to conduct electrical work on authorisation of a manager. It was highly relevant 'that Dean was the quarry electrician, and that this brought him within the statutory jurisdiction of the [defenders'] quarry manager' – here, the deceased.[55] Additional evidence suggested that Dean 'became part of the defenders' workforce': always on call at an hourly rate, he was the only electrician at the quarry, work for which took up most of his time.[56] Furthermore, 'the weight of the evidence showed that Dean was indeed under the *supervision and control* of the defenders as *part of their workforce* when working at the quarry'.[57] They relied upon Dean as an expert, and he would be in charge of electrical work. However, and as Dean himself recognised, general oversight and direction was with the defenders through the deceased.[58] For these reasons, 'although Dean was an independent contractor or a contractor with a degree of independence, the defenders were in the circumstances vicariously liable for his negligence'.[59]

According to *Marshall*, then, one may be vicariously liable for the negligence of a contractor who is so integrated into one's business as effectively to be part of one's workforce. The decision could usefully have underpinned the recognition by more junior Scottish courts that a relationship 'akin to employment' gives rise to vicarious liability. Yet its influence upon this development has been near-imperceptible. To some extent this is understandable. For example, holding that an action against an archdiocese for sexual abuse by a priest was time-barred in *CW v Trustees of the Roman Catholic Archdiocese of St Andrews and Edinburgh*,[60] Temporary Judge Arthurson QC acknowledged, *obiter*, that factually similar English decisions had 'state[d] a significant development of the law of vicarious liability, in particular as it pertains to the relationship of priest and Archdiocese'; and he saw 'no reason why these principles should not be applicable fully in this jurisdiction in that context'. If it was even contemplated, reference to *Marshall* here might have seemed superfluous.

More revealing is that *Marshall* barely figured in *Grubb v Shannon*.[61] There, the pursuer had an allergic reaction to the eyebrow tint which Higgins, a beauty

[55] ibid 121.

[56] ibid 121; see also the observation of Lord Dunpark, concurring, that 'the only difference between Dean and an electrician employed as a full-time servant of the defenders in the quarry workforce was that Dean worked part time at an hourly rate instead of full time at a weekly wage': ibid 125.

[57] ibid 121, emphasis added.

[58] The core evidence on this point is omitted from the *Scots Law Times*' reproduction of Lord Ross' opinion, but is partly quoted and summarised by Lord Dunpark: 1991 SLT 114, 123, 125; and fully reproduced at 1991 SCLR 104, 114–15.

[59] *Marshall* (n 2) 121 (Lord Ross, with whom Lord Maxwell agreed). See also the conclusion of Lord Dunpark, concurring, that 'while one may say that Dean was a contractor of his own labour, he cannot reasonably be classified as an independent contractor, for whose negligence the defenders are not liable': (n 2) 125–26.

[60] *CW v Trustees of the Roman Catholic Archdiocese of St Andrews and Edinburgh* [2013] CSOH 185 [15], [17]; citing *CCWS* (n 42); and *E* (n 14). Similarly understandable are the brief remarks in the employee-wrongdoer case of *Kennedy* (n 3) [55]–[56]; citing *Various Claimants v Barclays Bank Plc* [2020] UKSC 13, [2020] AC 973 [1]; and *E* (n 14).

[61] *Grubb* (n 3).

therapist, applied without conducting an initial skin test, or enquiring about allergies or experiences with similar treatments. Shannon leased and ran the salon in which the injury was caused. Though not Higgins's employer,[62] Shannon was vicariously liable for Higgins's negligence based on a relationship between them 'akin to employment'. The facts were 'unremarkable'.[63] The case is significant for Sheriff Reid's approach to and account of the law. He outlined a 'modern theory of vicarious liability', to 'be found in a quartet of landmark Supreme Court' cases,[64] with 'reinforcing ground breaking decisions of the English Court of Appeal' also meriting consideration.[65] The policy incidents identified by Lord Phillips in *Various Claimants v Catholic Child Welfare Society*[66] served *only* as convenient headings under which to consider many factual details of Higgins's relationship with Shannon, by extensive reference to previous authorities.[67] After this analysis, which – if necessary – could be described comfortably as compliant with the UK Supreme Court decision in *Various Claimants v Barclays Bank Plc*,[68] it was held that:

> Ms Higgins did indeed carry on activities, entrusted to her by the defender [Shannon], as an integral part of the defender's business activities, and for the benefit of the defender; that her activities were not attributable to the conduct of a recognisably independent business of her own, or of a third party; and that the negligence which forms the basis of the action was a risk created by the defender by assigning those activities to Ms Higgins.[69]

Marshall was the only Scottish case cited for the pursuer on the 'akin to employment' point. Whether anything was made of it in argument is unclear from Sheriff Reid's summary of submissions.[70] The only reference to it in his note was with another case, when observing that vicarious liability may arise, 'exceptionally, in the context of a contract for services, as between an employer and independent contractor'.[71] The brevity is probably explained by the fact that it was *not* actually

[62] ibid [87].
[63] ibid [2].
[64] Each of which he later summarised: ibid [74]–[84].
[65] ibid [15], [61]–[73], citing *CCWS* (n 42); *Cox* (n 27); *Mohamud v WM Morrison Supermarkets Plc* [2016] UKSC 11, [2016] AC 677; *Armes v Nottinghamshire County Council* [2017] UKSC 60, [2018] AC 355; noted B Lindsay (2018) 22 *Edinburgh Law Review* 294; *Viasystems* (n 28); *E* (n 14); and noting, by reference to *Lister v Hesley Hall Ltd* [2001] UKHL 22, [2002] 1 AC 215 [27]–[28], the earlier influence of *Bazley v Curry* [1999] 2 SCR 534 (SCC); *Jacobi v Griffiths* [1999] 2 SCR 570 (SCC).
[66] *CCWS* (n 42) [35], [47], discussed in more detail by Giliker in chapter three.
[67] See *Grubb* (n 3) [86]–[111], where refinements in *Cox* (n 27) and *Armes* (n 65) permitted Sheriff Reid, for example, to test for control by Shannon over *what* Higgins did, not *how* she did it; and to place no weight on 'deeper pockets' or insurance considerations.
[68] See *Barclays* (n 60) [27]. Less convinced is Reid (n 4) [3.29].
[69] *Grubb* (n 3) [112].
[70] Assembling facts on which '[p]articular reliance was placed' to establish a relationship 'akin to employment', before authorities referred to were simply listed: ibid [46].
[71] ibid [48], also citing *Stephen v Thurso Police Commissioners* (1876) 3 R 535 (IH), and in discussing the 'traditional theory of vicarious liability', ie, separately from the 'modern theory', found in English cases.

contended for Shannon that relationships 'akin to employment' were unknown to, or could not give rise to vicarious liability in, Scots law.[72] The possibility of a concession based on *Marshall* aside – that would surely have been noted – it seems that its main potential contribution in this case was uncalled-for because of assumptions by counsel and the Sheriff.

This state of affairs is broadly similar to that highlighted above, with *Park*. Scottish authority relevant to another not-inevitable development[73] was effectively passed over. Neither the parties nor the Sheriff in *Grubb v Shannon* brought domestic learning to bear on an essential condition of a claim that, '[p]erhaps as little as five years' prior, would have been struck out on the pleadings, but in 2018 came 'in the dizzying wake of a sea change in the law relating to vicarious liability', wrought by English cases.[74] However, *Park* is a forgettable, thinly reasoned first instance case running counter to more recent judicial and academic opinion on dual vicarious liability. Its near-disappearance may have been acquiesced in by those remembering it who disagree with its holding. *Marshall*, by contrast, is a fully reasoned appellate decision that positively *favours* the proposition that a relationship 'akin to employment' gives rise to vicarious liability. Yet it was not drawn upon by or, it seems, before, a junior first instance court to support what was acknowledged to be a considerable extension of established doctrine.[75] The reality is elementary: 'the busy practitioner' – and, we would add, the hard-pressed judge – 'must use the readiest tools to hand, and these, whatever their jurisprudential origin, … will tend to mould the development of [Scots] law'.[76] *Marshall* is, then, an even starker example than *Park* of the strong gravitational pull which English authority can exert on vicarious liability north of the border.

B. Linking Delictual Conduct to the Defenders' Relationship

Turning to Scottish learning on the second stage of the basic inquiry since *Lister v Hesley Hall Ltd*,[77] we note initially that the gravitational pull just mentioned has not been all one-way. A little of the Caledonian punctuated three important English movements on the close connection test. First – and though of course

[72] Instead, her solicitor argued unsuccessfully that Shannon and Higgins's relationship was 'more akin to that of landlord and tenant … than to employment': *Grubb* (n 3) [47], [116].

[73] Authorities conflict in Australia, for example: *DP v Bird* [2021] VSC 850 [120]–[214]; *PCB v Geelong College* [2021] VSC 633 [289]–[312].

[74] *Grubb* (n 3) [15], [61].

[75] See ibid [66]: a 'significant innovation' that relationships 'akin to employment' give rise to vicarious liability.

[76] TB Smith, 'Strange Gods: The Crisis of Scots Law as a Civilian System', in his *Studies Critical and Comparative* (Edinburgh, W Green, 1962) 87; A Rodger, '"Say Not the Struggle Naught Availeth": The Costs and Benefits of Mixed Legal Systems' (2003) 78 *Tulane Law Review* 419, 421.

[77] *Lister* (n 65).

not decisive – Scottish cases did inform the position taken in *Lister*. One was a 'good illustration of the correct approach'.[78] Another showed 'the importance of the existence of a sufficient connection' between delictual conduct and the defenders' relationship.[79] Second, we can recall the Scottish origin of a specific phrase:[80] 'the field of activities' assigned to a wrongdoer,[81] praised for its malleability in *Mohamud v WM Morrison Supermarkets Plc*.[82] Third, that same language received further attention[83] in 2020, when the Supreme Court addressed the close connection test in *Various Claimants v WM Morrison Supermarkets Plc*,[84] and endorsed a formula like that approved *prior* to *Mohamud*: the court must generally decide whether

> wrongful conduct was so closely connected with acts the employee was authorised to do that, for the purposes of the liability of his employer, it may fairly and properly be regarded as done by the employee while acting in the ordinary course of his employment.

As well as deserving a small portion of the (dis)credit for these movements, Scots law has tracked them. The first stage in this further reception of English learning was the acceptance of *Lister* in cognate instances of sexual abuse of minors in care,[85] and in cases concerning other wrongdoing, negligent and intentional.[86] This stage has already been charted by Bogle, whose 2019 article also notes the second stage:[87] the account of the law in *Mohamud* was applied in *Grubb v Shannon*.[88] A third stage in the process commenced in 2021. Following a tacit *obiter* application in an employee negligence case,[89] *Morrison* was explicitly taken as authoritative

[78] *Lister* (n 65) [18] (Lord Steyn); discussing *Williams v A & W Hemphill Ltd* 1966 SC (HL) 31.

[79] *Lister* (n 65) [39], [41], [44] (Lord Clyde); discussing *Kirby v National Coal Board* 1958 SC 514 (IH). One of the then-serving Scottish Law Lords, Lord Clyde mentioned other Scottish cases in his speech: *Lister* (n 65) [34], [48]. See also *Lister* (n 65) [59] (Lord Hobhouse).

[80] Also noted by D Brodie, 'Vicarious Liability and Bifurcation: Reflections on *WM Morrison Supermarkets v Various Claimants*' (2020) 24 *Edinburgh Law Review* 389, 390, though we would not date the phrase's further lease of life to its mere appearance in a lengthy quotation in *Lister* (n 65).

[81] See *Central Motors (Glasgow) Ltd v Cessnock Garage and Motor Co* 1925 SC 796 (IH) 802; discussed by Lord Clyde in *Lister* (n 65) [47].

[82] n 65 [35]–[36], [44]. See further *Group Seven Ltd v Notable Services LLP* [2019] EWCA Civ 614, [2020] Ch 129 [140]–[145].

[83] To use deliberately a neutral expression.

[84] *Various Claimants v WM Morrison Supermarkets Plc* [2020] UKSC 12, [2020] AC 989 esp [22]–[23], [25], [30]–[31]; citing, eg, *Dubai Aluminium Company Ltd v Salaam* [2002] UKHL 48, [2003] 2 AC 366.

[85] *J v Fife Council* [2008] CSIH 63, 2009 SC 163 [38] (an appeal as to quantum; vicarious liability was undisputed). The same is observable in many of the limitation cases mentioned in section IV.A. below, eg, *Kelly v Gilmartin's Executrix* 2002 SC 602 (OH) [46].

[86] *Vance v North Lanarkshire Council* [2008] CSOH 70, 2008 Rep LR 90 [25]; *Wilson v Exel UK Ltd (t/a Exel)* [2010] CSIH 35, 2010 SLT 671 [24].

[87] S Bogle, 'Responsibility for Another's Wrong in Scotland: Stick with *Lister* or Twist with *Mohamud*?' [2019] *Juridical Review* 211, 218–26, 230.

[88] *Grubb* (n 3) [61], [64], [80]–[84], [117]–[122].

[89] See *SH v Care Visions Group Ltd* [2021] SC EDIN 28, 2021 Rep LR 83. Though vicarious liability was undisputed, Sheriff Dickson took care to make a relevant finding that was plainly modelled on *Morrison* (n 84) [23].

in *Kennedy v Bonnici*,[90] which concerned the vicarious liability of school trustees for historic sexual abuse.

This shadowing of English law looks fortuitous today. No hard case has seriously tested the close connection analysis.[91] In the only case to apply *Mohamud*, the pursuer's success did not depend on any particular test.[92] *Grubb v Shannon* was a clear-cut instance of authorised functions negligently discharged. Whatever the wider potential of that decision, therefore, we in Scotland may simply bypass costly debate involving the courts about whether a *Mohamud*-type analysis is too permissive,[93] at least for usual application.[94] Based on *Kennedy*, and given pleaders' understandable habit of referring judges to more recent English cases,[95] *Morrison* looks set quietly to become the core authority on the close connection test.

If this is what occurs, it will be possible to say that the past two decades or so have seen the close connection test rather smoothly embraced in Scotland. This is further apparent when one considers the main Scots appellate authorities since *Lister*: *Wilson* and *Vaickuviene*. These cases actually support the *Morrison* test,[96] recognise that a tailored test has been applied in sexual abuse cases[97] and provide guidance like that highlighted in *Morrison* as conducive to principled decision-making.[98] For example, the question whether it is fair and just to impose vicarious liability is not generally at large in individual cases.[99] Analytically similar previous decisions guide the application of the close connection test in an instant case.[100] Temporal or causal links between a wrong and the defenders' relationship do not themselves establish a close connection.[101] Wrongdoing in the course of an

[90] *Kennedy* (n 3) [57]–[59] (Lady Wolffe).

[91] Compare, eg, *Mohamud* (n 65); *Bellman v Northampton Recruitment Ltd* [2016] EWHC 3104 (QB), [2017] ICR 543; reversed [2018] EWCA Civ 2214, [2019] ICR 459; *Various Claimants v WM Morrison Supermarkets Plc* [2017] EWHC 3113 (QB); affirmed [2018] EWCA Civ 2339, [2019] QB 772; reversed (n 84). (It is, of course, impossible to know how many Scottish disputes might settle due to reliance by practitioners on the English position, reducing litigation north of the border and the chances of difficult cases.)

[92] Even as against a more traditional 'scope of employment'-style analysis, as Sheriff Reid all but stated: *Grubb* (n 3) [118]–[120].

[93] Among many sources, see D Ryan, '"Close Connection" and "Akin to Employment": Perspectives on 50 Years of Radical Developments in Vicarious Liability' (2016) 56 *Irish Jurist* 239, 247–51.

[94] P Giliker, 'A Revolution in Vicarious Liability: *Lister*, the *Catholic Child Welfare Society* Case and Beyond' in S Worthington, A Robertson and G Virgo (eds), *Revolution and Evolution in Private law* (Oxford, Hart Publishing, 2018) 134–39.

[95] With less emphasis on Scottish cases, as noted in *Wilson* (n 86) [31]. See the discussion of English authority as it appeared in *Vaickuviene v J Sainsbury Plc* [2013] CSIH 67, 2014 SC 147; *Grubb* (n 3); then *Kennedy* (n 3).

[96] Most clearly in *Wilson* (n 86) [7]–[8] (Lord Hamilton, with whom Lord Reed agreed), [25]–[30] esp [26]–[27] (Lord Carloway, with whom Lord Reed agreed). See also *Vaickuviene* (n 95), [29], [34] (Lord Carloway), [43] (Lord Brodie), [45], [50] (Lord McGhie).

[97] *Vaickuviene* (n 95), [22]–[23], [26]–[27], [38] (Lord Carloway, with whom Lord Brodie and Lord McGhie generally agreed).

[98] *Morrison* (n 84) esp [22]–[26], [29]–[31], [35]–[47].

[99] *Wilson* (n 86) [12]–[13] (Lord Hamilton); *Vaickuviene* (n 95) [25] (Lord Carloway).

[100] *Wilson* (n 86) [13] (Lord Hamilton), [31] (Lord Carloway); *Vaickuviene* (n 95) [28], [37] (Lord Carloway).

[101] *Wilson* (n 86) [28]–[29] (Lord Carloway); *Vaickuviene* (n 95) [20]–[21], [37] (Lord Carloway).

independent, self-interested venture, is not regarded as closely connected with the defenders' relationship.[102]

What, however, of the Inner House's assertions that the so-called Salmond test remains relevant '[w]ithin the context of the broad test' of close connection?[103] So placed, the Salmond test is redundant. It neither adds anything to the close connection test, nor alters the outer limits of liability. Unsurprisingly, pleaders and judges in lower courts consistently prefer straightforwardly to apply the close connection test and associated guidance.[104] Having previously attracted comment,[105] the Inner House's composite approach appears destined to be forgotten, along with other potentially distinctive features of the Scottish case law.[106] It may be expected that continuity, not change, will largely characterise this area of vicarious liability in Scotland.

III. Particular Issues in Vicarious Liability

This section addresses two matters related to those examined so far. Having given a sense above of what the law is, where it is going and what has influenced it, we identify problems on the horizon, and the sources on which Scottish courts might draw in future.

A. Future Difficulties

Scholars have noted English law's strong historical influence on vicarious liability in Scotland.[107] It is unsurprising that it has persisted. We hazard that there exists in this field, as it more clearly does in certain others,[108] a general inclination among

[102] *Wilson* (n 86) [30], [32]–[34] (Lord Carloway); *Vaickuviene* (n 95) [28], [37] (Lord Carloway).

[103] *Wilson* (n 86) [25]–[27], [29]–[30] (Lord Carloway); *Vaickuviene* (n 95) [19]–[21], [24]–[25], [32] (Lord Carloway); citing, eg, RFV Heuston and RA Buckley, *Salmond and Heuston on the Law of Torts* 21st edn (London, Sweet & Maxwell, 1996) 443.

[104] In addition to *Grubb* (n 3) [119]–[120], see *Scottish Water Business Stream Ltd v Automatic Retailing (Scotland) Ltd (in admin)* [2014] CSOH 57 [94]; *Somerville v Harsco Infrastructure Ltd* [2015] SC EDIN 71 esp [22]. Slightly more ambiguous is *Shields v Crossroads (Orkney)* [2013] CSOH 144, 2014 SLT 190 [56]–[58].

[105] S Arnell, 'Employers' Vicarious Liability – Where Are We Now?' [2010] *Juridical Review* 243, 258–61; M Campbell, '*Somerville v Harsco Infrastructure Ltd*: Transferred Intent and the Scope of Vicarious Liability' (2016) 20 *Edinburgh Law Review* 211, 213–16.

[106] See those discussed post-*Mohamud* (n 65), which no longer stand out as distinctive post-*Morrison* (n 84), by Bogle (n 87) esp 228–30; and D Brodie, 'Vicarious Liability: The Net Tightens' (2016) 129 *Reparation Bulletin* 1, 3. Correctly, Brodie later reassessed the position: 'Vicarious Liability and Practical Jokes' (2020) 156 *Reparation Bulletin* 5, 7.

[107] E Reid and M Loubser, 'Strict Liability' in R Zimmermann, K Reid and D Visser (eds), *Mixed Legal Systems in Comparative Perspective: Property and Obligations in Scotland and South Africa* (Oxford, Oxford University Press, 2004) 626–27.

[108] See, eg, HL MacQueen, *MacQueen and Thomson on Contract Law in Scotland* 5th edn (London, Bloomsbury 2020) [1.56].

Scots lawyers to keep pace where possible with their neighbouring jurisdiction,[109] which is much larger.[110] Whether or not this is so, practitioners seem regularly to envisage, sometimes tacitly,[111] that relevant English developments will be emulated in due course. For example, a leading Scottish law firm's note on *Grubb v Shannon* observes that its 'most significant implication … is that Scottish law is following changes in England[:] we might anticipate that any further changes south of the border will be adopted here'.[112] As appears from the previous section of this chapter, we agree, especially so far as concerns further developments driven by the Supreme Court. Though its decisions in English appeals are technically non-binding,[113] the Inner House's 'deferential attitude'[114] to them is readily understandable from a practical point of view.[115]

If our prediction is correct, then, in the realm of vicarious liability, Scots lawyers will in future encounter problems like those in store for their English counterparts.[116] Most importantly, how do we detect the 'doubtful cases' in which, *Barclays* suggests,[117] policy reasoning 'may be helpful in identifying a relationship which is sufficiently analogous to employment to make it fair, just and reasonable to impose vicarious liability'? Can or should there *really* be a bright

[109] There is some evidence of it in relation to sexual abuse cases, specifically: Junor (n 43) 65; Lord Hope, 'Tailoring the Law on Vicarious Liability' (2013) 129 *LQR* 514. By *keep pace* we mean *at least* to develop similarly detailed doctrine, rather than *always* to align wholesale, though this will sometimes be desired and often results.

[110] We take as given the reader's awareness that senior courts in England and Wales give thousands of judgments yearly. In Scotland, it is hard reliably to establish how many disputes give rise to *written decisions*. Of these, there are, of course, fewer than there are *disposals* of disputes, official statistics on which not assist. (See, eg, the detailed decennial tables in *Civil Justice Statistics in Scotland 2019–20* (April 2021).) A 31 August 2021 Westlaw search for 2017–20 inclusive yields, respectively, 235, 206, 170 and 178 written decisions of the Court of Session (Outer and Inner Houses); and 201 in total for the Sheriff Appeal Court (Civil). (Cross-checking this search using Bailii yields figures of 224, 226, 171, 167; and a surely partial 81.)

[111] There is no hint that Supreme Court decisions in English appeals do not state Scots law in, eg, A Forsyth, 'Vicarious Liability Supreme Court Judgements', *Insights* (15 April 2020) www.burnesspaull.com/insights-and-events/news/vicarious-liability-supreme-court-judgements.

[112] Brodies, 'Vicarious Liability – Scotland Moves in the Same Direction as England & Wales', *Insights*, (3 July 2018) https://brodies.com/insights/insurance-and-risk/vicarious-liability-scotland-moves-in-the-same-direction-as-england-wales. See also the admission of vicarious liability in *A v Glasgow City Council* [2021] CSOH 102, 2021 SLT 1577, a foster abuse case.

[113] *AJ Allan (Blairnyle) Ltd v Strathclyde Fire Board* [2016] CSIH 3, 2016 SC 304 [31].

[114] Bogle (n 87) 230. More generally, judges and academics often cite English cases 'without specific warning that they do not determine Scots law': M Dewart, *The Scottish Legal System* 6th edn (London, Bloomsbury, 2019) [12.19]. Note, though, that borrowing from England is sometimes doctrinally inappropriate: *Joint Liquidators of Simclar (Ayrshire) Ltd v Simclar Group Ltd* [2011] CSOH 54, 2011 SLT 1131 [31].

[115] See Lord Hope, 'Scots Law Seen from South of the Border' (2012) 16 *Edinburgh Law Review* 58, 75–76.

[116] For the first two questions, see P Giliker, 'Can the Supreme Court Halt the Ongoing Expansion of Vicarious Liability? *Barclays* and *Morrison* in the UK Supreme Court' (2021) 37 *PN* 55, 61–62, 67. For the third, see C Beuermann, 'Vicarious Liability for Football Scouts' (2022) 138 *LQR* 170, 172–75.

[117] *Barclays* (n 60) [27]; not yet applied on this point in Scotland, but cited for general propositions in *Kennedy* (n 3) [55]–[56].

line between cases of sexual and other kinds of abuse,[118] on the former side of which the tailored close connection test will stay?[119] And might some reasoning permitted by the tailored test sit ill with elements of the reasoning understood to assist with whether a relationship between defenders gives rise to vicarious liability in the first place? These questions having emerged very recently, we can do no more than ask them. When they arise in Scotland, English learning will doubtless assist, if available.

Yet for all we have said about the reasonable use in Scotland of English sources on vicarious liability, they are no panacea. Consider briefly a further unanswered question: how does vicarious liability interact with agency? In 2013 Macgregor noted, inter alia, that the English position could be clearer, and that a different approach on the matter might be adopted north of the border.[120] The ground may have shifted since she wrote. But English law still furnishes no model for *easy* adoption.[121] We leave aside the detail. The point here is that this sparks interest in whether Scottish courts might look to jurisdictions *other* than England to develop their doctrine of vicarious liability. To this prospect we now turn.

B. Glancing Furth of England

Some might think that the first port of call should really be mixed legal systems,[122] among which Scotland's has been counted.[123] We overlook those in respect of which a 'language problem' arises, like Quebec,[124] on the basis that it is 'unrealistic

[118] The court, for example, was unwilling to apply a different test to racist harassment in *Vaickuviene* (n 95) [2], [17], [38]. The question in the main text is distinct.

[119] *Morrison* (n 84) [23], [36]; accepted at first instance in *Kennedy* (n 3) [57]–[59] for the tailored test in the sexual abuse context, but *without excluding* that test on different facts. Though tailored test reasoning may escape the sexual abuse context (*Chell v Tarmac Cement and Lime Ltd* [2022] EWCA Civ 7 [27]), it need not: see the caution in *Ali v Luton Borough Council* [2022] EWHC 132 (QB) [30]–[33], [47]–[48].

[120] L Macgregor, *The Law of Agency in Scotland* (Edinburgh, W Green, 2013) [13-01]–[13-02], [13-10]–[13-25]; citing, eg, *McE v De La Salle Brothers* [2007] CSIH 27, 2007 SC 556 [132] (Lord Osborne). Subsequent cases yield little. But see Lord Glennie's fleeting observations in *British Sky Broadcasting Group Plc v Avalonbar Ltd* [2014] CSOH 39 [55], in the context of breach of interdict and the statutory wrong of copyright infringement.

[121] See PG Watts and FMB Reynolds, *Bowstead & Reynolds on Agency* 22nd edn (London, Sweet & Maxwell, 2021) [8-176]–[8-204]; C-H Tan, 'Vicarious Liability in the Law of Agency?' [2022] *Journal of Business Law* 164. (Neither source examines *only* English authority.)

[122] See generally J Du Plessis, 'Comparative Law and the Study of Mixed Legal Systems' in M Reimann and R Zimmermann (eds), *The Oxford Handbook of Comparative Law* 2nd edn (Oxford, Oxford University Press, 2019).

[123] S Thomson, 'Mixed Jurisdiction and the Scottish Legal Tradition: Reconsidering the Concept of Mixture' (2014) 7 *Journal of Civil Law Studies* 51.

[124] For the main legislative regimes, see the *Code civil du Québec*, arts 1459–1464 (standard categories, including employers' liability), 2164 (mandator's liability). For a statement and application of employers' liability principles to facts involving historic child abuse, see *Lachance v Institut séculier Pie X* [2021] QCCS 1064 [180]–[339]. As appears from that judgment (ibid [198]–[204]),

to expect lawyers to cite, and judges to digest, decisions from other jurisdictions in foreign languages'.[125] We also leave aside systems like Louisiana,[126] which, though certainly of general comparative interest,[127] have not seen their doctrines of vicarious liability examined by Scots lawyers. Such jurisdictions are less likely to attract the attention of pleaders and judges working on the subject at hand.

Realistically, the likeliest source of inspiration among mixed systems is South African law, enthusiasm for which among Scottish academic lawyers is well-known.[128] A short 2004 account of vicarious liability in both jurisdictions noted their 'predominantly English … derivation' and similarity in many respects.[129] Naturally, more recent South African literature repays careful study.[130] But what might *primary* sources add to a Scottish court's decision-making? Section II.A of this chapter showed that, on relationships giving rise to vicarious liability, Scots law is quite developed.[131] So any examination of South African learning would probably be aimed at illuminating the close connection test. Whether this would often bear fruit unavailable elsewhere may, however, be doubted. For example, apex decisions on vicarious liability for sexual offences by police officers could clarify the *tailored* close connection test.[132] Normally, though, cases applying the test itself will surely be more helpful.[133]

Moreover, because the tailored test is confined in *Morrison* to sexual abuse cases, it is likely that risk-based reasoning will be heavily circumscribed in Scots (and English) law. Such reasoning is not so bridled in South Africa. There, courts can reach results which – *currently* – their Scottish counterparts might not.

Quebec courts sometimes rely on policy reasoning derived from common law Canadian cases: see further N De Stefano, 'A Comparative Look at Vicarious Liability for Intentional Wrongs and Abuses of Power in Canadian Law' (2020) 98 *Canadian Bar Review* 1. Where this is so, some Scots lawyers may rather simply tap that source directly.

[125] J Blackie and N Whitty, 'Scots Law and the New *Ius Commune*' in HL MacQueen (ed), *Scots Law into the 21st Century: Essays in Honour of WA Wilson* (Edinburgh, W Green, 1996) 74–75.

[126] For the main legislative regimes, see the Louisiana Civil Code, arts 2318, 2320.

[127] See VV Palmer and E Reid, 'Preface' in VV Palmer and E Reid (eds), *Mixed Jurisdictions Compared: Private Law in Louisiana and Scotland* (Edinburgh, Edinburgh University Press, 2009).

[128] See generally D Carey Miller, 'Sibling Mixed Systems: Reviewing South African/Scottish Comparative Law' (2016) 20 *Edinburgh Law Review* 257, but esp 280, addressing the fleeting second-hand reference to a South African vicarious liability decision in *Vaickuviene* (n 95) [23].

[129] Reid and Loubser (n 107) 626–36.

[130] See, eg, that available to practitioners and judges in Edinburgh's Advocates Library: M Loubser and R Midgley (eds), *The Law of Delict in South Africa* 3rd edn (Cape Town, Oxdord University Press, 2018) ch 33; M Loubser, *Tort Law in South Africa* (The Hague, Kluwer Law International, 2020) [443]–[465]. The *South African Law Reports* are held in the same location.

[131] Except on the unanswered agency question, alluded to above. But 'diversity of opinion' on this topic means that South African law may not greatly assist: S Wagener, 'The Relationship(s) Giving Rise to Vicarious Liability in South African Law' (2014) 131 *South African Law Journal* 178, 190.

[132] See *K v Minister of Safety and Security* [2005] ZACC 8, 2005 (6) SA 419; *F v Minister of Safety and Security* [2011] ZACC 37, 2012 (1) SA 536.

[133] See, eg, *Barry Congregation of Jehovah's Witnesses v BXB* [2021] EWCA Civ 356, [2021] 4 WLR 42 (permission to appeal granted 30 March 2022); *Blackpool Football Club Ltd v DSN* [2021] EWCA Civ 1352. Predictably, such cases have come to attention in Scotland. See, eg, use of *BXB* in *Kennedy* (n 3) [58].

In *Stallion Security (Pty) Ltd v Van Staden*,[134] a security company was vicariously liable when its site manager robbed and murdered a person working late in premises he oversaw. Relying on Canadian and English decisions, and eschewing 'references to a link with the duties, authorised acts or employment of the employee' whose wrongdoing 'did not in any manner constitute the exercise' of those duties or acts,[135] the court held 'that the creation of risk of harm by an employer may, in an appropriate case, constitute a relevant consideration in giving rise to a sufficiently close link between the *harm* caused by the employee and the *business* of the employer'.[136] On the facts, the employee's 'special position created a material risk that [he] might abuse his powers', which 'risk rendered the deceased vulnerable and produced the robbery and consequently the murder'.[137] Further, Stallion's security services contract with the company for which the deceased worked 'provide[d] a significant normative link between Stallion's business and the harm suffered by' the deceased's widow.[138]

In *Vaickuviene*, a 2013 case about racially motivated harassment culminating in an employee-on-employee murder, the Inner House opined that such wrongdoing did not itself justify 'any more generous an interpretation of the general' close connection test, like that observable in the sexual offences context.[139] If adhered to, this view entails that a Scottish court would decide *Stallion Security* differently. And it is not the only case about which this may be said.[140] Based on the foregoing, we doubt whether South African case law would *presently* assist much in difficult Scottish litigation on the close connection test – in respect of which the experience of other jurisdictions will most probably be surveyed. As has been said before, the benefits of intra-mixed-system study are by no means guaranteed.[141]

So where will Scottish pleaders and judges look to in future, if not simply south, to England? How will they employ decisions from different jurisdictions? Going by the cases, the most likely answers are: to other *common law* countries; and to refine the close connection test.[142] It is perhaps improbable that Scots

[134] *Stallion Security (Pty) Ltd v Van Staden* [2019] ZASCA 127, 2020 (1) SA 64; noted J Scott [2020] *Tydskrif vir die Suid-Afrikaanse Reg* 338.

[135] *Stallion Security* (n 134) [19]; an analysis at the core of the connection test in *Morrison* (n 84).

[136] *Stallion Security* (n 134) [17], [27]–[32] (emphasis added); citing, eg, *Bazley* (n 65); and *CCWS* (n 42).

[137] ibid [36].

[138] ibid [37].

[139] *Vaickuviene* (n 95) [22]–[23], [26]–[27], [38] (Lord Carloway, with whom Lord Brodie and Lord McGhie generally agreed). Because the tailored test was straightforwardly accepted in *Kennedy* (n 3) [57]–[59] as 'the correct' one, the decision does not determine whether it is confined to the sexual abuse context in Scotland.

[140] See, eg, *Fujitsu Services Core (Pty) Ltd v Schenker South Africa (Pty) Ltd* [2020] ZAGPJHC 111; reversed on other grounds [2022] ZASCA 7. The court applied the *Stallion Security* (n 134) risk-based analysis to an employee theft where it would not arguably be so used in English law: see Giliker (n 116) 69–70.

[141] K Reid, 'The Idea of Mixed Legal Systems' (2003) 78 *Tulane Law Review* 5, 38.

[142] See the references by pleaders and judges to Canadian (by far the most frequent), Australian and United States authority in *Wilson* (n 86) [11], [13], [23], [32]–[33]; *Vaickuviene* (n 95) [12], [15], [19], [22], [28]; *Somerville* (n 104) [19], [24]–[27], [30]; *Grubb* (n 3) [15].

law will ever differ fundamentally from English law on general questions of vicarious liability.[143] However, the courts' observable intellectual openness is sure to persist. We would be unsurprised if it increased, both in terms of legal systems considered, and the matters of principle on which foreign learning is brought to bear.[144]

IV. Responding to Historic Child Abuse in Scotland

Turning to the legal response in this jurisdiction to the evil of historic child abuse, this has at least three dimensions: inquisition, legislation, and litigation. This first aspect – reflecting on the incidence and causes of abuse and recommending best practice for the future – presently is being performed in respect of children in care by the Scottish Child Abuse Inquiry,[145] and the report of the Scottish Football Association's *Independent Review of Non-Recent Sexual Abuse in Scottish Football*[146] was published in February 2021. While more legislation may be expected in light of the above, so far the Scottish Parliament has passed the Limitation (Childhood Abuse) (Scotland) Act 2017 and recently established a compensation scheme for those alleging abuse in institutional care with the Redress for Survivors (Historical Child Abuse in Care) (Scotland) Act 2021. Furthermore, the Civil Litigation (Expenses and Group Proceedings) (Scotland) Act 2018 now provides for group proceedings, a possibility recently availed of by survivors of alleged child sex abuse.[147] As for litigation, the influence of English law is apparent in setting the test for vicarious liability. But very few cases have explored how that test will be applied by the Scottish courts in the specific context of historic child abuse.[148]

[143] See Bogle (n 87) 212, 230.

[144] See, eg, the discussion of an overall test for relationships giving rise to vicarious liability, and the relevance of control, in the *Irish* case of *Morrissey v Health Service Executive* [2020] IESC 6, [2020] PNLR 17 [12.7]–[12.20], reference to which may transpire to be instructive. *Morrissey* is discussed in more detail by Ryan in chapter five.

[145] Established in 2015, the inquiry has issued a series of case study findings, but is not due to deliver its final report until 2023 at the earliest. The SCAI's website is available at https://childabuseinquiry.scot.

[146] Available at www.scottishfa.co.uk/media/7516/independent-review-of-sexual-abuse-in-scottish-football-final-report.pdf.

[147] Permission has been granted under this legislation for proceedings to be brought by 22 former Celtic Boys Club players against Celtic FC plc. No written opinion is available, but see www.dailyrecord.co.uk/news/scottish-news/celtic-boys-club-victims-given-26355604. This high profile case, involving one of Scotland's largest football teams, likely will lead to judicial consideration of the issues raised in this section, and of vicarious liability more generally.

[148] See most explicitly *Kennedy* (n 3) [59]. There may also be difficult issues of proof, given that it has been recently noted that the use of similar fact evidence is precluded in the civil context by Inner House authority: *EG v The Governors of the Fettes Trust* [2021] CSOH 128, 2022 Rep LR 26 [22].

A. Limitation

The primary reason for this is that most litigation has not proceeded to a determination of liability because of the strict limitation period applicable to such claims. Until recently, historic abuse claims were subjected to the general, three-year limitation period,[149] with the Scottish courts hesitant to either defer this on the basis of subsequent discovery of the severity of a pursuer's injuries[150] or find it 'equitable' to extend the limitation period.[151] Often, the prejudice caused to the defender by the inability of the alleged abuser to give evidence – usually by reason of death – would undermine any attempt to have the limitation period extended.[152] This was so even if there existed limited evidence from other sources: what mattered was any material – even if not total – loss of evidence.[153]

Concerns about the strictness of the limitation regime led to the passing of the Limitation (Childhood Abuse) (Scotland) Act 2017. It disapplies[154] the three-year limitation period in relation to claims by those who suffered personal injury caused by abuse perpetrated, or which began, while they were children.[155] It is retrospective in effect,[156] and can resuscitate claims previously disposed of on the basis of the old limitation regime or settled correspondingly.[157] There are, however, exceptions to the operation of the Act.

The first, internal to the Act, is that a defender can argue that an action nevertheless should not proceed for one of the two reasons stated in section 17D: (i) that it would not be possible for a fair trial to take place; and/or (ii) that the defender would be substantially prejudiced, and that prejudice would outweigh

[149] Prescription and Limitation (Scotland) Act 1973, s 17(2)(a). The general rule is that the period runs from the later date between when the injuries were sustained and when the injured party reached the age of 16 (s 17(3)). Subsequent revelations or realisations do not amount to fresh injuries: *Aitchison v Glasgow City Council* [2010] CSIH 9, 2010 SC 411, disapproving *M v O'Neill* [2006] CSOH 93, 2006 SLT 823. On the differences between this regime and the Limitation Act 1980, see *McE* (n 120) [155]–[161] (Lord Osborne). For the continuing difficulties posed by limitation in England and Wales in this context, see *TVZ v Manchester City Football Club Ltd* [2022] EWHC 7 (QB) (a case which can be distinguished from the context of the Celtic Boys Club case (n 147)).

[150] Suppression of the relevant abuse will not be treated as within the rule that 'unsoundness of mind' allows the court to defer computation under s 17(3): *McE* (n 120) [173]–[175] (Lord Osborne). See also *K v Marist Brothers* [2016] CSOH 54; affirmed [2017] CSIH 2, 2017 SC 258 [7] (non-disclosure prompted by threats of spiritual condemnation).

[151] 1973 Act, s 19A. The sole reported example of an extension – which was not a vicarious liability case – is *A v N* [2013] CSOH 161, affirmed [2015] CSIH 26, 2015 SLT 289. See also the tentative conclusion in *Gorrie v Marist Brothers* 2002 SCLR 436 (OH).

[152] See, eg, *B v Murray (No 2)* 2005 SLT 982 (OH) [120]–[122]; affirmed [2007] CSIH 39, 2007 SC 688, [2008] UKHL 32, 2008 SC (HL) 146; *CW* (n 60) [19]; *F v Quarriers* [2015] CSOH 82, 2016 SCLR 111 [148]–[149]; *K* (n 150) [90]–[91].

[153] *B v Murray* (OH) (n 152) [30] (Lord Drummond Young).

[154] By inserting a new s 17A-D into the 1973 Act.

[155] 'Abuse' is defined in s 17A(2) as including 'sexual abuse, physical abuse, emotional abuse and abuse which takes the form of neglect …'

[156] 1973 Act, s 17B.

[157] ibid, s 17C.

the pursuer's interest to such a degree that the action should not proceed. A note of caution has been sounded against generalising from previous decisions,[158] and the relevance of cases decided under the prior regime remains unclear,[159] and opinions diverge on whether fair trial issues are preliminary matters, or should rather be determined after at least some evidence is heard.[160] However, some general points may be distilled from the decided cases. It has been accepted that the expansion of vicarious liability, and the introduction of the 2017 Act itself, may constitute substantial prejudice to a defender.[161] But these alone will not be particularly weighty factors in the face of a pursuer with financial and personal interest in the adjudication of a claim supported by some, albeit incomplete, evidence.[162] The extent and effects of the abuse will be considered in assessing the interest of the pursuer, whose reasons for delaying the action will not be relevant to that enquiry.[163] However, the death of an alleged abuser still usually will prevent a fair hearing,[164] unless the allegations have been admitted or there exists testimony from the abuser against which the allegations can be tested.[165] If there is 'no basis on which the defender can properly assert that the alleged abuse did not occur', then that will be a 'very significant matter' affecting the fairness of the trial.[166] This especially will be so where unspecified allegations are made against unnamed individuals.[167]

The second, external, exception is that the Act does not affect the position in relation to claims in respect of abuse suffered before 26 September 1964. Claims in respect of such abuse have been extinguished by the operation of the doctrine of prescription.[168] Given the restrictions on the competence of the Scottish Parliament,[169] human rights concerns moved the legislature to not seek to disturb

[158] *A v XY Ltd* [2021] CSOH 21, 2021 SLT 399 [53] (Lord Woolman).

[159] Compare *B v Sailor's Society* [2021] CSOH 62, 2021 SLT 1070 [240] (Lady Carmichael) (s 19A cases 'provide no useful guidance in relation to what constitutes substantial prejudice' and not tasked with specifically considering fairness of hearing) with *JXJ v The Province of Great Britain of the Institute of Brothers of the Christian Schools* [2020] EWHC 1914 (QB) [101] (Chamberlain J) (reasoning in s 19A cases regarding fairness of hearing 'relevant' and 'helpful'). In *Kennedy* (n 3) [60], Lady Wolffe preferred the former view; whereas in *B v Congregation of the Sisters of Nazareth* [2022] CSOH 8, 2022 Rep LR 31 [85], Lord Weir was more agnostic.

[160] Compare *LM v DG's Executor* [2021] SAC (Civ) 3, 2021 SLT (Sh Ct) 87 [15] (fair hearing 'cannot be held over until the end of a proof') with *Kennedy* (n 3) [64]–[66], [68] (fair hearing issues may remain live throughout proof).

[161] *A v XY* (n 158) [41]–[43].

[162] ibid [46]–[51] ([51]: scales tipped 'decisively in favour of the pursuer').

[163] *JXJ* (n 159) [101].

[164] ibid [107]–[111], [113]–[115]; *B v Sailor's Society* (n 159) [242], [255], [273]; *B v Sisters of Nazareth* (n 159) [108]

[165] *JXJ* (n 159) [104]–[106]; *B v Sailor's Society* (n 159) [236] (referring to the police interview of the alleged abuser in *LM* (n 160)).

[166] *B v Sailor's Society* (n 159) [273].

[167] *B v Sisters of Nazareth* (n 159) [104]-[109].

[168] *Kelly* (n 85) [29]–[43]; *K* (n 150) [71]–[77], discussing the effect of the Prescription and Limitation (Scotland) Act 1984. Note that the s 19A discretion also cannot be employed to revive a claim which is prescribed, as it is part of the law of limitation only.

[169] Scotland Act 1998, s 29(2)(d).

this position.[170] A limited remedy for those abused in institutional care will be provided by the Redress for Survivors (Historical Child Abuse in Care) (Scotland) Act 2021, which will establish a compensation fund made up of contributions from care providers which have signed up to the redress scheme. But not all survivors will have been abused in that context; nor will the scheme's capped recoveries sufficiently compensate all conceivable injuries.

Limitation inevitably requires that hard and fast lines be drawn, and the 2017 Act has at least ensured that those lines are drawn less harshly against those alleging historic abuse. A pursuer seeking compensation for a deceased pursuer's delicts still, however, faces an uphill struggle. A historic abuser might well have challenged the competence of the Scottish Parliament to pass bolder limitation legislation on human rights grounds,[171] and this weighed heavily in the minds of the architects of the reform when fixing its contours.[172] In framing this native legislative solution, the Scottish Government strongly was influenced by reforms in several Australian states following the Australian Royal Commission into Institutional Responses to Child Sexual Abuse.[173] However, given that the Scots and various Australian measures differ in formulation, Australian case law is probably of limited significance to interpreters of the 2017 Act.[174]

B. Legal Personality / Unincorporated Associations

A further question, particularly important in historic child abuse litigation, is how principles of vicarious liability apply where the defender alleged to be in the requisite relationship with the wrongdoer is an unincorporated association bereft of legal personality. Unincorporated associations 'occupy an anomalous and unsatisfactory position' in Scots law.[175] This is more acute given the historic importance of such associations – religious and secular – in the provision of residential care, schooling,[176] sports coaching and other recreational and social opportunities to Scottish children, increasing their potential incidence as defenders in cases involving historic child abuse. However, despite sustained analysis and recommendations by the Scottish Law Commission, the precise nature of

[170] See, eg, the Justice Committee of the Scottish Parliament, *Stage 1 Report on the Limitation (Childhood Abuse) (Scotland) Bill* (2017 7th Report) [69]–[74], [99].

[171] eg under the Convention for the Protection of Human Rights and Fundamental Freedoms, art 6 and protocol 1, art 1.

[172] Stage 1 Justice Committee Report (n 170) [23]–[26], [73].

[173] See the Policy Memorandum to the Limitation (Childhood Abuse) Bill [13]–[14], [32], [41], [87]. The Australian provisions are discussed by Beuermann in chapter four.

[174] Compare *JXJ* (n 159) [101(i)] with *LM v DG's Executor* [2020] SC DUN 1, 2020 SLT (Sh Ct) 11 [29], [33]; reversed on other grounds (n 160).

[175] *Gloag & Henderson* (n 41) [47.01].

[176] See eg T O'Donoghue, 'The Role of Male Religious Orders in Education in Scotland' in SJ McKinney and R McCluskey (eds), *A History of Catholic Education and Schooling in Scotland: New Perspectives* (London, Palgrave McMillan, 2019) 81–102.

unincorporated associations' potential liability remains unsettled.[177] It recently has been observed that, generally, 'the application of concepts such as vicarious liability … may be less than straightforward or, indeed, inapt' in the context of unincorporated associations.[178] That being said, there is support for the view that 'a person.[179] who is injured through the fault of such an association or its servants or agents has a right of action in delict against the association',[180] with specified members capable of being 'constituted as agents for the whole of the membership for certain purposes', including defending litigation.[181] These formulations do not reflect the post-*CCWS* expansion of the test for vicarious liability: can it be said that there is a relationship 'akin to employment' between a body without legal personality and its members?

Nevertheless, there is recent Scottish authority holding an unincorporated religious order vicariously liable for assaults perpetrated by a member,[182] but neither the personality point nor the relationship point receives any discussion in the reported decision. The sheriff held the defender association – in the singular – 'jointly and severally liable' for the assault. This terminology perhaps reflects the fact that, procedurally, a judgment against the 'association' in such circumstances technically is a judgment against the members called before the court, who thereafter have a right of relief against the association's property.[183] This can be contrasted with the position in England, where *CCWS* apparently has settled that an unincorporated association can be liable for the torts of its members, without need for recourse to the concept of agency or procedural workarounds.[184] The English position specifically was rejected by the Supreme Court of Ireland in *Hickey v McGowan*,[185] where the position adopted was broadly in line with that in Scotland: a religious order, lacking legal personality,

[177] Scottish Law Commission, *Discussion Paper on Unincorporated Associations* (Scot Law Com DP No 140, 2008); *Report on Unincorporated Associations* (Scot Law Com No 217, 2009). See further *Kershaw v Connel Community Council* [2018] CSOH 111, 2019 SLT 121 [13]–[18], [33].

[178] *The Shore Porters' Society of Aberdeen v Brown* [2021] CSOH 37 [16] (Lady Wolfe).

[179] The picture is complicated if the injured party also is a member of the association, as vicarious liability is said not to arise among co-principals: *Harrison v West of Scotland Kart Club* 2004 SC 615 (IH).

[180] *Gorrie* (n 151) [8.5].

[181] *McE* (n 120) [130] (*obiter*). cf *Kershaw* (n 175) [33] which reads this case as holding that vicarious liability cannot arise between an unincorporated association and its members. What was decided in *McE* was that a vicarious liability case had been improperly pleaded. In the passage cited in the main text, such liability *in principle* was accepted.

[182] *T v The English Province of the Congregation of Christian Brothers* 2020 SLT (Sh Ct) 108.

[183] *Harrison* (n 179) [23].

[184] *CCWS* (n 42) [61]. However, the imposition of vicarious liability on unincorporated association for all connected wrongs of their members has been criticised: P Morgan, 'Vicarious Liability on the Move' (2013) 129 *LQR* 139, 140–41; P Morgan, 'Vicarious Liability and the Beautiful Game – Liability for Professional and Amateur Footballers?' (2018) 38 *Legal Studies* 242, 255–58.

[185] *Hickey v McGowan* [2017] IESC 6, [2017] 2 IR 196.

cannot itself be vicariously liable for the tort of a member,[186] but a member may vicariously be liable for the torts of another to the extent this was carried out in the 'common interest' of the association[187] or 'sufficiently connected to the object and mission of the order'.[188]

What remains unclear is which members may be held vicariously liable for the delict of another in Scots law. The position in English law – which equates for these purposes an unincorporated association to that of a body corporate – would be to treat all members of the association at the time of the initiation of litigation (or, perhaps, the execution of the ensuing judgment) as liable.[189] However, in *Hickey*, the Supreme Court of Ireland held that only those who were members of the association at the time of the wrongdoing would be fixed with liability.[190] In *Gorrie v Marist Brothers*, the Outer House outlined these two possible approaches without deciding between them, simply stating that the former was 'not *prima facie* incompetent'.[191] The Scottish Law Commission made no recommendation bearing on the question. Clearly, there may well be situations where there simply are no contemporaneous members alive to be held liable, and this approach would increase the chance of a defender being able to establish, in terms of the limitation provisions discussed above, that no fair trial could take place. That – and the interests of justice generally – favour treating all members at the time of the litigation as liable, but this admittedly goes against the logic of sustaining the unincorporated nature of associations. The Scottish Parliament already has in other areas proven willing to correct injustices caused by quirks of legal personality.[192] Legislation framed for the particular context – as the 2017 Act is for limitation purposes – providing for recovery from unincorporated associations for historic child abuse,[193] may be a proportionate way to secure justice without wider disruption to the legal regimes in play.

[186] ibid [46]–[52] (O'Donnell J).
[187] ibid [56].
[188] ibid [38].
[189] The result of Lord Phillips' reasoning in *CCWS* (n 42) is that *Campbell v Thompson* [1953] 1 QB 445 (QB), which reflects the Irish position discussed below – at least for the purposes of granting a representative order under CPR r 19.6 – now does not stand.
[190] *Hickey* (n 185) [56], although it is recognised that this default rule may be departed from by the rules of the association. For the practical implications of this – and the possibility of having the names of other potential members disclosed by order of the court – see *Grace v Hendrick* [2021] IEHC 320.
[191] *Gorrie* (n 151) [8.6]. In *T* (n 182), the point was not discussed, and it is not clear precisely against whom decree was granted.
[192] See the Partnerships (Prosecution) (Scotland) Act 2013, removing the possibility of a partnership evading criminal liability by dissolving in the period between the criminal act and the ensuing prosecution (which occurred infamously in *Balmer v HM Advocate* [2008] HCJAC 44, 2008 SLT 799).
[193] See, relatedly, *Hickey* (n 185) [57] (O'Donnell J): '[w]hether this is a desirable position as a matter of law and whether further changes should or could be made, is a matter which might usefully be considered by those charged with law reform'.

V. Conclusion

The basic principles of vicarious liability in Scotland are quite well-settled, especially given a relative paucity of case law on the subject. Though Scottish learning has occasionally been forgotten, borrowing from England is frequent, understandable and likely to continue. It is to be hoped that this will not come at the expense of insights available elsewhere, particularly from the wider common law world. Quite apart from this, the Scottish Parliament has already shown itself willing to alter general rules in responding to the widespread social ill of child abuse. Further such local and targeted intervention may yet prove necessary.

10

Vicarious Liability in the Common Law World

Comparative Conclusions

PAULA GILIKER

I. Introduction

The aim of this edited collection has been to give the reader a clearer understanding of the operation of vicarious liability, its contemporary development, its (contested) theoretical underpinnings and an awareness of ongoing areas of tension that are likely to trouble courts, lawyers and indeed law students in the next 10 years. However, a comparative study aims for more than a summary of the state of play. As Siems has pointed out:

> Going beyond mere knowledge of foreign legal rules, comparative law broadens the understanding of how legal rules work in context … If a comparative researcher identifies unexpected similarities, she may want to find out whether there are any common historical roots or recent globalising trends of which she had been unaware. And, if there are unexpected differences, she may want to explore the political, cultural and socio-economic reasons that may explain them.[1]

The contributors to this work have therefore sought to go beyond the rules of substantive law to discuss the 'why' question – why is the law relating to vicarious liability in tort still uncertain despite extensive judicial consideration and to what extent do policy or other factors influence the tests the courts apply today?

In this chapter, I will seek to reflect on the similarities and differences between the doctrine of vicarious liability as applied in Canada, England and Wales, Australia, Ireland, Singapore, Hong Kong, New Zealand and Scotland.[2] What insights can

[1] M Siems, *Comparative Law* 3rd edn, (Cambridge, Cambridge University Press, 2022) 4.

[2] Scotland is, of course, a mixed legal system, but English law's strong historical influence on vicarious liability in Scotland has been noted by leading commentators: see E Reid and M Loubser, 'Strict Liability' in R Zimmermann, K Reid and D Visser (eds), *Mixed Legal Systems in Comparative Perspective: Property and Obligations in Scotland and South Africa* (Oxford, Oxford University Press, 2004) 626–27.

we draw as to the operation of vicarious liability as a doctrine in the law of torts from study of these different primarily common law jurisdictions? Two key questions will be addressed. First, to what extent can we identify a 'common law' of vicarious liability, that is, rules that are interpreted similarly across the common law world? If there are differences, what do they signify in terms of legal policy? In examining how different common law jurisdictions have applied the 'relationship' and 'scope of employment' tests for vicarious liability, this chapter will provide the reader with a valuable overview of legal development in vicarious liability across different common law jurisdictions. In so doing, it will provide guidance as to the operation of the two-stage test for vicarious liability and insights into the future operation of this doctrine. Second, this chapter will enquire why there has been significant cross-citation in this particular area of law. Why have the legal systems discussed in this book regarded reference to case law from other common law jurisdictions as beneficial, even if, as we shall see, it is not always followed? What is it about vicarious liability that has provoked this response? In examining how the common law courts have looked overseas for inspiration in interpreting the test for vicarious liability and its theoretical underpinnings, I will examine *why* vicarious liability has provoked such a vibrant cross-jurisdictional debates and why some jurisdictions have proven more influential than others.

II. Vicarious Liability in the Common Law World

Vicarious liability holds a special place in the common law of torts. As a strict liability doctrine, it conflicts with notions of corrective justice and the dominance of fault-based reasoning,[3] and yet continues to thrive in all the systems examined in this book. It is by its very nature, therefore, controversial; a factor no doubt that explains the debates outlined in this book. Vicarious liability as a rule of tort law raises three obvious questions: (i) what is the scope of the doctrine; (ii) how can its scope be justified and (iii) why has it been 'on the move'[4] for the last 20 years?

In this section, I will reflect on the answers to these questions provided in the earlier chapters of this book and consider, comparatively, what insights they give us as to the nature of vicarious liability in contemporary tort law.

[3] See, for example, criticism from academics such as Stevens who advocate a rights-based account of the law: R Stevens, *Tort and Rights* (Oxford, Oxford University Press, 2007) 244. His answer is a radical one: 'The answer to this challenge is that the nature of "vicarious liability" has been commonly misunderstood. What is attributed is not the liability, but the action'. See also EJ Weinrib, *The Idea of Private Law* (Oxford, Oxford University Press, 2012) 186. Both authors rely on the master's tort theory by which the employer can in some sense be regarded as the doer of the wrong by imputation or attribution, although such reasoning has been rejected by the common law courts, see, eg, *Majrowski* [2006] UKHL 34, [2007] 1 AC 224 [7].

[4] *Various Claimants v Catholic Child Welfare Society* [2012] UKSC 56, [2013] 2 AC 1 [19] per Lord Phillips (*CCWS*).

How, then, has the common law world responded to the two-stages that make up the test for vicarious liability: a relationship giving rise to vicarious liability *and* a connection linking the parties' relationship to the employee's tort (also known as the course of employment test). The application of these tests will be examined below.

A. What Relationships Give Rise to Vicarious Liability?

All the jurisdictions in this book regard the relationship of employer and employee to be the classic relationship that gives rise to vicarious liability.[5] As an Australian Court of Appeal judge stated in 2020:

> the principle of vicarious liability under the general law may be articulated by reference to a 'general rule', namely that an employer is vicariously liable for the negligence of its employee undertaken in the course of the employment, but not for the negligent conduct of an independent contractor.[6]

This statement is important in that it succinctly expresses certain accepted premises that underline the doctrine of vicarious liability, namely (i) the core application of vicarious liability is in relation to the employer/employee relationship; (ii) it does not apply to independent contractors;[7] and (iii) traditionally its core application has been in relation to the tort of negligence. Application of the doctrine beyond these accepted premises will raise questions as to the scope of the doctrine and has given rise to many of the debates outlined in this book.

Looking at the first two premises outlined above, this book has noted the willingness of most of the systems discussed in this book to look beyond the employment relationship. This is nothing new. Stoljar noted in 1960 the use of agency reasoning as a tool to extend the doctrine of vicarious liability beyond employees to those working gratuitously for the defendant.[8] Cases, for example, involving vicarious liability for the torts of drivers permitted to borrow the defendant's motor vehicle are long-standing[9] and can be traced back to case law concerning horse and buggy

[5] See, for example, *Hollis v Vabu Pty Ltd* [2001] HCA 44, (2001) 207 CLR 21 (Australia); *CCWS* (n 4) [35] per Lord Phillips: 'The relationship that gives rise to vicarious liability is in the vast majority of cases that of employer and employee under a contract of employment'. It should be noted that while the employer/employee relationship is the most common, other relationships will be recognised, for example, commercial partnerships, as giving rise to vicarious liability.

[6] *Hallmark Construction Pty Ltd v Harford* [2020] NSWCA 41 [87] per Basten JA.

[7] 'It is trite law that the employer of an independent contractor is, in general, not liable for the negligence or other torts committed by the contractor in the course of the execution of the work': Widgery LJ in *Salsbury v Woodland* [1970] 1 QB 324, 336.

[8] SJ Stoljar, *The Law of Agency* (London, Sweet and Maxwell, 1960) 9.

[9] See, for example, *Launchbury v Morgans* [1973] AC 127; *Soblusky v Egan* [1960] HCA 9, (1960) 103 CLR 215. See, in a different context, *S v Attorney-General* [2003] NZLR 450.

accidents in the early nineteenth century.[10] Australian judge McHugh J also argued in favour of the doctrine extending to 'representative agents', that is, drawing on agency cases, liability for a party working for and on behalf of the employer.[11] More recent cases, however, have not relied on what Gleeson CJ in *Scott v Davis*[12] termed 'the question begging label "agent"'.

Two approaches have been adopted by the courts. The first is to adopt a more generous interpretation of the employment relationship. McKendrick warned in 1990 of the dangers of adopting a rigid interpretation of the employer/employee relationship.[13] He highlighted the danger that if workers not satisfying a strict definition of 'employee' were treated as outside the scope of vicarious liability, the doctrine would be both curtailed and its policy justifications potentially undermined. However, the courts have increasingly accepted that the employer/employee relationship should be treated as a matter not of form but substance, looking at the economic reality of the parties' relationship.[14] On this basis, the court will ask whether the worker can realistically be said to be on business on his own account, taking the risk of profit or loss.[15] The Australian case of *Hollis v Vabu Pty Ltd*[16] demonstrates the potential of a more liberal test that focuses on the substance of the relationship rather than its form. Mr Hollis had been injured due to the negligence of a bicycle courier who was only identifiable by his uniform which bore the name of the owners of the business. Couriers had a degree of independence,[17] but the majority of the High Court of Australia, applying the economic reality test, found them to be employees. The company exercised a high degree of control over the cyclists,[18] and the Court found that the effect of Vabu's business model had been to

[10] See P Giliker, *Vicarious Liability in Tort: A Comparative Perspective* (Cambridge, Cambridge University Press, 2010) 110–16.

[11] See the judgments of McHugh J in *Hollis* (n 5) [73] and in *Scott v Davis* [2000] HCA 52, (2000) 204 CLR 333 [34], rejected, however, by the majority of the High Court of Australia. Note also similar ideas emerging from Canada of the 'dependent contractor': G Davidov, 'The Three Axes of Employment Relationships: A Characterisation of Workers in Need of Protection' (2002) 52 *University of Toronto Law Journal* 357.

[12] *Scott* (n 11) [14]. See also Gummow J [159]–[161].

[13] E McKendrick, 'Vicarious Liability and Independent Contractors – A Re-Examination' (1990) 53 *MLR* 770, 784. See also R Kidner, Vicarious Liability: For Whom Should the Employer Be Liable (1995) 15 *Legal Studies* 47.

[14] See *Viasystems (Tyneside) Ltd v Thermal Transfer (Northern) Ltd* [2005] EWCA Civ 1151, [2006] QB 510 (*Viasystems*) [55] (Rix LJ).

[15] *Ready Mixed Concrete (South East) Ltd v Minister of Pensions and National Insurance* [1968] 2 QB 497.

[16] *Hollis* (n 5), although the HCA more recently argued that the emphasis should be on whether a labourer is conducting his or her own independent business, as distinct from serving in the business of the employer, rather than an impressionistic checklist of factors representing the totality of the parties' relationship: *Construction, Forestry, Maritime, Mining and Energy Union v Personnel Contracting Pty Ltd* [2022] HCA 1 [34]–[35] (*CFMMEU*).

[17] Couriers were able to deal with the company as sole traders or members of a partnership and were paid fixed rates per job, using their own bicycles.

[18] 'Vabu's whole business consisted of the delivery of documents and parcels by means of couriers. Vabu retained control of the allocation and direction of the various deliveries. The couriers had little latitude': ibid [57] per Gleeson CJ, Gaudron J, Gummow J, Kirby J and Hayne J.

encourage pedestrians to identify the couriers as a part of Vabu's own working staff.[19] On this basis, it would be unrealistic to describe them as anything but *employees* for the sake of vicarious liability. There is a line to be drawn, however, between a more liberal view of the employee in light of changing employment practices and true independent contractors, as reiterated recently by the UK Supreme Court[20] and the Singapore Court of Appeal.[21] Lady Hale remarked on 'the classic distinction between work done for an employer as part of the business of that employer and work done by an independent contractor as part of the business of that contractor'.[22]

A second option has emerged from Canadian and UK law – the relationship 'akin to employment'. That is, a relationship not technically of employment, but closely resembling that of employment, should fall within the doctrine of vicarious liability. This argument, based on an incremental approach to employment relations and deemed consistent with the underlying policy justifications for vicarious liability, gained favour initially as a means of ensuring that the Roman Catholic church could be held vicariously liable for historical sexual abuse by priests who are not technically employees of the church.[23] The Supreme Court of Canada in *Doe v Bennett* in 2004[24] argued that the relationship between the bishop and a priest in a diocese was not only spiritual, but temporal:

> The priest takes a vow of obedience to the bishop. The bishop exercises extensive control over the priest, including the power of assignment, the power to remove the priest from his post and the power to discipline him. It is akin to an employment relationship.

This 'akin' to employment test was followed by the English Court of Appeal in *JGE*[25] (later confirmed in *CCWS*).[26] Drawing on *Bennett*,[27] the English court argued that it was a question of the closeness of the parties' relationship and that courts should look carefully at all the surrounding facts and circumstances to determine the true nature of the relationship. The UK Supreme Court in later decisions confirmed that even prisoners serving in the prison kitchen as part of their rehabilitation could be regarded as 'akin to employees' (*Cox v Ministry of Justice*),[28]

[19] ibid [52].
[20] *Barclays Bank plc v Various Claimants* [2020] UKSC 13, [2020] AC 973.
[21] *Ng Huat Seng v Mohammad* [2017] SGCA 58 [63].
[22] *Barclays* (n 20) [22].
[23] This argument is still used successfully by the Church in Australia, see *Trustees of Roman Catholic Church v Ellis* (2007) 70 NSWLR 565, [2007] NSWCA 117, although in some States legislation has been introduced to deal with this problem eg in 2018, NSW passed legislation to allow the term 'employee' in the context of vicarious liability claims against organisations for child abuse to include an individual who is akin to an employee (see Civil Liability Act 2002 (NSW) Part 1B ss 6G–6H). This has not, however, been implemented in all States eg Victoria.
[24] *Doe v Bennett* 2004 SCC 17, [2004] 1 SCR 436 [27].
[25] *JGE (or E) v English Province of Our Lady of Charity* [2012] EWCA Civ 938, [2013] QB 722.
[26] *CCWS* (n 4) [47].
[27] ibid [32]–[35]. *Bennett* was found to sit comfortably with the reasoning of the English Court of Appeal in *Viasystems* (n 14).
[28] *Cox v Ministry of Justice* [2016] UKSC 10, [2016] AC 660.

as were foster parents volunteering to undertake the care of children placed under local authority control (*Armes v Nottinghamshire CC*).[29] It drew the line, however, at a doctor undertaking health checks for a bank as part of its recruitment policy which was a minor part of his practice and which took place in the doctor's own consulting rooms.[30]

In extending the 'akin to employment' beyond religious organisations to defendants generally, the Anglo-Canadian approach responds to changing modes of employment practice, notably the casualisation of the workforce, the introduction of the gig economy and increasing sub-contracting of key operations which are integral to the successful operation of a business. The appeal of the 'akin to employment' model has spread beyond these two jurisdictions, being adopted in Ireland,[31] Singapore,[32] Hong Kong,[33] Scotland[34] and arguably New Zealand.[35] Menon CJ in the Singapore Court of Appeal commented that the akin to employment model enables the courts to fine-tune the existing framework underlying the doctrine so as to accommodate the more diverse range of relationships which might be encountered in today's context.[36] None of these courts have accepted, however, an extension of the doctrine to true independent contractors.

Neyers and Kiss in chapter two note, however, concerns in Canada that undue emphasis on the policy underlying vicarious liability, notably the theory of enterprise risk, might place the vital distinction between relationships 'akin to employment' and independent contractors in jeopardy.[37] Similar fears have been expressed in the UK.[38] In both jurisdictions, the apex courts have sought to provide reassurance that the traditional distinction between employees and

[29] *Armes v Nottinghamshire CC* [2017] UKSC 60, [2018] AC 355. Here the UK Supreme Court went further than the Supreme Court of Canada: *KLB v British Columbia* 2003 SCC 51, [2003] 2 SCR 403 (foster parents are independent contractors).

[30] *Barclays* (n 20).

[31] *Hickey v McGowan* [2017] IESC 6, [2017] 2 IR 196 (relationship between the wrongdoer and the Marist Order). The judgment in *CCWS* (n 4) was considered at length (and not uncritically) by the Irish Supreme Court.

[32] *Ng Huat Seng* (n 21) [66].

[33] Although it has yet to be argued successfully in that most of the attempts in the Hong Kong case law to argue for the imposition of vicarious liability in circumstances other than an employment relationship have concerned cases in which the wrongdoer was plainly the defendant's independent contractor or the independent contractor's employee: see Glofcheski in chapter seven.

[34] *Grubb v Shannon* [2018] SC GLA 13, 2018 SLT (Sh Ct) 193.

[35] Todd argues in chapter eight that the leading case of *S v Attorney-General* [2003] NZLR 450 would in the light of developments elsewhere in the common law world be better analysed as finding a relationship 'analogous to contract'.

[36] *Ng Huat Seng* (n 21) [66].

[37] See 30. They cite, for example, AE Spafford, 'The Enterprise Risk Theory: Redefining Vicarious Liability for Intentional Torts' (LLM thesis, University of Toronto 2000) 71–73.

[38] See, for example, A Silink, 'Vicarious Liability of a Bank for the Acts of a Contracted Debtor' (2018) 34 *PN* 46 and A Silink and D Ryan 'Vicarious Liability for Independent Contractors' (2018) 77 *CLJ* 458.

independent contractors continues to exist.[39] In *Sagaz*,[40] the Supreme Court of Canada reaffirmed that the traditional distinction was consistent with the policies of fair compensation and deterrence, and proposed an amalgamated test which incorporates what it saw as the best elements of the traditional control, organisation and entrepreneur tests.[41] However, the UK court in *Barclays Bank* went a step further than *Sagaz*, seeking to confine discussion of policy to what it described as 'doubtful' akin to employment cases.[42] This suggests a distinction between the two approaches, although we might question to what extent UK courts will be able to keep policy out of the relationship question.[43]

Australia, however, has to date resisted the lure of 'akin to employment'.[44] Although, as indicated above, *Hollis* indicates a broad interpretation of the 'employee' test, the status of 'employee' is still required at common law to trigger vicarious liability. However, change has occurred and, in 2016, the High Court of Australia in *Prince Alfred College*[45] indicated that a more liberal approach should be taken to the Stage 2 'course of employment' test. Although the case did not deal with Stage 1, this has led to calls to rethink the Stage 1 test. In chapter four, Beuermann outlined the 2020 case of *Plaintiffs A, B, C and D v Bird*[46] in which a volunteer (and minority shareholder) of a childcare centre (Little Pigeon) had been accused of abusing two infants. Bird had been actively involved in managing the centre, supervising the playground, cooking and undertaking some maintenance. The judge, applying *Hollis*, was prepared to treat Bird as an employee having considered the totality of the parties' relationship,[47] but significantly also commented that she saw no reason why, in principle, following *Prince Alfred College*, vicarious liability could not have arisen even if Bird could only be viewed as a volunteer.[48] Reference was noticeably made to the UK decisions of *Cox*[49]

[39] See *Barclays* (n 20) and *671122 Ontario Ltd v Sagaz Industries Canada Ltd* 2001 SCC 59, [2001] 2 SCR 983 (*Sagaz*).

[40] *Sagaz* (n 39) [35].

[41] ibid [47]. See also later case law: *Canada Post Corp v Carroll* (2012) 383 NBR (2d) 326 (CA) [55]; *Rush v De Ruiter* 2018 ONSC 1210 [73]-[80]; *Braiden v La-Z-Boy Canada Ltd* 2008 ONCA 464; *Sytsma v Keleshian* 2016 ONSC 460 [37].

[42] *Barclays* (n 20) [27]. It is interesting the Court seemed to regard the *Armes* case as a 'doubtful' case – a case where the UK Supreme Court took a different approach to the Canadian courts sparking a division in the common law world, as discussed in n 29 above.

[43] Recent case law does not bode well: see, for example, Stuart-Smith LJ in *Blackpool Football Club Ltd v DSN* [2021] EWCA Civ 1352 who commented at [129] that despite being what he regarded as a clear case on Stage 1 of the test, he nevertheless felt obliged to justify his decision by reference to policy in addition to the details of the parties' relationship.

[44] See *Sweeney v Boylan Nominees Pty Ltd* [2006] HCA 19; (2006) 226 CLR 161 [33]. For criticism, see J Burnett, 'Avoiding Difficult Questions: Vicarious Liability and Independent Contractors in *Sweeney v Boylan Nominees*' (2007) 29 *Sydney Law Review* 163.

[45] *Prince Alfred College Incorporated v ADC* [2016] HCA 37, (2016) 258 CLR 134.

[46] *Plaintiffs A, B, C and D v Bird* [2020] NSWSC 1379.

[47] See, generally, [426]–[447]. Although Bird was unpaid, the Court found Mr Bird was remunerated by the various benefits he received: [432].

[48] ibid [418]–[424].

[49] *Cox* (n 28).

and *CCWS*.[50] While conceding that the principles in these cases did not entirely accord with those established in *Prince Alfred*, the judge held:

> [these principles] do demonstrate how the common law develops, when new situations arise for consideration. I consider that application of the Australian principles to the facts I have found, would permit the conclusion that Little Pigeon was vicariously liable for Mr Bird's acts, even if he provided his services to Little Pigeon as a volunteer, rather than as an employee.[51]

In the later (and unrelated) case of *DP v Bird*,[52] the Supreme Court of Victoria was again prepared to rethink how Australian courts should approach vicarious liability claims, this time in a claim against the Catholic church for abuse by a priest. Here applying the *Hollis* criteria, the court found it impossible to treat the priest as an employee.[53] Influenced by *Cox*, the judge then proceeded to engage in a holistic and broad inquiry into the totality of the circumstances surrounding the relationship between the Diocese and the priest and relied upon comments from the decision of the High Court of Australia in *Prince Alfred* to support an extension of the Stage 1 test to include that of an assistant priest's relationship with his diocese.[54]

Such cases, while of limited authority, indicate that Australian courts are both aware of the 'akin to employment' test as promulgated by the UK and Canadian courts and are conscious of the limitations of *Hollis* in straining to respond to new forms of casual employment. It remains to be seen whether the spirit of change in the lower courts will spread to the High Court. In 2022, Gleeson J (with Gageler J) cited with approval the view of the HCA in *Sweeney* that the common law distinction between employees and independent contractors was 'too deeply rooted to be pulled out'.[55] Australia provides an interesting example of the common law world providing a resource for national courts but one, notably, that is counter-balanced against domestic, and directly authoritative, case law: in both of the lower court judgments, the courts were keen to attribute legal development to the inspiration of the High Court of *Australia* in the *Prince Alfred* case. It remains to be seen whether the HCA regards this as a legitimate inference. One conclusion can,

[50] *CCWS* (n 4). *Barclays Bank* (n 20) was also cited.

[51] (n 46) [424] per Her Honour Justice Schmidt.

[52] [2021] VSC 850 (J Forrest J). See N Foster, 'Vicarious Liability of Bishop for abuse committed by clergy': https://lawandreligionaustralia.blog/2021/12/30/vicarious-liability-of-bishop-for-abuse-committed-by-clergy/ who argues that the decision is wrong, as inconsistent with clear High Court of Australia authority.

[53] ibid [211].

[54] ibid [205]–[206]: 'The Court could not and should not be bound by observations in [the *Ellis* case (n 23)] a case which have now been overtaken by highly persuasive judicial statements in this country and other Commonwealth jurisdictions, in particular, those of the High Court in Prince *Alfred College*, the Supreme Court of Canada in *Bazley*, and the Supreme Court of the United Kingdom in the [*CCWS*] case. To adopt Lord Phillips' statement in [*CCWS*]: "The law of vicarious liability is on the move", and *Ellis* has been left in its wake'.

[55] *CFMMEU* (n 16) [94], citing *Sweeney* (n 44) [33] per Gleeson CJ, Gummow, Hayne, Heydon and Crennan JJ.

however, be reached. The influence of the common law world in the interpretation and application of the 'akin to employment' and Stage 1 test is remarkable.

B. Modernising the 'Course of Employment' Test: From Salmond to Close Connection to Occasion

The notion of a functional limit on the scope of the doctrine of vicarious liability seems to have developed from the late seventeenth century onwards,[56] and is thus found in all the common law jurisdictions discussed in this book. As indicated above, however, its application, perhaps inevitably, has been contested in that it sets a limit to which strict liability can be invoked against an innocent defendant. While all systems have come to accept that all torts potentially can fall within the scope of vicarious liability, the Stage 2 test asks: to what extent does the tort in question have to be connected to the relationship that binds the tortfeasor and the innocent defendant to make it fair and just that vicarious liability should be imposed? While the defendant employer will not be responsible for the employee going on a 'frolic of his own',[57] the question remains to what extent horseplay in the workplace and intentional criminal acts can (and should) be regarded as actions for which vicarious liability should apply. Three tests stand out.

i. The Salmond Test

The so-called Salmond test states that vicarious liability will only arise if the employee's tort represented 'either (a) a wrongful act authorised by the master or (b) a wrongful and unauthorised mode of doing some act authorised by the master'.[58] First stated in 1907, it proved influential across the commonwealth.[59] The Salmond test was embraced across the common law world: in Canada,[60] Ireland,[61]

[56] J Baker, *Introduction to English Legal History* 5th edn (Oxford, Oxford University Press, 2019) 437, citing *Turbervile v Stamp* (1697) B & M 611, 612, per Holt CJ; *Jones v Hart* (1699) 2 Salk. 441. Discussed in Giliker (n 10) 147–49 who also traces ideas back to Roman law.

[57] To use the traditional language of *Joel v Morrison* (1834) 6 C & P 501, 503, 172 ER 1338, 1339 per Parke B.

[58] JW Salmond, *The Law of Torts* 1st edn (London, Stevens and Haynes, 1907) 83. This test was repeated in each edition until its final edition in 1996: RFV Heuston and RA Buckley, *Salmond and Heuston on the Law of Tort*, 21st edn (London, Sweet and Maxwell, 1996) 443.

[59] As described in Lunney's excellent essay: M Lunney, 'Professor Sir John Salmond (1862–1924): An Englishman Abroad' in D Nolan and J Goudkamp (eds), *Scholars of Tort Law* (Oxford, Hart Publishing, 2020) 125. See also chapter one of this book.

[60] See *WW Sales Ltd v City of Edmonton* [1942] SCR 467. For a discussion of the use of the test in Canada pre-*Bazley* see S Wildeman, 'Vicarious Liability for Sexual Assault: The Two New Tests for Scope of Employment in *B(PA) v Curry* and *T(G) v Griffiths*' (1998) 7 *Dalhousie Journal of Legal Studies* 1, 34ff.

[61] *O'Keeffe v Hickey* [2008] IESC 72, [2009] 2 IR 302 highlights ongoing resistance in 2008 to moving away from the Salmond test.

Singapore,[62] Hong Kong,[63] New Zealand[64] and Australia.[65] Lunney suggests that the longevity of the Salmond formulation can be attributed to its elegance and seductive systemising of the law. 'It is a good example', he comments drily, 'of how seductive Salmond's systemising could be, even if the law itself had taken a different turn'.[66]

Yet the judicial prominence of the Salmond test came to be threatened by the increasing willingness of the courts to permit vicarious liability for intentional and self-serving tortious misconduct that was difficult to reconcile with the wording of the test. Cases such as *Lloyd v Grace, Smith &Co*[67] indicated, for example, that torts such as fraud, civil theft and battery could be within the doctrine of vicarious liability. In the 1990s, it was sexual abuse that challenged the courts to fit such acts within the Salmond test. The English Court of Appeal in 1998 maintained that such criminal activities amounted to 'an independent act of self-indulgence or self-gratification'[68] and could not be regarded as able to satisfy the Salmond test.

If, therefore, vicarious liability were to apply to intentional torts such as sexual abuse, a new test was needed. While the Canadian Supreme Court and UK Supreme Court adopted the close or sufficiently close connection test – and were followed by courts in Ireland,[69] Singapore,[70] Hong Kong,[71] New Zealand[72] and Scotland[73] – Australia chose a different test. These two tests will be examined below.

ii. The Close Connection Test

This test finds its origins in the 1999 and 2001 cases of *Bazley v Curry*[74] and *Lister v Hesley Hall Ltd.*[75] In *Bazley*, McLachlin J argued that vicarious liability would

[62] See Tan in chapter six.

[63] Until *Ming An Insurance Co (HK) Ltd v Ritz-Carlton Ltd* (2002) 5 HKCFAR 569. For comment, see R Glofcheski, 'A Frolic in the Law of Tort: Expanding the Scope of Employers' Vicarious Liability' (2004) 12 *Tort Law Review* 1.

[64] See Todd, chapter eight. The first edition of Salmond was actually printed in New Zealand where Salmond was a Professor of Law under the imprint of London firm Stevens and Haynes.

[65] *Deatons Pty Ltd v Flew* [1949] HCA 60, 79 CLR 370.

[66] Lunney (n 59) 125, noting, however, that Salmond did not regard *Lloyd v Grace, Smith & Co* [1912] AC 716 as correctly decided. Lord Diplock was perhaps less polite in referring to the Salmond formula as 'that infelicitous but time-honoured phrase': see *Morris v CW Martin & Sons Ltd* [1966] 1 QB 716, 737.

[67] *Lloyd v Grace, Smith &Co* [1912] AC 716.

[68] *Trotman v North Yorkshire CC* [1998] ELR 625, 632.

[69] *O'Keeffe v Hickey* [2008] IESC 72, [2009] 2 IR 302.

[70] *Skandinaviska Enskilda Banken AB v Asia Pacific Breweries (Singapore) Pte Ltd* [2011] SGCA 22, [2011] 3 SLR 540.

[71] *Ming An* (n 63).

[72] *S v Attorney-General* [2003] 3 NZLR 450 (CA).

[73] *Wilson v Exel UK Ltd (t/a Exel)* [2010] CSIH 35, 2010 SLT 671.

[74] *Bazley v Curry* [1999] 2 SCR 534, 174 DLR (4th) 45 (*Bazley*).

[75] *Lister v Hesley Hall Ltd* [2001] UKHL 22, [2002] 1 AC 215 (*Lister*), although the court claimed that the germ of the *Bazley* close connection test could be traced back to the traditional Salmond test: [15]. Lord Steyn referred to *Bazley* as a 'luminous and illuminating' judgment which would henceforth be the starting point for consideration of similar cases: [27].

generally be appropriate where there was 'a significant connection between the creation or enhancement of a risk [of injury] and the wrong that accrues therefrom, even if unrelated to the employer's desires'.[76] Under the connection test, as articulated by the UK House of Lords, vicarious liability will arise where the employee's torts could be said to be so closely connected with his employment that it would be fair and just to hold the employers vicariously liable.[77] Under this more generous test, vicarious liability could extend to intentional torts such as sexual abuse without the problems that arose under the Salmond test.[78] The 'close connection' test has been adopted subsequently by most of the jurisdictions discussed in this book.[79] Australia, however, remains an outlier.[80]

While the great advantage of the 'close connection' test is its ability to explain how intentional torts might satisfy the Stage 2 test, it left open a number of questions. One obvious question that arose immediately was whether it should also apply to non-intentional torts or whether this latter category would continue to be governed by the Salmond test. While Canada and Hong Kong were immediately willing to apply the new test to all torts,[81] this question took some time for the UK courts to resolve. The UK courts were also reluctant initially to address the policy basis for the close connection test, but eventually, in *CCWS*, accepted at the highest level that its justification lies, primarily, in arguments of enterprise risk. This policy justification – that having created or enhanced the *risk* of the wrong being committed, it is appropriate and just that the employer or operator of the enterprise be held responsible, even though the wrongful act may be contrary to its desires[82] – comes from the Canadian courts and demonstrates the power of cross-citation in this area of law. The idea that vicarious liability can be explained and justified by reference to enterprise risk theory has swept the common law world. The UK,[83] Irish,[84] Hong Kong[85] and Singaporean[86] courts have shown their willingness to adopt this rationale. And yet enterprise risk has been subject to criticism, not least for permitting over-extensive liability placing an increasingly

[76] *Bazley* (n 74) [41]

[77] *Lister* (n 75) [28] per Lord Steyn.

[78] As noted in *Trotman* (n 68).

[79] See cases cited above. It is interesting to see how quickly it was adopted after *Lister* (2001).

[80] *Prince Alfred College* (n 45).

[81] See *Ming An* (n 63) (Hong Kong) and the discussion of Canadian law in chapter two. The same result has been ultimately reached in other common law jurisdictions.

[82] *Blackwater v Plint* 2005 SCC 58, [2005] 3 SCR 3 [20] per McLachlin CJ.

[83] *CCWS* (n 4) (UK). See J Bell, 'Vicarious liability for child abuse' (2010) 69 *CLJ* 440, 442: 'the ultimate justification of vicarious liability is really the risk which an employer creates for those who encounter his business or enterprise'. Note doubts, however, arising in Scotland: *Vaickuviene v J Sainsbury Plc* [2013] CSIH 67, [22]-[24] per Lord Carloway. See, further, S Bogle, 'Responsibility for Another's Wrong in Scotland: Stick with *Lister* or Twist with *Mohamud*?' [2019] *Juridical Review* 211.

[84] *Hickey* (n 31) [41] per O'Donnell J.

[85] *Ming An* (n 63).

[86] *Skandinaviska* (n 70). See D Tan, 'Internalising Externalities: An Enterprise Risk Approach to Vicarious Liability in the 21st Century' (2015) 27 *Singapore Academy of Law Journal* 822

onerous burden on innocent defendant employers.[87] Australian academic Gray has pointed out that, as a theory, it fails to explain key elements of the vicarious liability test, for example, if an enterprise is expected to internalise the risks created by its workers as a cost of the enterprise, it 'does not explain why vicarious liability is dependent upon proof that the employee committed a tort'.[88] Logically it should cover all harmful acts. We can go beyond this – why does it need to be confined to employees/those akin to employees rather than all actors that act on behalf of the employer?[89] Is it always the case that vicarious liability represents the most efficient way of distributing losses caused by wrongful employee behaviour (are employers always the better risk-bearers?)?[90] And finally to what extent are the courts best placed to appraise this question?[91]

In rejecting enterprise risk reasoning as a basis for the doctrine, the Australian High Court in *Prince Alfred College* remarked that reference to such general principles left the law depending on policy choices which are matters upon which minds may differ.[92] In particular, it expressed its concern that enterprise risk reasoning might render the connection test one of mere causative connection rather than requiring a 'significant' connection between the parties' relationship and the tort.[93] The HCA on this basis rejected the test stated by the UK Supreme Court in *Mohamud v Morrison Supermarkets plc*[94] which had seemed to argue that a 'sufficient' connection between the field of activities entrusted to the employee and the wrongful conduct would suffice.[95] The UK Supreme Court

[87] However, it also has its advocates, notably, D Brodie, *Enterprise Liability and the Common Law* (Cambridge, Cambridge University Press, 2010) and S Deakin, '"Enterprise Risk": The Juridical Nature of the Firm Revisited' (2003) 32 *Industrial Law Journal* 97 and has provoked extensive discussion in US literature: see, for example, GC Keating, 'The Idea of Fairness in the Law of Enterprise Liability' (1997) 95 *Michigan Law Review* 1266.

[88] A Gray, *Vicarious Liability Critique and Reform* (Oxford, Hart Publishing, 2018) 138. See also C McIvor, 'The Use and Abuse of the Doctrine of Vicarious Liability' (2006) 35 *Common Law World Review* 268.

[89] D Brodie, 'Enterprise Liability: Justifying Vicarious Liability' (2007) 27 *OJLS* 493.

[90] H Hansmann and R Kraakman, 'Toward Unlimited Shareholder Liability for Corporate Torts' (1991) 100 *Yale Law Journal* 1879 argue that enterprise liability can only justify liability to the extent that corporations appear to be the cheapest cost avoiders and/or insurers: 1918–19. We might also question the assumption that the imposition of vicarious liability in such circumstances serves the policy ends of promoting deterrence given limited empirical evidence of this effect.

[91] R Merkin and J Steele, *Insurance and the Law of Obligations* (Oxford, Oxford University Press, 2013) 204. It is also problematic that vicarious liability renders the tortfeasor and the employer jointly liable meaning that it permits the employer (subject to legal and practical limitations) to shift liability back to the actual tortfeasor as a joint tortfeasor at law.

[92] *Prince Alfred College* (n 45) [45].

[93] A fear shared by a number of commentators eg P Morgan, 'Certainty in Vicarious Liability: A Quest for a Chimaera?' (2016) 75 *CLJ* 202, 205.

[94] *Mohamud v Morrison Supermarkets plc* [2016] UKSC 11, [2016] AC 677, in particular [44]–[45] per Lord Toulson.

[95] As discussed in chapter three of this book. See also D Ryan, '"Close Connection" and "Akin to Employment": Perspectives on 50 Years of Radical Developments in Vicarious Liability' [2016] *Irish Jurist* 239; J Plunkett, 'Taking Stock of Vicarious Liability' (2016) 132 *LQR* 556.

in the later case of *Various Claimants v Wm Morrison Supermarkets plc*[96] was quick to reassure lawyers that the test remained one of 'close connection', reverting back to the test traditionally stated by Lord Nicholls in *Dubai Aluminium*.[97] As discussed in chapter three, in advising the courts to refer to previous court decisions to identify the factors or principles which point towards or away from vicarious liability in the case before the court, it sought to provide a more principled and consistent basis for the Stage 2 test. More radically, the Court held that enterprise risk arguments should be confined to the akin to employment test (as seen in *Barclays*) and sexual abuse cases where a 'tailored' version of the close connection test would apply.[98]

The interplay of the common law courts on the connection test is notable, not least the apparent change in the UK court's position post-*Prince Alfred College*. A comparative overview enables us to examine key struggles with the close connection test and the extent to which policy reasoning has influenced its operation. While in *CCWS*, for example, the UK Supreme Court acknowledged that enterprise risk was one of the key justifications for vicarious liability, in *Morrison* an attempt seems to be made to encourage courts to adopt a more cautious approach that focuses on the closeness of the connection to what the employee was actually authorised to do. For common law jurisdictions that have sought to follow the *Bazley/Lister* test, *Morrison* raises a difficult question: do they too adopt a more cautious approach or continue to follow their pre-*Morrison* approach?

One outstanding question still awaiting resolution is how to deal with binding UK authority indicating the close connection test should not be used for cases of fraudulent misrepresentation.[99] While the Canadian[100] and Singaporean[101] courts have simply extended the close connection test to fraud, this has led to confusion in some common law jurisdictions seeking to follow *Lister*. Glofcheski, for example, notes in chapter seven that while Bokhary PJ in *Ming An* argued that the close connection test is 'the basic criterion for vicarious liability in regard to all torts committed by an employee during an unauthorised course of conduct, whether intentional wrongdoing or mere inadvertence is involved',[102] this has caused tension with earlier authority imposing stricter conditions for vicarious liability for financial fraud. Post-*Ming An* case law has failed to resolve this tension.[103]

[96] *Wm Morrison Supermarkets plc v Various Claimants* [2020] UKSC 12, [2020] AC 989 (*Morrison*).

[97] *Dubai Aluminium Co Ltd v Salaam* [2002] UKHL 48, [2003] 2 AC 366 [23].

[98] *Morrison* (n 96) [23] and [36], citing *CCWS* (n 4) [83] and [85]. Later authority has clarified that it should apply in both child and adult sexual abuse cases: *Trustees of the Barry Congregation of Jehovah's Witnesses v BXB* [2021] EWCA Civ 356, [2021] 4 WLR 42 [84] (*BXB*).

[99] *Armagas Ltd v Mundogas SA* [1986] AC 717 (HL); *Hockley Mint Ltd v Ramsden* [2018] EWCA Civ 2480, [2019] WLR 1617.

[100] See chapter two.

[101] See *Skandinaviska* (n 70).

[102] *Ming An* (n 63) 581.

[103] Compare, for example, *Ronia Ltd v Clarke* HCA 3972/2000, [2005] HKEC 326; *Wan Kwok Ling v Hou Tak Securities Ltd* [2006] 4 HKLRD 525 and *Luk Wing Yan v CMB Wing Lung Bank Ltd* (2021) HCA 1249/2016, [2021] HKCFI 279, discussed in chapter seven.

Glofcheski argues in his chapter that this confusion leaves the current state of the law of employee fraud in Hong Kong in an unacceptable state with no explanation for the different approaches. Here following UK law includes adopting its own doctrinal uncertainties; the onus falling on the recipient jurisdiction to recognise the difficulty and find its own solution.

One final source of controversy has been created recently by the UK courts. In *Morrison*, as indicated above, the Court indicated that a distinct 'tailored' approach should be taken towards cases alleging sexual assault.[104] Logically this would mean that a different version of the close connection test would apply to a serious physical assault to that of a minor sexual assault, despite the devastating impact of both occurrences on the victim. Such a line is not necessarily easy to draw, and it remains unclear to what extent UK courts will resist discussion of policy concerns in non-sexual abuse cases. Again, jurisdictions keen to follow *Lister* and its subsequent interpretation may wish to pause while UK law resolves the uncertainties created by the *Morrison* case.

Stepping back, we can see that the close connection test provides a good example of courts following case law from other jurisdictions but inadvertently bringing with it certain baggage: loose phraseology, unresolved doctrinal conflicts and policy rationales that may or may not transplant easily into the recipient jurisdiction. Relying on *Bazley* and *Lister*, in reality, has meant that common law jurisdictions are seeking guidance from a far from foolproof model. The Australian courts have, in particular, been suspicious of the apparent simplicity of the 'close connection' test as a means to resolve problems with the Salmond test. Instead, it has recommended its own test: the 'occasion' test.

iii. The Occasion Test

In the sexual abuse case of *Prince Alfred College v ADC*,[105] the High Court of Australia (HCA) rejected the Anglo-Canadian close connection test in favour of the occasion test, that is, whether the apparent performance of the employee's role could be said to provide the '*occasion*' for the abuse. The close connection test it argued, as evidenced by its liberal interpretation in the UK case of *Mohamud*,[106] was likely to result in the imposition of vicarious liability for wrongful acts for which the employment provided no more than an opportunity.[107] On this basis:

> in cases of this kind, the relevant approach is to consider any special role that the employer has assigned to the employee and the position in which the employee is

[104] For detailed critiques, see D Nolan, 'Reining in Vicarious Liability' (2020) 49 *Industrial Law Journal* 609; P Giliker, 'Can the Supreme Court Halt the Ongoing Expansion of Vicarious Liability? *Barclays* and *Morrison* in the UK Supreme Court' (2021) 37 *PN* 55; J Lee, 'The Supreme Court, Vicarious Liability and the Grand Old Duke of York' (2020) 136 *LQR* 553.

[105] *Prince Alfred College* (n 45).

[106] *Mohamud* (n 94)

[107] *Prince Alfred College* (n 45) [83]. The HCA did, however, argue that *Lister* would have satisfied the occasion test.

> thereby placed vis-à-vis the victim. In determining whether the apparent performance of such a role may be said to give the 'occasion' for the wrongful act, particular features may be taken into account. They include authority, power, trust, control and the ability to achieve intimacy with the victim. The latter feature may be especially important. Where, in such circumstances, the employee takes advantage of his or her position with respect to the victim, that may suffice to determine that the wrongful act should be regarded as committed in the course or scope of employment and as such render the employer vicariously liable.[108]

Rather than relying on Canadian or UK law, the HCA found inspiration in the judgment of Owen Dixon J in *Deatons Pty Ltd v Flew*[109] who had argued that employers should only be liable for acts where the apparent performance of the employment 'gives occasion' for the wrongful act.[110] Dixon J had been, of course, influenced by the Salmond test so the 'occasion' test may be regarded as an Australian variant of this test,[111] but one intended to provide a narrower alternative to the 'close connection' test.

Thinking comparatively, it is interesting to see the Australian courts favour what appears at face value to be a 'home-grown' alternative, but one that inevitably draws on the cross-jurisdictional Salmond test. The 'occasion' test has had a mixed reception, however, both domestically and outside Australia from commentators who have questioned whether the division between occasion and opportunity for wrongdoing (for which it is commonly accepted that no liability arises) is any clearer than that specified in the 'close connection' test.[112] Beuermann in chapter three also notes that the specific guidance mentioned above is directed at 'cases of this kind' (that is, sexual abuse cases). She questions, therefore, to what extent this guidance will apply in other types of case; the High Court reserving its position as to how the law might be developed in relation to other torts.

Nevertheless, *Prince Alfred*'s expression of caution, notably in relation to the use of policy arguments to determine the scope of liability, and advocacy of 'the orthodox route of considering whether the approach taken in decided cases furnishes a solution to further cases as they arise'[113] is a message that seems to

[108] ibid [81].

[109] *Deatons* (n 65). Some indication of the stature of Sir Owen Dixon can be found in the fact that the Melbourne location of the High Court of Australia is called the Owen Dixon Commonwealth Law Courts.

[110] ibid 381.

[111] Beuermann argues in chapter three that reliance placed by the judges on the judgment of Dixon J in *Deatons* indicates that the High Court did not intend to shift the general approach to determining vicarious liability in Australia away from the traditional Salmond test. I would be more equivocal in arguing *Prince Alfred College* indicates a willingness to modify the Salmond test but agree that it is seen more as a modification than rejection of the test.

[112] See, for example, Australian scholar C Beuermann, 'Vicarious Liability: A Case Study in the Failure of General Principles?' (2017) 33 *PN* 179, 187: 'At best, the distinction between forms of employment that provide the "occasion" as opposed to the "opportunity" for wrongdoing by an employee is very fine; at worst, it is semantic'. See also J Goudkamp and J Plunkett, 'Vicarious Liability in Australia: On the Move?' (2017) 17 *Oxford University Commonwealth Law Journal* 162, 167.

[113] *Prince Alfred College* (n 45) [46].

have resonated with the UK Supreme Court in its 2020 decisions on vicarious liability (albeit not openly acknowledged). It also has the potential to influence the common law world. In contrast, it seems less likely that its test of 'occasion' will prove as persuasive. Ryan, for example, has argued that it is not at all easy to find a meaningful difference between the terms 'occasion' and 'opportunity' given that they are often used interchangeably in ordinary parlance. We might share his doubts that 'occasion' is any less open-ended than that of 'connection'.[114] In my view, what is important about *Prince Alfred College* is its advocacy of a focus on the details of the employment relationship rather a more general survey of the employee's 'field of activities'. Whether one terms it 'occasion' or 'connection', this provides a stronger justification why vicarious liability should be imposed on an employer. The key point is that the courts are seeking to identify an acceptable substantive approach. Australia therefore may not have solved the dilemma of how to provide a clear and workable test for defining the scope of employment,[115] but it has succeeded in highlighting the need for caution and consistent case law in an area of law threatened by the broad approach of Lord Toulson in *Mohamud*. If it has succeeded in preventing *Mohamud*'s sufficient connection test from sweeping over the common law world, it should be welcomed on this ground alone.

III. Factors Favouring Common Law Comparisons

In Section II, I highlighted the extent to which the common law jurisdictions discussed in this book have drawn inspiration from other common law jurisdictions in developing the law of vicarious liability. While Australia has chosen to go its own way, we have seen similarities both in reasoning and citation of authority in Canada, England and Wales, Ireland, Singapore, Hong Kong and New Zealand. Inevitably, differences of emphasis exist at a local level, but what is remarkable in this area of law is the degree of cross-citation between different jurisdictions. Even where the judges do not agree – the UK and Australia being the obvious example – cross-citations exist.[116] As indicated above, UK case law has been particularly influenced by Canadian case law, notably *Doe v Bennett*[117]

[114] D Ryan, 'From Opportunity to Occasion: Vicarious Liability in the High Court of Australia' (2017) 76 *CLJ* 14, 17.

[115] A point conceded by Gageler and Gordon JJ: 'The Court cannot and does not mark out the exact boundaries of any principle of vicarious liability in this case': (n 45) [131].

[116] *Hollis* (n 5), *NSW v Lepore* [2003] HCA 4, (2003) 212 CLR 511 and *Prince Alfred College* (n 45) all discuss UK and Canadian authorities. Australian law, in turn, is regularly discussed by the UK Supreme Court eg in *Lister* (n 75) [81]; *Dubai Aluminium* (n 97) [32]; *Mohamud* (n 94) [29] but dismissed in *CCWS* (n 4) [82] in 2012 for having 'shown a bewildering variety of analysis'.

[117] *Doe* (n 24).

and *Bazley v Curry*.[118] The influence of UK case law on Singaporean, Hong Kong, Irish and indeed Scots law has been noted also in this volume. While occasional references are made to US[119] and South African law,[120] these comparisons are rare, indicating that differences in these legal systems render them less useful to courts.[121]

In this section, I will examine why the common law courts have found cross-citation of common law authority useful in this area of law. While a shared system of *stare decisis* renders case law authority important, it will be submitted that cross-citation will be triggered by a finding that the common law authority in question is of sufficient quality and prestige to influence the domestic court's reasoning. Further, vicarious liability has faced a number of challenges in the last 20 years and these have encouraged the courts to look to other esteemed common law jurisdictions for guidance in how to approach difficult questions of law.

A. Providing a Source of Persuasive Authority

Jurisdictions that have shared history, a common mode of thought in legal matters, similar institutions, similar use of legal sources and a shared ideology will typically regard themselves as part of a shared legal tradition.[122] The existence of a common language (English), accessible materials, statutes and cases in a familiar style, together with the perception of a shared culture and ideology will encourage judges to utilise material from common law jurisdictions with which they feel confident and familiar.[123] We know that common law jurisdictions are naturally selective in the material they cite, giving priority to domestic case law. Yet the act of citation indicates recognition; that the court has placed particular weight on this source.[124] D'Andrea et al argue that cross-citation is far from just a matter of a common language and ease of access, but represents something deeper: that judges and lawyers perceive themselves as forming part of a common legal culture

[118] *Bazley* (n 74).

[119] US law is perhaps unsurprisingly cited more frequently in Canada: see, for example, *Jacobi v Griffiths* [1999] 2 SCR 570, 174 DLR (4th) 71 [55]–[56], [58], [64].

[120] For example, MacDuff J in *JGE* (n 25) cited *Minister of Police v Rabie 1986* (1) SA 117. The possible use of South African law as a comparator in Scots law as a fellow mixed (common law/civil law) legal system is considered in chapter nine.

[121] Not least that the South African law of delict derives from a mixed common/civil law system. US law (found in the US Restatement of Agency), while manifesting some similarities, is largely state-based rendering it far less useful as an authoritative source.

[122] K Zweigert and H Kötz, *An Introduction to Comparative Law* 3rd edn (Oxford, Clarendon Press, 1998) 68.

[123] It should be noted that this does not signify all common law jurisdictions will be regarded as helpful, discussed further in P Giliker, 'The Influence of EU and European Human Rights Law on English Private Law' (2015) 64 *ICLQ* 237, notably 253.

[124] 'the fact of citation gives a work authority to some degree and thus it will exert some influence on the way the law grows': JH Merryman, 'The Authority of Authority: What the California Supreme Court Cited in 1950' (1954) 6 *Stanford Law Review* 613.

in which cross-fertilisation of ideas will be beneficial in improving the quality of legal reasoning.[125] As Sir Anthony Mason (former Chief Justice of Australia) has commented: '[Australian judges] should fashion a common law for Australia that is best suited to our conditions and circumstances … The value of English judgments, like Canadian, New Zealand … depends on the persuasive force of their reasoning'.[126]

What, then, renders a judgment *persuasive*? It is more than just finding a system that has a similar idea of what we mean by vicarious liability, but in finding a system for which the courts have esteem.[127] Such systems will not be regarded as 'foreign' laws, but rather as systems that represent 'living' law which *may* be useful in the practical process of dispute resolution.[128] What is of interest here is that despite the end of formal ties and termination of appeals to the Privy Council, jurisdictions in this book continue to find cross-citation beneficial in terms of legal development. The difference in its modern form is that the relationship between the courts is no longer hierarchical but rather represents a cross-jurisdictional dialogue in which the UK Supreme Court might follow the case law of the Supreme Court of Canada; or the High Court of Australia consider but ultimately reject the case law of the Canadian and UK courts. Cases, therefore, will only be received as persuasive authority when the courts believe that they may assist in framing their own domestic dialogue,[129] or can trigger debate as to the right domestic solution.[130] As Slaughter remarks:

> looking abroad simply helps [the judges] do a better job at home, in the sense that they can approach a particular problem more creatively or with greater insight. Foreign authority is persuasive because it teaches them something they did not know or helps them see an issue in a different and more tractable light. It provides a broader range of ideas and experience that makes for better, more reflective opinions.[131]

We might also note the importance of cross-citation for smaller legal systems such as Singapore, Ireland and Hong Kong where limited domestic case law makes the discussion of tort law principle in larger jurisdictions particularly

[125] S D'Andrea et al, 'Asymmetric Cross-Citations in Private Law: An Empirical Study of 28 Supreme Courts in the EU' (2021) 28 *Maastricht Journal of European and Comparative Law* 498, 534.

[126] A Mason, 'Future Directions in Australian Law' (1987) 13 *Monash Law Review* 149, 154.

[127] See HP Glenn, 'Persuasive Authority' (1987) 32 *McGill Law Journal* 261.

[128] ibid, 289. Contrast, for example, the treatment of civil law systems that do possess a doctrine of what a common lawyer would term 'vicarious liability' but whose authority is not perceived as meeting these requirements, discussed in Giliker (n 10). For hostility to such comparisons, see J Stapleton, 'Benefits of Comparative Tort Law Reasoning: Lost in Translation' (2006) 1(3) *Journal of Tort Law* 1–44.

[129] See A-M Slaughter, 'A Global Community of Courts' (2003) 44 *Harvard International Law Journal* 191, 195–96. This will lead, she hopes, to deliberation rather than gap-filling.

[130] J Bell, 'Researching Globalisation: Lessons from Judicial Citations' (2014) 3 *Cambridge Journal of International and Comparative Law* 961, 967.

[131] Slaughter (n 129) 201. For recent recognition, see M Arden and J Edelman, 'Mutual Borrowing and Judicial Dialogue Between the Apex Courts of Australia and the UK' (2022) 138 *LQR* 217 who emphasise that it is not just a case of borrowing from one another but by a process of dialogue and mutual learning.

helpful.[132] Larger jurisdictions, here Canada, England and Wales and Australia, have therefore proven more influential than their smaller counterparts; the courts finding assistance from jurisdictions with which they are familiar and regard as having prestige. While English appeals to the UK Supreme Court are technically non-binding in Scotland, the UK Supreme Court also provides a natural reference point for Scots private lawyers. Campbell and Lindsay have noted a general inclination among Scots lawyers to keep pace where possible with their larger neighbouring jurisdiction, particularly in this area of law.[133] The high level of citation of English case law by the Irish Supreme Court has also been identified in a recent citation study.[134] Tan, in his chapter on Singaporean law, notes that the courts in Singapore do often take their cue from English developments, while, he argues, confidently and quietly charting their own path through this labyrinthine area of tort law. However, cross-citation does not mean, he argues, that smaller jurisdictions are deferential. While Singapore frequently refers to the UK Supreme Court, its courts will reject solutions that do not fit within domestic legal policy.[135] Equally, the Irish Supreme Court in *Hickey v McGowan*[136] reviewed and rejected the view of the UK Supreme Court in *CCWS* that an unincorporated association, despite lacking legal personality, could be held vicariously liable for the torts of its employees as if it were a corporate entity. Glofcheski in chapter seven highlights nevertheless the practical assistance that can be derived in common law systems based on a system of *stare decisis* where there is a dearth of domestic precedents. Hong Kong, for example, has yet to rule on vicarious liability for sexual abuse in that such cases have yet to come to court. This is not, as Glofcheski hastens to add, to say that such abuses do not take place in this jurisdiction, but only that legal remedies have yet to be sought.[137] In such cases, common law comparisons can provide a vital life-line to lawyers seeking to gauge what the law is likely to be when such cases finally come to court.

Regarding authority as persuasive does not signify, however, that it will always be followed. It will be consulted, often cited, but is still subject to domestic law. In

[132] This is a commonly recognised phenomenon: 'Larger countries often influence smaller countries in a variety of ways, particularly when they are culturally relatively similar … Moreover, since larger countries normally produce a larger number of cases, new legal problems surface there first': M Gelter and M Siems, 'Citations to Foreign Courts – Illegitimate and Superfluous, or Unavoidable? Evidence from Europe' (2014) 62 *American Journal of Comparative Law* 35, 53.

[133] See chapter nine, section III.

[134] D'Andrea et al (n 125) 507. See also E Carolan, 'The Supreme Court of Ireland' in A Jakab, A Dyevre and G Itzcovich (eds), *Comparative Constitutional Reasoning* (Cambridge, Cambridge University Press, 2017) 458.

[135] The Singapore Court of Appeal, for example, has previously rejected the assumption of responsibility test for duty of care cases involving pure economic loss: *Anwar Patrick Adrian v Ng Chong & Hue LLC* [2014] SGCA 34; [2014] 3 SLR 761.

[136] *Hickey* (n 31) [49]. Note also the position in Scotland described in chapter 9.

[137] For the only reported case in which a legal remedy was sought, although apparently not pursued to trial, see *H v Lau Ka Yee* [2006] 4 HKLRD 579 (application to strike out the claim of vicarious liability against the diocese for a deacon's sex assaults on an altar boy dismissed on the basis that the minimum standard of an arguable case was met by the plaintiff).

this book, Australia has proven an interesting example of a system that regularly cites English law,[138] but which has rejected the approach of other common law jurisdictions discussed in this book both at the relationship stage (Stage 1) and the course of employment stage (Stage 2). Its reasons for doing so have been discussed above, but it is important here to recognise that despite following its own path, the case law of Canada and the UK continues to be cited and relied upon by reformers as a basis for liberalising the law.

Persuasive authority, therefore, may assist in shaping domestic jurisprudence. We can see that authority must be earned and that while historical factors may encourage cross-citation, case law may nevertheless be rejected if deemed inconsistent with domestic policy. Nevertheless, it can prove useful in filling gaps in domestic jurisprudence, providing authority that may not exist domestically or is out of date. It can assist also in developing a 'living law' that responds to contemporary needs and in framing or stimulating (although, as we have seen, not always resolving) legal debates. In so doing, a second factor comes into play: that the law of vicarious liability has had to respond to a number of challenges in the last 20 years, notably to changes in employment relations and to revelations of historic institutional child sexual abuse. In seeking to determine an appropriate domestic response to such changes, consideration of developments across the common law world has proven particularly useful.

B. Responding to Global Change: Cross-Citation as a Resource in Troubled Times

As we have seen in Section II, both stages of the vicarious liability test have been subject to considerable judicial activity in the last 20 years. Two main triggers can be identified that have caused the courts to review the scope of vicarious liability during this period. First, an influx of cases raising vicarious liability in the context of historic institutional child sexual abuse have raised questions whether sexual abuse should be regarded as 'within the course of employment' and, if so, how to reframe the vicarious liability test to include intentional torts that do not in any way benefit an employer. Second, changes in workplace hiring have stimulated a rethinking of the relationship test. As employment practices evolve with a move to casual and temporary workers in the 'gig' economy, courts are being asked whether the stage 1 relationship test should extend to workers 'akin' to employees. This, in turn, triggers a related question: if a more flexible approach is to be taken, how can this be justified in terms of policy?

[138] Although not as much as in the past, see R Smyth and I Nielsen, 'The Citation Practices of the High Court of Australia, 1905–2015' (2019) 47 *Federal Law Review* 655.

Reflecting on the substantive law discussed in Section II, we can identify general acceptance in the common law world that the law of vicarious liability is on the move.[139] The significance of these changes has been recognised by apex courts across the common law world. In *Hickey* v *McGowan*,[140] O'Donnell J, for example, recognised that:

> The law of vicarious liability was relatively stable, narrow and well understood for most of the 20th century until recently, and much if not all of the development of the law has occurred because of the necessity of addressing the phenomenon of historic sexual abuse of children in an institutional context … [T]here has been a number of carefully analysed, but not always consistent, attempts in the courts of the highest level in the common world, to provide a framework in which to address claims of historic sexual abuse.

The High Court of Australia has noted that despite divergent views on how to respond to these questions, the catalyst is the same: how to deal with claims of vicarious liability concerning the sexual abuse of children in educational, residential or care facilities by persons who were placed in special positions with respect to the children.[141]

The courts have further reflected on how structural changes in the labour market have been a trigger for change. This has led to a realisation that the doctrine is 'not a static concept and has adjusted over the centuries to provide just solutions to the challenges of changing times'.[142] As we have seen, changes to the relationship test derive both from the casualisation of labour and also due to the fact that sexual abuse cases involving religious institutions often involved parties such as priests who were not strictly 'employees' in the strict sense of the word. As recognised by the Singapore Court of Appeal, most courts (Australia again being a notable exception) agree on the need 'to fine-tune the existing framework underlying the doctrine so as to accommodate the more diverse range of relationships which might be encountered in today's context'.[143]

A doctrine on the move also needs a justification beyond the pragmatic – safeguarding the interests of victims of sexual abuse or those injured by casual workers often identifiable only by their uniform indicating their work for a particular employer.[144] Enterprise risk has swept from Canada (*Bazley*) via England and Wales (*CCWS*) to Ireland in *Hickey v McGowan* where O'Donnell J

[139] *CCWS* (n 4) [19]. This phrase has inspired commentary around the common law world, see, eg J Counsell, 'Historical Sexual Abuse Claims: Is Vicarious Liability "on the Move" Again?' [2020] *Journal of Personal Injury Law* 225; D Ryan, 'Vicarious Liability for Independent Contractors: Orthodox Principles "on the Move"?' (2019) 16 *Irish Employment Law Journal* 4; Goudkamp and Plunkett (n 112).

[140] *Hickey* (n 31) [42] (with whom Denham CJ, MacMenamin and Dunne J agreed).

[141] *Prince Alfred College* (n 45) [38].

[142] *JGE* (n 25) [60] per Ward LJ.

[143] *Ng Huat Seng* (n 21) [63].

[144] The context as *Hollis v Vabu* (n 5).

specifically identified it as the core theoretical basis for the imposition of vicarious liability[145] and Singapore where the Court of Appeal in 2011 gravitated towards an overarching rationale of 'enterprise risk'.[146] For the Hong Kong courts, enterprise risk reasoning is a relevant consideration that has permitted an expansion of vicarious liability.[147] The High Court of Australia in *Prince Alfred College* acknowledged the influence of the UK and Canadian courts in promoting enterprise risk as a justification for vicarious liability. While resisting its appeal, the HCA was nevertheless induced to provide an alternative justificatory framework. Participation in the dialogue does not necessarily signify assent. Enterprise risk reasoning continues to provoke an active debate in all the jurisdictions included in this text.

It is these developments that have been influential in creating the incentive for the cross-jurisdictional dialogue outlined in this book. They raise questions for the courts (and lawyers) to resolve and the answers are not straightforward or cut-and-dried. This presents a fertile environment for cross-citation which explains why we see common law courts seeking persuasive authority from the other common law jurisdictions. As Lord Phillips acknowledged in *CCWS*, the changes we have seen in this area of law in the last 20 years are fundamental and have led to revision of each limb of the test for vicarious liability and its justifications. We have seen changes made to the scope of vicarious liability, the burden imposed on employers and the role tort law plays in terms of victim compensation. While Lord Phillips was adamant in defending such changes, he made one concession which perhaps explains much of the law discussed in this book and why the debates to which it gives rise is so important:

> The law of vicarious liability is on the move … [T]hese developments of the law of vicarious liability … represent sound and logical incremental developments of the law. They have, however, made it more difficult to identify the criteria that must be demonstrated to establish vicarious liability than it was 50 years ago.[148]

The need for guidance from esteemed and persuasive authority is therefore self-evident.

IV. Conclusion

In *Jones v Kaney*,[149] Lord Collins commented that: 'It is highly desirable that … in cases where issues of legal policy are concerned, the court should be informed about the position in other common law countries'. It is submitted that this advice

[145] *Hickey* (n 31) [41] per O'Donnell J.
[146] *Skandinaviska* (n 70).
[147] *Ming An* (n 63).
[148] *CCWS* (n 4) [19]–[21].
[149] *Jones v Kaney* [2011] UKSC 13; [2011] 2 AC 398 [76].

continues to hold true in relation to the common law doctrine of vicarious liability. It is a doctrine that crosses common law jurisdictions which have faced similar challenges in relation to the two stages of the test – determining the relationship giving rise to vicarious liability and the scope of the connection that links the parties' relationship to the employee's tort. Faced with demands for change, we have seen the utility of a 'common law' approach. As noted above, all systems have been prepared to examine the economic realities of the employment relationship and accept that changes in employment practices require a more flexible approach that focuses on substance rather than form. However, extending the employment relationship to include relationships that are not technically those of employment but factually proximate has raised debate as to the scope of the doctrine and split jurisdictions. Australia (in the High Court at least) is resisting the 'akin to employment' extension and the UK Supreme Court in *Barclays Bank*[150] has recently stressed the need to focus on the details of the relationship to avoid too generous an approach. Equally, at Stage 2 of the vicarious liability test, there has been a general movement from the commonly applied Salmond test to the 'close connection' test. If Australia has again opposed this development in preferring its own occasion test, it has nevertheless demonstrated a willingness to respond to common law authority coming from Canada and the UK. The High Court of Australia has also provided valuable feedback on the weaknesses of authority such as *Mohamud*,[151] to which the UK Supreme Court arguably responded in the later case of *Morrison*.[152]

At both stages of the test, we have seen a debate crossing jurisdictions with cross-citation of cases encouraging legal development. While Australia has to a certain extent resisted change, its lower courts have seized on authority from other common law jurisdictions as a spur for reform while, and this is important, framing the debate within domestic precedents. Yet there are limits to the benefits of cross-citation. At its best, in responding to an area of law in which the courts are facing uncertainty and difficulties in application, cross-citation should create an active dialogue amongst judges – a counterfactual world in which consequences of change can be tested, not merely hypothetically, but in some form of grounded reality – to assist in shaping and reinvigorating legal principle in domestic law.[153] However, much will depend on the quality of the sources used. Ryan, while recognising that, due to limited Irish case law, reference to English case law is a reality, questions to what extent it has proven helpful in providing clear and coherent rules. The Irish approach is one he characterises as caution and incrementalism. This view is shared by other contributors who have criticised the UK courts for providing doctrinally unclear authority with which the courts have had to struggle

[150] *Barclays* (n 20).
[151] *Mohamud* (n 94).
[152] *Morrison* (n 96).
[153] J Bell, 'The Relevance of Foreign Examples to Legal Development' (2011) 21 *Duke Journal of Comparative and International Law* 431, 460.

(Glofcheski pointing out, for example, in chapter seven, uncertainty on how to apply the close connection test to cases of fraudulent misrepresentation). What is interesting, however, is that we have seen little of what is often contemptuously termed 'ornamental' comparative law, that is, reference to case law merely to confirm a view already taken.[154] Rather we have seen an ongoing debate as to the nature of the two-stage test for vicarious liability and how courts should respond to the challenges facing this doctrine. This has taken place both in the academic literature (involving many of the contributors to this book) and in the courts themselves.

More than 20 years after *Bazley* and *Lister*, questions remain unanswered as to the application of the test for vicarious liability, its scope and relationship with parallel doctrines such as non-delegable duties, its policy justifications and its ability to respond to the needs of victims. As demonstrated by this chapter, the dominant jurisdictions (Canada, England and Wales, Australia) have been unable to provide foolproof guidance and ongoing doctrinal uncertainties have been shared amongst the common law community. It remains important that each jurisdiction provides a test attuned to its own particular needs, responding to domestic precedents and statutory frameworks, the needs of litigants and domestic policy concerns. There is not therefore (and neither should there be) a 'common' law of vicarious liability. However, if we are to resolve these uncertainties, we can all benefit from a common law dialogue on vicarious liability – a dialogue concerning its legal development and its policy justifications that resonates across the common law legal family. It is this dialogue that provides a valuable resource to lawyers, practising or otherwise, across the common law world and beyond. As a common lawyer working in the field of vicarious liability, I continue to learn from my fellow common lawyers across the world. Such a dialogue enriches us as lawyers and deepens our understanding of this important, if often doctrinally frustrating, doctrine of vicarious liability. If we are to understand vicarious liability and anticipate its legal development, then the need to review its operation across the common law world is more important than ever.

[154] Gelter and Siems (n 132) 80, although they acknowledge that, at a modest level, even ornamental comparative law can stimulate comparative legal discussions. For a more critical view, see J Husa, *A New Introduction to Comparative Law* (Oxford, Hart, 2015) 33 who questions its value beyond the decorative.

INDEX

www.ingramcontent.com/pod-product-compliance
Ingram Content Group UK Ltd.
Pitfield, Milton Keynes, MK11 3LW, UK
UKHW020802290926
15470UKWH00003B/907

9 781509 939077